Public Service Ethics

Ethics—in all its exemplary and exhausting forms—matters. It deals with the most gripping question in public life: "What is the right thing to do?" Now in a thoroughly revised second edition, *Public Service Ethics: Individual and Institutional Responsibilities* introduces readers to this personally relevant and professionally challenging field of study. No matter the topic—the necessity of ethics, intriguing human behavior experiments, the role of ethics codes, whistleblowing incidents, corruption exposés, and the grandeur and decay of morality—there is no shortage of controversy. The book enables readers to:

- appreciate why ethics is essential to leadership,
- understand and apply moral development theory at the individual and organizational levels of analysis,
- differentiate between ethical problems and ethical dilemmas, and design creative ways to deal with them,
- develop abilities to use moral imagination and ethical reasoning—to appraise, argue, and defend an ethical position, and
- cultivate individual and institutional initiatives to improve ethical climate and infrastructure.

Authors James Bowman and Jonathan West capture reader interest by featuring learning objectives, skill-building material, discussion questions, and exercises in each chapter. The authors' narrative is user-friendly and accessible, highlighting dilemmas and challenging readers to "own" the book by annotating the pages with one's own ideas and insights, then interacting with others in a live or virtual classroom to stretch one's thinking about the management of ethics and ethics of management. The ultimate goal is to bolster students' confidence and prepare them for the ethical problems they will face in the future, equipping them with the conceptual frameworks and context to approach thorny questions and behave ethically.

James S. Bowman is Professor and Director of the Masters of Public Administration Program at the Askew School of Public Administration and Policy, Florida State University, USA.

Jonathan P. West is Professor and Chair of Political Science and Director of the Graduate Public Administration Program at the University of Miami, USA.

"The second edition continues with the same comprehensive format and chapters, with lots of updated information and more developed insights on key theoretical topics. The authors offer many useful analytic tools and methods for engaging in ethical analysis, with numerous real-world examples and cases. Students will continue to find the book very useful."

– **Richard Green**, *University of Utah, USA*

Public Service Ethics

Individual and Institutional Responsibilities

Second Edition

James S. Bowman and Jonathan P. West

Routledge
Taylor & Francis Group

NEW YORK AND LONDON

Second edition published 2018
by Routledge
711 Third Avenue, New York, NY 10017
and by Routledge

2 Park Square, Milton Park, Abingdon, Oxon OX14 4RN

Routledge is an imprint of the Taylor & Francis Group, an informa business

© 2018 Taylor & Francis

[First edition published by CQ Press 2014]

Library of Congress Cataloging-in-Publication Data
Names: Bowman, James S., 1945- author. | West, Jonathan P. (Jonathan Page), 1941- author.
Title: Public service ethics : individual and institutional responsibilities / James S. Bowman and Jonathan P. West.
Description: Second Edition. | New York : Routledge, 2018. | Previous edition: 2015. | Includes bibliographical references and index.
Identifiers: LCCN 2017059733| ISBN 9781138578180 (hardback : alk. paper) | ISBN 9781138578197 (paperback : alk. paper) | ISBN 9781351265126 (ebook)
Subjects: LCSH: Civil service ethics. | Public administration--Moral and ethical aspects. | Political ethics. | Civil service ethics--United States. | Public administration--Moral and ethical aspects--United States. | Political ethics--United States.
Classification: LCC JF1525.E8 B69 2018 | DDC 172/.2--dc23
LC record available at https://lccn.loc.gov/2017059733

ISBN: 978-1-138-57818-0 (hbk)
ISBN: 978-1-138-57819-7 (pbk)
ISBN: 978-1-351-26512-6 (ebk)

Typeset in Minion Pro by
Servis Filmsetting Ltd, Stockport, Cheshire

Visit the eResources: www.routledge.com/9781138578197

For Loretta
JSB

For Colleen
JPW

Contents

List of Tables, Figures, and Exhibits

TABLES

FIGURES

EXHIBITS

Preface to the Second Edition

As with the first edition, there remains a pressing need to address this vital area of study. Ethics—in all its exemplary and execrable, exhilarating and exhausting forms—*matters*. It deals with the most gripping question in life: "What is the right thing to do?" As important as it may be to "do things right," it is essential to "do right things." Indeed, regardless of how many things a person does in life, what will be remembered is how he or she responded to ethical challenges. The imperative nature of the topic, then, invites investigation. Since most existing public service ethics books do not report recent research or bring other material up to date, we have expanded our treatment of the subject. The aim is to capture reader interest by featuring in each chapter learning objectives, essential knowledge, skill-building material, telling endnotes, discussion questions, exercises, and appendices.

The intent is to make the narrative user-friendly and accessible by highlighting dilemmas, challenging readers to resolve them, and enticing them to go beyond the text to discover and confront new issues. In so doing, we trust that readers will contact us with their suggestions for improvement in the book (jbowman@fsu.edu; jwest@miami.edu). The ultimate goal is to contribute to student confidence as he or she confronts ethical issues in the future. In so doing, truly "own" this publication by annotating these pages with *your* ideas, disputes, satisfactions, discomforts, experiences, comparisons, applications, and insights. Then interact with others in a live or virtual classroom to stretch your thinking about the management of ethics and ethics of management.

As in the first edition, *Public Service Ethics: Individual and Institutional Responsibilities* Second Edition introduces readers to this personally relevant and professionally challenging field of study. No matter the topic—the necessity of ethics, intriguing human behavior experiments, provocative approaches to decision making, new theories to understand ethical actions, the role of ethics codes, whistleblowing incidents, corruption exposés, and the grandeur and decay of morality—there is no shortage of controversy. This book discusses these issues, explains how they arise, and suggests what can be done about them. Be advised, however, that it will not, and cannot, provide answers for every case; the study of ethics is not like a cookbook full of recipes.

We have crafted a volume that:

- assumes that readers are or will be line managers or technical experts,
- presents a comprehensive range of topics and issues,

- illustrates these discussions with a blend of current events from business, government, and the not-for-profit sectors, and
- encourages students not merely to peruse the material, but also to apply it.

As members of the American Society of Public Administration, who have widely published in the field (see "About the Authors"), we believe that while no one is perfect, most people care deeply about ethics, and are willing to think about basic issues when given the opportunity. To that extent, all of us are ethicists. Professionals, it follows, need not only technical and leadership competencies, but also well-honed ethical skills to effectively conduct the public's business. That belief also motivated us to write the type of text described below.

The initial chapter—the first of three in Part I that explores the foundations of public service ethics—discusses the multiple rationales for examining ethics. Knowing why one is undertaking an activity is the first step to understanding. New material includes: further discussion of the relationship between technical and ethical competence; the nature of the market economy, additional discussion questions, YouTube resources, journal-writing guidance, and the utility of the text to the Network of Schools of Public Affairs and Administration ethics guidelines.

The second chapter probes multiple frames of reference in comprehending how to study the subject area, now augmented with more on the Enlightenment as well as a case analysis of the 2017 Grenfell Towers fire in London. The third exploratory chapter defines values and ethics. Fresh information includes what ethics is not, multiple sources of ethical obligation, as well as new cases and exercises, including the Amazon headquarters location controversy and the first of five Bad Actor tabletop exercises.

With foundations in mind, Part II investigates approaches to ethics. These strategies emphasize individual-centered (cognitive and virtue) schools of thought. To gain a perspective on this material, Chapter 4 focuses on an inclusive and hierarchical theory of moral development that can be applied to individuals and organizations. It also introduces a recent contrasting theory from behavioral ethics that relies on psychological tendencies to explain human conduct. Among the revisions are: updates on "willful blindness" and "trolley-ology," as well as new information on critiques of the Milgram experiment, tragedies on Facebook, Nazi concentration camps, baby ethics, ethics quizzes, and exercises. Since people do not necessarily make ethically sound choices, Chapter 5 presents a problem-solving strategy that showcases two cognitive decision-making methods: results and rule. More information on moral courage in making decisions is provided, and the second Bad Actor tabletop assignment complements this chapter. Chapter 6, the third and final individual-premised approach to ethics, turns the discussion from results and rule cognitive philosophies to virtue theory, from "head" to "heart." The theory is further defined and profiles of exemplary public servants are brought up to date.

Chapter 7 then consolidates the three individual-centered methods to ethics into a tripartite framework—the ethics triad—that provides a comprehensive tool to analyze difficult work issues. This framework is used to examine selected cases throughout the balance of the book. The chapter also introduces the field of behavioral ethics, which directly challenges the usefulness of traditional views of ethical decision making such as those found in the triad. This school of thought argues that the prescriptive character of cognitive and virtue ethics does not adequately explain how people really act in ethical situations. Based on experimental and experiential evidence, the claim is that emotion is at least as important as logic—indeed, may be the basis of rationality—in decision making. This in depth discussion has been thoroughly revised and expanded.

Part III, beginning with Chapter 8, shifts from individual cognitive ("head") and virtue ("heart") ethics to organization-centered ("body") approaches. That is, while the mastery of personally focused ethics explored in Part II is necessary, it is not sufficient for understanding the full scope of ethics, as individual conduct is affected by the environment within which it occurs. The chapter scrutinizes the ethical infrastructure in organizations, and is followed by subsequent chapters dealing with corruption control and whistleblowing in institutions. Changes include: material on organizational structure and institutional ethics; an auditing profession point–counterpoint feature; an update on the torture controversy; the value in "asking for trouble," corruption rationalizations; new studies on the Flint, Michigan water disaster and the Wells Fargo scandal; as well as Red Cross problems, gift giving, examples of "failing upward;" and the third Bad Actor exercise.

Selected issues in public service ethics constitute Part IV of the book, with separate chapters on ethics of elected officials, organizational gaming and performance measurement, at-will employment doctrine, and a case study in open government. These discussions represent a diverse set of topics that illustrate the all-encompassing character of topic area. Chapters 11 and 12, respectively, examine behaviors of political figures and an important dimension of improper institutional conduct, gaming the system. Added are "fake news," elected officials' falsehoods, courage awards, and bridge-building leaders plus two more Bad Actor exercises. Chapters 13 and 14 explore, in depth, two different issues using the ethic triad. Part V consists of the closing chapter that serves as a capstone for the text. It emphasizes that all people are ethical agents who have the choice between moral grandeur or decay, and provides guidelines for honorable action in the years ahead. In addition to updates, especially on white-collar crime, coverage of "post-truth politics," the evolution of ethics, and self-development exercises are new to this edition.

Each chapter, then, includes case studies drawing on actual and hypothetical events that give students the opportunity to apply the concepts and analytical frameworks in the chapters. Some cases present scenarios that are then followed by questions to consider; others are applied case studies in which we guide the reader through the application of a decision-making framework to show the thought process behind how a decision might be made. Chapters 13 and 14 are the exception, in that the entirety of the chapter is essentially a case analysis. In addition, end-of-chapter discussion questions and exercises give students further opportunity to think more deeply about ethical issues, as well as apply what they have learned.

Welcome to public service ethics in a book whose subject will affect the future of all readers in their careers. And now for the adventure!

James S. Bowman and Jonathan P. West

Acknowledgments

We take pleasure in acknowledging the contributions and assistance of the anonymous referees, Qian Huang, Stephanie M. Belaustegui, Sam McCall, Jasmine Atkinson, and Jacqueline Porter. In addition, our past students, both on campus and online, have helped us clarify thinking about ethics.

Taylor & Francis, as well as the authors, would also like to thank the reviewers for their time and insights.

Finally, appreciation is due to M. E. Sharpe Publishers, SAGE Publications, Taylor & Francis, and Elsevier for granting permission to adapt some of our previous work to this book.

About the Authors

James S. Bowman is professor of public administration at the Askew School of Public Administration and Policy, Florida State University. Noted for his work in ethics and human resource management, Dr. Bowman is author of nearly 150 journal articles and book chapters, as well as editor of six anthologies. He is co-author of the prize-winning *Human Resource Management in Public Service: Paradoxes, Processes and Problems* (6th ed., in press) and *Achieving Competencies in Public Service: The Professional Edge* (2nd ed., 2010). He is the immediate past editor-in-chief of *Public Integrity*, a journal owned by the American Society for Public Administration. A past Network of Schools of Public Affairs and Administration Fellow, as well as a Kellogg Foundation Fellow, he has experience in the military, civil service, and business. Bowman was elected to the National Academy of Public Administration in 2017.

Jonathan P. West is professor and chair of political science and director of the graduate public administration program at the University of Miami. His research interests include ethics, public administration, and human resource management. He has published nearly 150 peer-reviewed articles and book chapters as well as nine books. In addition to the two books mentioned above co-authored with Bowman and others, he has co-edited *American Public Service: Radical Reform and the Merit System* (Taylor & Francis, 2007) and *The Ethics Edge* (ICMA, 2nd ed., 2006) and co-authored *American Politics and the Environment* (SUNY Press, 2nd ed., 2016). For 16 years he has been managing editor of *Public Integrity* journal. He served as a captain in the U.S. Army as a management analyst in the Office of the Surgeon General.

PART I

Foundations of Public Service Ethics

1 Pertinence, Practicality, and Poppycock

Always do right. This will gratify some people and astonish the rest.

—Mark Twain

This chapter—the first of three that explore the foundations of public service ethics—explores the multiple rationales for examining ethics as well as reasons behind the reluctance to discuss ethics in policy and administration. Knowing why one is undertaking an activity is the first step to understanding any situation. The chapter objectives are to:

- appreciate personal reasons for studying ethics,
- recognize the pervasiveness of ethics,
- acknowledge that professional public service has never been solely a technical enterprise,
- understand that the exercise of power is immediate, real, and vital,
- distinguish the costs associated with ethical pitfalls, and
- evaluate credulous poppycock that claims ethics is impossible, unnecessary, and simple.

PERTINENCE: REASONS TO STUDY ETHICS

There is no guarantee that anyone will make more effective choices by studying ethics. But such study helps to contemplate them on your own and to speak intelligently about ethical matters with others. Reflecting on ethics issues encourages the recognition of moral duty and obligations. Ideally, it serves to make prudent judgments that can be publicly justified. This understanding is the basis for at least five reasons to explore ethics: it is personal, pervasive, professional, powerful, and full of pitfalls where the costs of ethical failure are high.

Personal

While the word *ethics* may provoke fear and loathing as a dull topic, or one that takes people out of their comfort zone, in fact, it stimulates thinking people with life's most compelling questions—those that deal with what is right and wrong, good and bad. As Thomas Schelling (1984, 38) writes, "Often the question is not 'Do I want to do the right thing?' but rather 'What is the right thing to want to do?'" The initial observation, then, is that humans are the only creatures that are struck by the difference between *is* and *ought*, and wonder about what sort of creatures they are and could be. *Homo sapiens* are, in other words, unique moral agents because they have the capacity to think about thinking, to ponder about what is "right" and "proper" and "fair" (Wilson, 1993).

In public service, the "what is" question seeks to discern what is actually occurring in a particular setting. This seemingly obvious factual or descriptive question aims to better understand or make judgments about ethical behavior. However, describing "what is" is complicated by the varying ethical perceptions, beliefs, values, and biases found at the individual, organizational, and societal levels. The "ought to be" question is normative and focuses on what should be done in a given situation (e.g., how to treat a long-time employee when downsizing). The issue for managers and leaders is how to get from "what is" to "what ought to be" in practice. It is challenging because it requires weighing what can be done with what ought to be done. This is where you come in.

You count, and can make a difference in the movement from what is to what ought to be by adding to—or subtracting from—excellence and joy in the workplace. What you do matters. This book is aimed squarely at readers, inviting everyone to actively engage ethics— to take it personally. It will help prepare for the day when you are called upon to juggle these considerations and then decide: "This is what should be done, this is why it should be done, and this is how it will be done." When that time comes, it will be important to be confident that the action taken is ethically feasible and desirable.

This leads to a second observation: People unabashedly make decisions about what is best. Henry Ford said, "Believe in your best, think your best, study your best, have a goal for your best, never be satisfied with less than your best, try your best—and in the long run, things will work out for the best." You need to know what is right, and that the choices you make are good. If an unexamined life is not worth living, following Socrates, then, an examined life is lived for a good reason. Every act of every person is a moral act, to be tested by moral criteria; to study ethics is to learn not only how people make good judgments, but also why they make bad ones. Readers are bid to probe the empowering, if inherently controversial, choices about meaning and value in public service. Managers and employees without a carefully considered set of public service values are likely to be poor decision makers; they are inclined to dither when confronted with decisions presenting ethical implications.

The third observation of a personal nature is that individual values are the final standard, as there are many, sometimes conflicting, determinants of action. "To the question of your life," wrote Jo Coudert in *Advice from a Failure*, "you are the only answer. To the problems of your life, you are the only solution." Individual responsibility and accountability, therefore, are inescapable (notice the "i" in "ethical"). But note that people typically perceive themselves as more ethical than others and that consensus regarding proper behavior diminishes when proceeding from abstract to specific circumstances. Actual human contact can change everything, clarifying some issues while confounding others. Black and white can, in fact, look like two shades of gray.

The implications of the personal reason for studying ethics are that they can be both enabling (it is not mere sentimentality) and debilitating (being questioned about ethics can strike at the core of one's moral being). Either way, how you handle an ethical dilemma may be the only thing remembered about you ("The decision of a moment," it has been said, "lasts a lifetime"). The question, in short, is not whether we will die, but how we will *live*. Existence is defined by choices, as French philosopher Albert Camus asked, "Should I kill myself, or have a cup of coffee?"

Pervasiveness

Not only is ethics a highly personal concern, but it is also a pervasive one. It is part and parcel of the activities of everyday life, encompassing and affecting almost everything that happens. Indeed, as technology has further interconnected with others around the globe, it has also made us more ethically interdependent. Ethics is a fundamental, familiar component of all walks of life: business, government, religion, sports, academe, and nonprofit organizations. Newspaper headlines, television and radio broadcasts, and Internet coverage provide story after story of wrongdoing in business, government, and nonprofit sector organizations. Heroes and heroines plummet from their exalted status by making poor choices (e.g., see the compelling saga of the rise of New York State Attorney General Eliot Spitzer vs. the fall of Governor Spitzer in Eimicke, 2005, and Eimicke & Shacknai, 2008). Likewise, organizational brands are tarnished by immoral actions. In both, citizen trust is lost and financial resources squandered for short-term gain. Ethical leadership is lacking and sorely needed, particularly in the civil service where public-regarding ethics is so central to the core of democracy: government by, for, and of the people.

And ethical concern is probably greater than ever before as ethical issues have a tendency to be magnified and expanded today for three interrelated reasons:

- The *scale effect:* Modern technologies make it possible to do misdeeds on a massive scale.
- The *display effect:* Communications systems (particularly the advent of social media) can dramatically package, instantly distribute, and repeat incidents.
- The *PR effect:* Public communication has become professionalized public relations as a result of polling, focus group research, image management, news event "spin," "damage control," "spontaneous" grassroots mobilization, and related marketing techniques. (Adapted from Heclo, 2008, 26–28)

Velocity, in short, can readily trump veracity. As Mark Twain said, "A lie can travel halfway round the world while the truth is putting on its shoes."

Additionally, as the post-industrial service economy shifts emphasis from products to people, higher moral standards are expected. People have learned to become sensitive to the natural environment, and today they are also becoming sensitive to the ethical environment. Yet while a broader range of activities are seen as unethical today, conditions for employee abuse continue to grow, exacerbated by rapid societal change.

Professional

Public servants, accordingly, must not only do technical things right but also do ethically right things. Professional work is value intensive as it focuses on goals, synthesis, and priorities; leaders take responsibility for what is done as they serve as models and represent others. Someone without basic ethics skills is professionally illiterate. Indeed, ethical competence encompasses technical competence. The classic definition—and often oath—of a *professional* is someone who shows leadership in technical ability and ethical character. A professional is not a professional merely because of her expertise, but also because of her adherence to ethical standards. The ability to contemplate, enhance, and act on these faculties is the essence of professional life. It is unthinkable for a professional not to do her best; it is her duty. (See Appendix 1.2, Book Chapters and NASPAA Professional Competencies in Public Administration.)

This is what makes scandals so devastating. Scandals result when professionals in a variety of fields have demonstrated a lack of understanding of this basic precept. Namely, the question "Management for what?" seems to have been misunderstood. Management is not an end; rather, it is a means to an end. Thus, while process and policy often overlap, the ethics of process—regardless of the policy issues involved—is key. If process is ably done, policy is likely to be ethical as well. A focus on "why" when making decisions may lead to recognition of ignorance, followed by the acquisition of knowledge, resulting in expansion of moral imagination. The aptitude for critical judgment is the *sine qua non* of a professional. Those who treat management and ethics apart will never understand either one.

One attempt to keep management focused on ethics is the appointment of a chief ethics and compliance officer in an organization. Criticized by some as window dressing, while praised by others as a way to highlight ethical issues and promote right behavior, these officials have become commonplace in large firms, nonprofit organizations, and governments (see Exhibit 1.1 on a week in the life of Marisol Lopez, an ethics and compliance officer). A critical question is whether these positions have the power and resources to make a difference (see Chapter 8).

Power

A fourth reason for interest in ethics is found in the capacity of government and its agents to exercise power. The study and practice of public administration has never been regarded as only a technical matter. Moral reform is the impetus of modern public administration as values are at its soul (Frederickson, 1996). Governance is both a democratic and a moral

A Week in the Life of Ethics Officer Marisol Lopez

Marisol Lopez is an ethics and compliance officer for XYZ, a large nonprofit organization in a big southeastern city. Like most nonprofit ethics officers, Lopez faces a thorny set of issues that creates challenges, threats, and opportunities for her and for her charitable organization. Her work is complicated by a downturn in the economy, declining charitable donations, a rapidly changing workforce, an increasingly cumbersome legal and regulatory environment, pressures for higher productivity, and pending layoffs. Lopez earned her MPA degree with a concentration in law and ethics more than 20 years ago. She has been working in the nonprofit arena since that time, progressing up the ranks to become the organization's first ethics and compliance officer, a position she has held since its creation 10 years ago. She is a strong communicator, politically savvy, and able to assimilate information quickly.

After arriving at the office on Monday morning, Marisol is told about a breaking news story on a financial scandal involving another major employer in the city. She is aware that any large organization, whether in business, a nonprofit, or government, can have its reputation tarnished by the unethical actions of managers or employees. She is grateful to be working for an organization that has long recognized the importance of ethics and proactively created her office to reduce the risk of any scandal or wrongdoing. Other nonprofits, such as the American Cancer Society, American Red Cross, and American Arbitration Association, have created ethics officer positions to supplement their ongoing ethics programs. She feels fortunate that she reports directly to the CEO and makes regular presentations to the board of directors, unlike some chief ethics officers in her professional association (the Ethics and Compliance Officer Association), who report indirectly through the general counsel. Her direct reporting channel helps her to be strategically relevant and independent, a key to her effectiveness.

As she reviews her schedule for the week, she notes several important matters that must be attended to:

- *Today*—She needs to put the finishing touches on an article for her organization's newsletter, a Q&A-style piece regarding hypothetical ethical situations and how to deal with them. Then she is giving a briefing to a small group of board members at lunch highlighting several good examples of ethical behavior by organization members. In the afternoon, she is meeting with staff to review final revisions of their "no-gifts" policy.
- *Tuesday*—She is working with staff to complete a risk assessment study of the organization's fund-raising effort; in the afternoon, she is overseeing with the HR director an internal investigation of charges involving unfair hiring practices; later that day, she intends to sit in on a new employee orientation where she will be speaking about standards of behavior and the code of ethics.
- *Wednesday*—She is briefing the CEO and his staff regarding the implications of a compliance initiative affecting international operations. That afternoon, she is scheduled to attend an outside consultant's briefing on an assessment of program effectiveness in the budget office.
- *Thursday*—She is planning to review revisions to the policies and procedures manual; later, she will convene an ethics committee composed of representatives

from human resources, finance, fund-raising, and operations. They will be discussing ways in which the organizational culture creates risks and how to mitigate them to stay out of trouble. The committee is trying to get away from the "one-and-done" checklist mentality for improving ethics, which simply tallies how many people certify that they've read the code of conduct or participated in mandatory ethics training.

- *Friday*—She is scheduled to examine ethics hotline messages that report misconduct to see if there are any red flags needing attention. After that, she is meeting with a group of mid-level supervisors to discuss how to make people feel comfortable in reporting problems. Marisol remembered how impressed she was by a recent article written by another ethics officer that said, "If employees believe reporting bad news equates to failure, that organization is building a toxic culture." She wants to avoid spending all of her time and her staff's "firefighting" in response to compliance problems, and instead focus on building a culture that promotes ethics. She will encourage the committee to benchmark their practices against peer group nonprofits with similar histories.

Lopez's schedule shows the broad range of issues and events that might be encountered by ethics and compliance officers. In the corporate arena, chief ethics officers emerged in the early 1990s when the Federal Sentencing Guidelines for corporations were implemented. Under this legislation, firms with effective compliance and ethics programs receive preferential treatment during prosecutions for white-collar crime. The 2002 Sarbanes-Oxley Act and the 2010 Dodd-Frank Act further accelerated this trend to help identify potential problems. Nonprofit organizations and governments have taken a similar path by establishing ethics officer positions as part of their ethics program.

endeavor. The argument for democracy is not that it is efficient, but that it is the right form of government. If questions of right and wrong are answered by the state, those decisions are the immediate, real, and vital official allocation of values. When citizens, advocacy groups, and lobbyists demand government intervention, they seek an authoritative resolution of a conflict of values. This distribution of values—promoting particular values while minimizing others—is significant because it has far-reaching ethical consequences. The results range from human health to social and corporate welfare to government regulation. Democracy provides accountability mechanisms for such value allocations, which can permit careful consideration of competing interests by decision makers.

Social control of ethical behavior in public service can be assessed by considering the types of power being exercised, the source of the power within or outside the organization, and the locus of social control mechanisms applied to individuals and organizations. Table 1.1 shows social influence exercised through three types of power: symbolic, economic, or coercive. Symbolic power is linked to values and beliefs and it invokes emotional reactions (e.g., internal: praise; external: publicity), which can be used by an organization to appeal to

| TABLE 1.1 | Social Control of Ethical Behavior in Organizations: Type, Source, and Focus of Power | | |

Source of Power	Type of Power Used	Applied to the Individual	Applied to the Organization
Internal to the Organization (Organization Culture and Structure)	• Symbolic Power	• Letter of commendation, award, praise, criticism, humiliation, storytelling	• Code of ethics, policies and processes that generate behavioral norms
	• Economic Power	• Bonus, raise, promotion, firing, pay freeze	• Mission, strategy
	• Coercive Power	• Not legally available (But: kidnapping, forceful threat, beating, forced exposure to toxins, etc.)	• Not relevant (unless organization is "suicidal")
External to the Organization (Nongovernmental Stakeholders)	• Symbolic Power	• Minority proxy resolution to remove firm's officers	• Publicity, news
	• Economic Power	• Bribe, kickback, award, reward	• Purchase, boycott, strike, slowdown
	• Coercive Power	• Not legally available (But: disruptive picketing of executive homes, terrorist attacks, vandalism)	• Not legally available (But: violence accompanying strike, vandalism, sabotage, terrorism)
External to the Organization (Legal and Government Pressures)	• Symbolic Power	• Jawboning, warning, use of social networks	• Warning, citation, testimony at congressional hearing
	• Economic Power	• Fine, tax	• Fine, tax, contract, quota, tax credit, tariff, regulatory barriers to entry
	• Coercive Power	• Jail, execution	• Forced shutdown

Source: Wood (1994, 305). Reprinted by permission of Pearson Education, Inc., Upper Saddle River, NJ.

its members, the media, and other stakeholders, and to incentivize action on ethical issues. Economic power involves material rewards or sanctions to achieve ethical objectives. It is exercised by those inside or outside of the organization in the form of pay raises or adverse personnel actions, in the case of the former, and budget cuts, in the case of the latter. Coercive power entails the use of force or threat (e.g., incarceration) to control behavior. Internal social controls seek to generate behavior norms (e.g., mission statements); external social controls are applied by government regulations or stakeholders who seek to influence policy.

Price of Ethical Pitfalls

A final consideration in studying ethics is the substantial costs that ethical problems can incur. It is difficult to put a dollar figure on the costs of such failures because they are not reported on a balance sheet. However, the expenses can be considerable and, as Thomas, Schermerhorn, and Dienhart (2004, 58–59) demonstrate, they can occur at three levels (Figure 1.1). Level 1 costs are less problematic to calculate, and are often overemphasized by leaders. They include fines and penalties occurring as a consequence of ethical breakdown. These levies may be significant, but are often bearable, even nominal, notably for those organizations that are well insured. Level 2 costs are "clean-up" expenditures (audit, attorney, investigator fees) that are usually as high as, or higher than, Level 1 costs. Level 3 outlays are typically underappreciated by executives and harder to quantify, but often devastating. They can take the greatest toll because the costs include multiple adverse effects: loss of reputation and morale, and increase of cynicism and regulation. Given the high price of ethical failure, preventive strategies are a wise investment.

| FIGURE 1.1 | Price of Ethical Failure |

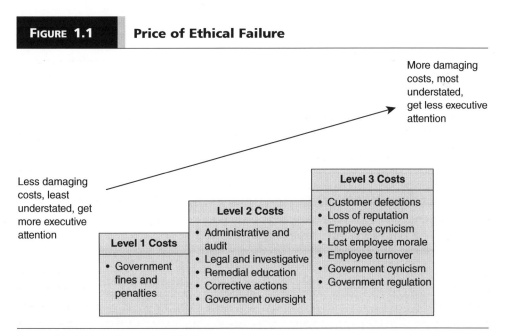

Source: Adapted from Thomas et al. (2004).

In short, all of these reasons—with their personal, pervasiveness, professional, power, and pitfall implications—account for the salience of issues such as business fraud, question-able Red Cross management and accounting practices, the FBI not heeding terrorist warn-ings, firefighters setting fires, clergymen and coaches abusing children (and their superiors covering up the problem), Olympic judges and school teachers rigging scores, ballplayers taking steroids, Wall Street insider trading, document shredding, off-shore tax havens, media moguls sexually harassing co-workers, Wells Fargo creating fake customer accounts, auto makers cheating on emission standards, cyber bullying, businesses dumping toxic waste and hundreds of financial officers "restating" misleading company audits. Ethics and violations of ethics, in short, are based on the actions of people.

PRACTICALITY: COMMITMENT AS A PRIVILEGE AND OBLIGATION

Accordingly, ethics cannot be achieved unless all people in the organization practice it at a personal level. A personal commitment to honorable behavior is both a privilege and an obligation (see Newell, 2015). Most people want to be ethical and to follow through on personal and professional commitments. They intend to do the right thing but sometimes make wrong choices or remain uncertain about which course of action is the right one. Success ultimately depends on what we know, what we do, and what we become as a result. Excellence, as Aristotle saw, cannot be attained without studying and mastering the art of achievement. As a manager or future manager, you cannot delegate that responsibility; you must show the way by example. This requires careful thought, clarification of one's values, and a willingness to do what it takes to achieve ethical competency. An ounce of practice, Gandhi observed, is worth more than tons of preaching. It is in this spirit that we challenge readers to develop an "ethics journal" that includes the creation of an individualized checklist to help supply material for the journal. (See Exercise 4 at the end of the chapter.)

POPPYCOCK: MYTHS ABOUT ETHICS

Despite the compelling reasons to study ethics and its practicality, there is often a reluctance to discuss ethics in policy and administration. This hesitation—or outright rejection of ethics—rests on three contentions: that ethics is impossible, unnecessary, and simple.

Ethics as Impossible

It is contended that ethics is unattainable. Relativism maintains that all judgments are subjective and private, a matter of taste and opinion. Yet causal support for relativism, with the desire to be tolerant and respectful of others, is clearly deficient and misleading. Yes, different people have different codes and norms, but this truism proves little. There may be, for instance, different views about science (e.g., flat earth, evil spirits cause disease, global warming). Most people, however, do not therefore conclude that there is no truth in geography, medicine, or meteorology. Similarly, why assume that for an ethical truth to exist everyone must know it (Rachels & Rachels, 2014)? People are fallible and cultures change; making reasoned, ethical judgments is not only appropriate, but also morally responsible.

William J. Bennett (1978, 22), former U.S. Secretary of Education, tells of his visit to a classroom where his colleague encounters a student who is skeptical of a class on ethics. The dialogue illustrates that ethics is inescapable:

> *Student:* Mr. Jones, I don't think you can teach ethics, because there really aren't any in any real sense. Each person's values are as good as anybody else's. Values are subjective.
>
> *Instructor:* No, that's not true. Some people's values are better than others.
>
> *Student:* No, they're subjective. No one can impose his values on somebody else.
>
> *Instructor:* That's not true.
>
> *Student:* Yes, it is.
>
> *Instructor:* No, it isn't.
>
> *Student:* Well, that's your opinion and I have mine and it's just like I'm saying we disagree and you can't impose your viewpoint on me.
>
> *Instructor:* Well, I'm the teacher here and I say values are not subjective.
>
> *Student:* So what? I'm a student and I say they are.
>
> *Instructor:* Well, what do you think of this? I say values are not subjective and if you don't agree with me then I'll flunk you.
>
> *Student:* (gasp) What? What? You can't do that! Are you crazy?
>
> *Instructor:* No, I can do that. Why not?
>
> *Student:* Well, (sputtering) because it's not fair.
>
> *Instructor:* "Fair," "fair," what do you mean "fair"? Don't impose your values and sense of right and wrong on me.
>
> *Student:* (pause, and eventually) I see your point.

The instructor was able to parry back and forth with his student effectively to make a point, namely, suggesting that all values are equally valid because they are personal is simply not tenable. Adolph Hitler and Martin Luther King are not moral equivalents.

It also may be that some values are relative to culture, but others are not. It is a mistake to say that if some values are relative, all must be. Why? It would mean that there are no cultural practices that are wrong (torture and slavery are widely accepted as wrong independent of culture). As Nietzsche famously wrote, "Nothing is true, all is permitted." To assert that no reasons need be given for one's beliefs is self-defeating—that is, to defend such a view requires giving reasons for it. If norms are impossible, then how does one defend her own standpoint (Rachels & Rachels, 2014)? If everything is relative, then, *reductio ad absurdum*, relativism has no foundation; everything loses meaning—including relativism.

Aristotle summarized the situation in this manner: Differences between traditions have enough in common—by virtue of shared humanity—to make achievement of common norms a realistic goal. With relativism, however, there is no basis to condemn evil, no hope that people can work together to address humanity's problems. The goal in thinking about ethics is to generate progress, tolerate diversity without moral recklessness, and encourage moral imagination to find common ground between disparate views. Nonetheless, the relativity debate continues because rights are normative aims, not descriptive facts—a vision for a better world will always be contested (Boghossian, 2017).

It is, of course, true that many arguments—scientific and moral—cannot be definitively proved by logic or evidence. They can, however, be rational. Short of finality, there is ample scope for rationality in discussions. Decisions are objective in the sense that they can be defended and criticized by logical arguments. The irony today is that people often have strong convictions about minor issues (sports, fashions, weather), while holding weak convictions about major issues (what is right and wrong).

While personal preferences in food and drink may be the ultimate point as they require no public justification ("I like *nachos*" is inconsequential), an official's attitude toward whistleblowers does matter. If an opinion has no basis in reason, then it is unlikely to be very persuasive. And if ethical arguments cannot be conclusively resolved, this only indicates how fundamental they are.

Ethics as Unnecessary

In addition to the claim that ethics is impossible, a second contention is that ethics is simply unnecessary. The proposition is that society is a market system in which participants have only to look out for themselves and let the "invisible hand" handle all conflicts. Oblivious to ethical concerns, morality has nothing to do with anything. This self-operating, "automatic," nonjudgmental approach explains the appeal of commercial reasoning. Even arch global capitalist George Soros, however, points out that "[W]e can have a market economy, but we cannot have a market society" (Sandon, 2002). The embrace of the marketplace, along with the reluctance to engage moral issues, enfeebles discourse in the public square (Sandel, 2012, 14). Former U.S. Secretary of Labor Robert Reich (2012) provocatively recounts abuses of public trust seen on Wall Street and in corporate suites, concluding that these "are not matters of private morality. They're violations of public morality. They undermine the integrity of our economy and democracy. They've led millions of Americans to conclude the game is rigged." Markets, stated differently, are at least as susceptible to erratic performance and emotional reaction as those in politics and government. To combat declining trust and rising cynicism in all sectors of the economy, moral imperatives must not be obscured.

The market, left on its own, is an arena of antagonistic, autonomous, isolated, selfish figures; ethics is irrelevant, impractical, and inappropriate. The idea of public life, in contrast, encourages citizens to see themselves as living with others in common purpose, and to see leading an ethical life as contribution to a just polity. In a democratic society, value differences are resolved by the political process. The economy serves society; society does not serve the economy. If society exists to serve the market, then any moral limits that introduce market inefficiencies should be eliminated. Adam Smith, who after all was a professor of moral philosophy, knew this. Capitalism may make the world a better place, but only when it is a servant not a master of human needs.

When economists talk about self-regulating markets, what they mean is that markets reach an equilibrium between supply and demand. This says nothing about whether this equilibrium is good for society. Unfortunately, morality is not built into markets; they are fine, for instance, with child labor and slavery. Ethics is not only optional, but also vulnerable to a variation of Gresham's Law—like counterfeit currency, bad ethics drives out good ethics. This is why markets must be subject to other forces such as ethics and government. The "invisible hand" operates for the public good only if directed by the social values the political system enacts by its laws. Governments do not intrude on free markets; they organize and maintain them. As Peter Drucker (1954) famously wrote, "Free enterprise cannot be justified as being good for business. It can be justified only as being good for society."

Perhaps the first two contentions—that ethics are impossible and unnecessary—can best be countered in this way: Be bold in what you stand for and careful for what you fall for. The next justification to avoid ethics is that it is a clear-cut matter like the difference between day and night, so that discussing it is not worth the effort.

Ethics as Simple

Ethical decision making is difficult and multifaceted, not as obvious and easy as concluding that everything is either black or white. Such judgments are often:

- troublesome (conflicting standards may apply when confronting situations),
- hard to recognize (crucial information may be unavailable or deliberately withheld), and
- submerged in everyday workplace behavior (harassment and intimidation).

Many moral problems in institutions involve individuals, groups, or organizations, some of whom will be helped and others hurt as a result of factors beyond their control. Some may have their rights recognized, respected and expanded; others may have their rights denied or ignored. Ethical resolution of issues related to benefits and harms, rights and wrongs for different stakeholders are complex and require careful deliberation.

There are five reasons why ethical decision making is not a straightforward process, as these decisions have:

1. extended consequences—there is often a ripple effect, noted previously, as first-level consequences have multiple impacts both within and outside the organization (e.g., downsizing),

2. multiple alternatives—they are not usually just dichotomous options such as A vs. B decisions (tell the truth or lie?), but involve more complex choices,

3. mixed outcomes—results are seldom clear, unambiguous, and "win–win," but frequently knotty and murky, with winners and losers,

4. uncertain impacts—unanticipated outcomes (greater costs, lower benefits) are not unusual, and

5. personal implications—decision makers often face real disadvantages and advantages (job loss, reputation enhancement). (Adapted from Hosmer, 1987, 12–14)

As suggested by the first two statements, leaders should seriously ponder the possible second- and third-order consequences of all available alternatives. In doing so, they need to garner the advice from those who have relevant knowledge and experience to anticipate the likely differing reasons given the uncertain consequences. However, even the best intentioned leaders often encounter two potentially dangerous pressures when facing decision deadlines: the need to craft timely solutions before all of the facts are in, and the temptation to be more confident than circumstances warrant (also see Chapters 5 and 10). In these situations, Jean Lipman-Blumen (2005, 95) suggests following the old dictum "make haste slowly" and cites Steven Sample's recommendation to "think gray, see double, never completely trust an expert."

Studies of well-regarded "high reliability" organizations have examined the concept of "mindfulness." Weick, Sutcliffe, and Obstfeld (1999), for example, refer to this as *enriched awareness* among those in an organization concerned about the potential for a catastrophe. This awareness results in heightened consciousness and a sense of personal responsibility to prevent its occurrence. Such *reflective conduct* linking ethical thinking with action should promote "right-doing" and avoid wrongdoing. It requires open lines of communication from the bottom up, not just the top down. Sears, Roebuck & Company, for instance, has as part of its ethics program an employee survey called "My Opinion Counts." Among the questions are "Do you believe unethical issues are tolerated or not tolerated here?" and "Do you know how to report an ethical issue?" The program may enable the reporting of problems without fear of reprisal (subsequent chapters, especially Chapter 5, describe some additional tools to use when confronting thorny ethical choices).

A final reason people mistake ethics as elementary is that they fail to distinguish between what ethics is and what it is not. Ethics is not only complying with the letter of the law, religious beliefs, our feelings, and prevailing social norms or scientific formulas. While ethics is related to each of these claims, it is not as simple as they suggest. If ethics is not derived solely from feelings, law, religion, social norms or science, where do we derive standards of behavior to act in the many situations encountered in personal and professional lives? The chapters that follow explore this question as the many facets of ethics and ethical decision making are examined.

CONCLUSION

The observations on pertinence, practicality, and poppycock in this chapter can produce personal discomfort because ethics exists in the sphere of aspiration where one's reach exceeds one's grasp—the gap between the "is" and the "ought." Ethical quandaries are both hauntingly unavoidable and maddeningly intractable. To create this awareness produces some anxiety, and thoughtful people already have plenty of that. Yet, for Aristotle, public service is not merely one calling among others, but rather essential for the good life, to form good character and cultivate responsible communities. Moral excellence does not consist of maximizing pleasure over pain, but rather is the result of taking pleasure and pain in the right things (Sandel, 2009).

Although ethical problems cannot be easily "solved" (Aristotle's admonition not to demand greater clarity than a subject permits is relevant here), their importance remains. The fact that decisions are hard to make does not stop them from being made. Striving for excellence, if not perfection, is essential. It is better to be aware of troubling arguments that bear on workplace issues than to act on simplistic generalizations and unexamined premises.

It should not go unnoticed that no definition of the term *ethics* has been offered in this chapter, a task deliberately delayed for later discussion. The goal here has been to engage, enrich, and elevate an essential inquiry into the self. "Goodness without knowledge is weak and feeble," according to John Phillips, the founder of Exeter Academy, "but knowledge without goodness is dangerous."

***

Since most of us spend our lives doing ordinary tasks, the most important thing is to carry them out extraordinarily well.

—Henry David Thoreau

FOR DISCUSSION

1. Critically examine the reasons for studying ethics discussed in this chapter, modify as needed, and offer additional ones.

2. Critique these statements:

   - A technically incompetent manager is as unprofessional as an ethically incompetent one.
   - An ethically competent manager will be working on technical competence; the opposite may not be true.
   - Ethical competence may be more important, harder to come by, and more difficult to recognize than technical competence.
   - "A professional is someone who can do his best work when he doesn't feel like it." —Alistair Cooke.

3. The chapter rebutted claims that ethics is impossible, unnecessary, and simple. Refute the rebuttal.

4. Identify a headline scandal or an incident in an organization you are personally familiar with. Discuss how the problem is being handled. Ensure that some context for the case is briefly provided, such as the type of organization and its size (the organization does not have to be named), when the problem occurred, and the exact nature of the issue.

EXERCISES

1. Complete at least two sentence stems. For instance:

   - "I disagree with___."
   - "I wonder about___."
   - "I was surprised by___."
   - "I re-learned that___."
   - "I did not understand___."

   A completed stem, then, would be, "I think that there is at least one other reason to study this subject; this additional reason is___." Next, add a one- or two-sentence explanation to the stem so that others can ascertain your reasoning. Another example would be, "I doubt that the contention in the chapter about topic X is accurate. Instead,___."

2. There are a number of websites that attempt to verify the truth claims surrounding current event controversies, such as:

   - http://www.factcheck.org
   - http://www.politifact.com/truth-o-meter
   - http://snope.com
   - http://www.truthorfiction.com

   Identify at least one other site as well as two sites dedicated to the study of ethics. Be sure to provide the complete URL, the purpose of the organization, and the range of issues it covers.

3. The 21st century began with Enron Era that set off a wave of corporate scandals involving scores of flagship corporations in many sectors of the economy—and leading banks that facilitated the dubious transactions for them and many other less well-known businesses. In fact, many of the debacles implicated not just individual firms, but entire industries. The widening scandal involved illegal manipulation of company stock options at the expense of investors (among the charges were racketeering, fraud, obstruction of justice, money laundering, tax evasion, insider trading, grand larceny, destruction of evidence, and misuse of company funds). For some commentators, the things that were done that were legal were just as troubling (Labaton, 2006).

   By 2007, the worst home mortgage crisis since the Great Depression (the subprime crisis) emerged as a result of deregulation, predatory lending, and risky investments that undermined the housing sector and the nation's financial institutions. The shockwaves impacted the entire U.S. economy and the world banking system. Indeed, the $65 billion involved in the Bernie Madoff Ponzi scheme would be dwarfed by the over $2.5 trillion paid by citizens to bail out Wall Street firms deemed "too big to fail." As the nation entered the second decade of the new century, it experienced the deepest recession since the 1930s, which has yet to be resolved as the recovery has been one of the weakest on record.

Nonprofits (such as the United Way and the Red Cross) as well as chronically under-staffed government entities (e.g., the Securities and Exchange Commission) also did not go uncriticized during these episodes. In fact, these sectors are often led by former business executives—some of whom engaged in dubious practices.

To prepare for class participation, include, as needed, information from the commentary immediately above and consider the claim that Americans are socialized to believe that their economic system is inherently superior, which leads to little consideration of its morality.

4. The book began with four reasons—personal, pervasiveness, professional, and power—to study ethics. Apply these factors to the case below in order to help understand what is at stake here. What would you do? Why? Hints: Is your participation actually needed? What is in the best interest of your supervisor with whom you wish to maintain a good relationship?

> A work colleague has been able to succeed despite a pattern of poor performance. She does not seek feedback or take it well when received; the result is that projects are regularly submitted late and contain problems that others must fix. She has also been dishonest about relationships with co-workers and their duties. She is able to retain her position because she reports to an executive who has not held her accountable.
>
> Recently she terminated a competent subordinate who had attempted to assist in correcting her mistakes. This upset other employees as they felt the individual was treated unfairly: the low-level worker was in an impossible situation of trying to ensure that the work was done competently, while her boss wanted it done in an inferior manner that would require rework by others. The discharged employee has retained an attorney to show that the adverse action was retaliatory. The lawyer has asked me to tell what I know of the situation (and I may be required to testify under oath); my employer will tell me that I am not authorized to discuss personnel matters. I feel as though I should speak up for "the little guy," but am concerned that I will just hurt myself. (Adapted from Appiah, 2017, June 21)

5. Ethics Checklist and Journal

> Although at the start I thought the journal and checklist exercise was going to be a waste of time, I have found that they have proved to be one of the most useful tools I have ever used. They have taught me more about both the material and about myself than I ever could have hoped to learn just by reading.
>
> *When we were given the personal checklist and journal assignment, my first thought was, "How on earth is this supposed to help? I know how to stay on*

track with what I need to do; I don't need this checklist to help me do it." Oh, how wrong I was!

The checklist serves as a guide; I learned early on that procrastination decreases any time allotted to perform at my greatest ability. The journal served to assist in application of the material. Understanding the text became easier once I began to write in my journal and apply the literature to current events and personal experiences. Considering these tools, there is no reason why an individual should neglect to perform at his/her best.

The above comments demonstrate how past students, who may once have been skeptical, profited from the checklist and journal assignments. The checklist, once customized as desired, becomes a useful way to track activities that you identified as important. Accordingly, make the reading material personally meaningful by launching the ethics journal (Exhibit 1.2). An initial entry might be a challenging case you have experienced; it should identify the dilemma in one sentence, describe it in several paragraphs, analyze the outcome, and indicate what was learned. If the readings shed light on the case, then that might be noted.

EXHIBIT 1.2   Ethics Journal

In addition to reflections on current events, personal experiences, your work or school habits, course readings, and class discussions, here are more prompts that may be helpful as you journal:

- How did you plan your activities for today? What values underlie your plan?
- Draft a message that describes your favorite moral exemplar.
- Describe the way you solve problems.
- What is the most important thing you did today? Why?
- Develop and complete several sentence stems (see Exercise 1, above) and then supply a short explanation or commentary to elaborate on your stems.

Like a new physical exercise, keeping a journal and checklist may seem a bit awkward and uncomfortable at first; if so, this feeling is likely to diminish as you continue to practice and benefit from the activity. Remember the Rule of the Trumpet: You get out what you put in.
    The positive outcomes of this exercise include:

- ownership (taking responsibility for your own learning),
- enhanced awareness of personal growth,
- self-confidence,
- good study habits,
- focusing on the subject area as a whole, and
- "reflectivity" (digging deeper to examine meanings rather than taking things at face value).

If you are not having fun doing this project, then start anew!

Throughout the term, illustrate the journal with a current events file based on a search of ethics websites, newspaper stories, blog reports, magazine articles, scholarly publications, and television reports (this material likely will help inform your contributions to discussions with colleagues). As well, include your reactions to this book and emphasize interesting, surprising reflections about what you (dis)agreed with. Complete a copy of the Personal Checklist form (Appendix 1.1) as part of the journal each week. Note that the sample checklist should be modified as needed.

Journaling is straightforward: Simply put words on a page. Because this is your personal log, there is no right or wrong way to keep it. While there are no rules or limits in this assignment, you can seek a comfortable place for sketching your entries, talk about what was significant today, write from the heart, and, if you like, pretend you are scribbling a note to your best friend.

Write what you know, and think of your diary as an old buddy you are having coffee with. Just ask, "What's up?" and start recording your thoughts (http://www.journalingsaves.com/how-to-journal/). The value of this exercise is in the process, not necessarily the product. Frequent entries help gain perspective. Get to know yourself. There is power in the written word, sorting through the events, recognizing patterns, generating energy for change, and seeking control over your environment. A journal is a gift we give to ourselves.

6. Access and watch the 60-minute video, "Do Unto Others" from the Ethics in America series as part of the Annenberg/CPB Collection at https://www.learner.org/vod/vod_window.html?pid=191

REFERENCES

Appiah, K. (2017, June 21). Should I help an unjustly fired co-worker? *New York Times Sunday Magazine*, pp. 22–23.

Bennett, W. J. (1978, July 25). What values are substituted for truth? *Wall Street Journal*, p. 22.

Boghossian, P. (2017). The moral maze of relativism. In Catapano, P. & Critchley, S. (Eds.), *Modern ethics in 77 arguments: A stone reader*. New York: Liveright Publishing Corporation.

Drucker, P. (1977). *People and Performance*. NY: Routledge, p.29.

Eimicke, W. (2005). Eliot Spitzer: "The people's lawyer." *Public Integrity*, *7*, 353–372.

Eimicke, W., & Shacknai, D. (2008). Eliot Spitzer: "The people's lawyer" disgraced. *Public Integrity*, *10*, 365–380.

Frederickson, H. (1996). *The spirit of public administration*. San Francisco: Jossey-Bass.

Heclo, H. (2008). *On thinking institutionally (on politics)*. Chicago: Paradigm.

Hosmer, L. (1987). *The ethics of management*. Boston, MA: Richard D. Irwin.

Labaton, S. (2006, December 17). A push to fix the fix on Wall Street. *New York Times*. Retrieved from http://www.nytimes.com/2006/12/17/weekinreview/171abaton.html

Lipman-Blumen, J. (2005). *The allure of toxic leaders*. Oxford: Oxford University Press.

Newell, T. (2015). *To serve with honor: Doing the right thing in government.* Crozet, VA: Loftland Press.

Rachels, J., & Rachels, S. (2014). *Elements of moral philosophy* (8th ed.). New York: McGraw-Hill.

Reich, R. (2012, March 14). The difference between private and public morality. *Huffington Post.* Retrieved from http://www.huffingtonpost.com/robert-reich/the-difference-between-pr_b_1344690.html

Sandel, M. (2009). *Justice: What's the right thing to do?* New York: Farrar, Straus & Giroux.

Sandel, M. (2012). *What money can't buy: The moral limits to markets.* New York: Farrar, Straus & Giroux.

Sandon, L. (2002, September 10). Common or excessive, greed is a sin. *Tallahassee Democrat,* p. 1D.

Schelling, T. (1984). *Choice and consequence.* Cambridge, MA: Harvard University Press.

Thomas, T., Schermerhorn, J., & Dienhart, J. (2004). Strategic leadership of ethical behavior in business. *Academy of Management Executive, 18,* 56–66.

Weick, K., Sutcliffe, K., & Obstfeld, D. (1999). Organizing for high reliability: Processes of collective mindfulness. *Research in Organizational Behavior, 21,* 81–123.

Wilson, J. (1993). *The moral sense.* New York: Free Press.

Wood, D. (1994). *Business and society.* New York: HarperCollins.

Appendix 1.1
Personal Checklist

The premises of this exercise include the following:

- People want to do a good job; one way to know if someone is doing a good job is *to find out* by keeping records ("the strongest memory is weaker than the palest ink").
- Problems are opportunities to improve quality (check marks on the accompanying checklist are facts, and facts *are* friends).
- It is more effective to fix the process that is the cause of the problem rather than to fix blame on a person.

Benefits of the checklist:

- Its mere presence on your desk not only is a continuing reminder of your commitment, but also may actually prevent problems from arising in the first place.
- Properly constructed (see below), the list should have a "calming effect" as it is a way to bring order to personal activities, thereby harnessing initiative and motivation.

Tips for developing and using the list:

- Use the KISS principle (keep it sweet and simple), since a complex, lengthy list will likely lead to frustration.
- Seek a balance between new standards that may result in less time wasted and those that may expand time commitments.
- Recognize that not all specific problems can be dealt with by a checklist (e.g., a frustrating experience with a checklist may reveal for the first time an over-commitment to activities that may lead to a general cutback in responsibilities).
- Note that the list is subject to change and continuous improvement.
- Watch for synergy (e.g., being on time for an activity [in]directly contributes to a state of mind that leads to improved participation).
- Know that analyzing "why" something happens leads to "how" to improve.

Sample Checklist

Instructions: Modify the checklist as needed and use regularly.

Checklist, Week of _____

Problem Category	M	T	W	Th	F	Sa	Su	Total
Complete reading on a timely basis								
Review notes at the end of the week								
Keep up with current events								
Study at least __ hours/day								
Devote significant time to projects								
Spend so much time improving own activities that none is left for griping or blaming others								
Exercise and maintain a balanced diet								
Refer to this checklist								
Customized entry here								
Customized entry here								

Appendix 1.2
Book Chapters and NASPAA Professional Competencies in Public Administration

The Network of Schools of Public Policy, Affairs and Administration (NASPAA) requires MPA programs to identify learning outcomes and competencies for all courses and program objectives. The aim is to provide students with concepts and techniques needed to think through ethical issues, and to understand the kinds of questions that should be asked in decision making. The table below shows chapters of the book that introduce material to help develop the five managerial competencies of public service professionalism.

Chapter	NASPAA Competencies				
	To Lead and Manage in Public Governance	To Participate in the Policy Process	To Analyze, Synthesize, Think Critically, Solve Problems, and Make Decisions	To Articulate and Apply a Public Service Perspective	To Communicate and Interact Productively with a Diverse and Changing Workforce and Citizenry
1	✗		✗	✗	
2	✗		✗	✗	
3	✗		✗	✗	
4	✗	✗	✗	✗	
5	✗	✗	✗	✗	✗
6	✗		✗	✗	✗
7	✗		✗	✗	
8	✗	✗	✗	✗	✗
9	✗	✗	✗	✗	
10	✗	✗	✗	✗	
11	✗	✗	✗	✗	✗
12	✗	✗	✗	✗	✗
13	✗		✗	✗	
14	✗		✗	✗	
15	✗	✗	✗	✗	

2 Perspectives on Ethics

Macro, Meso, Micro

Successful leaders see the opportunities in every difficulty rather than the difficulty in every opportunity.

Reed Markham

LEVELS OF ANALYSIS

Since ethics is personal, pervasive, professionally important, powerful, practical, and full of pitfalls (Chapter 1), it is not about to go away. It is important, therefore, to move beyond the consciousness raising in the initial chapter to an understanding of ethics. This second foundational chapter examines the three levels of analysis in ethics: macro (intellectual and historical societal concerns), meso (organizational), and micro (individual). Gaining an appreciation for multiple frames of reference is helpful in comprehending the nature of the subject area. The chapter objectives are to:

- understand different levels of analysis and their implications,
- analyze interactions at the macro, meso, and micro perspectives on ethics,
- recognize the need for integration of the three levels in promoting ethics,
- appreciate factors that influence admirable behavior,
- know that ethical inquiry can be explored as readily as any other type of management analysis,
- embrace ethics as both the easiest and hardest topic anyone encounters, and
- apply chapter concepts to real cases.

This chapter shows how developments at the macro level (society, markets, government) interact with those at the micro (individual) and meso (organizational) levels. At each point, conflicts may be encountered, and people must decide how to resolve them. In some cases, societal and organizational ethical climates will be compatible with individual ethics, reducing the likelihood of discord.

Conflicts, however, may occur when there is a clash of societal, organizational, and individual ethics. One of the most common issues is conflicts of interest, where an employee has to weigh personal interests against the public good. Such dilemmas raise the question, "How should I handle this situation?" When interest compatibility is absent, cynicism may result, especially if the employee wants to make right choices, but the organization demands wrong choices. The dynamic interaction that exists among the three levels adds complexity to decision making (Figure 2.1). The letters A–D in the figure indicate the dyadic and triadic relationships that exist. Specific kinds of issue that can arise at each level are shown in Table 2.1 opposite.

FIGURE 2.1 | **Interactions Among Macro, Meso, and Micro Levels**

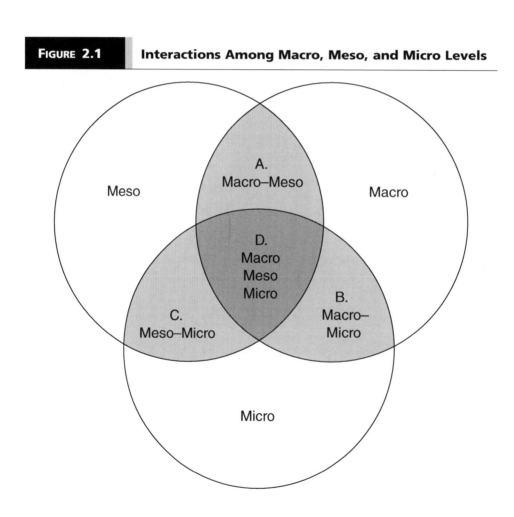

TABLE 2.1	Levels of Ethical Issues

Profession-Wide/Public Sector-Wide (Macro) Level

- Is the established public hearing process really fair to citizens and truly democratic in nature?
- Is the procurement process sufficiently insulated from political concerns and undue influence?
- Are unelected bureaucrats sufficiently responsive to the needs of the citizenry?
- Are the viewpoints of all affected parties (i.e., stakeholders) considered in the course of decision making?

Organizational (Meso) Level

- What kinds of values am I communicating to my peers and subordinates by my behavior? And do these values cohere with my organization's values? Are they supportive of the public welfare/common good?
- Should I deploy standards of evaluation stricter than those required by law because I know that the legal standard is grossly inadequate?
- Should I overlook the misdeeds of my colleagues in the interest of organizational cohesion?
- Should I blow the whistle on the wrongdoings in my organization, knowing that there will be detrimental political consequences for the organization?
- Is my use of organizational resources mainly for the benefit of the public or for personal gain?
- Should I give the promotion to my sister's husband because I know they are having financial troubles even though someone else deserves it more?
- Should I use my work car on family road trips because I don't want to pay for the expensive gas and put miles on my personal leased car?
- Should I tell my supervisor the project is almost finished when in reality I haven't begun?
- Should I hire the person I like or the person who is most qualified?
- Should I tell my manager that my co-worker has been taking confidential financial statements home?

Individual (Micro) Level

- Should I leave or wait until the person whose car I hit in the store parking lot comes back?
- Should I run the stop sign because nobody is around?
- Should I tell the waitress she forgot to charge me for my meal?
- Should I return the sunglasses I accidentally left the store with even though no one noticed?
- Should I leave a restaurant without paying because the service was poor?
- Should I cheat on my taxes by overstating my charitable contributions?
- Should I tell the cashier that she gave me change for a $20 when I paid with a $10?
- Should I tell my bank that they deposited someone else's money in my account?
- Should I lie to a friend or family member to avoid hurting their feelings?

Source: Adapted from Carroll and Buchholtz (2000). Reproduced by permission, www.cengage.com/permissions

The discussion here starts with a brief intellectual and historical perspective on the large-scale, macro level of analysis: the study of knowledge and political history. This is followed by an examination of contemporary research on the three analytical levels, bolstered by focusing on societal, organizational, and individual ethics.

Macro Level of Analysis: Historical Dimensions

The Study of Knowledge. Until the end of the 19th century, ethics was integral to higher education; its purpose was to develop mind and soul, to cultivate character and morality.

TABLE 2.2	Classical and Modern Worldviews

Classical World View

Religious belief
God exists
Future-world orientation
World as a mysterious garden
Centralized authority
Intuition
Sense of community
Charity
Justice
Routine
Just price

Modern worldview

Religious skepticism
God may or may not exist
This-world orientation
World as scientific project
Diverse moral authorities
Rationality
Sense of individualism
Self-interest
Liberty
Innovation
Market price

Source: Adapted from an anonymous source.

Teddy Roosevelt's observation, "To educate a man in mind, but not morals is to create a menace to society," captures the spirit of this perspective. Universities were cathedrals of learning devoted to probing the meaning of life. The academy, using the Oxford/Cambridge model, was where morality and philosophy were taught: The supreme end of education was to distinguish right from wrong, to seek the good life, and to become model citizens.

This classical organic view—that the world was an enchanted garden and people an integral part of it—would be confronted with the modern mechanistic view that nature can be understood and controlled through experimental manipulation; God created the universe and science would define it (Table 2.2). A positivist theory of knowledge based on the Newtonian paradigm denied attention to the moral and social nature of knowledge. The Enlightenment created an intellectual world of skepticism, reason, and evidence-based change. The central lesson of the Enlightenment was that facts matter, especially when they conflict with dogma. The result was C. P. Snow's (1959/1993) "two cultures"; science (with its emphasis on questions of "how") superseded the humanities (forever fascinated by questions of "why"). Since, historically, religion had provided moral guidance in institutions of higher learning, the study of ethics was relegated to philosophy and religion departments as an afterthought. Mandatory attendance at chapel services was dropped. Academic research and teaching replaced character formation at the core of the university's mission. Virtue was divorced from knowledge.

The modern mystique of science would eventually fade as it became evident that scientists were often effective in addressing questions of how, but not why (e.g., see Kuhn, 1962; Watson, 1969). People realized that scientism—science as the only way to discover truth—could not deal with the most fundamental aspects of reality: its values, meaning, and purpose. Scientific inquiry never produced standards to adjudicate moral claims. Science and religion simply ask different questions with the former emphasizing the "is" and the latter focusing on the "ought." "Science without religion is lame;" said Einstein, and "religion without science is blind."

Political History. Arthur Schlesinger (1986/1999) analyzed 20th-century America in terms of two types of alternating periods. *Public purpose eras* were times of high idealism, commitment to the public good, new programs to benefit others, reform movements (provoked by issues that the market could not resolve), and a relative absence of corruption (the early 1900s, 1930s, 1960s). *Private interest eras* were times when people became exhausted by intense public action, displeased with its consequences, and pursued their own interests. Materialism, personal satisfaction, privatization, cult of the market, and sanctity of private property were the watchwords; there was a priority of wealth over commonwealth that nourished a propensity for corruption (the 1920s, 1950s, 1980s–present). Each phase flows out of the conditions and contradictions of the phase before it, as there is always a desire to better the socio-political condition. Citizens are never fulfilled for long with either cycle—eventually, a time for a change emerges.

Whether one is operating in the public interest or private interest era, the insights gleaned from both the humanities and science—from asking questions about "why" and "how" and about "what ought" and "what is"—are important in understanding ethics. From a historical perspective, the analysis now moves to the contemporary period and summarizes selected studies germane to the three levels of ethics.

CONTEMPORARY RESEARCH ON LEVELS OF ETHICS

While macro-level influences obviously affect meso and micro ethics, Applebaum, Vigneault, Walker, & Shapiro (2009) stress that critical interactions occur at the macro–meso upper boundary and at the meso–micro lower boundary (Figure 2.2). Here, law and ethics policy interact with organizational responses, such as conduct codes and ethics training, and ethical leadership seeks to cultivate "individual and organizational ethical congruence" (528).

Appelbaum et al. (2009) emphasize that the meso level is pivotal in creating and sustaining an organization's ethical culture because it is a critical link between macro and micro levels. However, by stressing the organization–individual relationship (i.e., meso–micro; Figure 2.1, dyad C) as the most important one in building a shared and lasting ethic with its employees, the authors neglect the influence of the macro level, particularly the impact it has on the micro level (the "Macro–Micro Interface" in Figure 2.2 fills in this gap in their model). For example, they maintain that the strategic significance of the macro level is difficult to verify empirically as having positive and observable behavioral effects on individuals.

Nielsen and Massa (2012), in their examination of the ineluctable pull of societal factors, provide support for the crucial influence of macro forces. They point out that macro-level

---

FIGURE 2.2   **Integration of the Three Levels**

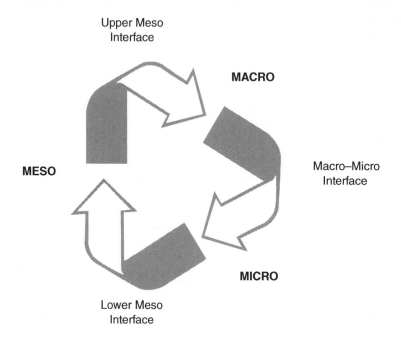

Source: Adapted from Applebaum et al. (2009).

---

developments can influence meso- and micro-level ethics; they can be both the cause of problems and the locus of solutions. This is exemplified in blowing the whistle and the Great Recession.

Whistleblowing (see Chapter 10) shows the relationship between macro and micro ethical issues. Nielsen and Massa (2012, 142) contend that the structure of macro "U.S. finance capitalism" creates barriers for whistleblowers: First, regulatory agencies are understaffed due to "the logic of minimal regulation"; second, junior regulators have financial incentives "to learn on the job and then leave . . . to work in lobbying firms"; third, lobbyists contribute considerable amounts of money to the politicians who appoint regulators.

The 2008 recession illustrates how organizational ethics problems can originate at the macro level. Specifically, the central cause of the macro financial crisis is the system of today's capitalism and its emphasis on short-term profit maximization. If organizational ethics problems are caused primarily by the macro level, then long-range solutions may necessitate systemic reforms. As these two cases suggest, macro developments should not be discounted and understanding the interfaces at each of the three levels is essential.

An example of macro–meso–micro relationships (Figure 2.1, intersection D) is changes in the global economy (resulting from competition, technological innovation, and pricing mechanisms) that impact the meso level (layoffs, contingent workers, privatization) with repercussions at the micro level for employees (modification of the "psychological contract," the unwritten understanding about mutual goals and expectations). When individuals see a breach in their psychological contract—which heretofore led them to expect a reciprocal relationship between hard work and loyalty—this can lead to detrimental repercussions in job satisfaction, performance, commitment, and retention (Berman et al., 2015; Rigotti, 2009; West, 2012; Zhao et al., 2007). Coupled with the risk shifting of costs from employers to employees (health co-pays, higher deductibles, replacement of defined benefit pensions to defined contribution pensions), this departure from the hard work–loyalty norm can further affect employee attitudes and behaviors.

What can be done in response to these trends? At the meso level, cost cutting does not have to take the form of layoffs. There are many alternative strategies that can be used before resorting to more drastic measures that depress employee satisfaction and commitment (West & Condrey, 2011). Indeed, it is possible to increase productivity by establishing closer employee–management relationships, and competency-development options (Matzler & Renzl, 2006; Mayfield & Mayfield, 2002; Olson-Buchanan & Boswell, 2002). Using economic and non-monetary incentives also may bring about a decline in opportunistic behavior and augment employee effort due to a mutual desire to see the organization flourish (Brown et al., 2011; Green, 2008; Pfeffer, 1994).

At the micro level, another response to recent trends involves micro changes affecting macro (Figure 2.1, dyad B). One illustration is ethical investing in which investors decide where to put their money by considering the social impacts created by the businesses. Emphasis on areas like human rights, the environment, and arms production have become important considerations by investors when supporting socially responsible mutual funds (which are generally competitive with other funds). Consumers could be motivated as well to examine the record of producers before deciding to purchase their products. The assumption is that businesses will have to respond to ethical investors and critical customers who seek to hold firms accountable (Jeurissen, 1997, 249). Organizations such as Greenpeace, Corporate International Accountability and Amnesty International, for instance, have pressured multinational corporations to be more socially responsible. However, Robert Reich (2007, 181), former U.S. Secretary of Labor, is skeptical about the extent to which business will pursue social goals:

> Making companies more "socially responsible" is a worthy goal, but it would be better served by making democracy work better. Pressuring companies to be more virtuous is an unaccountable mechanism for deciding complex social issues better left to legislators . . . the democratic process and courts at least provide means for weighing and balancing claims. Not so in the private sector.

Government is often slow to act on social problems, but it would be more likely to respond if citizens and service recipients aggressively made their wishes known. The Tea Party and

Occupy Wall Street movements showed the potential impact of an aroused citizenry as the former was effective in electing candidates to Congress and the latter in changing the national conversation about who actually benefits in today's economy. In short, the macro-level developments both affect and are affected by meso and micro behaviors, including relationships depicted in Figure 2.1, vectors A, B, and D. Attention now shifts to meso-level analysis.

MESO LEVEL OF ANALYSIS: THE ORGANIZATION

In thinking about ethics in the world of work, it is possible to rely on everyday morality. Yet the workplace has features that limit the applicability of ordinary ethics. The most obvious example is the mission of the military in dealing with enemies when under fire. What people ought to do on the job depends to some extent on the organizational roles that they occupy, as Miles's Law states, "Where you stand depends upon where you sit." Ethical dilemmas confronting soldiers are likely to differ considerably from those facing journalists, professors, physicians, attorneys, and people in other occupations. And those in public service have important, specialized ethical issues to deal with as well.

Integrating meso- and micro-level ethics (Figure 2.1, dyad C) in public service is challenging. While designing and implementing ethics codes and offering training are not easy tasks (see Chapters 3, 4, 8), it is critical to undertake them as codes and training promote integrity at work. They are especially important in the public sector from which citizens expect accountability and transparency. Yet while internalizing ethics is a key component to an organization's success, it is often under-emphasized, a problem that frequently results in questionable activities. For example, the behavior of some police forces in recent years has resulted from officers abusing their roles (see e.g., Mclean & Poisson, 2015). By wearing their uniforms when shopping off-duty to get reduced prices or, more importantly, using deadly force for minor traffic violations, these personnel taint the character of civil servants and consequently public trust. Transgressions among employees occur elsewhere as well: college admissions officers who lower standards for the children of wealthy donors, charity fundraisers who allocate gift moneys to projects that violate the donor's intent, and social service providers who fudge the data from evaluation studies to make their program appear more successful than it is (see Chapter 12).

To mend deterioration of standards, organizations must take action. It is not enough for managers to devise codes and offer training for an ethics program to be effective, just as it is not sufficient for those charged with serving the public to decide whose interests should be privileged. Rather, both meso and micro strategies must be employed in unison to combat unethical behavior. The agency should promote ethical awareness and responsibility while, simultaneously, the public servants themselves must internalize moral consciousness.

What can be done to avoid improper behavior? Two strategies, one micro level and one meso, are needed. At the micro level, employees should be encouraged to discuss integrity issues. More open lines of communication among co-workers about ethical dilemmas and personal responsibilities at work should occur in an atmosphere not of recrimination, but of continuous improvement. In turn, at the meso level, the department should clarify norms of proper behavior and provide guidance. Thus action is required, as Jeurissen (1997, 251) suggests, by "a combination of responsible autonomy from below, and control from above." Communicative process and norm clarification throughout the organization necessitates meso and micro integration of ethics, whereby individuals internalize institutional values, making them a part of their moral consciousness.

Meso strategies such as codes, training, audits, and ombudspersons can be useful aids in promoting moral sensitivity (the ability to recognize ethical issues), moral analysis skills (the capacity to analyze moral problems), and moral creativity (the talent to weigh decision options in light of conflicting values). Clearly, there are actions organizations can take to cultivate an ethical environment, but employees have a responsibility as well to uphold ethics and avoid wrongdoing, as discussed below.

MICRO LEVEL OF ANALYSIS: THE INDIVIDUAL

The question is, "How does one apply his values, learned as a child, in the workplace?" The quip, "I learned ethics at my mother's knee, but she did not tell me about highly leveraged derivative transactions," illustrates that basic intuitions developed in the family may not be easily applied to many issues. Stated differently, while there are important affective forces in value formation, there is also a significant cognitive component that depends on analysis and reflection.

The good news is that most people want to be ethical, most organizations want to be ethical, and most employees and organizations want to be treated ethically—indeed, they demand it. The bad news is that many individuals and institutions just are not very good at applying shared values to decision making. The glory of the human story is that the capacity for good makes ethics possible. The tragedy is that the propensity for evil makes ethics necessary (Preston, 1994).

Does a good ethical match between individuals and organizations make a difference in the life of both? Research by Ambrose, Amaud, and Schminke (2008, 329) examines "ethical fit," or congruence, between the individual and the institution. By adopting a phenomeno-logical approach—that is, focusing on the unique perspectives encapsulated in each of the three levels of analysis—they find that this "fit" does make a difference: Ethical congruence strengthens employees' and employers' commitment. Why? An ethical climate that creates a sense of community—a "corporate family" working together for the common good—coheres with employees who exhibit conventional levels of moral reasoning, focusing on mutual benefits and obligations (see Kohlberg's theory of moral development in Chapters 4 and 8). The effect is an increase in commitment to the organization and job satisfaction, and reduced turnover. The practical implication from this work is that ethical person–organization (P-O) congruence deserves attention by managers when crafting learning, development, and selection strategies (Ambrose et al., 2008, 330–331).

Training and development efforts coupled with judicious hiring are crucial. For ethics to become a predominant factor in organizational life means gaining ethics skills as one would develop other management skills. The goal is to manage, not moralize. Ethical analysis can be learned as readily as other forms of policy analysis. As in policy decisions, conceptual tools to examine the ethical dimension of decisions are needed. The objective, consistent with the Aristotelian notion of human flourishing, is to explore how one could act by increasing resources for decision making and not reducing ethics to non-ethical criteria (Chapter 5).

Without ethics education, new members of the profession will likely rely on values such as unthinking organizational loyalty, technical competence (untempered by moral judgment), or passive obedience to authority. Professionals bring both idealism and cynicism to their work; the hope here is to reinforce the former and minimize the latter. In our efforts, let us seek the middle ground between:

- naive utopianism ("we can change the world," a morality model that is unrealistically optimistic and ineffectual), and
- cynical pessimism ("we can't change anything," a fatalistic model that permits the worst to prevail).

It is between these two poles—optimistic realism—where progress is made: The Arab saying, "Trust in Allah, but tie your camel," demonstrates the utility of this approach. Trust is fine, but being informed is also prudent. Consider the case below (Exhibit 2.1).

EXHIBIT 2.1	**Ethical Dilemma: Macro, Meso, Micro Ethics in Action**

I support the Other 98, 99% Power, and Occupy Wall Street movement, and I am aghast at the predatory behavior of corporate banking. Although I do not work on Wall Street, I own stock in a mutual fund that includes these firms. Am I a hypocrite?

Taking offense at a dilemma and doing nothing about it defines a hypocrite. But a hard look at the situation suggests that you do not qualify. Your conduct, so far, may not be up to your convictions, a very common human condition. "In the real world, ethical standards have to accommodate some degree of ambivalence" (Kaminer, 2011). No one can do everything. If there were no room for hesitation, no one would ever meet ethical ideals, or have much reason to try. The movement itself has no qualifications for membership, as it tolerates contradictions and welcomes everyone; it definitely does not demand that people sell their stock.

The first obligation, then, is to determine if stock ownership is actually part of the problem or part of the solution. Is it preferable to stay with the mutual fund and learn what policy, if any, it has toward diversification and support for reform? If it is decided that the situation is untenable, then change is mandated. But even such an action will not stop investment bankers from enriching themselves off you: The financial sector is so entwined in every aspect of the economy that it is difficult for any individual to be isolated from it. Some form of compromise is inevitable. Its precise nature depends on the economy, the firm's investments, and personal values.

Source: Adapted from Kaminer (2011).

What are some factors that can influence ethics at the meso and micro levels? That is the topic of the next section.

FACTORS INFLUENCING MESO–MICRO ETHICS

Narrowing the focus to interactions at the meso–micro level (Figure 2.1, intersection C), there are four meso forces that can promote or impede individual behavior (Figure 2.3): leadership, strategic policies, organizational culture, and individual characteristics.

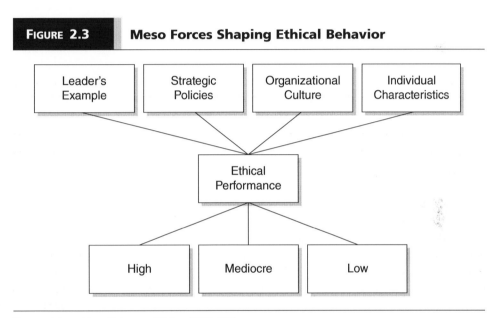

FIGURE 2.3   Meso Forces Shaping Ethical Behavior

Source: Adapted from Steiner and Steiner (2006, 196).

Leadership

The importance of top leadership in setting the tone and providing role models in public service settings is well documented (Dobel, 1998; Johnson, 2012; Kaptein, Huberts, Avelino, & Lasthuizen, 2005; Van Wart, 2005; West & Berman, 2006). A recent study charting ethics in six Asia-Pacific countries and four U.S. states stresses the important role of senior managers in setting high performance expectations and displaying exemplary leadership (West, Beh, & Sabharwal, 2013). People look to leaders to signal, through their actions and words, the values that are important to the organization. Unethical signals or unclear standards of behavior can lead to employee distrust and compromised performance standards. If leaders engage in ethically dubious behavior, it becomes easier for personnel to rationalize doing the same thing.

Most managers, as noted, want to do a good job. The grandfather of one of the authors of this book used the words "right" and "good" in a redundant way by saying things such as, "That was a right-good idea" or "You did a right-good job." He meant to convey "very good" by using this phrase, but it is helpful to keep the relationship and distinction of the double adjectives in mind between ethics and economics. Government managers have a job to do as stewards of public monies and administrators of public projects, and they need to do these things ethically to uphold the citizen trust. They want to produce good not bad economic results and to do so in ways that are ethically right not wrong (Bowman, 1995, 65).

Strategic Policies

Managers are responsible for implementing the goals and objectives of their organizations. They want to aggressively pursue performance targets, without pushing so hard that their efforts erode standards. Organizations should encourage employees to perform, while simultaneously articulating and implementing policies about appropriate behavior (e.g., conduct codes, ethics training, ethics audits). By promoting strategies that put too much stress on performance and too little on ethics, the results could compromise both. This is a way of reiterating Dennis Thompson's (1992, 255) caution, "[B]ecause other issues are more important than ethics, ethics are more important than any issue." Ethics, in other words, is a precondition for good government.

Unwelcome compromises can also result from reward and pay policies. Setting inflexible numerical quotas for performance and allocating rewards based on attaining the quota can lead to perverse outcomes (see Chapter 12). For example, compensating solid-waste collectors for the weight of their load can lead them to water down the garbage to add weight to the truck. Incentivizing police for the number of traffic tickets issued can result in questionable traffic stops and justified citizen complaints. Penalizing, instead of rewarding, teachers for accurately grading students can result in compromised standards, dishonest grades, and grade inflation.

Organizational Culture

The culture of an organization—the third meso-level factor affecting micro behaviour—encompasses its values, norms, rules, and rituals. Culture, like leadership and strategic policies, communicates what is important, often through informal and subtle ways. If the accepted practice is that "anything goes, so long as it is not illegal" or "get it done, no matter what," then dishonorable behavior is likely to occur. Under such circumstances, employees will be fearful and unwilling to sound the alarm on dubious behavior. Manipulating figures to make performance look good could be one consequence; failing to recognize the ethical dimension of one's actions could be another. In both instances, "culture eats strategy for breakfast": the action could be framed as a "good" economic decision, discounting any "wrong" ethical implications. The actions of one local government to positively influence the ethical culture in its jurisdiction are exemplified by Miami-Dade County (Exhibit 2.2).

EXHIBIT 2.2 | **Miami-Dade Commission on Ethics and Public Trust**

On March 12, 1996, the voters of Miami-Dade County, Florida, opted to amend the county's Home Rule Charter to create an ethics commission. Following the amendment, the county created the Commission on Ethics and Public Trust to help guarantee the honesty of both the electoral process and the governmental decision making. Acting as a safeguard for county residents, the commission's purpose is to educate the citizenry on the standards of conduct and to impose them on public officials.

Its unique membership comprises five people appointed by different stakeholders in the community. The Chief Judge of the Eleventh Judicial Circuit appoints two members: one former federal or state court judge and one past U.S., state, or county attorney or assistant. Next, the deans of the University of Miami Law School and St. Thomas School of Law alternately select a third member from his or her law school. Additionally, the director of Florida International University's Center for Labor Research and Studies designates the fourth representative. Finally, the Miami-Dade County League of Cities, Inc. names a fifth individual who has held elected office at the local level in the past.

Among the powers and duties outlined in the Code of Metropolitan Miami-Dade County, the commission is authorized to review, interpret, and render advisory opinions regarding the Citizens' Bill of Rights. In addition, it is empowered to appoint and remove the inspector general and conduct both preliminary investigations and public hearings. By a two-thirds vote of all members, it can subpoena witnesses, take evidence, compel attendance, and administer oaths.

In the first half of 2012, the commission wielded its power of investigation and quasi-judicially conducted hearings, and delivered opinions on a variety of issues and complaints. For example, the commission found that a supervising attorney and University of Miami lecturer cannot contract with the university (as an attorney or lecturer) while serving on the county's Financial Recovery Board because the university has a financial interest in the board's decisions. In so doing, they established that they are prohibiting relationships that could be seen as conflicts of interest that could impact stakeholders. The agency also evaluated and answered several of City of North Miami Mayor Andre Pierre's questions regarding issues such as arms-length transactions, quarterly gift disclosures, and voting on matters brought by an entity with whom he has debtor–creditor relations.

In addition, the Ethics Commission investigated an issue sweeping across the entire county. As reported by *The Miami Herald,* local politicians and public officials in several Miami-Dade county municipalities had been using free tickets to sporting events, concerts, and festivals for their personal benefit, tickets meant to be set aside for underprivileged children, the elderly, and the needy. The commission decided to call a public discussion on the issue and established guidelines prohibiting officials from using these tickets in their self-interest.

Since its creation in 1996, the Commission on Ethics and Public Trust has proved its essential and central role in local government. Acting as an independent agency, it has provided opinions and answered questions on various ethical issues regarding public officials, elections, and ethical standards.

Sources: Smiley (2012); Miami-Dade Ethics Commission; Code of Metropolitan Dade County.

Individual Characteristics

Employee and managerial behavior is related to both incentives in the meso environment and personal internal dispositions at the micro level. When working in an ethically troubling environment with incentive systems that unintentionally encourage wrongdoing (e.g., amoral or corrupt leaders, unrealistic deadlines or pressures to "achieve your numbers," overly permissive departmental culture), employees might succumb to temptations to violate their ethical code. Personal characteristics (age, experience, gender, education, religion) may have a bearing on their willingness to engage in unethical behavior, but researchers have achieved mixed results when exploring these relationships. A final example showing the interactions of the three levels and their impacts is the 2011 Pennsylvania State University sexual abuse case (Case Study 2.1) and the 2017 London fire disaster (Case Study 2.2).

CASE STUDY 2.1

The Pennsylvania State University Athletic Sex Abuse Scandal

On June 22, 2012, former Penn State assistant football coach Gerald "Jerry" A. Sandusky was found guilty of 45 criminal charges, including nine counts of unlawful conduct with minors, 10 counts of corruption of minors, 10 counts of endangering the welfare of children, and eight counts of involuntary deviant sexual intercourse. For some university employees—ranging from locker room janitors to high-ranking administrators, and all the way up to the university's president—it was hardly a shock. In 1998, the first incident was reported to university officials, and they swept it under the rug. As the years went on, more reports came in, and still nothing was done. For over a decade, officials were aware of Sandusky's crimes and yet continued to give him the very access to university facilities and football events he needed to groom young boys for sexual abuse. If rank-and-file workers at the bottom of the university hierarchy had come forward, or if those at the top had taken action, the childhoods of almost a dozen boys would have been unsullied and the integrity of an institution would still be intact.

Although, at first glance, it seems inconceivable that such heinous negligence and blatant disregard for the welfare of children could have persisted for so long, a closer look reveals a situation that is entirely understandable, though nevertheless inexcusable. It is the age-old story of the corrupting influence of organizational dynamics, but in an unexpected setting and with devastating consequences. As the details of who knew what and when, and failed to act on it, became evident, the picture that emerged is less one of malicious individuals engaged in a conspiracy and more of a tragic tale of the pernicious effects of an insulated, hierarchical, and publicity-minded organization, which enabled the key actors to make the wrong decisions at each step. While the failures of Penn State illustrate how an unscrupulous organizational infrastructure (meso) can mislead individual decision making (micro) and overwhelm cultural factors (macro), it also suggests what measures should be taken to ensure that meso-level factors exert a positive ethical influence both above and below.

Zooming in on the micro-level decision making of the actors involved, it can be seen how a rotten organizational infrastructure not only encouraged individuals to shirk their sense of responsibility, but also, more fundamentally, clouded their very perception of ethical issues. This was evident in the 2001 incident, when assistant coach Mike McQueary witnessed Sandusky molesting a boy in the shower. Although McQueary reported what he saw to head football coach Joe Paterno the next day, things went awry from then on. McQueary said that the encounter between Sandusky and the boy was "extremely sexual in nature" and he "thought that some kind of intercourse was going on."

Yet according to Athletic Director Timothy Curley and Senior Vice President Gary Schultz, when Paterno conveyed the account to them, details were lacking, and they were under the impression that the encounter was disturbing but not criminal. And even though Curley and Schultz later met with McQueary directly, by the time they informed University President Graham Spanier, the account had morphed into "horsing around" in the shower. Moreover, Spanier himself described the situation of an employee showering with a child as "unique," even though he was well aware of Sandusky's shower room behavior with another boy in 1998.

What can account for such a blatant disregard for the truth and such an egregious failure to identify the situation as an ethical issue? Loyalty plays a big part here, for, as J. Patrick Dobel observes, "the mind will often perform surgery and reinterpret what they see into a frame compatible with their respect and trust for the person." Moreover, to admit that Sandusky, a man they trusted and admired for so long, was a child molester would force them to confront their own moral failures for befriending him—and, in the case of Schultz, Curley, and Spanier, for continuing to trust him after the 1998 incident. Predictably, the failure to properly categorize the situation as ethical allowed these men to rationalize their decision not to report Sandusky, opting instead to offer him "professional help," which they framed as the more "humane" approach.

Yet even those who did perceive the ethical issue at hand found their ethical duty hindered by organizational factors. McQueary himself was wrongfully absolved of his responsibilities by the strict hierarchy of the football team, since he was told by Paterno, "[Y]ou did what you had to do. It's my job now to figure out what we want to do" (quoted in Freeh, Sporkin, & Sullivan, LLP, 2012, 65). Likewise, the dominant status of the coaches discouraged a janitor from reporting a similar incident he witnessed a year earlier. The janitor feared he would be fired if he came forward because, as he explained, "football runs this University" (65). If any of these individuals had spoken up at the time, at least two more assaults of young boys could have been prevented.

Nevertheless, if macro-level safeguards had been functioning properly, the ethical lapses at the meso and micro levels, although regrettable, would not have been so disastrous. As an insulated and highly prized part of the university, the football program existed outside the boundaries of standard operating procedure. Although the Office of Human Resources is regularly notified of incidents involving employees, officials like VP Schultz failed to report the 1998 incident so they could handle it themselves and keep it from getting out. Moreover, from 2000 to 2008, even though he was retired, Sandusky was allowed to operate summer youth football camps on campus without a Memorandum of Agreement, which is required of all third parties using university facilities.

Far more notable than these infractions, however, is the fact that, for nearly two decades, the university had failed to implement the federal Clery Act, which requires all institutions of higher learning to collect and report crime statistics and warn the community of ongoing threats to safety. Thus, as athletic staff falling under the purview of the statute, Paterno, Curley, and McQueary were obligated by federal law to report the 2001 incident to the University Police. But since the university was not in compliance with the act until 2012, institutional checks that could have averted future abuses were not in place. Indeed, Schultz and Spanier should have been concerned with guaranteeing compliance with the Clery Act, rather than with protecting Penn State's image.

Had individuals displayed greater moral courage at the micro level, or had institution-wide, macro-level policies been more strictly enforced, the tragedy might never have happened. In the final analysis, however, it becomes clear that the situation did not call for supererogatory behavior or a perfectly functioning bureaucracy, but rather accountability, transparency, and integration at the meso level. According to the report of the investigation by former FBI Director Louis Freeh, the key is to have a "values- and ethics-centered community where everyone is engaged in placing the needs of children above the needs of adults; and . . . an environment where everyone who sees or suspects child abuse will feel empowered to report the abuse" (129). A more ethically aware organizational culture, paired with institutionalized training and guidelines—as well as the integration of the athletic program into the broader university administrative and human resource structure—can help ensure that, in the future, organizational factors do not lead otherwise good people astray.

QUESTIONS TO CONSIDER

1. How can you relate the material in this chapter to the Pennsylvania State scandal?

2. How do macro, meso, and micro ethics come into play in this case?

Sources: Freeh, Sporkin, & Sullivan, LLP (2012); Dobel (2011).

CASE STUDY 2.2

Ethical Dilemmas During the Grenfell Tower Fire
Stephanie M. Belaustegui, University of Miami MPA Student

Introduction. In 2017, a freezer malfunctioned and caught fire in a West London apartment building (Malkin & Siddique, 2017). The fire spread rapidly due to a layer of very flammable insulation that enveloped the entire high rise. It took more than 200 firefighters over 12 hours to extinguish the resulting blaze (London Fire Brigade, 2017). It was so dangerous that nearby buildings were evacuated, and riot police units, using their ballistic shields, were called to protect firefighters and victims from falling debris (Towers, 2017). At least 71 people died; more than 70 were injured (Yeginsu, 2017). The BBC reported that the fire was the worst single loss of life since the end of the Second World War (Rushton, 2017, June 6).

The building had been renovated in 2016, but a resident action group had been calling for a full safety overhaul since 2013. Not only was the polyethylene material flammable, hundreds of fire doors did not meet code (Booth & Wahlquist, 2017). In the aftermath, one firefighter wrote an anonymous letter to the press, describing his or her experiences (Anonymous, 2017). It detailed the life-altering choices that this individual made, decisions that would have irrevocable repercussions.

Micro Dilemmas. The letter particularly highlights dilemmas that factor into the decision encountered in trying to evacuate victims from the building. The firefighter faced a nearly impossible decision after reaching the 19th floor with their partner and locating two victims. The victims were delirious, but said that there were five more people trapped four floors above. The firefighter had to weigh the situation and explain every thought that he or she had before deciding what to do. The decision had to be made in seconds as is typical in so many life-threatening situations, and the firefighter reveals the high level of stress experienced in choice making:

> Micro dilemmas each have consequences: Was there enough air left in the breathing apparatuses to reach the 23rd floor? Since the victims are delirious from smoke inhalation, is their report accurate? If we let them carry on down the stairs alone, could they find their way out? If we went up another floor, would we actually find five? If we found them, what state would they be in? Could the two of us get that many out, especially if one or more were unconscious? How would we decide who to take? Did we have enough air to make it back down to safety ourselves from where we were? Could I live with the thought that saving two lives is better than taking the risk to go up and potentially save no one?" (Anonymous, 2017)

The letter writer expressed the difficulty of suppressing growing panic as the situation obviously became dire. Although never explicitly stated, the firefighter seems to have made the decision to save the two people and called for another team to go up and attempt to retrieve the remaining victims on the 23rd floor.

The rescuer describes a second dilemma that occurred once outside the building, as a saved victim was talking on a phone with her friend and her child on the 11th floor, and begged the first responder to save them. She was told to stay on the line with her friend, while another team was dispatched to get her and her child (Anonymous, 2017). There were scores of these dilemmas over the 12-hour period. The firefighter teams went back again and again despite exhaustion and pain, retrieving as many people as was possible before the building was too unsafe to enter. This experience gives credence to why ethical dilemmas are studied: No one ever wants to believe they will have to make a decision about someone's life, but people may have to do just that.

The situation faced here compares to the trolley dilemma (Chapter 4): the concern of exchanging some lives for others, the factor of direct action versus indirect action, and the intervention of a third party who must make the decision. But more like the MIT moral machine (Chapter 4, Exercise 8), there are numerous factors beyond the number of people who came into play for the London fire case. Although the firefighter does not describe the final decision, it is clear that the two people on the 19th floor were rescued. The caveat is that the decision was made once another team was called to retrieve the other five people on the 23rd floor, but it is never made clear if that team makes it up there or what they found. The mayor of London issued a statement that the full report will not be available for quite some time. It may take months just to determine the identity of all the victims and the status of all the missing people.

The initial dilemma is apparently decided, but unlike the trolley dilemma, no final outcome is ever described. Regardless, the firefighter who authored the letter weighed the options and evidently determined the risk was too great to himself, to his partner, and to the two victims they were already attending to. All the markers would indicate that this decision was arrived at through utilitarian means, but that assumption rests on the lack of details provided in the letter. In short, the author might have felt other emotions that affected the decision which were not defined as bluntly as the quantifiable risks of attempting to retrieve the other people.

It is difficult to determine whether this decision was an adequate response. As with all first responders and soldiers, it was made in the heat of battle; to judge such a choice in hindsight—without overwhelming evidence that the decision was incorrect—may be unjust. Based on the letter, the utilitarian approach would dictate that – while the greatest good needs to be achieved—the firefighters did exactly that. They guaranteed two lives over the seemingly remote possibility of saving five lives. The unknown condition of the other five people might have been the most influential factor. If all five were no longer conscious, the firefighters would have had to choose whom to save. They made a prudent decision that guaranteed the lives of the two people they knew were still alive.

Micro, Meso, Macro Implications, and Consequences. As mentioned, the implications are difficult to discern since the letter writer did not provide further notation regarding the fate of the other five or even the fate of the two that he or she brought out. When considering the three levels of ethical influence, the immediate dilemma and subsequent decision executed on a micro level in that the firefighter had to make the decision for him or herself. There were, however, significant meso- and macro-level decisions occurring as well.

Most intriguing was an unusual interaction between micro- and macro-level ethical decision making. This can be seen through the scale and display effects (Chapter 1). The letter provided to the media allowed thousands to experience the visceral nature of the firefighter's decision-making process. Importantly, it acted as further ammunition for citizen groups calling for responsible parties to face consequences for allowing this building to become a death trap.

A meso-level result might be revising how the London Fire Brigade handles large-scale vertical fires, although it is unclear that they could have done any more than what was done. Months after the disaster, the medical examiners are still working through the site and investigators have warned the public not to even to look at the site as it could cause psychological trauma, a reminder to the populace of how horrendous this event was (Hardy & Cooper, 2017). This grim reality could be interpreted as a meso- or macro-level interaction.

This could explain the mounting pressure on local leadership and the community to hold the responsible parties accountable. Initially, the building designers and material manufacturers were thought to be accountable, but as the weeks passed, the community's desire for justice shifted focus to community leadership, predominantly at the meso level, the "Royal Borough of Kensington and Chelsea and the Kensington and Chelsea Tennent Management Organization." The police have stated that these two organizations are being investigated for "corporate manslaughter," which is punishable by fines, but not imprisonment (Dodd & Sherwood, 2017). While this may not constitute justice in the eyes of victims' families, the ripple effect to other communities and their leaders has been undeniable. Here, the connection between meso- and macro-level ethics, and how they interact, is on display. Fire safety had been an ongoing concern for this community for some time. Now, pressure to test and prepare for fire safety is a focus for many communities across the UK and abroad.

This effect may not be long-lasting, but if it reduces the risks of large-scale fire incidents like this one, then the benefits are tangible. Naturally, it would be ideal for community leaders to be more proactive, seeking solutions without external pressure, but ethics does not exist in a vacuum. Behavioral factors play a significant role. Meso- and macro-level decisions are influenced by events and public outcry. The two levels impact each other as meso-level decisions can lead to national lawmakers changing their position. Macro-level changes can lead to meso-level changes in communities that might not have otherwise given consideration to this issue.

Testing for fire safety has become a top priority for local councils and members of Parliament. By late July, the BBC reported that at least 82 buildings failed their fire safety inspections; more than half are owned and managed by housing authorities like the one at Grenfell (2017). A new test is more comprehensive, consisting of three parts—all of which must be passed. Members of Parliament worked with fire fighters to devise the new tests, while councils struggle with the immense costs to complete the upgrades necessary to safeguard thousands of homes (BBC, 2017). A full public report on Grenfell Tower is pending.

While top-down political pressure on councils has been significant, fire safety experts and community organizers are already concerned that the fervor will cool and that local governments will not act. Indeed, as Dame Judith Hackitt of the Manufacturers Organization explained, upgrades for Grenfell were on a two-year schedule, a completely unacceptable timetable (BBC, 2017). Hackitt welcomes all recommendations to improve the situation, but already, councils in outlying areas of London and beyond are losing awareness of the issue. The meso-level impact cannot affect independent organizational meso-level actors absent continuous macro-level support that may diminish over time.

Upshot. The micro-level impact, however, could remain strong among homeowners, residents, and first responders who will not soon forget what occurred. Grenfell teaches the lesson that some catastrophes are too difficult to overcome without the necessary resources and support, but proper preparation could reduce the chance of such occurrences. Conveying and sustaining that message at the meso and macro levels is difficult with so many other issues competing for the attention of decision-makers. Still, the choices of fire fighters will have long-lasting impacts on the lives they touched, a quality that cannot be measured.

CONCLUSION

Ethics is exalting and eviscerating; it is both the easiest and most difficult of subjects: People want to praise good actions and condemn bad ones, but there often is no one best way, no bottom line. The questions are easy, the answers are hard. This book makes the topic easier, but not easy.

Moral issues are encountered at each of the three analytical levels discussed here. Contrasting the historical and modern worldviews shows the shift in emphasis over time from morality to reason, from questions of "why" to "how" and from a focus on "ought" to "is." Nonetheless, normative questions of morality and ethics continue to be compelling. The macro–meso–micro interfaces are significant, complex, and dynamic, as actions between and within these levels affect ethics in myriad ways. As demonstrated, macro-socioeconomic forces influence meso-level actions (e.g., regulators) and micro-level actions of individuals (e.g., whistleblowers), with implications for ethics. Macro-level change also can have a cascading effect on organizational response strategies (cost cutting) and individual job prospects (job insecurity), ultimately raising ethical concerns. However, meso- and micro-level activism (Greenpeace) can impact the macro level (multinationals, government). It is at the personal and organizational level, in fact, where much of the action on ethics is played out in the workplace with institutions seeking to clarify norms of right behavior and individuals grappling with issues of personal responsibility. Exemplary leadership, strategic policies, organizational culture, and individual characteristics are important factors influencing ethical behavior. The fit between the ethical values of agencies and their members affects desired policy outcomes and employee well-being.

***

The simplest truths often meet the sternest resistance and are slowest in getting general acceptance.

—Frederick Douglass

For Discussion

1. The question "Can ethics be taught?" is a conceptually confused one. Ethics and values are taught—the urgent questions are, "Which ones?" and "How can the lessons be sustained?"

2. Different incentives drive organizations in each sector of the economy: economic self-interest in business, power in government, virtue in nonprofit agencies. Be ready to identify some ethical implications at each of the three analytical levels of this statement.

3. Analyze these topics:

    *   Teddy Roosevelt's quote near the start of this chapter
    *   C. P. Snow's "two cultures" discussed early in the chapter
    *   Knowledge is knowing what; perspective is knowing why
    *   Ethics as the easiest and hardest topic in management

4. Today the tension between Snow's "two cultures" (classical view vs. the modern view of education) has morphed into a disdain for science and for education in general. Belief trumps reason and ideology overwhelms politics, with the result that the findings of nonpartisan research organizations (e.g., the Government Accountability Office, the Congressional Budget Office) are ignored and draconian budget cuts are levied on departments that rely on science (such as the National Institutes of Health, the

National Oceanographic and Atmospheric Administration, the Department of Energy, the Environmental Protection Agency). Discuss.

5. If Schlesinger is correct in finding a cyclical pattern in the arc of American history, a new *public purpose era* should have emerged by now. Discuss.

6. Comment on the Douglass quote found at the end of the chapter, and invite others to respond to your views.

EXERCISES

1. Norman Bowie, professor of philosophy at the University of Delaware, makes the following comparison of management philosophies:

   • Boss in organization A says to employees, "You will never be fired without cause, but if the economy turns sour, some of you will have to be let go."
   • Boss in organization B says to employees, "You will never be terminated without cause neither will you be fired in the event of an economic downturn. If the company should go under because of circumstances beyond our control, we will all go under together." (Adapted from Bowie, 1988, 111)

   If you were an employee, which employer would you prefer? Why? If you were an investor, which firm would you prefer? Why? Which management philosophy is closer to the classical view of a corporation's purpose? Explain.

2. Summarize your notes (made in the page margins of this text, a notebook, or your journal) and establish links between this chapter and the overall book objectives. Continue to do this as self-study exercise throughout your work. While doing so, create sentence stems (see Chapter 1) for discussion.

REFERENCES

Ambrose, M., Amaud, A., & Schminke, M. (2008). Individual moral development and ethical climate: The influence of person-organization fit on job attitudes. *Journal of Business Ethics*, *77*, 323–333.

Anonymous. (2017, June 20). *"I was a firefighter at Grenfell Tower – and this is what it was really like." Independent.* Retrieved from http://www.independent.co.uk/voices/grenfell-tower-fire-fighter-what-it-was-like-a7798766.html

Applebaum, S., Vigneault, L., Walker, E., & Shapiro, B. (2009). (Good) corporate governance and the strategic integration of meso ethics. *Social Responsibility Journal*, *5*, 525–533.

Berman, E., Bowman, J., West, J., Van Wart, M. (2015). *Human resource management in public service* (5th ed.). Thousand Oaks, CA: Sage.

Booth, R., & Wahlquist, C. (2017, June 14). *"Grenfell Tower residents say managers 'brushed away' fire safety concerns." the guardian.* Retrieved from theguardian.com

Bowie, N. (1988). The paradox of profit. In N. D. Wright (Ed.), *Papers on the ethics of administration* (pp. 97–120). New York: State University of New York Press.

Bowman, J. (1995). Ethics and quality: A "right-good" combination. In J. West (Ed.), *Quality management today* (pp. 64–72). Washington, DC: International City/County Management Association.

Brown, S., McHardy, J., McNabb, R., & Taylor, K. (2011). Workplace performance, worker commitment, and loyalty. *Journal of Economics & Management Strategy, 20*, 925–955.

Carroll, A., & Buchholtz, A. (2000). *Business and society: Ethics and stakeholder management* (4th ed.). Cincinnati, OH: South-Western College.

Code of Metropolitan Dade County, Florida, Chapter 2: Administration Article LXXVI Commission on Ethics and Public Trust.

Dobel, J. P. (1998). Political prudence and the ethics of leadership. *Public Administration Review, 58*, 74–81.

Dobel, J. P. (2011, November 11). The Penn State scandal: How good men become moral failures [Web log post]. Retrieved from http://pointofthegame.blogspot.com/2011/11/penn-state-scandal-how-good-men-become.html

Dobel, J. P. (forthcoming). *Value driven leading: A management approach*. New York: Routledge.

Dodd, V., & Sherwood, H. (2017, July 28). *Grenfell council "may have committed corporate manslaughter" – Met police. the guardian*. Retrieved from theguardian.com

Freeh, Sporkin, & Sullivan, LLP. (2012, July 12). *Report of the Special Investigative Counsel regarding the actions of the Pennsylvania State University related to the child sexual abuse committed by Gerald A. Sandusky*. Retrieved from http://progress.psu.edu/assets/content/REPORT_FINAL_071212.pdf

Green, F. (2008). Leeway for the loyal: A model of employee discretion. *British Journal of Industrial Relations, 46*, 1–32.

Grenfell Tower: 82 buildings fail new fire safety test. July 28, 2017. BBC. bbc.com

Hardy, J., & Cooper, G. (2017, October 15). *Grenfell Tower fire: Work begins to screen stricken high rise. getwestlondon*. Retrieved from getwestlondon.co.uk

Jeurissen, R. (1997). Integrating micro, meso and macro levels in business ethics. *Ethical Perspectives, 4*, 246–253.

Johnson, C. (2012). *Meeting the ethical challenge of leadership: Casting light or shadow* (3rd ed.). Thousand Oaks, CA: Sage.

Kaminer, A. (2011, October 28). Occupational hazard. *New York Times Sunday Magazine*. Retrieved from http://www.nytimes.com/2011/10/30/magazine/the-ethicist-occupational-hazard.html?_r=0

Kaptein, M., Huberts, L., Avelino, S., & Lasthuizen, K. (2005). Demonstrating ethical leadership by measuring ethics: A survey of U.S. public servants. *Public Integrity, 7*, 299–311.

Kuhn, T. (1962). *The structure of scientific revolutions*. Chicago: University of Chicago Press.

London Fire Brigade. (2017, June 19). *Grenfell Tower fire update*. Retrieved from london-fire.gov.uk

Malkin, B. & Siddique, H. (2017, June 14). *"What we know so far about the London tower block fire." the guardian*. Retrieved from theguardian.com

Matzler, K., & Renzl, B. (2006). The relationship between interpersonal trust, employee satisfaction, and employee loyalty. *Total Quality Management & Business Excellence*, *17*, 1261–1271.

Mayfield, J., & Mayfield, M. (2002). Leader communication strategies critical paths to improving employee commitment. *American Business Review*, *20*(2), 89–94.

Mclean, J., & Poisson, J. (2015, September 21). Police officers caught using their position for personal gain in recent years. *The Toronto Star*. Retrieved from https://www.thestar.com/news/canada/2015/09/21/police-officers-caught-using-their-positon-for-personal-gain-in-recent-yers.html

Miami-Dade Ethics Commission. (2012). *Ethics opinions*. Retrieved from http://ethics.miamidade.gov/opinions.asp

Nielsen, R., & Massa, F. (2012). Reintegrating ethics and institutional theories. *Journal of Business Ethics*, *115*, 135–147.

Olson-Buchanan, J. B., & Boswell, W. R. (2002). The role of employee loyalty and formality in voicing discontent. *Journal of Applied Psychology*, *87*, 1167–1174.

Pfeffer, J. (1994). *Competitive advantage through people*. Boston, MA: Harvard Business School Press.

Preston, N. (Ed.). (1994). *Ethics for the public sector*. Leichhardt, Australia: Federation Press.

Reich, R. (2007). *Supercapitalism: The transformation of business, democracy and everyday life*. New York: Vintage Books.

Rigotti, T. (2009). Enough is enough? Threshold models for the relationship between psychological contract breach and job-related attitudes. *European Journal of Work and Organizational Psychology*, *18*, 442–463.

Rushton, S. (2017, June 6). Greed caused London's worst fire since WWII, occupy.com. Retrieved from http://www.occupy.com/article/greed-caused-london-s-worst-fire-wwii#sthash.e4T6xwPR.qRAYuNPx.dpbs

Schlesinger, A. (1986/1999). *Cycles of American history*. New York: Mariner.

Smiley, D. (2012, February 21). Miami-Dade ethics report rips ticket freebies. *Miami Herald*. Retrieved from http://ethics.miamidade.gov/library/Publications/no-more-freebies_herald.pdf

Snow, C. P. (1959/1993). *The two cultures*. Cambridge: Cambridge University Press.

Steiner, G., & Steiner, J. (2006). *Business, government and society* (11th ed.). New York: McGraw-Hill.

Thompson, D. (1992). Paradoxes of government ethics. *Public Administration Review*, *52*, 255–256.

Towers, T. (2017, June 14). *"Riot police protect firefighters from falling debris: Grenfell Tower block fire." Metro News*. Retrieved from metro.co.uk

Van Wart, M. (2005). *Dynamics of leadership in public service: Theory and practice*. Armonk, NY: M. E. Sharpe.

Watson, J. (1969). *The double helix*. New York: Mentor.

West, J. (2012). Employee-friendly policies and development benefits for millennials. In R. Sims & W. Sauser (Eds.), *Managing human resources from the millennial generation* (pp. 201–228). Charlotte, NC: Information Age Press.

West, J., Beh, L., & Sabharwal, M. (2013). Charting ethics in Asia-Pacific: Does East meet West, ethically? *Review of Public Personnel Administration*, *33*, 185–204.

West, J., & Berman, E. (Eds.). (2006). *The ethics edge*. Washington, DC: International City/County Management Association.

West, J., & Condrey, S. (2011). Local government strategies for controlling personnel costs. *Journal of Public Budgeting, Accounting and Financial Management*, *23*, 423–454.

Yeginsu, C. (2017, November 17). British authorities put final death toll of Grenfell Tower at 71. *New York Times*. Retrieved from https://www.nytimes.com/.../europe/uk-grenfell-tower-death-toll.html

Zhao, H., Wayne, S., Glibkowski, B., & Bravo, J. (2007). The impact of psychological contract breach on work-related outcomes: A meta-analysis. *Personnel Psychology*, *60*, 647–680.

3 Values, Ethics, and Dilemmas

The time is always right to do what is right.

—Martin Luther King, Jr.

This third chapter in Part I defines values, ethics, and dilemmas. Understanding these terms is a prerequisite to the rest of the book. Indeed, as Socrates believed, "The beginning of wisdom is the definition of terms." Chapter objectives include:

- identifying values and outlining them as found in American culture,
- applying values in public service,
- defining ethics,
- discerning when an issue is an ethical one,
- differentiating an ethical problem from an ethical dilemma,
- analyzing the domains of human action, and
- recognizing factors that endanger a concern for ethics.

As with so much of Western civilization, it is helpful to go back to ancient Greece to gain a perspective on contemporary times. The Greek root word for ethics is *ethos*, which includes an emphasis on individual character as well as on the citizen as part of the city-state. The moral development of a person and group is a mutual responsibility in the community; the good life (*eudaimonia*, flourishing or living well as a human being) is achieved in the environment of the polity. "Without civic morality communities perish," wrote philosopher Bertrand Russell, "without personal morality their survival has no value." Given this essential perspective, ethics is nonetheless hard to define. The attempt can be initiated by first understanding values, then ethics.

DEFINING VALUES

It is said the most important thing in life is to decide what is important, to decide how to live our lives. Values are what matter. They determine who a person is and what gives meaning to life. Everything that is done is influenced by values. They are core beliefs that shape one's worldview and impact the character of an individual and the community; a shared value is a kind of "cement" that brings and holds people together. Such norms can be found at three levels: culture, the workplace, and public service. First, values—latent and espoused—distinctive to American culture as a whole include:

- enterprise and hard work (challenges rooted in the pioneer experience emphasized competitiveness and achievement),
- independence or love of freedom (derived from the founders and immigrants),
- humanitarianism or concern for others (a belief that few people in history are as sensitive to appeals on behalf of the needy as Americans),
- cooperation (teamwork by individuals, e.g., sports), and
- honesty (the number-one value in most public opinion surveys). (Manning, Curtis, & McMillen, 1996, 202–203)

Second, contemporary American values at work include recognition of competence, individual respect and dignity, personal choice and freedom, employee involvement, pride in one's work, individual lifestyles, financial security, self-improvement, and wellness (Jamieson & O'Mara, 1991). Third, key values for public service ethics are (a) regime values (constitutional foundations as repositories of values), (b) organizational culture (consistent with regime values, which is not the case, as most American organizations are not run by democratic principles), and (c) personal values (in the Western tradition, the individual should not be submerged by the organization) (Cooper, 2000).

Additional values composing the traditional public service ethos include transparency, accountability, responsiveness, humility, service, compassion, fairness, integrity, caring, social trust, altruism, equality, democratic participation, and civic duty that ennoble daily civil service (Houston & Cartwright, 2007, 91; McConkie, 2008; Newell, 2015, 14). These concepts are widely considered to be the source of ethics codes that can guide "right behavior." Public service norms, grounded in a wider moral context, can create a strong foundation on which to make ethical judgments by developing expertise, offering continuity, and speaking truth to power. The motivation to "do the right thing" emanates from deeply held beliefs that are part of a larger orientation to work toward a common good:

> Judgments about right behavior must be rooted in a "vision of the good," . . . from which our moral intuitions flow. Public-service values are the means by which we articulate this vision of the good. . . . Taken as a whole, they describe not just what it is right to do but—which comes first—who public servants are: what a public service is for, what it stands for, what it means, what it wants to be. . . . Public-service values re-awaken our sense of public service as a "special calling." (Heintzman, 2007, 594–595)

APPLYING VALUES IN PUBLIC SERVICE

Conflicts among these value sets are inevitable. Ideally, the function of government is to maintain conditions of life in which morality is possible. Recall Thompson's (1992) ethics paradox from the last chapter: Because other issues are more important than ethics, ethics is more important than any issue—that is, ethics provides the preconditions for the making and implementing of good public policy. It is to be expected that high-level public servants should be socialized to the core values of honor, benevolence, and justice in exercising their bureaucratic responsibilities. These internal controls—personal beliefs and professional values—are buttressed by external controls—legislative oversight, citizen participation, judicial review, law and legal traditions—to help ensure promotion of the public interest. Indeed, Dwight Waldo (1980) lists no fewer than 12 features of ethics terrain for the public servant, with obligations to: the constitution, the law, the country, democracy, public agency norms, professionalism, family and friends, self, other institutions and interests (e.g., party, church, class, race, union), the public interest, human rights, and religion or God). In any case, bureaucratic pathologies promoting maladministration can and do occur when these controls and obligations break down or conflict, resulting in actions that are undemocratic, unfair, unethical, and illegal.

Two contrasting examples are provided below: The first shows how a public servant, I. "Scooter" Libby, sought to protect his superiors from political embarrassment and sacrificed values of ethics and honesty in the process; the second demonstrates how another official, James Loy, used ethical values as a consistent guide to action in his responsibilities (the accounts that follow are based, respectively, on Stewart, 2011, 123–262, and Getha-Taylor, 2009, 200–206).

Exemplar Profile: Scooter Libby Compromising Values

Once news reached the country that weapons of mass destruction (WMDs) had not been found in Iraq, skepticism spread throughout the nation. President George W. Bush led the country to war because he had received news that Iraq had been building nuclear weapons in violation of United Nations agreements made in 1991. The president's 2004 State of the Union address included 16 words that would cause controversy throughout the White House, news organizations, and intelligence agencies: "The British government has learned that Saddam Hussein recently sought significant quantities of uranium from Africa" became headline news when investigations failed to produce nuclear weapons. In an atmosphere of speculation, commentators and journalists set out to find the truth about government intelligence—was the WMDs argument just a ploy used to invade Iraq for political reasons? The evidence pointed to the office of the vice president.

Scooter Libby became a central figure in the scandal that engulfed the administration. As Vice President Richard Cheney's chief of staff, he became responsible for finding out what happened and for dealing with the press. News stories surfaced that the vice president had requested and authorized a covert operation to send a retired ambassador to Niger to discover whether Iraq had been buying uranium in African markets. The results of the alleged operation: There was no Iraqi effort to obtain uranium. Reporters began publishing articles that the Bush administration knew the information they were telling the public was false, and that information Cheney claimed he never knew about was untrue.

Libby, acting at the personal or micro level of ethics, met with media contacts and the Central Intelligence Agency (CIA) to uncover the sources of the operation and prove Cheney's and Bush's innocence and integrity. He quickly discovered that the former ambassador was Joe Wilson, the husband of CIA agent Valerie Plame. In efforts to clear the vice president and president of the blame, Libby informed reporters that Wilson's wife worked for the CIA to discredit Wilson's operation and findings. Implying that nepotism was responsible for the operation, Libby told journalists that this was a CIA operation involving Plame that was never reported to the White House. Libby did not realize that he had revealed the identity of a CIA agent, a leak jeopardizing national security and constituting a federal crime.[1]

Libby's actions resulted in an extensive investigation by the Federal Bureau of Investigation, which found that he covered up the truth and provided several versions of the same story. Libby was tried and convicted under federal statutes for perjury, obstruction of justice, and compromising the identity of a covert agent and national security. Although Libby was convicted and disbarred, his actions mirrored a pattern, according to critics, that characterized the macro-level "culture" of the administration—lies trump truth. His sentence was commuted (a reduction in legal penalties), but not pardoned (nullification of conviction) by the president. In contrast to these events, James Loy provides an example of uncompromising ethical values in action as a public servant.

Exemplar Profile: James Loy Embodying Values of Honor, Respect, Duty

In the wake of the September 11 attacks the public was forced to come to terms with the post-9/11 world, as government confronted the dangerous, emerging security issues facing the nation. This shift spawned new governmental agencies in a context that was without precedent. The task of reorganizing the bureaucracy was daunting and riddled with obstacles. James Loy was up to the challenge, for he knew the one thing that could guide public servants through uncharted waters: values. As commandant of the U.S. Coast Guard, administrator of the nascent Transportation Security Administration (TSA), and deputy secretary of the Department of Homeland Security (DHS), Loy has been an exemplar of norms-based leadership. His achievements are a testament to the power of values in an organization. In each of these administrative settings, Loy retained the same focus on core organizational values, while the role that such tenets played varied considerably. Examining Loy's efforts sheds light on how to lead by identifying and operationalizing organizational values, as well as the considerable advantages of the resultant leadership style.

As chief of personnel and training for the Coast Guard in the early 1990s, Loy set out to specify the service's defining values, which had not yet been infused into the organizational infrastructure. Working alongside civilians, enlisted members, and officers, Loy isolated three key premises: honor, respect, and devotion to duty. While Loy recognized that these values resonated with individuals throughout the Coast Guard, he saw that this was not enough: They needed to be integrated into the very fabric of the institution. Under his leadership, the three values were incorporated into official documents and became a central component of training. As a result, the Coast Guard exhibits a high degree of internal cohesion and unparalleled levels of performance and employee satisfaction. Loy brought these same leadership techniques when he led the 9/11-era agencies, with very different applications.

When Loy was asked in 2002 to assume leadership of the TSA, the task was a far cry from merely discerning the already existing values of a longstanding organization. In fact, when he took the reins, core values were not his central concern. Loy and his colleagues had only a year and a half to implement 36 congressional mandates, which included screening all checked baggage for explosives and setting up and managing security checkpoints at every airport to screen passengers. Loy attributed the agency's success in meeting the deadline to the zeal for public service that characterized the aftermath of 9/11. Once the lion's share of the work had been accomplished, he had the foresight to turn to defining values in an effort to preserve the atmosphere that had energized the organization. Having made explicit the values that helped the TSA surmount the considerable challenges of its formative years—integrity, innovation, and team spirit—he better positioned the organization to meet future challenges to its goal: safe air travel.

Loy was faced with an even more formidable assignment at the DHS: organize the efforts of 180,000 individuals across 22 different agencies to effectively safeguard the nation. If formulating the character of an organization from scratch was hard, piecing together a common vision from a diverse combination of differing agendas, cultures, and legacies was exponentially more difficult. But Loy was undeterred. He knew that the DHS would devolve into factionalism unless each component agency could "see their puzzle piece fitting into the greater design effort" (Getha-Taylor, 2009, 203). Loy embedded in the organization's strategic plan six values directly germane to employees at all hierarchical levels: awareness, prevention, protection, response, recovery, and preparedness. Thus, through values-based leadership Loy was able to unite multiple agencies with a multiplicity of viewpoints and direct them toward a common purpose. In so doing, he helped create organizations capable of ethical action. Unlike Libby, Loy succeeded in acting upon his personal convictions at the micro level of ethics, while operating within the organizational (meso) level of the TSA and DHS.

Suppose that two people with very different values—Libby and Loy—are close friends. Should Loy break off the friendship? Being friends with others does not condone everything they do; so long as he does nothing to contradict his values (e.g., lying, covering up), the relationship is valid. Ending the relationship is unlikely to have much impact; remaining friends holds the potential that Libby could be influenced by a different way of thinking. Part of being a good person is being open to others; indeed, a person cannot be sure who he is until he interacts with others (see discussion of the Milgram experiments in the next chapter). If someone associates only with those who share similar views, the scope of life experiences has been significantly reduced (commentary is based on a parallel case in Klosterman, 2013, 16).

In short, Albert Einstein said, "Try not to become a man of success, but rather try to become of man of value." Public service is noble work, but ensuring that civil servants serve in a worthy manner requires an individual internal moral compass, an organizational culture that cherishes honor, and a nation that confers respect for those who live up to the ideals of democracy (Newell, 2015, 177).

DEFINING ETHICS

Ethics in theory is grounded in values that are general, constant, and internally derived. In contrast, ethics in practice is specific, changing, and situationally determined. Stated differently, ethics translates values into action. A leader like Admiral Loy must understand and internalize a definition of management before he can begin to manage effectively. Unlike Scooter Libby, an administrator needs to adopt a definition of ethics to make effective, defensible, value-based decisions, and to stand by those judgments in times of difficulty.

Ethics might be defined as the way values are practiced, the way "business is done around here." It is both a process of inquiry (deciding how to decide) and a code of conduct (a set of standards that govern action). It is a system of right and wrong and a means to live accordingly. It is a quest for the good life. "Sometimes," as Wayne Heinrichs wrote, "all it takes for you to start making right choices is the spark of realization that your life was meant for something better." Ethics, then, studies how one ought to live, principles of right and wrong, and what it is to live a fulfilled life.[2]

Ethics begins with care, namely, caring about human and natural life, the welfare of others, honest and trustworthy communication, and fundamental individual and group freedoms. Relevant performance standards are to do no harm, enable informed choice, solve problems, seek the common good, and engage in continuous improvement (DiNorcia, 1998). An issue is an ethical one when it is genuinely important, conflicting rights are at stake, and harms and benefits are involved. Yet ethics is not always, or even often, about problems that involve choosing between right and wrong. Rather, it is frequently about genuine ethical dilemmas: choosing between two different rights or between two different wrongs. Thus, advice to "do the right thing" may not be very helpful. While ethical problems may have a straightforward answer, ethical dilemmas are complex moral mazes with no easy answers. That is, decisions are distinguished from one another based on the premises on which they are made.

Ethics asks us to think mindfully, and challenges emotions by asking why we feel the way we do and if that feeling is fair. It demands that we not only feel, but *think* through the situation. Ethics, then, is about creating strength (to turn a phrase, "right makes might"). It is not primarily about staying out of trouble, although avoiding misdoing is often a beneficial side effect of worthy behavior. A person need not be an angel or a hero to behave ethically. The only moral requirement is to do good and avoid doing evil. Ethics does not demand sainthood, just ordinary decency, a readiness to wrestle with fundamental issues in human relations and to learn enough to make informed decisions. Put another way, Justice Potter Stewart noted that ethics is knowing the difference between what you have the right to do and what is right to do (Caccese, 1997, 14).

It may also be useful to indicate what ethics is not (Markkula Center for Applied Ethics, n.d.). It is not the same as feelings (emotions are important, but people can feel good when doing wrong), religion (religions advocate high standards, but may not address all problems confronted), law (statutes, as the lowest common dominator, may or may not be ethical), culture (culture can be blind to some ethical problems) and science (it cannot tell people what they ought to do). Case Study 3.1 portrays an issue in everyday organizational life (what should you do?) that calls for sound judgment—knowing what ethics is and what it is not. Case Study 3.2 offers a compelling look at what might constitute hypocrisy. End-of-chapter Exercise 5 takes into account the importance of the decision-makers' obligations and role constraints in addressing an ethical scenario.

CASE STUDY 3.1

Challenge the Leader

I worked for a nonprofit organization that ran an international leadership program for high school students. I had access to the president's contact list, which included many names from an escort service. I feel that the parents of the students would want to know this about a man who will be with their children overseas. What should I do?

Parents likely would want to know this fact; indeed, they might want his medical history, credit rating, and other personal information. But those things, including his choice of whom to have sex with, are not job related. Breaking the law, however, is a different matter. Someone who routinely does that has an appetite for risk, which is not a desirable qualification for this position. Still, it is unknown if he gets a thrill from perusing the list but goes no further. Likewise, perhaps the people on the list are volunteers at an AIDS community program. Since he gave you access to the file, why not just ask him, "Did you mean for me to see it? I am concerned that you might be putting children at risk."

QUESTIONS TO CONSIDER

1. What do you think? Why? Remember, you can judge his answer for yourself, but "judge carefully: chaperoning children is a scary business, but so is endangering someone's career."

2. Is easing the worker's conscience in revealing the list (individual, micro ethics) what is best for the organization (meso)—and ultimately for students who benefit from the program?

Source: Adapted from Kaminer (2011).

CASE STUDY 3.2

Hypocrisy or Humanity?

In 2017, Amazon sent governmental officials across the nation scrambling to respond to its announcement to build a headquarters, promising tens of thousands of jobs and billions in investment to the winning location. Governments are mobilizing to devise lucrative incentive packages. I know how this works, because I spent eight years supporting these types of incentive as the governor of Delaware from 2009 to 2017.

The bidding war highlights a competition that state and local governments engage in every day. But it's a self-defeating war that should stop. A *New York Times* investigation in 2012 found that states, counties, and cities were handing out more than $80 billion a year in incentives to attract and retain companies, money better spent on education, roads, and parks.

The result is a market failure in which neither side is motivated to fix the problem. State and local policymakers can't unilaterally opt out without potentially negative consequences for their constituents, while businesses have a fiduciary obligation to pursue these short-term incentives.

There's a better way to compete for business: a federal tax of 100 percent on every dollar a business receives in state or local incentives. This tax would end payouts that go to a corporation's bottom line and would eliminate the pressure these companies are under to divert tax monies to themselves. States would still compete for these jobs but they would do so in a way that better aligns with the long-term interests of taxpayers and the businesses themselves. This approach would provide a significant victory for taxpayers. Instead of making payments to businesses, states and municipalities would invest in and compete based on factors that make the most difference for an area's economic potential and for a company's ultimate success: the abilities of the workforce, the excellence of schools, the physical infrastructure, and quality of life. That is a competition worth having.

DISCUSSION QUESTIONS

1. What do you think of desirability of such a tax (is it a good idea)? Why? Is the tax feasible (given political realities, could it be approved)? Explain.

2. Join this conversation:

   - Bob: "The governor is being a hypocrite for advocating change that he could have fought for while he was in office."
   - Sally: "Just because someone made a mistake and belatedly admits it, that does not mean we cannot learn from him; indeed, if humans lived by that rule, there would be a lot of silence."

Source: Narrative adapted and condensed from Markell (2017, September 21).

DOMAINS OF HUMAN ACTION: LAW VS. FREE CHOICE

Law is one domain of action (the obedience to the enforceable) and free choice (the complete freedom for spontaneity, originality, and energy) is the other. But the cardinal question remains, "How is free will used?" Between the two domains lies ethics. Where law is silent, ethics should speak. Ethics is self-enforced obedience to the unenforceable obligation. Simplified, ethics is what one does when no one is watching. Law is external, mandatory, and objective, whereas ethics is internal, voluntary, and subjective. Law is imposed, ethics is inspired. Table 3.1 shows the distinction between law, ethics, and values.

Ethics is at risk of destruction from both law ("regulate everything") and free choice ("anything not illegal is permissible"). The greatness of a nation is measured by not mere obedience to law (timorous people) and not by "letting it all hang out" (resulting in anarchy). Rather, the true test of distinction is the extent to which citizens can be entrusted to obey self-imposed law, for without ethics civilization perishes (Kidder, 1994, 67). Another test for citizens is the ability to puzzle through myths to discern reality. Which of these statements is a "myth" or a "reality"?

- Ethical people are always ethical no matter what happens.
- Ethics cannot be learned or taught.
- Ethical values are personal and are not expressed within the organization.
- Focusing on ethics does little to improve productivity, morale, or problem solving.
- When an ethics code is written and distributed, there is no need to do anything else.
- The appearance of wrongdoing and actually doing wrong are two entirely different things.
- An ethical organization can be created quickly.
- Morality cannot be legislated. Law is judged by ethics.

Some of these claims represent "common sense"—which itself may be a myth. In short, a heavy burden rests on the shoulders of the populace as they ponder law, ethics, and values.

TABLE 3.1	Distinctions Between Law, Ethics, and Values	
Law	**Ethics**	**Values**
• Defined as a rule established in a community by authority or custom	• Defined as the determinant of morality	• Defined as an individual's driving force
• Exists to remedy wrongs	• Focused on right and wrong	• Used in individual decision making
• Based on Common Law	• Maintains that every profession has its own code	• Are subject to change
• Defines community standards	• Upholds peer and professional oversight	
• Can conflict with ethics	• Can be incongruent with law	
• Maintains that ignorance is not a defense		

Source: Adapted from DeChello (2003, 4).

SOCIAL FORCES ENDANGERING ETHICS

Ethics is not just about definitions and distinctions, information and insight. It is about transformation: It requires performance and expects responsibility. As such, ethics is endangered not only by relativism (Chapter 1), but also by at least five other phenomena.

First, sensational scandals typically pit right against wrong. Seductively, they distract attention from important daily ethical issues which may not have ready answers. Second, grasping the best solution can be the enemy of the good (Aristotle wisely warns against setting impossible standards, a caution consistent with the recommendation to aim for the "middle ground," as discussed in Chapter 2). Ongoing improvement of character development and decision making is the objective as ethical problems can be progressively managed, if not solved, provided ideals are kept in mind. Third, the topic of ethics can be easily trivialized (e.g., worrying excessively about accidentally taking pencils home from work). Fourth, cherished myths can act as a powerful deterrent to thinking about ethics: The capacity of self-deception and moral illusion should not be overlooked (Chapter 7).

A fifth factor menacing public service ethics is the increasing importance of private sector values, including the advent of the New Public Management (NPM), and its growing emphasis on market norms. As Turo Vertanen (2000, 338) notes, "Self-interest is the key coordination mechanism of markets and the basis of performance-related pay, privatization and consumer choice." Under NPM-inspired managerialism (and its assumptions that people are money-driven rather than value-driven), he cautions, there is a weakening of the commitment to the public interest and egalitarian principles that have long been associated with public service. These changes also require different competencies of managers. While there is some evidence that managerial commitments to public and business-like values are complementary (cf. Berman & West, 2012), concerns that government administrators may be overly responsive to and influenced by private interests dominate. The shift of values under NPM and the resulting tensions—specifically, the greater weight increasingly given to "a lean state, citizen activism and markets" at the expense of longstanding commitments to "public service ethics and the specificity of the public sector"—demand attention (Vertanen, 2000, 340–341). The commitment to public service as a vocation serving the common good is at risk by deference to an unquestioning faith in markets and instrumental values.

Yet the appeal of market values is understandable: The market system does not judge the ethical quality of decisions. Instead, the legitimacy of an exchange is based on its efficiency in the broad framework of the marketplace. The problem is that such market "imperialism"—the reduction of every activity and value to a corporate commodity—tends to erode nonmarket ethical norms, thereby impoverishing moral and civic life. The manner in which a society structures its institutions affects how people behave; corporatization usually means centralization, consolidation, and homogenization at the expense of public participation and democratic governance. In the decision to commercialize and commodify a good or service, intrinsic commitments—not just extrinsic motivation—warrant consideration. Michael Sandel's (2012) *What Money Can't Buy: The Moral Limits of Markets* examines, *inter alia*, blood collection systems and life insurance policies.

Despite the assumed efficiency of markets, they "not only lead to chronic shortages, wasted blood, high costs, and significant risks of contamination" (Sandel, 2012, 123), but also exploitation of the poor by for-profit blood banks as well as the decline in the sense of obligation to donate blood. Blood collected for transfusion in the United States is given by volunteer blood donors. In contrast to the hybrid commercial and nonprofit American system, the highly effective British blood collection is based on unpaid volunteers.

In the second case example, *dead peasant* or *janitor's insurance* (formally known as *corporate-owned life insurance*) companies secretly insure the lives of their employees so that they profit from their deaths. Sandel writes that this creates "conditions where workers are worth more dead than alive" and treats them as commodities, not people "whose value to the company lies in the work they do" (136). These policies, which constitute approximately a quarter of all life insurance sold, have become a strategy for tax-free, windfall corporate finance. After 9/11, for instance, some of the first insurance payouts went to the victims' employers, not their families. In spite of some recent changes, "it is hard to see why," Sandel continues, "the tax system should encourage companies to invest billions in the mortality of their workers rather than in the production of goods and services" (136).

There has been a shift, Sandel believes, "from *having* a market economy to *being* a market society" (10). In both the blood supply and life insurance cases, what was once largely an endeavor that had public benefits increasingly has become an instrument of private gain. Commodification is seen as good in itself, irrespective of its effectiveness or its impact on the daily lives of people. In the process, the moral meaning of blood collection and life insurance systems has been eroded. Since these transformed activities serve little social good beyond profit, their corrosive nature suggests the need for decommodification, the reclaiming of certain goods—water, genes, seeds, education, health care, and politicians—from market logic and failure. Inevitably, tradeoffs will be made in any such decisions. Figure 3.1

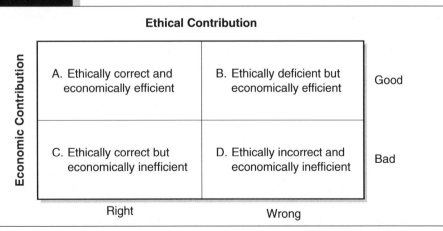

FIGURE 3.1   **Ethical Principles vs. Economic Imperatives**

Ethical Contribution

	Economic Contribution		
	A. Ethically correct and economically efficient	B. Ethically deficient but economically efficient	Good
	C. Ethically correct but economically inefficient	D. Ethically incorrect and economically inefficient	Bad
	Right	Wrong	

Source: Adapted from West and Bowman (2008, 32).

poses tradeoffs between competing values of economic imperatives versus ethical principles (further discussion of such tradeoffs is found in West & Bowman, 2008; see Exercise 4 to apply this matrix of tradeoffs to different scenarios).

CONCLUSION

Terms such as *values, ethics, dilemmas,* and *law* are fundamental concepts examined here and explored further in the chapters to follow. Public service provides the opportunity to act on American values in advancing the commonwealth. Especially challenging for administrators is the management of norms in an increasingly diverse world and an ever changing public service where value conflicts are inevitable (Case Study 3.3). Some public servants like Admiral Loy make core values the singular focus; others such as Scooter Libby lose their value moorings and succumb to pressures that compromise public values. Between the arenas of law and free choice lies ethics. Officials can choose to be obedient to the enforceable (law) or the unenforceable (ethics). Libby failed to obey either, and Loy was guided by both. But adherence to ethics is challenging given the social forces that provide seductive distractions. Nonmarket norms are sometimes subverted by the encroachment of market values, resulting in the degradation and devaluation of the public good.

CASE STUDY 3.3

Value Conflicts in World Affairs

Ethical dilemmas arise out of value conflicts—instances when the courses of action open to a decision maker support equally legitimate but opposing or incompatible goals. In the chapters that follow, you will be exposed to different resources to draw on when mediating challenging dilemmas. But, for these tools to be useful, it is necessary to first be familiar with the contours of value conflicts as they occur in the practice of public management. Examining two high-profile incidents—the run-up to the U.S. invasion of Iraq and the Danish cartoon controversy—will help to understand how to identify value conflicts as well as the sometimes dire consequences of failing to acknowledge such a conflict when it occurs.

The Bush administration's decision to invade Iraq in 2003 provoked public uproar when it was later discovered that the primary justification for the invasion—Saddam Hussein's stockpile of weapons of mass destruction (WMDs)—was never proved to exist. According to Fredrik Bynander (2011), the fraudulence of the justification renders the decision an ethical failure, not just because it constituted an act of deception, but also because it neglected the multiplicity of values at stake (see Chapter 11 for more on presidential deception and foreign policy).

In Bynander's analysis, the leveraging of a tenuous WMD claim as incontrovertible reflects how the administration "overemphasized internal values domestically and internationally (how to sell the war, rather than establish a cause for war that would hold up across time)" (46). While this tactic was nevertheless successful in mobilizing domestic support, its use displayed a disregard for a core international affairs value: multilateral action grounded in international law (clearly present due to Iraq's noncompliance with United Nations weapons inspection requirements). The interplay of domestic and international values requires a tactful balancing act, but this was eschewed by the administration's steadfast resolve to unseat a tyrant. Thus, its justification proved to be unsustainable, as "the state-centric value of standing up to challengers came out as grossly over privileged (and dishonestly so) to audiences in arenas that support other values" (Svedin, 2011, 221).

While both cases presented here entail diplomatic crises, unlike the domestic–international hybrid WMD incident, the Danish cartoon incident is largely a domestic ethical dilemma. It illustrates how a values conflict can spiral out of control if not handled with discretion. In October 2005, the Danish newspaper *Jyllands-Posten* published political cartoons of the Prophet Muhammad, the representation of whom in any manner (let alone wearing a turban in the shape of a bomb) is forbidden by Islamic law. When Muslim organizations sought a meeting with the country's prime minister to address their outrage, he dismissed their request, citing Denmark's longstanding commitment to freedom of expression (Olsson, 2011, 146–148).

After months of demonstrations by religious leaders throughout the Muslim world, the prime minister realized the issue was not simply one of freedom of speech, but also of freedom of religion. By that point it was too late. Calls for boycotts of Danish products were already circulating around the Internet. The burning of Danish flags gave way to the burning of Denmark's embassy in Lebanon. The prime minister resorted to hiding behind the efforts of the European Union and Danish Imams to appease the Muslim community and eventually defused the crisis (Olsson, 2011, 151–154).

These two incidents demonstrate failure to take the crucial first steps in tackling an ethical dilemma: identifying the value conflict and isolating those values that clash. Evident in these cases, the stakes in ethical dilemmas are high: Failure to recognize a collusion of values in a timely manner can be disastrous.

QUESTIONS TO CONSIDER

1. What ethics principles were violated in the run-up to the U.S. invasion of Iraq?

2. How does the Danish cartoon incident illustrate Dennis Thompson's observation, made earlier, "Because other issues are more important than ethics, ethics are more important than any issue"?

Sources: Bynander (2011); Olsson (2011); Svedin (2011).

Both sets of values have their place. Each can contribute to social betterment, but, as shown, excessive reliance on commercial premises can undermine the civic goods that should not be on sale. In short, values and ethics are of paramount importance: Almost anything a manager does has ethical implications. Ethics is much like tennis: Those who fail to master the basics of serving well usually lose. And like good tennis playing, ethics takes practice. Take this opportunity to *carpe diem*.

***

Ethical managers must know what's right, value what's right, and do what's right.

—Carl Skoogland

NOTES

1. Winston Churchill once said of a colleague: "He has all the virtues I dislike and one of the vices I admire."
2. Ethics are principles by which one is guided in relationships with others (what people do in society), while morals have to do with principles that guide the behavior of individuals with respect to their own integrity. The two inform one another, although their focus is different. The terms, following their classical origins (Latin: morality; Greek: ethics) whose definitions are synonymous, are frequently used interchangeably since both have to do with right conduct and good character.

FOR DISCUSSION

1. Every organization has values, but they may not be the dominant purpose of business or government. Nonprofits, however, arose to meet societal needs not addressed by the other sectors (indeed, they were often created to right a societal wrong). Explore this statement.

2. Dennis Thompson's belief that ethics are more important than any other issue is discussed in this chapter. Do you agree or disagree? Why?

3. If ethics is defined as a system of right and wrong, and as a means to live accordingly, how does etiquette differ from ethics?

4. Comment on these observations:

   - "Are you taking responsibility for taking responsibility?"
   - "Everyone knows right from wrong." Right?
   - "The habit of not thinking something is wrong, gives it the appearance of being right." (Thomas Paine)
   - "Values are critical guides for making decisions. When in doubt, they cut through the fog like a beacon in the night." (Robert Townsend)

5. Traditional public administration values emphasize consensus, shared ideals, democracy, and social equality. An emergent anti-government paradigm advocates self-interest, individualism, competition, Machiavellianism, and survival of the fittest (Abels, 2017, July 17). Discuss.

6. Is it ethical for a student to cut her ethics class?

EXERCISES

1. Complete the following sentence: "Ethics is like . . ." and explain your sentence in a one-page paper. This assignment is intended to help you think about ethics in a metaphorical sense. Ethics might be seen as an icy street, with people slipping and sliding on the verge of falling. It could be like an apple—bright and shiny and full of promise on the outside, but rotten to the core. Perhaps ethics is like the Golden Rule, "Do unto others as you would have them do unto you," a guiding principle for life, or "He who has the gold rules," a cynical, if insightful, commentary on contemporary human affairs. However you see ethics, be creative with your metaphor and enjoy discussing it with others. (Courtesy of Professor Ramona Ortega-Liston, University of Akron)

2. What are some of your most important values? What is the basis of them (did they derive from family, religious, or school experiences)? Record your thinking in your journal.

3. Use the topics below as catalysts for journal entries:

   - Your personal definition of ethics
   - At least three values you value and describe one professional experience when one of those values was realized or tested
   - How dramatic news stories may distract from genuine ethical dilemmas
   - How "the best can be the enemy of the good"
   - How ethics can be trivialized
   - How economic imperatives can compromise ethical principles

4. Read the following scenarios and decide which quadrant in Figure 3.1 is the best fit. Put the appropriate letter (A–D) next to each of the items below:

   - Paying an extra fee to skip security lines at the airport
   - Freeways creating special lanes that allow those willing to pay to skip rush hour traffic
   - A university accepting donations from a donor who has strong, public feelings against interracial and interreligious marriages
   - A lobbyist paying in excess of $1,000 to a line-stander to arrive minutes before a congressional hearing that is open to the public free of charge with limited capacity
   - Paying someone to stand in line for you to get otherwise free tickets to a performance held by New York City's Public Theater with limited capacity
   - Hiring someone to camp out in front of the Supreme Court days before the Affordable Care Act arguments begin, although the hearing is free to the public (with limited capacity)
   - A business that does not discriminate against customers belonging to a racial/ethnic minority group

- Rejecting a lucrative contract with Chick-Fil-A because their anti-gay contributions offend your university's student and faculty population
- A business that does discriminate against customers belonging to a racial/ethnic minority group
- The City of Miami allowing community redevelopment agencies to redraw lines to include both affluent and slum-and-blight areas, and then only improve the already affluent areas
- Paying $200 to receive seven football tickets at the beginning of the season rather than wait in line for free student tickets the day before games
- Paying $15,000 a year to a concierge doctor who is available around the clock, doesn't make you wait, and has only 600 patients rather than 3,000
- Prisoners paying a fee for an upgrade to a cleaner, nicer jail cell
- An employee telling a supervisor that progress has been made on a project when none has
- States selling naming rights to state parks

[Note: Some items are adapted from Sandel (2012).]

5. Bad Actor Exercises

   Instructions: The tabletop exercises serve to provide students with a framework for the application of ethical decision making in real-world scenarios. For the scenario below (and those that follow in Chapters 5, 9, 11, and 12), you will be assigned a role to assume. After reviewing the scenario and the role, form a response outlining your decision and the reasoning behind it. Be sure to consider ethical theories and principles and answer in earnest. Your decision may not always be the most ethical choice; however, you should explain the constraints in your decision making and state relevant reasons for your response.

   Tabletop Exercise 1: The Bad Parent

   Jane Weber is a single mother of five children. She is currently raising one teenager, two pre-teens, and two children under the age of nine. None of the children's fathers is involved financially or otherwise. Jane is on welfare and has a tendency to bounce between several minimum wage jobs including bartending and housekeeping. She often works odd hours and is forced to leave the children home alone. With little income, Jane struggles to provide the essentials for her family, and they often have to go without simple amenities. Jane is on the verge of eviction, and was recently laid off from her housekeeping job.

   Role 1: Teacher

   You are a teacher for one of Jane's oldest children. You have noticed that the child is often wearing clothes that do not fit, and appears distraught and distracted in class. The child is teased for his appearance regularly. After talking to the child, you learn that his free lunch at school is often his only meal, and he stays awake watching his siblings most nights. The child's grades are slipping and he is now at risk academically.

Do you feel obligated to act in this situation? How would you respond? Consider your obligations, ethical and otherwise. To whom are you accountable as an educator? What factors impact your decision?

Role 2: Friend

You are Jane's friend and former co-worker, and you have intimate knowledge of her financial situation. Having met her children, you are aware of the struggle that they face on a daily basis. You know that Jane does not intend to endanger her children, but she is irresponsible and often neglectful in her duties as a mother. You do not have the capacity to help Jane yourself, but you know that she needs assistance. What do you do? Do you report Jane to family services? Consider your obligations, ethical and otherwise. To whom are you accountable as a friend? What factors impact your decision?

Role 3: Close Relative

You are Jane's only living relative and have become aware of her escalating situation. You have offered your help in the past, but Jane has refused out of pride. In your last conversation, Jane reveals that she is nearing eviction, and she again refuses your help. You know about the children's issues at school, and feel the situation is worsening. What do you do? Consider your obligations, ethical and otherwise. To whom are you accountable as a family member? What factors impact your decision?

Role 4: Neighbor

You have been Jane's neighbor for the past year. You often see Jane coming and going at odd hours and know that she has 5 children at home. You notice the children often leave for school late and are dressed poorly, sometimes the children don't go to school at all. Your children are friends of Jane's kids, and they admit they sometimes sneak food to the neighbors when they don't have enough. You saw an eviction notice on Jane's door last week and know that the family needs more help than you can offer. What do you do? Consider your obligations, ethical and otherwise. To whom are you accountable? What factors impact your decision?

6. View the You Tube video with Damon Horowitz, "Moral Operating Systems" (16 minutes) and Ted Talk by Monica Lewinsky: "The Price of Shame" (22 minutes).

REFERENCES

Abels, M. (2017, July 17). A new public administration paradigm is emerging. *PA Times*. Retrieved from https://patimes.org/public-administration-paradigm-emerging

Berman, E., & West, J. (2012). Public values in special districts: A survey of managerial commitment. *Public Administration Review, 72,* 43–54.

Bynander, F. (2011). Value conflicts in foreign policy crises: How the United States and the U.K. wrestled with the ethical dilemma of going to war in Iraq. In L. Svedin (Ed.), *Ethics and crisis management* (pp. 37–56). Charlotte, NC: Information Age.

Caccese, M. S. (1997). Ethics and the financial analyst. *Financial Analysts Journal, 53*(1), 9–14.

Cooper, T. (2000). *Handbook of administrative ethics.* New York: Marcel Dekker.

DeChello, P. (2003). *Law and ethics: A clinician's guide to legal and ethical practice.* Middlefield, CT: D&S Associates.

DiNorcia, V. (1998). *Hard like water: Ethics in business.* New York: Oxford University Press.

Getha-Taylor, H. (2009). Managing the "new normalcy" with values-based leadership: Lessons from Admiral James Loy. *Public Administration Review, 69,* 200–206.

Heintzman, R. (2007). Public-service values and ethics: Dead end or strong foundation? *Canadian Public Administration, 50,* 573–602.

Houston, D. J., & Cartwright, K. E. (2007). Spirituality and public service. *Public Administration Review, 67,* 88–102.

Jamieson, D., & O'Mara, J. (1991). *Managing workforce 2000: Gaining the diversity advantage.* San Francisco: Jossey-Bass.

Kaminer, A. (2011, June 14). Challenge the leader. *New York Times Sunday Magazine.* Retrieved from http://www.nytimes.com/2011/06/12/magazine/the-ethicist-challenge-the-leader.html

Kidder, R. (1994). *Shared values in a troubled world.* San Francisco: Jossey-Bass.

Klosterman, C. (2013, March 17). My cheating friend. *New York Times Sunday Magazine,* p. 16.

Manning, G., Curtis, K., & McMillen, S. (1996). *Building community: The human side of work.* Duluth, MN: Whole Person Associates.

Markell, J. (2017, September 21). Let's stop government giveaways to corporations. *New York Times.* Retrieved from https://www.nytimes.com/2017/09/21/opinion/incentives-businesses-corporations-giveaways.html?emc=edit_th_20170921&nl=todaysheadlines&nlid=63449989

Markkula Center for Applied Ethics. (n.d.). A framework for ethical decisionmaking. Retrieved from https://www.scu.edu/ethics/ethics-resources/ethical-decision-making/a-framework-for-ethical-decision-making/

McConkie, M. (2008). Spirituality and the public sector. *International Journal of Public Administration, 31,* 337–341.

Newell, T. (2015). *To serve with honor: Doing the right thing in government.* Charleston, SC: Loftlands Press.

Olsson, E. (2011). Communication in crises of public diplomacy: The quest for ethical capital. In L. Svedin (Ed.), *Ethics and crisis management* (pp. 141–162). Charlotte, NC: Information Age.

Sandel, M. (2012). *What money can't buy: The moral limits of markets.* New York: Farrar, Straus & Giroux.

Stewart, J. (2011). *Tangled webs: How false statements are undermining America: From Martha Stewart to Bernie Madoff.* New York: Penguin.

Svedin, L. (2011). Conclusions. In L. Svedin (Ed.), *Ethics and crisis management* (pp. 217–246). Charlotte, NC: Information Age.

Thompson, D. (1992). The paradoxes of government ethics. *Public Administration Review, 52,* 254–259.

Vertanen, T. (2000). Changing competences of public managers: Tensions in commitment. *International Journal of Public Sector Management, 13,* 333–341.

Waldo, D. (1980). *The enterprise of public administration: A summary view*. Novato, CA: Chandler & Sharp.

West, J., & Bowman, J. (2008). Employee benefits: Weighing ethical principles and economic imperatives. In C. Reddick & J. Coggburn (Eds.), *Handbook of employee benefits and administration* (pp. 29–54). Boca Raton, FL: CRC Press.

PART II

Individual-
Centered
Approaches to
Ethics

4 Moral Development Theory

The perfecting of one's self is the fundamental base of all progress and all moral development.

—Confucius

This chapter initiates Part II of the book, "Individual-Centered Approaches to Ethics." The chapters included in this section present philosophically based approaches to ethics (cognitive and social intuition) as well as psychologically based ethics. To gain perspective on this material, this chapter focuses on an inclusive and hierarchical theory of moral development that can be applied to both individuals and institutions. It also offers a critique of this theory. Chapter objectives are to:

- comprehend Kohlberg's theory of moral development,
- apply moral development theory,
- relate the theory to professionalism,
- explore the implications of two classical laboratory experiments,
- understand Haidt's critique of Kohlberg, and
- distinguish between utilitarian and deontological approaches.

KOHLBERG'S MORAL DEVELOPMENT THEORY: A RATIONAL APPROACH

The leading theory of moral development was formulated by Lawrence Kohlberg, shown in Table 4.1. Kohlberg posited that people may mature morally by moving from stage to stage in each of three levels, although they may stop at any time. He argued that most people reason at the "conventional" level.

The levels and stages of Kohlberg's theory are hierarchically ordered: Level 1, Stages 1 and 2 constitute preconventional morality. Stage 1 is characterized by a punishment and obedience orientation, wherein obedience is linked to externally imposed punishment, deference to power, and fear

TABLE 4.1	Kohlberg's Stages of Moral Development With Behavioral Orientation			
Level	Self-Perception	Stage Orientation	"Right" Behavior	Reference Frame
Level 1: Preconventional	Outside Group	1. Punishment and obedience	1. Avoid punishment, defer to power	1. Physical consequence of actions
		2. Instrumental–relativistic	2. Satisfaction of own needs	2. Human relations are like a marketplace
Level 2: Conventional	Inside Group	3. Good boy–nice girl	3. That which pleases/helps others	3. Majority or "natural" behavior
		4. Law and order	4. Duty, maintenance of social order	4. Authority and fixed rules of society
Level 3: Postconventional	Above Group	5. Social contract	5. In terms of individual rights, free agreement	5. Constitutional/democratic agreement, social utility
		6. Universal–ethical	6. Choice of conscience, ethical principles	6. Universal imperatives, justice, human rights

Source: Adapted from Kohlberg (1971).

of pain or loss of love. Here, morality is determined by avoiding punishment and receiving rewards. Stage 2 is characterized by instrumentalism and deal making with negotiated exchanges of favors for personal benefit ("you scratch my back and I'll scratch yours"). Morality is seen as advancing self-interest and honoring agreements.

Level 2, Stages 3 and 4 reflect conventional morality. Stage 3 highlights the approval of others (family, friends, co-workers) as a determinant of behavior. Living up to the expectations of others (the childhood desire to be a "good boy/nice girl") and winning the acceptance and approval of one's social group is a primary value. Stage 4 emphasizes compliance with laws, policies, and legitimate authorities. Orientations focus on complying with authority, doing one's duty, and maintaining social order. Reasoning at level 2 is conventional and not critical, responding to pressures to conform to accepted expectations, standards, and rules.

Level 3, Stages 5 and 6 represent postconventional morality. Stage 5 gives emphasis to due process, individual rights, and social consensus. Cognition at the fifth stage can lead to challenges to legitimate authority. Critical reflection, independence of mind, and a more impartial view are evident. Stage 6 is grounded in universal ethical principles, wherein right actions are determined based on individual conscience and commitments to abstract concepts such as justice, care, and freedom.

Kohlberg built on the work of Jean Piaget, developing an empirically based moral development theory premised solely on moral reasoning. For Kohlberg, the levels at which people operate when confronting moral issues vary as they pass through different phases of their lives. Children, adolescents, and some adults dominate the preconventional level, while most of the population operates at the conventional level, and a much smaller percentage reach the postconventional level. Upward movement from lower to higher stages in the hierarchy can occur through a maturation process that leads to a more sophisticated and complex understanding of ethical problems and solutions.

Kohlberg posed case dilemmas to his research subjects, asking them what they would do in such situations. However, he was less concerned with their answers than in their response to a second question: "Why?" He was interested in the moral *reasoning* subjects used in addressing the issue. Kohlberg's question was why do people behave in certain ways at each level of moral development? A well-known case used by Kohlberg involved a man, Heinz, who had to decide whether to steal a drug he couldn't afford to buy but that would save the life of his ailing wife. Kohlberg observed variation in the way people reacted to, interpreted, and dealt with Heinz's and other dilemmas. Kohlberg's theory of cognitive moral development grew out of the recorded responses to such hypotheticals posed to different respondent groups. Analysis of the contemporary hypothetical case in Case Study 4.1 illustrates the thought processes using Kohlberg's three-level, six-stage schema that might be provoked by an ethically challenging situation confronting military Private X.

Twenty years in the making, Kohlberg's theory presumes that careful moral reasoning can—and should—affect one's ethical perspective, and that moral judgment has cognitive features. His theory, while extraordinarily influential, has been challenged on many fronts. Among the criticisms are the narrow focus on moral judgment, inattention to issues of conflict of interest or confidentiality, insufficient evidence of postconventional thinking, overemphasis on macro and under emphasis on micro morality, a hard "staircase" approach to stage development, undue reliance on verbal responses, an implication that higher stages are morally preferable to lower stages, the restriction of samples to males, and its inclusion of certain ethical approaches while excluding others (Rest & Narrvaez, 1994; Rest et al., 1999; Swisher, Rizzo, & Marley, 2005; Velasquez, 1998). Other researchers refer to "schemas" and "orientations" rather than stages in describing moral development.

Carol Gilligan, a student of Kohlberg's, finds that while men may pass through the developmental stages as described, the moral thinking patterns of women are not the same. The "male" perspective on ethics addresses issues using "impersonal, impartial, and abstract moral rules," relying on principles of justice and rights that Kohlberg associates with postconventional thinking. Gilligan's research identifies an alternative "female" viewpoint wherein subjects see themselves as "part of a 'web' of relationships with family and friends," which gives emphasis to addressing moral issues stressing "sustaining these relationships, avoiding hurt to others . . . and caring for their well being." Caring and being responsible are more important in the "female" approach while "adhering to impartial and impersonal rules" is closer to the "male" perspective (Velasquez, 1998, 28). As Gilligan notes, for women, "morality is conceived in interpersonal terms and goodness is equated with helping and pleasing others" (quoted in Singer, 1994, 55–56). Gilligan's work suggests the need to be cautious in making blanket generalizations about moral development.

CASE STUDY 4.1

Applying Kohlberg's Stages of Moral Development

A low-ranking military serviceman (Private X) is ordered to kill innocent civilians by his superior (albeit crazed) officer. How might the private analyze his ethical requirements?

In early stages of development, a *punishment/obedience orientation* (similar to that of a young child) compels Private X to comply with stated rules (in this case, the requirements to unquestioningly follow the orders of his superior). This imperative is reinforced through a fear of consequences of noncompliance. In this case, the private believes that disobedience will result in a range of unpleasant consequences, ranging from physical harm to court martial.

He may feel that it is necessary to conform to the norms of his peer group soldiers, who, he believes, will also follow such orders, soldiers who have been trained to use violence without prejudice. In doing so, the soldier affirms his loyalty to his group of peers, and is thus gratified by his sense of belonging. Here, he has traded his feelings of concern for the value of belonging. This dynamic illustrates the second stage in Kohlberg's development: the *self-gratification orientation*.

Private X has likely (up to this point) developed a substantial level of trust and loyalty toward his leader. Further, a similar level of trust and loyalty has no doubt developed among the soldiers—whose lives depend on it. An orientation toward Stage 3, *approval of others*, directs him to do the "right thing"; do what the lieutenant and the other men "expect"; do what the others would presumably do. He is compelled by this need for the support of his leader and of his friends. In this approval, he may find adequate justification for questionable actions.

Having been indoctrinated into the military culture, Private X is ever aware of the chain of command. The hierarchy of rank within this community and the authority that stems from it are at the very foundation of this military culture. The laws, rules, and customs of the organization are necessarily inflexible; they are constant and demand compliance. This compliance is essential for the efficient function and stability of its culture. It may be that, regardless of other judgments, Private X is compelled by this Stage 4 orientation that prioritizes *law and order* above all else. In this context, obedience to the directives of his superior (regardless of reservation) is given the greater moral weight.

Approaching the later stages of moral development, the private may begin to loosen his previous commitment to the expectations of his lieutenant and platoon, and the authority of military protocol and convention. Oriented in this way, toward a greater social contract, he relies more on his own personal standards of social responsibility; he recognizes that it is not moral to follow a directive (such as killing innocent civilians) that lacks legitimacy. Here, the values of his platoon and perhaps of the military are judged with relativity. Outside of these organizations, perhaps, there exists an overriding social consensus on his own personal standards; Stage 5—*consensus/social contract*—allows him to more appropriately judge the legitimacy of the order.

If, however, Private X had developed to the last stage of moral development, he would apply a set of *universal ethical principles* to his analysis. His principles are not simple laws that map a course of action, but rather represent a host of abstract ideas that address the concepts of justice, reciprocity, equality, and respect for others. Based on his personal morality, these principles provide guidance beyond the dictates of the conventions of the military establishment. He understands the rights of the innocent civilians and places value on their lives. His principles provide a compass that guides his questioning.

The hypothetical in Case Study 4.1 reveals different reactions Private X might have experienced at each stage of moral development when confronted with an extraordinarily stressful situation. Now, two classical laboratory trials—Stanley Milgram's "shock" experiment and Philip Zimbardo's Stanford prison experiment—further illustrate Kohlberg's theory of moral development. They both suggest the importance of "getting in touch with your inner psychopath" (see Exhibit 4.1).

EXHIBIT 4.1   **Getting in Touch With Your Inner Psychopath**

We all loathe the psychopaths of the business world. They use others, they see themselves as deserving more and better than everyone else, and they feel entitled to do things the way they want rather than doing as they really should. Sometimes impulsively and sometimes planfully, they're looking out for "Number 1" above all else. Psychopathy can look like all kinds of things but we just hate it when we see it.

Here's the problem with that loathing of ours: Every one of us carries around those very same wishes and impulses. All that makes us different from the psychopaths we read about, or perhaps see each day a few offices down from us, is really just a matter of degree and our personal level of self-control—pretty thin tethers to both our ethics and much-loved feelings of virtue.

Here's the other problem with that loathing: The more we refuse to see those impulses and desires in ourselves, the less control we actually have over them. Shunning them because "I could never be like that" is simply a combination of wishful thinking and blind faith. A far more effective way to prevent ethical lapses is to look hard and deep at yourself and see what your particular wishes and impulses actually are, however unsavory some of them may sometimes feel to you. That will then allow you to begin to see the places where you might have previously unseen risks for loosening your self-control or needed attention to ethics.

Lest it need to be said, the goal is not to befriend those inner psychopathic impulses—they obviously need to not be encouraged! However, to acknowledge their presence is the foundation for actually controlling them as opposed to simply choosing to assume that your behavior is—and will somehow always magically be—appropriate. As Ralph Waldo Emerson observed, "the only person you are destined to become is the person you decide to be."

Sources: ethicsthought@aweber.com. Used with permission.

MILGRAM'S SHOCK AND ZIMBARDO'S PRISON EXPERIMENTS: ETHICS UNDER PRESSURE

Milgram: Situation Ethics

The objective of Milgram's work was to discover conditions under which people would defy authority to honor the moral imperative not to inflict harm on a helpless individual. Two individuals are taken to a room where one (the "learner") is strapped in a chair and an electrode is placed on his arm. The other (the "teacher") is taken to an adjoining room where she reads word pairs and asks the learner to read them back. If the learner gets the answer correct, then they move on to the next word pair. If the answer is incorrect, the teacher shocks the learner, starting at 15 volts and gradually going up to 450 volts in 15-volt increments. Although the teachers believed they were administering shocks, the learners were Milgram's confederates and were not harmed.[1]

The key micro relationship, then, was not between the teacher and the learner, but between the teacher and the experimenter—that is, whether or not the teacher would obey Milgram, who relied solely on verbal commands for persuasion. The experiment is oceanic because it extends beyond mere speculation and written tests; it is one thing to discuss in the abstract individual rights and authority, and quite another to examine moral choice in an actual situation.

Psychiatrists, students, and middle-class adults interviewed by Milgram prior to the experiment all predicted that only a lunatic fringe, perhaps one in 1,000 people, would go all the way and administer 450 volts. The experiment was conducted with hundreds of individuals aged 20–50 from various walks of life, and there were few demographic variables associated with obedience (Milgram, 1974; also see Blass, 2000 and McLeod, 2007, which include video excerpts of the experiment). The subjects were not blindly obedient (although many seemed more concerned about their own stress than that of the learner). But they were obedient as nearly two-thirds of "teachers" went to 450 volts; in fact, none of the participants who refused to administer the final shocks (everyone went to at least 300 volts) insisted that the experiment itself be stopped. Consider too what might have happened if the learner, on meeting the teacher prior to the beginning of the experiment, had been unpleasant to him. Here the teacher's personal ethics (micro) were subverted by the permissive ethic of the meso, Milgram-led organization. Predictions about what would happen in the experiment were so far off because they focused on the autonomous individual rather than the situation in which she finds herself. Ethics is a question not only of belief, but also of action. The problem is not knowing right from wrong, but doing it.

Unwelcome insights into human behavior derived from the experiment include the following:

- It is not so much the kind of person one is as it is the type of situation she or he is confronted with that determines how one will act.

- Those in the experiment who carried out their tasks were dominated by an administrative, rather than a moral, outlook; they were a component of a system ("just doing my job"), not autonomous individuals.
- People can become an instrument of organizational authority in the presence of an authority and may be unable to free themselves from it (the superior–subordinate relationship—and the control panel itself—overwhelms any other consideration).
- It is psychologically easy to ignore responsibility when one is only an intermediate link in a chain of action.

The results of Milgram's work, one of the most well-known psychological experiments in history, are disquieting, so much so that some researchers believe that he manipulated and mistreated subjects and misinterpreted or exaggerated the findings. In reviewing the experiment's archives, the records of all 24 variations of the experiment (each with a different protocol), one scholar found that in over one-half of them 60 percent of the teachers *disobeyed* the authority figure. "The high percentage rate compliance results was made famous since it was the initial interaction that Milgram reported . . . that involved only 40 subjects" (Perry, 2013).

What is disconcerting about the experiment is that many of the subjects were not perverted or sadistic, but rather terrifyingly normal. As one analyst noted, they were nothing more—and nothing less—than "desk murderers," as they were unable to balance the two components of being a professional: technical and ethical competence (see Chapters 1 and 3). It is befitting that professionals make moral decisions at Kohlberg's Level 3 of moral development. A professional cannot make moral decisions solely from the self-interested Level 1 perspective. The Level 2 perspective may be inadequate because some social roles are unjust (e.g., police in the Jim Crow American South, Nazi doctors, U.S. intelligence officials torturing prisoners during the Iraq War). Level 3 reasoning, however, checks abuse of one's skills for either one's own advantage or the advantage of one's social group.

The task of professionalism is not to eliminate self- and group interest, but to balance them in light of a higher claim of human dignity. Advancing from Level 1 to Level 2 is a common psychological development requiring little deliberate decision. Professional life, however, requires a conscious commitment to both the technical and moral standards of excellence. It is unthinkable for a professional to do otherwise (Snell, 1993).

Zimbardo: The Stanford Prison Experiment

In another well-known experiment, Philip Zimbardo, like Milgram, investigated the pressures of social conformity, arguing that situations can induce unexpected responses to the extent that nearly any deed may be committed by anyone. The infamous "Stanford Prison Experiment" that placed students in a mock jail can be viewed at http://prisonexp.org. One difference between the two classic experiments is that Milgram's work emphasized short, one-on-one sessions, whereas Zimbardo's work involved the "total immersion" of multiple subjects for six days and nights.

In August 1971, Zimbardo turned the basement of the Stanford psychology department into a mock prison. Twenty-four college students were arbitrarily assigned to roles as either prisoner or guard by the flip of a coin. Once they had been arrested and processed, the prisoners were stripped of all their clothing, and given uniforms and an identification number. With three small cells each housing three of the nine total prisoners and a two-by-two closet representing solitary confinement, the inmates experienced harsh and dehumanizing conditions. The guards began exerting their power by forcing prisoners to endure physical activity when they believed the convicts misbehaved. The inmates began showing signs of emotional distress to the point that one of them had to be released. Soon the prisoners believed that they could never leave the institution and that it was no longer just an experiment. Educated young men were transformed into cruel prison guards or emotionally tortured inmates. Astonishingly, even Zimbardo lost himself in his role as superintendent, forgetting his role as experimenter. After only six days, Zimbardo had to call off his two-week experiment because both the guards and prisoners had completely fallen into their roles, having forgotten reality and their personal identities. Participants subverted their ethics—and even their identities—in pursuit of a task.

Analysis

Both Milgram's and Zimbardo's findings have withstood the test of time, as evidenced by compelling documentaries, popular movies ("The Experiment" [2010] with Adrian Brody and Forrest Whitaker and "Experimenter" [2015] with Peter Sarsgaard and Winona Ryder as well as "The Stanford Prison Experiment" 2015 drama), and continuations of their research. In 2006, Court TV's "Human Behavior Experiments" (45-minute) program demonstrated the relevance of obedience experiments today. It included cases including a criminally malicious "telephone strip search" of a restaurant employee by a person claiming to be a police officer (also portrayed in the 2012 movie "Compliance"), actions of a fraternity resulting in a hazing death, and torture at Iraqi prisons.[2]

Primetime's "The Science of Evil" (https://www.youtube.com/watch?v=HwqNP9HRy7Y) was a rare replication of Milgram's experiments conducted in cooperation with Santa Clara University (also see Rushton, 2004). Even though participants were advised that deception was involved (the only way the experiment could be legally redone), the findings were similar to the original trials. There have also been recent virtual replications of the experiments where human participants "shocked" virtual beings with comparable results (teachers had to be reminded that the virtual representations of people were not actually real). In popular culture, reality shows, video games, and hidden camera scenarios in ABC's "What Would You Do?" program often involve wrongdoing and how people respond to it. More scholarly updates of Milgram's work include Blass (2000) as well as Zimbardo (2007).

There are at least two themes common to all these materials. One is that while people think that they know how they would react to a given scenario, they are often bewildered once they find themselves confronted with an actual situation and submit to authority figures. The power of self-deception—when confidence is confused with competence—can be compelling. Indeed, thinking about moral dilemmas in World War II, Preston (2001) asks, how can I know that "I would not have deceived myself to avoid moral responsibility had I worked in Nazi Germany, just as I may presently deceive myself about my responsibility to victims of systemic poverty and oppression in our world?" (95).

The second commonality is "willful blindness" to problems in plain sight (Hefferman, 2012), such as Bernie Madoff's Ponzi scheme, British Petroleum's safety record, the pedophile scandal in the Catholic Church, the misbegotten Iraq War, subprime mortgages, or Volkswagon's emissions-cheating scandal. In every instance, and many more, why were repeated warnings not heeded? The impulse to obey and conform—as well as the fear and futility involved in challenging authority—make people blind to personal, organizational, and national tragedies. It takes considerable intestinal fortitude to doubt the official view. As in Hans Christian Andersen's *The Emperor's New Clothes*, few people are willing to appear unfit for their positions or ignorant by asking questions—even if the emperor *does* have no clothes. The results from the Milgram and Zimbardo protocols run counter to Kohlberg's findings that moral judgments are settled upon by moral reasoning. Clearly, contextual factors influence behavior in ethical dilemmas. Evil is done not only by monsters, but at least as frequently by normal people put in terrible circumstances.

HAIDT'S SOCIAL INTUITIONALIST APPROACH

In contrast to Kohlberg's moral development theory, which emphasized reasoning and not emotion, stands the work of Jonathan Haidt (2012). There are two central differences between Haidt's and Kohlberg's theories: One is process, the other substance.

Regarding process, Kohlberg finds that moral judgments are settled on by moral reasoning and that reasoning progresses from lesser to greater complexity in stages. Kohlberg's rationalism links morality to individual autonomy, rights, and justice, while paying little attention to authority, hierarchy, and tradition—factors important in the Milgram and Zimbardo experiments. Haidt sees things differently, apparent in his assessment of the Heinz case. Haidt views the dilemma ("Should Heinz steal a drug to save his wife's life?") as one constructed by Kohlberg to achieve an inevitable response: rational moral thinking that involves weighing "concerns about harm and life against concerns about law and property rights" (36). He found that 30 University of Virginia students were not dumbfounded by the Heinz case. They offered sound reasons for their assessment: Saving a life trumps property concerns. Instead, Haidt chose a brother–sister scenario involving a "taboo violation" that would elicit a "gut reaction."

> Julie and Mark, who are sister and brother, are traveling together in France. They are both on summer vacation from college. One night they are staying alone in a cabin near the beach. They decide that it would be interesting and fun if they tried making love. At the very least, it would be a new experience for each of them. Julie is already taking birth control pills, but Mark uses a condom too, just to be safe. They both enjoy it, but they decide not to do it again. They keep that night as a special secret between

them, which makes them feel even closer to each other. So what do you think about this? Was it wrong for them to have sex? (Haidt, 2012, 45)

Haidt used a second scenario involving another "taboo violation": A family's dog is killed by a car in front of their house. They have heard that dog meat is delicious, so they cut up the dog's body, cook it, and eat it for dinner. Haidt expected immediate moral condemnation from the same students in each case. He was right. Participants viewed sex between siblings and consumption of dogs as wrong, but when they were asked to explain why, they were flummoxed, responding with explanations like "I don't know, I can't explain it, I just know." When those vague explanations are challenged by researchers, participants flounder, grasping for reason after reason to justify their moral judgments. Haidt concluded that emotional reactions precede moral judgments. Participants made their moral judgment quickly and emotionally, then sought to develop a rational explanation for their decision. He maintains that morality does not come primarily from moral logic, but rather reasoning in these cases was simply an *ex post facto* search for ideas to justify the judgments they had already made. As Haidt has observed, "The emotional tail wags the rational dog" (quoted in Kahneman, 2011, 40).

Social Intuitionalism

Haidt contends that two separate processes are at work in thinking about (a) ethics judgment (seeing that) and (b) reasoning why (describing how one reaches the judgment). According to Haidt, while Kohlberg studied the "reasoning why," he neglected the "seeing that." Haidt, along with others (Margolis, 1987; Wason, 1960), maintains that rapid intuitive moral judgments precede carefully reasoned justifications. In the Heinz dilemma, it is contended that subjects can intuitively "see that" stealing the drug to save his wife's life was the preferred act and that the case was constructed to enable good arguments on both sides of the issue. In contrast, in the brother–sister and dog consumption cases, strong gut feelings about right and wrong influence a snap judgment that is later justified through moral reasoning. His rule: "[I]ntuitions come first, strategic reasoning second" (Haidt, 2012, 52). Reasoning does not seem to play a decisive role in formulating ethical judgments.

Such findings may cast doubt on the cognitive approaches to ethics (Chapter 5) or may just suggest that ethical reasoning is largely interpersonal. Haidt's model is referred to as the *social intuitionist approach*, because intuition is followed by *post hoc* ethical reasoning provided as a justification to others (see Chapter 7 on behavioral ethics). Thus, according to Haidt, the primary purpose of reasoning is not to guide an individual to an ethical judgment, but to provide support for an already held ethical intuition. As a result, if logic has any role in shaping judgments, it is primarily interpersonal: Presenting someone with a different perspective can trigger them to question their own beliefs. This reversal is less likely to happen, although still possible, on private reflection.

In a return to Milgram, the shock experiment has been replicated with a significant change. There are three teachers who are working together to administer shocks; two of the teachers are confederates of the experimenter. As the shocks become more intense, the confederates express concern for the welfare of the learner. This concern increases as the shocks continue to be administered. Eventually, the confederates, at different voltage levels, can take it no more and decide to leave the room with comments indicating their unhappiness with the actions taking place. Expressed disapproval ultimately influences the third teacher to question his own behavior—an example of the important influence of social context on ethical behavior.

Moral Foundations Theory

Haidt's work also can be contrasted with Kohlberg's on substantive grounds. Haidt finds the six stages of moral development to be deficient because they reflect only a portion of a broader domain of moral values (Haidt & Graham, 2007). Kohlberg's rationalism was "oversystematized and underempathized" (121). Haidt's ideas were influenced by Richard Schweder, a cultural psychologist whose work criticized rationalist thinking, on the grounds that Kohlberg's theories were valid only for individualistic cultures and not for others. Shweder's rival three ethics—autonomy, community, and divinity—were found to have cross-cultural applicability. Subsequent studies (Graham et al., 2011; Graham, Haidt, & Nosek, 2009; Iyer et al., 2011) confirmed the same, ultimately leading to the six foundations or intuitions of Moral Foundations Theory (MFT).

Two exemplary foundations are care/harm and liberty/oppression, which support ideals of social justice emphasizing compassion for the poor and the political equality of population subgroups. Care/harm empathizes with suffering and despises cruelty; liberty/oppression opposes abuse of power, abhors tyranny, and supports powerless groups. The third premise is fairness/cheating, which focuses on proportionality and people getting their just deserts. It seeks to punish cheaters and foster cooperation while avoiding exploitation. The remaining elements are:

- loyalty/betrayal (helps us discern whether someone is or isn't a team player, and to reward loyal members of the team while punishing those who betray us or others),
- authority/subversion (helps us discern rank or status and whether people are behaving appropriately), and
- sanctity/degradation (makes us sensitive to symbolic objects or threats and makes it possible to give objects irrational values).

These pillars round out the list of psychological systems that compose what Haidt (2012, 154, 181–184) refers to as "the universal foundations of the world's many moral matrices" (see data on the Moral Foundations Questionnaire at www.YourMorals.org). It is possible that MFT is simply the next step in what can be viewed as a gradual process of settling on a definition of morality by enlarging its frontiers.[3]

Two specific examples further indicate the importance of both rationality and emotion in moral decision making: the trolley and footbridge dilemmas (Exhibit 4.2).

EXHIBIT 4.2	The Trolley and Footbridge Dilemmas

Psychologists are fond of discussing the famous "trolley dilemma," and a variation of it referred to as the "footbridge dilemma" (see Bazerman & Tenbrunsel, 2011; Haidt, 2012). In the footbridge scenario, a runaway trolley can only be stopped from killing five people by a bystander pushing a heavy person with a large backpack off a footbridge onto the tracks below. Would it be acceptable to cause the death of one person to save many? The dilemma is often used to contrast two cognitive schools of thought regarding ethics: a utilitarian (consequentialist) approach and a deontological (rules or duties) approach (see Chapter 5). Utilitarian theory seeks the greatest total good, which in this case would lead to the conclusion that it was ethically justifiable to heave the man off the bridge in order to save the lives of the five others, assuming there was no other way to save them. Deontological theory, by contrast, focuses on the duties to respect individual lives and avoid harming others, and view shoving someone off the bridge to be immoral and violate the victim's rights.

Most people respond to this dilemma by judging the act of throwing the man as ethically unacceptable, justifying their judgment using such deontological arguments as that it would be breaching the victim's rights or that the ends do not justify the means. Bazerman and Tenbrunsel (2011) compare this response with the utilitarian strategy which includes totaling up the costs and benefits for all involved and opting to save the lives of many even if it meant sacrificing one.

The second related scenario, discussed by Bazerman and Tenbrunsel (2011), also involves a runaway trolley racing toward five workmen who are standing on the tracks and likely to die if it continues to race forward. In this instance, the five men could be saved if a switch were pulled to turn the trolley to a side track where it would kill one person rather than five. Is it ethically justifiable to pull the switch, killing one to save five? The response of most people is that it is morally justifiable, believing that causing the death of five is worse than one: a utilitarian rationale focusing on consequences.

But do people actually do what they say they will do? In 2003, a Union Pacificad employee faced a trolley-like decision: a runaway train was headed toward downtown Los Angeles. Should the train be diverted to a sidetrack to go to a less populated community knowing it would derail causing death and destruction? Consistent with utilitarian calculus, the switch was thrown, and 13 people were injured (including three children who were hospitalized) in the small suburb (Keysar & Costa, 2014, June 20).

For an update on "trolley-ology," using self-driving cars, consult Kaplan (2015, October 28)—viz., what if your self-driving car decides one death is better than two—and that that one is you? See also the moral dilemmas depicted in MIT Moral Machine (moralmachine.mit.edu), a platform for gathering a human perspective on moral decisions made by machine intelligence, such as self-driving cars. You will be presented with random dilemmas that a self-driving car is facing and you can select the outcome you feel is most acceptable.

For some, it is troubling to observe the contradiction between responses to the two cases. Haidt cites the work of Greene et al. (2001), who thought the two trolley cases were not morally equivalent. Greene and his colleagues suspected that gut feelings led people to make deontological judgments, while utilitarian judgments relied more on rationality (see

Chapter 5 for definitions of these two approaches). Absent the "bare-handed push" found in the first case, Greene contends, it was possible in the second instance to weigh the costs and benefits and select the one that saved the five men. A portion of Greene's research involved presenting participants with these cases while they were undergoing an MRI brain scan. He found that the portions of the brain involved in emotional processing were immediately activated, demonstrating a correlation between emotion and moral decision making, thereby offering support to the position of social intuitionists about the central role of emotion. The views of both rationalists like Kohlberg and social intuitionists such as Haidt provide valuable and competing insights on the nature of moral decision making.

Before leaving the discussion of moral development foundations, it would be remiss not to include the work of Paul Bloom (2014). Based on experimental data, he argues that babies can judge the goodness or badness of others' actions, feel compassion, and exhibit a sense of justice. Using puppet shows (see "60 Minutes" segment at https://www.youtube.com/watch?v=FRvVFW85IcU), he discovered that babies have the capacity for moral judgment: They see who they want to interact with and who they want to reward and punish. Babies are moral animals. To teach a child ethics, it is not necessary to start from scratch; they already know the basics. A complete theory of morality, then, consists of both innate capacities that humans are born with as well as cultural influences that affect individual development.

CONCLUSION

Kohlberg's emphasis on psychological rationalism led to his six-stage progression in moral reasoning. The rational approach suggests that sound reasoning about ethics causes morally upright behavior. Accordingly, Kohlberg had no interest in unconscious inferences or intuition. Haidt, in contrast to Kohlberg, suggests that emotion—not rationality—is the key to understanding moral judgments. In his view, social intuition provides a quick response to moral dilemmas and rational justifications are then conceived. On substantive grounds, Haidt's work differs from Kohlberg's as well. Haidt finds Kohlberg's emphasis on individual autonomy to be culture-bound, and his focus on justice, fairness, and harm to be too limited. Haidt maintains that his Moral Foundations Theory is more comprehensive and valid cross-culturally. Paradoxically, remember that "only those who understand their own potential for unethical behavior can become the decision makers that they aspire to be" (Banaji, Bazerman, & Chugh, 2003, 64). The important roles of rationality and emotion as explanations for moral judgments are explored more fully in subsequent chapters.

***

The omission of good is no less reprehensible than the commission of evil.

—Plutarch

NOTES

1. The preceding two paragraphs are adapted from an essay by Heather Miller (1997).
2. "Ghosts of Abu Ghraib" (HBO, 2007; 100 min.) is available from Netflix or other vendors. It begins and ends with excerpts from the original black-and-white films taken during the experiments.
3. Whether or not the conventional/postconventional distinction remains valid in spite of the contributions of MFT remains a matter of debate. Indeed, there is a clear similarity between Kohlberg's justice-centered picture of morality and the fairness/reciprocity and care/harm foundations. Prioritizing fairness and harm over the other three foundations (excluding the liberty/oppression foundation) is positively related to postconventional reasoning on the Kohlbergian Defining Issues Test (Baril & Wright, 2012). Thus, if the Kohlbergian narrative of moral development is true, then the authority, loyalty, and sanctity foundations would not be proper foundations at all, but rather relics of conventional reasoning. Haidt also observes that care and fairness are valued by liberals far more than the loyalty, authority, and sanctity foundations, whereas conservatives are more or less equal in their valuations of all the MFT foundations (Graham, Haidt, & Nosek, 2009; Haidt, 2012; Haidt & Graham, 2007).

FOR DISCUSSION

1. What were the key lesson(s) of the Milgram experiment?

2. Comment:

   - "The experiment was completely contrived and is therefore irrelevant and has nothing to do with real life."
   - "Only those who understand their own potential for unethical behavior can become the ethical decision-makers that they aspire to be. Simple conviction or sincere intentions are not enough" (Banaji et al., 2003, 64).

3. There are many similarities that the Milgram and Zimbardo experiments share as well as significant differences. Identify and critique. Hint: Consider such factors as the nature of participation by the subjects, the duration of the experiments, the importance of role-prescribed behavior, infliction of physical and psychological pain, and so forth.

4. Participate in discussion of these cases:

   a) In 2017, Miami teenager Naika Venant hanged herself live on Facebook. The *Miami Herald* reported that 1,000 people watch for nearly an hour as she prepared herself, and watched another hour as she dangled from the noose. They mocked her, called her names, posted laughing emoji, and produced parody videos pretending to hang themselves. Then they clicked their browers to see what else was on (Pitts, 2017, January 30).

      The same year, a Florida man drowned in a pool while a group of teens laughed and recorded the death; one of them yelled, "Ain't nobody going to help you." See Fifield (2017, September 19) for an insightful analysis of the ethics and legality in such incidents.

Comment, using moral development concepts and/or referencing the Kew Gardens case, discussed in chapter 5.

b) It is well-known that the Nazis operated death camps during World War II. One ethicist was recently asked by a colleague how many camps the Nazis had; he thought that is was about "three." At the beginning of this century, the US Holocaust Museum began cataloging all killing centers—ghettos, slave labor sites, brothels with sex slaves, prisoner-of-war camps, and concentration camps (Lichtblau, 2013, March 13). Based on post-war estimates, researchers believed that there might be about 7,000 sites. Over 42,500 throughout Europe, from France to Russia have now been documented. Discuss.

5. It is claimed that the vast majority of evil is not done by bad people. It is committed by ordinary men and women under certain circumstances; evil is knowing better, but doing worse. Agree or disagree and defend your view.

6. Klein (2008) recounts a scenario in "strategic ignorance:" you can earn money to buy a new flat screen by selling a homeless child to a business that will harvest his organs for transplants. It can be suggested that any time you buy a new TV instead of sending money to a homeless children's charity, you are doing essentially the same thing. Discuss.

7. One ethics class syllabus states that "ethics as practiced by the individual is the foundation upon which this course is built." A student indicated that:

> [I]f one of us is not doing our best, then that destabilizes the discussion for the rest of the class. Without authentic discussion, we cannot benefit from the deep thought required to have meaningful exploration of important issues. One strong effort can position us for the next success, as one builds upon another. The effectiveness of one student's contribution leads to the success of others. Our micro-level effort as scholars contributes to our meso-level success as a class. Comment.

EXERCISES

1. Summarize your notes (made in the page margins of the readings or a notebook) and establish links between chapter and course objectives. Continue to do this as self-study exercise. While doing this, create sentence stems (see Chapter 1) for possible use.

2. Watch the following brief videos and write a one-page essay describing the insights gained:

"Marc Hauser"
"Human Morality, Part 1": http://www.youtube.com/watch?v=KiUqBKGHp8o
"Human Morality, Part 2": https://www.youtube.com/watch?v=KiUqBKGHp8o
feature=related; (approximately five minutes each)

"Massimo Pigliucci"

"Neuroethics and the Trolley Dilemma": http://www.youtube.com/watch?v=NOfKyjyWiU0&feature=related (five minutes)

3. The plot of the movie "Unthinkable" (2010) is summarized below:

An American Muslim man, Yusuf, made a videotape in which he threatens to detonate three nuclear bombs in separate U.S. cities if his demands are not met. A special interrogator, H, is brought in to force Yusuf to reveal the locations of the bombs. He tortures the suspect, escalating his methods over time, justifying his acts by indicating that potentially disastrous consequences necessitate the extreme measures. Yusuf demands that the U.S. president announce a cessation of support for "puppet governments" and dictatorships in Islamic countries and a withdrawal of American troops from all Muslim countries. The demand is dismissed. When Yusuf is accused of faking the threat to make a point about the moral character of the U.S. government, he breaks down and admits that it was all a ruse. He provides an address to prove it. Investigators find a room that matches the scene in the video and locate evidence on the roof. A soldier removes a picture from an electrical switch, which triggers a tremendous explosion at a nearby shopping mall, killing 53 people. Yusuf justifies the deaths, stating that the Americans kill that many people every day.

H questions whether Yusef will reveal the bombs' locations unless Yusuf's wife is found. With some difficulty, she is found and detained. H brings her in front of her husband and threatens to mutilate her in front of him. H slashes her throat and she bleeds to death in front of Yusuf. Still without cooperation, H brings in Yusuf's two children. H makes it clear that he will torture them if the locations of the bombs are not divulged. Yusuf breaks and gives three addresses (in New York, Los Angeles, and Dallas), but H does not stop. Citing the amount of missing nuclear material Yusuf potentially had at his disposal, H insists that Yusuf has not admitted anything about a likely *fourth* bomb. H points out that everything Yusuf has done so far has been planned meticulously. He knew the torture would most likely break him, and he would have been certain to plant a fourth bomb, just in case. H makes it clear to Yusuf what would happen to his children if he did not cooperate.

H asks for the children to be brought back in for further interrogation. H then demands that the heretofore most ethically sensitive person, Brody, bring the children back in, because her decency will give him the moral approval that he needs to do the "unthinkable." When she refuses to retrieve the children for H, he unstraps Yusuf, sarcastically setting him free. An officer draws his pistol and aims it at H to coerce him into further interrogation. Yusuf grabs the officer's gun. He asks Brody to take care of his children and kills himself. In the final scene, Brody walks out of the building with Yusuf's children.

Analyze the situation depicted in the film as follows:

- Use one of the theories described in this chapter to analyze the plot from the perspective of (a) Yusef, (b) H, or (c) Brody.
- What moral justification might Yusuf have offered for his actions? What moral justification might H have offered for his actions? What moral justification might Brody, the female official, offer for her actions?

4. In the early 1980s, conferees at the International City/County Management Association national convention turned in a questionnaire that contained 10 cases. While many of the results demonstrated a high degree of consensus, several did not ("Ethics," 1982), including those below. Select at least two of these scenarios for analysis. Do you believe that the lack of agreement then would still be the same today? Why or why not?

- The chamber of commerce in a nearby city is hosting work panels at a resort, and you as the city manager are invited to go, all expenses paid. Do you accept?
- A physician friend asks you (the city manager) if you are interested in investing with him in a building in the city. Do you agree to do so?
- A highly valued employee recently told you that she borrowed money from the petty cash fund during the past year, wrote false receipts, and later returned the money. Under the personnel rules of the city, her behavior warrants an adverse personnel action against her. What would you do? Why?

5. The International City/County Management Association offers several ethics self-assessments and quizzes (http://icma.org). Take at least one and record the results in your journal and/or allude to them in class discussion.

6. Do you usually decide an ethical issue based on possible consequences of an action or on an ethical belief? Provide an example in your journal.

7. "Trolley-ology" (Exhibit 4.2) has fascinated philosophers for nearly 50 years and continues to do so (Cathcart, 2013; Edmonds, 2013). Do you agree that ethical responses are contingent depending upon circumstances and that basic instincts are fickle and readily manipulated?

8. Access MIT Moral Machine dilemmas at moralmachine.mit.edu. Choose between the two different options in 13 situations and then at the end compare your decisions based on others who took the test. Think about and be prepared to discuss the reasoning behind your choices.

9. View the following videos available on You Tube: "Philip Zimbardo: The Psychology of Evil" (23 minutes); "Marc Hauser-Human Morality Parts 1 & 2" (five minutes each); "Neuroethics and the Trolley Dilemma"; "Jonathan Haidt, Moral Roots of Liberals and Conservatives" (19 minutes); Dan Ariely, "Our Buggy Moral Code" (16 minutes).

References

Banaji, M. R., Bazerman, M. H., & Chugh, D. (2003). How (un)ethical are you? *Harvard Business Review, 81*, 56–65.

Baril, G., & Wright, C. (2012). Different types of moral cognition: Moral stages versus moral foundations. *Personality and Individual Differences, 53*, 468–473.

Bazerman, M., & Tenbrunsel, A. (2011). *Blind spots: Why we fail to do what's right and what to do about it.* Princeton, NJ: Princeton University Press.

Blass, T. (Ed.) (2000). *Obedience to authority: current perspectives on the Milgram paradigm.* Mahwah, NJ: Elbaum.

Bloom, P. (2014). *Just babies: The origins of good and evil.* New York: Broadway Books.

Cathcart, T. (2013). *The trolley problem, or would you throw the fat guy off the bridge?* New York: Workman Publishing.

Edmonds, D. (2013). *Would you kill the fat man? The trolley problem and what your answer tells us about right and wrong.* Princeton, NJ: Princeton University Press.

Ethics. (1982). *Public Management*, 20–21.

Fifield, J. (2017, September 19). Why it is hard to punish "bad Samaritans." *Stateline.* Retrieved from http://www.pewtrusts.org/en/research-and-analysis/blogsstateline/2017/09/19/why-its-hard-to-punish-bad-samaritans

Graham, J., Haidt, J., & Nosek, B. (2009). Liberals and conservatives rely on different sets of moral foundations. *Journal of Personality and Social Psychology, 96*, 1029–1046.

Graham, J., Nosek, B., Haidt, J., Iyer, R., Koleva, S., & Ditto, P. (2011). Mapping the moral domain. *Journal of Personality and Social Psychology, 101*, 366–385.

Greene, J., Sommerville, R., Nystrom, L., Darley, J., & Cohen, J. (2001). An fMRI study of emotional engagement in moral judgment. *Science, 293*, 2105–2108.

Haidt, J. (2012). *The righteous mind: Why good people are divided by politics and religion.* New York: Pantheon Books.

Haidt, J., & Graham, J. (2007). When morality opposes justice: Conservatives have moral intuitions that liberals may not recognize. *Social Justice Research, 20*, 98–116.

Hefferman, M. (2012). *Willful blindness: Why we ignore the obvious at our peril.* New York: Walker.

Iyer, R., Koleva, S., Graham, J., Ditto, P., & Haidt, J. (2011). Understanding libertarian morality: The psychological roots of individual ideology. Unpublished manuscript, Department of Psychology, University of Southern California. Available at http://papers.ssrn.com/sol3/papers.cfm?abstract_id=1665934

Kahneman, D. (2011). *Thinking, fast and slow.* New York: Random House.

Kaplan, S. (2015, October 29). What if your self-driving car decides one death is better than two—and that one is you? *Washington Post.* Retrieved from http://www.washingtonpost.com/news/morning-mix/wp/2015/10/28/what-if-your-self-driving-car-decides-one-death-is-better-than-two-and-that-one-is-you/

Keysar, B. & Costa, A. (2014, June 20). Our moral tongue. *New York Times.* Retreived from http://nytimes.com/2014/06/22/opinion/sunday/moral judgement

Klein, D. (2008). *Plato and a platypus walk into a bar*. New York: Penguin.

Kohlberg, L. (1971). From is to ought: How to commit the naturalistic fallacy and get away with it in the study of moral development. In T. Mischel (Ed.), *Cognitive development and psychology* (pp. 151–235). New York: Academic Press.

Lichtblau, E. (2013, March 13). The Holocaust just got more shocking. New York Times. Retrieved from https://www.nytimes.com/2013/03/03/sunday-review/the-holocaust-just-got-more-shocking.html?nl=todaysheadlines&emc=edit_th_20130303

Margolis, H. (1987). *Patterns, thinking and cognition*. Chicago: University of Chicago Press.

McLeod, S. (2007). The Milgram experiment. Retrieved from www.simplypsychology.org/milgram.html

Milgram, S. (1974). *Obedience to authority: An experimental view*. New York: McGraw-Hill.

Miller, H. (1997, May). *Stanley Milgram (1933–1984)*. Retrieved from http://muskingum.edu/~psych/psycweb/history/milgram.htm

Perry, G. (2013). *Behind the shock machine*. New York: New Press.

Pitts, L. (2017, January 30). The lonely death of Nakia Venant and what it says about us. *Tallahassee Democrat*. Retrieved from www.tallahassee.com/.../01/29/pitts-death-lonely-naika-venant/97196020

Preston, N. (2001). *Understanding ethics* (2nd ed.). Leichhardt: Federation Press.

Rest, J., & Narrvaez, D. (Eds.). (1994). *Moral development in the professions: Psychology and applied ethics*. Hillsdale, NJ: Erlbaum.

Rest, J., Narrvaez, D., Bebeau, M., & Thoma, S. (1999). *Postconventional moral thinking: A neo-Kohlbergian approach*. Mahwah, NJ: Erlbaum.

Rushton, S. (Ed.). (2004). *The Milgram re-enactment: Essays on Rod Dickinson's re-enactment of Stanley Milgram's obedience to authority experiment in collaboration with Graeme Edler*. Maastricht: Eyck Academie.

Singer, P. (1994). *Ethics*. New York: Oxford University Press.

Snell, R. (1993). *Developing skills for ethical management*. London: Chapman & Hall.

Swisher, L., Rizzo, A., & Marley, M. (2005). Update on moral reasoning research and theory in public administration: A new-Kohlbergian perspective. In H. G. Frederickson & R. Ghere (Eds.), *Ethics in management* (pp. 70–94). Armonk, NY: M. E. Sharpe.

Velasquez, M. (1998). *Business ethics: Concepts and cases*. Upper Saddle River, NJ: Prentice Hall.

Wason, P. C. (1960). On the failure to eliminate hypotheses in a conceptual task. *Quarterly Journal of Experimental Psychology, 12*, 129–140.

Zimbardo, P. (2007). *The Lucifer effect: Understanding how good people turn evil*. New York: Random House.

5 Cognitive Ethics Methods

Result and Rule Problem-Solving Approaches

We make our decisions, and then our decisions turn around and make us.
—F. W. Boreham

The personal, pervasive, professional, and powerful motivation (Chapter 1) behind much of ethics is the search for the good life, the life well-lived. There are many different conceptions of the good life, and it is not necessarily obvious which is superior. Since life is about making choices, and people do not necessarily make ethically sound decisions (Chapter 4), this chapter examines problem-solving strategies that highlight cognitive decision-making approaches to aid in making choices.

While the first question of philosophy is "How do I know?" the fundamental issue of ethics is, as Socrates said, "What ought one to do?" No single theory exists that will resolve ethical dilemmas. There is no unified theory, no secular "one best way" that tells someone what it is to be moral. Accordingly, the chapter objectives are to:

- recognize different approaches to ethics,
- understand a five-stage method to analyze issues,
- comprehend the role of moral courage in decision making,
- show the utility of several complementary decision-making strategies
- apply ethical philosophies to cases.

APPROACHES TO ETHICS

Approaches to ethics depend upon the "head," "heart," and "body." The first concerns the right decision, the kind of act one performs by identifying psychological and social cognitive factors that affect a decision. This cognitive school of thought includes two well-known philosophies (discussed further in Chapter 7). If one expects a theory to solve tough problems, then these strategies may be helpful. The second, "heart" perspective (Chapter 6) emphasizes the "right person," the kind of individual one is, by identifying and nurturing personal virtues of character that enable people to live an exemplary life. If a theory is expected to help people in their daily activities, then this viewpoint may be useful. Finally, the "body" strategy (Chapters 8–10) focuses on institutional circumstances, by discerning ways to structure organizations to enhance honorable behavior and combat corruption. If a theory is expected to help understand the impact of the environment on individuals, then this method may be appropriate.

These philosophies are quite different, but they are not wholly incompatible, as hybrid systems are possible. The idea is to strive for balance: Ethics is not geometry, but the art of the possible. In ethics, as in the rest of life, there are no magic answers. In addition, differences between theories should not lead one to despair or to the conclusion that one is as good as another. In this imperfect world, the best that can be done is to fully analyze the issues, develop the most complete arguments possible, and make a defensible choice. Administrators must be able to give credible reasons for their decisions. A five-stage model is presented below; this will be complemented by introducing several "shortcut" approaches, as well as additional decision-making aids for the key step—action—in the five-stage model.

A FIVE-STAGE METHOD FOR ANALYZING ETHICAL ISSUES

"I'm trying to figure out if I have an ethical conflict," a man said. "If you have to ask, then you do," replied his wife.

Consider this five-step method to deal with ethical issues: (1) attention, (2) perception, (3) processing, (4) action, (5) evaluation (Exhibit 5.1) (also see Figure 5.1). The focus of this strategy is on the head, or cognitive ethics.

Attention and Perception

One must initially "see," recognize, or attend to a problem, something some of Milgram's "teachers" failed to do in shocking the "learners" (Chapter 4). Indeed, this initial phase may well, by definition, be the most important one. Once—or if—the person's attention is gained, then it is up to the individual to perceive the underlying ethical issues (if any) and determine whether it is her responsibility, an obligation that many in the shock experiment subjects did not understand.

Processing

The third step is processing, or how one should cope with the problem. Responses include impulsive reaction ("just do it"), simple rule ("I just work here"), and ethical reflection (cognitive theories). The last reaction defers to philosophies that contend matters of right and wrong are a function of either (a) the weighing of expected results or consequences of an action (teleology, also known as *consequentialism*) or (b) the application of a universal rule (deontology or duty/rule ethics). Thus, deontology emphasizes doing one's duty or

EXHIBIT 5.1 **Five-Stage Problem-Solving Method for Confronting Ethical Situations**

ATTENTION →	PERCEPTION →	PROCESSING →	ACTION →	EVALUATION
Must "see" problem	See problem (i.e., who, when, where), but is it my responsibility?	How should I think about the problem?	OK to think about ethics, but do I need to act?	What did I learn?
		Levels of Analysis: 1. Expressive 2. Simple rule 3. Ethical reflection	**Kew Gardens Principles:** 1. Need 2. Proximity 3. Capability 4. Last resort (results/ ethical rules)	

Source: Adapted from McDanield (1985).

adherence to a moral imperative, whereas teleology emphasizes the results of an action. For instance, a deontologist would claim an absolute duty to abstain from murder, whereas a teleologist would contend people usually should not commit murder because it can cause undesirable consequences.

While these two strategies—deontology and teleology—are hardly perfect, their claimed strength is that they are superior to impulse, a simple rule, or an intuitive understanding of right or wrong—to say nothing of sheer expediency. However, the cardinal drawback in teleology is that predicting consequences is hazardous. "What we anticipate seldom occurs," Disraeli observed, "what we least expect generally happens." As for deontology, "ought" implies "can," but deciding what to do when duties conflict is no mean task. An undue emphasis on duty, with its "all or nothing" approach, also may deprive the individual of responsibility. Either way, very little in the world is exactly what it at first seems to be. As the old oracle said, "All things have two handles: beware of the wrong one."

Action

The fourth step is action. After processing the problem, the immediate question becomes, does the decision maker need to act? The Kew Gardens principles (named after an infamous 1964 murder in Kew Gardens, New York, in which 38 people purportedly witnessed a street

FIGURE 5.1   **Application of Flowcharting**

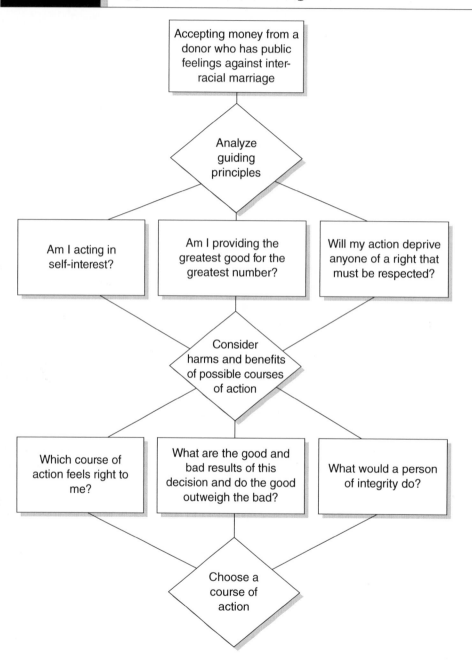

killing from the safety of their apartments—and did nothing)[1] may be helpful in answering the question (see e.g., Cook, 2014). Together, they offer assistance in determining action:

1. Need—is there a genuine requirement for action?

2. Proximity—is the actor nearby or in proximity?

3. Capability—does the person have some capacity to change the situation?

4. Last resort—if no one else is going to act, then the individual must decide to act and develop an action plan to execute the decision.

A moral agent, in short, is only responsible for problems he can do something about.

Depending on the issue under consideration, several additional methods—flowcharting and line drawing—might be useful as complements or substitutes for these Kew Gardens principles to assist in whether action should be taken (Exhibit 5.2).

EXHIBIT 5.2   Flowcharting and Line Drawing

Engineers use flowcharts in their projects to outline possible courses of action and to clearly view each of their effects. For instance, assume the president of a public university has just received a donation from a donor who is well known for her opposition to interracial marriage. Figure 5.1 analyzes a dilemma using the flowchart method. This involves considering principles—such as the decision–maker's motivations for action (self-interest, greatest good, individual rights, harms and benefits) as well as whether the action feels right. It assesses whether the positive consequences outweigh the negatives, and whether a virtuous person would act in this way. After careful deliberation, the decision maker may conclude that declining this donation is a prudent course. Such a thorough analysis may require more time than available in a fast-moving, time-pressed workplace; however, where a manager does have the luxury to ruminate at length over a dilemma, flowcharting is a useful method.

A second technique to consider when facing a decision is line drawing. This involves a process whereby a test case is placed along a continuum between an ethical action ("positive paradigm") and an unethical action ("negative paradigm") (Gotterbarn, 2007, 56; Harris, Pritchard, & Rabins, 2009, 80–84). The positive paradigm (PP, clearly acceptable) and the negative paradigm (NP, clearly unacceptable) are the outliers in the scenario, while the test case is the action under scrutiny. The individual confronted with a challenge, after brainstorming about the features of the paradigms, can draw a line for each feature and locate its positive and negative descriptions at either end of the continuum. The relevant aspects of the situation can then be plotted along the PP–NP continuum. This enables the decision maker to circle the features with the most ethical relevance and determine where the case falls on those scales.

Line drawing has both benefits and drawbacks. Gotterbarn (2007, 55) notes that, unlike approaches that examine the overall context and the broad ethical issues of the situation, line drawing examines the specific elements that help determine the ethical or unethical aspects of a decision. By plotting the significant aspects of the case and placing them on the continuum, then identifying the most relevant features and where they stand in relation to the polar points on the scale, policymakers can evaluate an action on a variety of levels and balance the positive and negative features in making a decision. It is especially useful when dealing with ethically "gray areas" where there is uncertainty about "where to 'draw the line' between permissible and impermissible actions" (Harris & Rabins, 1993, 412).

There are limitations of line drawing: It is necessary to know the details of the case, it is subjective and can be arbitrary, and factors under consideration may vary in weight. Nonetheless, since there is not always a bright line differentiating ethical from unethical actions, exercising prudent judgment through drawing lines can be useful. As Harris and his colleagues (2009) observe, "[S]ometimes arbitrary conventions to separate acceptable from wrong actions are in order" (84; see Appendix 5.3 for an application of line drawing).

Evaluation

The final stage in the five-step model is evaluation. That is, the policymaker considers what happened and what was learned. Evaluation is important because it provides a test of the utility of the analytical approach used, the reasoning behind the judgment, and a catalyst of change. For example, in Maria's situation (Case Study 5.1), she may have decided not to take action regarding harassment charges against her former employer as a result of reasoning guided by the Kew Gardens principles. While she satisfied the first three criteria in assessing her moral obligation to act—need, proximity, and capability—she may have concluded that she was not the last resort, and thus declined to pursue the matter. A post-decision assessment (evaluation) may have validated her judgment as other affected parties could have stepped up to resolve the problem. Alternatively, the harassment could have persisted or intensified, harming her former co-workers, leading her to question or regret her decision not to act. Lessons learned from evaluation provide valuable data—whether confirming one's judgment or refuting it—prompting continuous improvement that informs future decisions and actions.

While the five-stage model is useful for its comprehensive nature, Exhibit 5.3 offers three shortcut approaches that may be handy in some circumstances and may be regarded as a useful starting point in decision making. (Two other guides to decision making and action are described with applications in Appendices 5.1 and 5.2.) Exercise 3 provides another framework for the application of ethical decision making in real-world scenarios that takes into account the decision-maker's role.

| EXHIBIT 5.3 | Selected Decision-Making Tools |

Blanchard and Peale's (1988) "Ethics Check"

1. Is it "legal"? Will I be violating either civil law or agency policy?

2. Is it balanced? Is it fair to all concerned in the short term as well as the long term? Does it promote win–win relationships?

3. How will it make me feel about myself? Will it make me proud? Would I feel good if my decision was published in the newspaper? Would I feel good if my family knew about it?

Josephson's (1992) Code

1. Ethical people treat others the way they want to be treated.

2. Ethical values (honesty, fidelity, tolerance, self-discipline, integrity, promise keeping, and so forth) should always take precedence over nonethical ones (wealth, comfort, success).

3. It is proper to violate an ethical principle only to advance a more valid ethical principle (e.g., lying to a terrorist to save an innocent life).

Stone's (2009) Guidelines to Use When Contemplating Violation of Ethical Rules

1. Will you gain a personal benefit?

2. Is the decision simply taking the easy way out?

3. Does it serve the cause of justice?

Sources: Blanchard & Peale (1988); Joseph and Edna Josephson's Institute of Ethics (1992); Stone (2009).

MORAL COURAGE

Carefully proceeding through the five-step method—putting principles into practice—requires courage: "the readiness to endure danger for the sake of principle"; "knowing the right thing to do is not the same as doing the right thing" (Comer & Vega, 2011, xv, 4). Moral courage consists of moral principle, danger in adhering to principle, and endurance in service to principle despite danger (Kidder, 2006). Newell (2017, March 7) maintains that:

All three are required: principle and danger without endurance is timidity. Principle and endurance without awareness of the danger is foolhardiness. Danger and endurance with no moral principle at stake may be physical courage), but it is not moral courage.

The classical Greek concept of manliness emphasizes the virtue of courage: assertiveness, competitiveness, and confidence to be the best. He not only knows what to do and when to do it, but also is brave enough to follow through.

Public service, when viewed as a calling, demands moral courage. Newell (2017, December 4) continues:

> Ensuring government works is not for the faint of heart. It requires persistence and humility. It means paying more attention to doing the right thing than doing things right. It requires the ability to speak up for those without a voice and to speak against those, inside government, who would deny the value of that voice. You won't find moral courage — including the character and ability to establish justice – on lists of competencies for public servants or on job vacancy announcements. You won't see it referred to in performance appraisals. Yet without it, the public service is a vastly diminished institution, and America suffers as a result.

As the U.S. grows ever more divided and partisan, people are not used to honesty and courage. Seeing a leader stand up for what he or she believes is right is increasingly rare.

As evident during the athletic sex scandals at Pennsylvania State University (Chapter 2), organizational pressures inhibited individuals from taking the action they knew was ethically required. Those who wish to do good are frequently called on to exhibit moral valor: the resolve "to do what . . . is right, despite fear of social or economic consequences" (Peterson & Seligman, 2004, 216).

Those who kept quiet at Penn State were certainly lacking in moral boldness. Comer and Vega's (2011, 25) personal threshold concept—"what it takes for us to cross our proverbial moral line to act in a way that violates our standards and values"—explains how unethical outcomes persist in the face of sound ethical reasoning. Decision-maker thresholds were low: Their need to do what was right was easily overwhelmed by their narrower desire to promote the interests of the athletic program. For those with higher thresholds, the consequences of putting principles into practice can be significant (see Chapter 10 on whistleblowing). By constantly attuning one's self to elements of an organizational setting that can distract from doing the right thing, one's threshold can be heightened. And as it rises, moral bravery is nurtured to the benefit of professional and organizational development (Comer & Vega, 2011, 34). Moral competence, understanding how to address quandaries, likely will lead to greater levels of courage; if the issue is fully understood, then it is easier to address it with confidence.

CASE STUDY 5.1

Applying the Kew Gardens Principles

This scenario describes Maria's previous employment at an unnamed agency.

During her three years of employment at the agency, Maria experienced and witnessed acts of sexual and racial harassment. Having gained employment elsewhere, she now enjoys freedom from fears of termination by her past employer. Knowing that others continue to be the target of such abuses, she wonders if she has a micro-level ethical obligation to undertake actions against the meso-level organizational ethics of her former agency.

Maria seeks an answer; she reaches one by applying the Kew Gardens principles:

1. Given the well-known psychological and moral consequences of harassment, it is clear that it will result in social injury. As the severity of that injury is difficult to assess, it is also hard to determine whether need is increasing or decreasing. Increasing need will add to Maria's responsibility. Regardless, the potential—if not the certainty—of social injury exists. As such, a *need* for action exists.

2. Over a period of three years, harassment of both a sexual and racial nature was observed. Despite relocation to other employment, a responsibility may still exist. According to the Kew Gardens principles, such knowledge is defined as *proximity*. Further, having been immersed in such a hostile environment, it is safe to assume that knowledge of resulting risk and social injury exists.

3. Having established that need and proximity are present, it must be determined if there are actions available that might be expected to provide relief. In other words, is there a capability to purse such a remedy? Appropriate legal channels exist for such grievances, and, since these procedures may not produce substantial hardship, reasonable strategies are available. Therefore, the necessary *capability* exists.

4. Those employees who remain in the department feel helpless as fears of reprisal (including termination) prevent the filing of formal complaints. With this decreased likelihood comes greater obligation on an individual level. Although such determination is complex, and many variables exist, the level of responsibility grows as it becomes more and more likely that an individual is the last resort. In this case, however, it is difficult to imagine that there are no other possibilities. Other options may be complicated or unpleasant, but they likely exist. Here, the case may not adequately meet the criterion of *last resort*.

In short, by using the Kew Gardens principles to think through the dilemma, Maria may conclude that she is not obligated to take action against her former employer.

APPLYING THE FIVE-STAGE METHOD: A PERSONAL AND PROFESSIONAL CONFLICT

Having examined the five-stage problem-solving strategy and the central role of moral courage, this section offers an application of the approach. As noted in the last chapter, officials at an International City/County Management Association national convention turned in a questionnaire that contained 10 cases ("Ethics," 1982). While many of the responses demonstrated a high degree of consensus, several did not, including the scenario below:

> For years, you and a lifelong friend have celebrated your birthday with your families at an expensive restaurant, and she has always insisted on paying. This year, you have been elected to serve on the county commission. Your birthday is next week, and your friend has made reservations. Do you go?

Discussions through the years with in-service and pre-service students reveal the following findings, arrived at using the step method:

Step 1: Attention. The initial impulse of some students is to object to the case on the grounds that their personal life—their birthday for heaven's sake!—should not be a matter of public debate.

Step 2: Perception. In a similar vein, students reluctantly concede that perhaps there could be an issue here, but regard it to be sufficiently trivial as to be inconsequential.

Step 3: Processing. For those who attend to the issue and perceive it to be one that requires deliberation, robust argumentation often takes place based on results- and rule-oriented ethics.

Step 4: Action. Satisfaction of all four factors in the Kew Gardens principles is evident. The action taken, depending on the outcome of the discussion, could range considerably: to keep the custom "as is," to keep the tradition but split the check, to have the dinner at a private home, to suspend the party while in public service, to reject the invitation.

Step 5: Evaluation. Based on the above, this step reveals errors in analysis and judgment and suggests the need for an enhanced sensitivity to ethical matters.

Consider this: Would the responses differ if the research were replicated today? Why?

The sexual harassment case study (5.1) also demonstrates how application of the Kew Gardens factors can help in determining the responsibility to act. The same hypothetical case shows the utility of the five-step approach to analyzing ethical issues. The flagrant instances of sexual and racial misconduct surely captured Maria's *attention*; indeed, it was undoubtedly one of the factors pushing her to seek other employment. She *perceived* that this inappropriate, demeaning, and destructive workplace behavior created a hostile work environment. The *processing* of this situation involved assessing the four criteria associated with Kew Gardens principles—need, proximity, capability, and last-resort criteria—and could have involved the consideration of results and rules. Her *action* alternatives—doing nothing or intervening in an attempt to correct the situation—were mulled over before making a decision. Finally, she would likely *evaluate* in retrospect whether she made the right decision in light of subsequent events. Although not all four criteria are met in this case, it is important to remember that the principles foster awareness of legitimate need and ways to remedy a situation in a manner that compels a person to right conduct.

CONCLUSION

Chance favors the prepared mind.

—Louis Pasteur

Milgram found that untutored human nature cannot be trusted to protect people from inhumane treatment at the direction of malevolent authority. James Baldwin wrote that people do not wish to be worse. Rather, "they really wish to become better, but they often do not know how." An exploration of cognitive ethics suggests that selected strategies can be helpful to decision makers. The theories are analogous to rules of grammar—precise, accurate, and indispensable—while their application to—knowledge of—good writing may be loose, vague, and indeterminate.

Accordingly, it is best to use approaches to ethics to expand one's imagination: far better an imprecise answer to the right question than a precise answer to the wrong question—or not to even recognize the existence of a problem. If a situation is considered outside of its original context (a "figure–ground" reversal), then a coffee cup suddenly becomes a paper-weight, pencil holder, or a planter. Moral imagination, then, encompasses thinking anew, recognizing ethical problems, asking difficult questions about one's actions, and finding alternatives when those available are unacceptable.[2]

In short, the diverse forms of ethical reflection in Step 3 of the five-stage model are powerful ways to reframe problems, an ability lacking in many of Milgram's subjects. While such approaches have limitations, the objective is to clarify issues, enlarge one's vision, and seek enriched understanding. Like good maps, various theories offer choices, not a formula. Just as a map outlines a journey, a theory offers guidelines—landmarks, dangers, possible routes, but leaves the traveling to the travelers. These objective ethical belief systems provide help in making inevitable compromises. They do not eliminate need for judgment, but emphasize the significance of independent thinking.

These strategies are not mutually exclusive, but, rather, are complementary. Used in combination, they can result in improved decision making. It is entirely possible that contradictory guidance may result when analyzing a dilemma from multiple perspectives (see Chapter 7). Yet each encourages careful sifting of facts, thoughtful weighing of alternatives, and a willingness to exercise moral imagination by applying different lenses when exploring solutions to wicked problems. Expertise may be necessary, but it is not sufficient. As Einstein noted, "Logic will get you from A to Z; imagination will get you everywhere." Dilemmas raise crucial questions that demand answers. The cases included here show the range of ethical issues confronting public servants. These approaches provide a toolbox of strategies for dealing with these perplexing workplace issues.

***

The hardest task is not to do what is right, but to know what is right.

—Lyndon Baines Johnson

NOTES

1. The Kitty Genovese murder in 1964 is one of the most infamous in history; it inspired the creation of the 911 emergency call number, numerous story lines in television serials, a book (Cook, 2014), and a 2016 documentary. The event is evidence of bystander apathy and the diffusion of responsibility. While initial newspaper stories may have been misleading, a powerful cultural parable resulted. The incident, in any case, illustrates the stories that people tell themselves can justify their (in)action (Merry, 2016, June 29).

2. If you believe that you lack imaginative powers, reawaken the skill you had as a child when you used your imagination to play and daydream. This skill declined in school, which emphasized the logical, reasoning left side of the brain at the expense of the imaginative, creative right side. Visualizing interesting, outlandish scenarios (daydreaming) is one way to nurture your creativity. Another is to ask yourself, "What would I attempt to do if I knew I could not fail," or "If the obvious ways to deal with a problem did not exist, then what would I do?"

   In other words, seek different viewpoints, a changed basis for choices, and new assumptions by making unusual friends, engaging in new activities, and reading things that you do not normally read (also see Jacobs, 2018, January 12). It is no surprise that leading Japanese organizations encourage employees to learn flower arranging, practice the highly ritualized tea ceremony, and play team sports in order to appreciate the value of beauty, precision, and cooperation.

FOR DISCUSSION

1. "The five-stage decision-making method purports to be a comprehensive model, with most other approaches either part of, or supplementary to, it." Critique this statement.

2. The Moral Minimum is a negative injunction to avoid and correct social injury. This principle is not unlike a physician's obligation to do no harm. While useful, it is vague and lacks the specificity needed to be a precise guide to action. Brainstorm some circumstances in which social injury cannot be avoided or corrected. Identify an ethical problem and analyze it using the Moral Minimum in combination with the Kew Gardens principles. In what ways do the Kew Gardens principles become useful corollaries of the Moral Minimum?

3. Activist and politician Jeanette Rankin (1880–1973) said, "You don't do the right thing because of the consequences. If you're wise, you do it regardless of the consequences." Why or why not?

4. When asked about one of Saul Alinsky controversial community-organizing tactics—does the end justify the means?—he replied, "That is never the question, but rather do these particular ends justify these particular means?" Discuss.

EXERCISES

1. This chapter focuses on "deciding how to decide." Select any one of the scenarios in this chapter and examine it using a different analytical approach than the one provided in the chapter. For example, the harassment case was analyzed using the Kew Gardens principles and the five-step approach, but it could be analyzed using another strategy such as flowcharting, line drawing, the sensitivity–intensity matrix, or the ethical principles approach.

2. Complete an Unethical Performance Appraisal?
   Your supervisor has asked you to inflate the annual review of one of your staff members. To exercise moral courage and imagination, stand up for what is right without jeopardizing the relationship with your supervisor. To accomplish both goals, consider some of the options below and then provide a better one:

   • Calmly explain why you believe the assignment is wrong and it is just bad business (it is possible that he does not know it is imprudent or he may think that, because others have done it, it is acceptable). Agree that you wish to help your employee, but the evaluation will hurt both him and the agency in the long run. Importantly, provide some win–win solutions such as training or mentoring to enhance the subordinate's performance. Find a way to accomplish the objective without compromising personal integrity by consulting privately with those whom you respect.
   • Keep in mind that you may be wrong (seek a "reality check" with a trusted colleague; perhaps the employee's work is not as disastrous as you think it is).
   • Pick your battles. Refuse to fake the appraisal (if your boss is reasonable, he will rethink his approach, but if not, do not participate in the charade). However, take a hard line if convinced the issue is worth fighting for; it is a sign of integrity to stand firm, but for only truly egregious tasks should you prepare to walk away or suffer an adverse personnel action. (Adapted from Weinstein, 2011, pp. 110–111.)

3. Review Appendix 5.1, Figure 5.2, Figure 5.3, and Table 5.1, on the sensitivity–intensity matrix and complete assignments described there.

4. Examine Appendix 5.2, Table 5.2 and the example provided; on the ethical principles approach then complete the assignment at the end.

5. Read Appendix 5.3 illustrating the line drawing method. Identify an ethical scenario that might be appropriately analyzed using the line drawing approach, then identify the dimensions of the case and the negative and positive paradigms. How useful is this strategy in analyzing the scenario and arriving at a decision? Why?

TABLE 5.1	Ethical Dilemmas and Possible Solutions	
Ethical Dilemma	**Solution 1**	**Solution 2**
1. Allowing a toxic culture to exist	Adapt to environment and follow own ethical standards	Follow conscience and protect team as much as possible
2. Incivility	Require training courses on diversity	Open discussion to resolve differences
3. Harassment	Make changes to management style	Seek help from human resources
4. Violation of privacy	Find out circumstances and procedures to be followed	Seek assistance from human resources
5. Retaliation	Report any retaliation	Avoid retaliating against an individual
6. Coercion	Engender accountability	Apply participative management
7. Not respecting values	Respect cultural values	Do not alienate different values
8. Not providing honest feedback	Question remarks and assumptions	Publish reliable and frequent metrics on performance
9. Treating people inequitably	Ensure everyone has opportunity to speak and participate	Task and responsibilities can be assigned
10. Lacking personal responsibility	Offer opportunities to participate in planning and execution	Assign roles and responsibilities
11. Spreading malicious rumors	Hold meetings to confront and communicate	Collect facts and data that substantiate or counter
12. Misusing power and position	Obtain participation by key stakeholders	Ask stakeholders for feedback on performance
13. Discriminating	Encourage team member interaction	Provide diversity training
14. Encouraging or not dealing with infighting	Maintain independence and credibility	Apply conflict management
15. Not treating everyone fairly and respectfully	Give fair opportunity to participate	Ask for volunteers
16. Not stopping hidden agendas	Remove person from project	Call out agenda in meeting to uncover and verify or discredit
17. Exploiting people	Reemphasize vision of project	Ask what is best interest of project
18. Deliberately and maliciously damaging reputations	Address comments up front	Get human resources involved

Source: Adapted from Kleim (2012, 130–138).

TABLE 5.2	The Ethical Principles Approach

Ethical Principle	Ethical Reasoning
Consequences	*What course of action will do the most good and the least harm?*
Utilitarian ethics	What course of action brings the greatest good for the greatest number of people?
Proportionality ethic	What are the good and bad results of this decision and do the good outweigh the bad?
Theory of justice	Does this action apply impartially to each employee and organizational unit?
Golden rule	If I were in the position of another person affected by my decision, would my actions be considered fair by that person?
Reversibility rule	Would you be willing to change places with the person affected by my contemplated action?
Protect health, safety, welfare	What course of action will best protect the health, safety, and welfare of others?
Integrity	*What plan can I live with, which is considered with the basic values and commitments in my organization?*
Virtuous character	Would this action be undertaken by someone of exemplary or virtuous character?
Disclosure rule	What course of action would I be comfortable with if it was examined by my friends, family and associates?
Professional ethic	Can my action be explained before a committee of peers?
Intuition ethic	Which course of action feels right to me?
Rights	*Which alternative best serves others' rights, including stakeholders' rights?*
Principle of equal freedom	Will my contemplated action restrict others from actions that they have legitimate right to undertake?
Rights ethic	Will my action deprive any person affected by it of a right that must be respected?
Practicality	*Which course of action is feasible in the world as it is?*
Conventionalist ethic	What action will further my self-interest without violating the law?
Darwinian ethic	What course of action will enable me to succeed and survive in this organization?
Organizational vs. personal ethic	Is this action consistent with both organizational ethics and personal ethics and do organizational considerations override personal ones?
Organizational loyalty	What are the organizational goals and what can I do that is good for the organization?

Source: Cava, West, and Berman (1995).

6. Critique Klosterman's criticism of the Golden Rule (http://www.nytimes.com/2013/10/27/magazine/does-the-golden-rule-hold-up-in-modern-society.html?_r=0).

7. Ethics is like a muscle: the more it is used, the more it develops. Intentionally exercising it may seem strange at first, but with practice results it will become second nature. Start with small daily issues to strengthen your muscles; if you wait for a major event you may not be ready. Record efforts at exercising your ethics muscles in your journal and share at least one of them in class.

8. **Tabletop Exercise 2: The Bad Cop. Instructions (see Chapter 3, Exercise 5).**
Officer Bleakman has been on the police force in his city for five years. In that time, dozens of complaints have been lodged against him for harassing members of the community, particularly minorities. With the rise of the Black Lives Matter movement, the public has begun to record interactions with officers, and a video of Bleakman harassing a young Black man has surfaced on the Internet. In the video, Bleakman is clearly abusing his power and uses a racial slur when referring to the young man. Ultimately, Officer Bleakman lets him go after shoving and roughly restraining him. There appears to be no cause for the hostile interaction, and there was no report filed by Bleakman regarding the incident.

Role 1: Police Chief
You are the Chief of Police in Officer Bleakman's force. You are aware of his history of complaints and have seen the video of his interaction with the young Black man. How do you react? Do you take punitive action against Bleakman? If so, to what extent? Consider your obligations, ethical and otherwise. To whom are you accountable as the Chief of Police? What factors impact your decision?

Role 2: City Official
You are a city official in the same city as Officer Bleakman. After seeing the video of his interaction with the young Black man, you are made aware of his history of complaints. The public has not been informed of his background, and community members are demanding answers. Do you feel obligated to react in this situation? What would be your reaction, if any? Consider your obligations, ethical and otherwise. To whom are you accountable as a city official? What factors impact your decision?

Role 3: Partner
You have been Bleakman's partner on the force for the last year. In that time, you have witnessed several inappropriate acts, including the situation from the video. Bleakman often speaks in a derogatory manner about minorities, especially Blacks, and you have firsthand knowledge of his improper behavior while on duty. Do you blow the whistle on Bleakman? Why or why not? Consider your obligations, ethical and otherwise. To whom are you accountable as an officer of the law? What factors impact your decision?

Role 4: Community Member

You are a member of the community in which Officer Bleakman often patrols. You have heard about his abuse from fellow community members. You are a close family friend of the young man Bleakman assaulted in the video. Are you compelled to take action in this situation? If so, what action would you take? Consider your obligations, ethical and otherwise. To whom are you accountable as a member of the community? What factors impact your decision?

Role 5: Local News Reporter

You are a local news anchor and journalist reporting on the incident from the video recording. After working your sources, you have discovered that Officer Bleakman has a history of complaints from minorities within the community. What angle do you report in your story? Do you protect Bleakman's past? Why or why not? Consider your obligations, ethical and otherwise. To whom are you accountable as a reporter and journalist? What factors impact your decision?

REFERENCES

Blanchard, K., & Peale, N. (1988). *The power of ethical management.* New York: Morrow.

Cava, A., West, J., & Berman, E. (1995). Ethical decision-making in business and government: An analysis of formal and informal strategies. *Spectrum: The Journal of State Government, 68*, 28–36.

Comer, D. R., & Vega, G. (2011). The personal ethical threshold. In D. R. Comer & G. Vega (Eds.), *Moral courage in organizations: Doing the right thing at work* (pp. 25–34). Armonk, NY: M. E. Sharpe.

Cook, K. (2014). *Kitty Genovese: The murder, the bystanders, the crime that changed America.* New York: Norton.

Ethics. (1982). *Public Management*, 20–21.

Gotterbarn, D. (2007). Enhancing ethical decision support methods: Clarifying the solution space with line drawing. *SIGCAS Computers and Society, 37*, 53–63.

Harris, C., Pritchard, M., & Rabins, M. (2009). *Engineering ethics: Concepts and cases* (4th ed.). Belmont, CA: Wadsworth.

Harris, C., & Rabins, M. (1993, November). *Two methods for ethical case analysis.* Paper presented at Frontiers in Education Conference, Washington, DC.

Jacobs, R. (2018, January 12). Ethical curiosity: An essential dimension of ethical leadership. *PA Times*. Retrieved from https://patimes.org/ethical-curiosity-essential-dimension-ethical

Joseph and Edna Josephson's Institute of Ethics. (1992). *Survey of employee opinions, values, and behavior.* Los Angeles: Author.

Josephson, M. (1992). *Making ethical decisions.* Marina Del Ray, CA: Josephson Institute.

Kidder, R. (2006). *Moral courage.* New York: Morrow.

Kleim, R. (2012). *Ethics of project management.* Boca Raton, FL: CRC Press.

McDanield, M. (1985). Lecture, Ethics and Public Administration, Florida State University, Fall semester.

Merry, S. (2016, June 29). Her shocking murder became the stuff of legend. But everyone got the story wrong. *Washington Post*. Retrieved from https://hiwihhi.com/washingtonpost/status/748198366350278656

Newell, T. (2017, March 7). Abraham Lincoln's second inaugural: Moral courage in public life. *PA Times*. Retrieved from https://patimes.org/abraham-lincolns-inaugural-moral-courage...

Newell, T. (2017, December 4). Moral courage in public service: Lessons from the life of Susan B. Anthony. *PA Times*. Retrieved from https://patimes.org/moral-courage-public-service-lessons-life-susan-b-anthony/

Peterson, C., & Seligman, M. E. P. (2004). *Character strengths and virtues: A handbook and classification*. Washington, DC: American Psychological Association.

Stone, B. (2009, November 4). Go ahead, break a rule. *Governing*. Retrieved from http://www.governing.com/columns/mgmt-insights/Go-Ahead-Break-a.html

Weinstein, B. (2011). *Ethical intelligence*. Novato, CA: New World Library.

Appendix 5.1
Sensitivity–Intensity Matrix Approach

The sensitivity–intensity matrix, like the Kew Gardens principles and the Moral Minimum, helps answer the question of what action should be taken (i.e., following the five-step method, they focus on Step 4). For Ralph Kleim (2012), there are two signal considerations to be made when confronting an ethical dilemma: the sensitivity of the issue and the intensity of the response. Some transgressions will capture the immediate attention of decision makers because of their sensitivity (e.g., a pattern of racial discrimination), while others may not warrant immediate attention (a few instances of occasional tardiness) because of their relatively lesser intensity. These considerations assist to determine the suitable response. For instance, the need to act promptly in dealing with a late employee is not as compelling as the need to confront the person responsible for repeated instances of discrimination.

Kleim (2012, 36–37) specifies 12 factors in assessing the sensitivity of an ethical situation and gauging the intensity of the managerial reaction: the magnitude of the issue, scalability of the issue, context of occurrence, ramification of actions, control over the situation, accident or design, facts and data, impact on decision makers, consequences, assumptions, and the causes and the impact of response. Taking these elements into account will aid managers to determine both the issue sensitivity and response intensity, and whether the circumstances require action.

Applying the Sensitivity–Intensity Matrix

Figure 5.2 shows four situations, appropriate responses, and questions to consider in assessing the sensitivity of the issue and the intensity of the reaction. The second matrix (Figure 5.3) is purposefully blank. Identify two issues that can be classified in cells A, B, C, and D and devise two answers for each issue.

Questions to ask in determining the sensitivity of the issue and the intensity of the response to an ethical dilemma include the following:

- Is this an important or unimportant issue?
- What were the circumstances when this occurred?

FIGURE 5.2   **Sensitivity–Intensity Matrix**

Sensitivity of Ethics

	Low	High
High	A. Issue: Spread a rumor about a co-worker Response: Removal from project	B. Issue: Teacher altering student responses on standardized test Response: Investigation and termination
Low	C. Issue: Taking paper and pencils home from work Response: Verbal warning	D. Issue: Government official revealing identity of CIA agent Response: Presidential discretion used to mitigate prison sentence

(Intensity of Response — vertical axis label)

Source: Kleim (2012).

FIGURE 5.3   **Sensitivity–Intensity Matrix (blank)**

Sensitivity of Ethics

	Low	High
High	A. Issue: Response:	B. Issue: Response:
Low	C. Issue: Response:	D. Issue: Response:

(Intensity of Response — vertical axis label)

- How much control does the actor have?
- What facts and data are relevant?
- Is the situation severe enough to warrant attention?
- What caused the situation or transgression?
- What are the likely impacts of the response?
- What is the likely effect of the action?
- Does it affect one person or a larger group?
- Did the event occur by accident or by design?
- In what ways are stakeholders impacted?
- Can the assumptions be treated as facts?

The next application of the matrix approach (Table 5.1) also invites your decision making. Consider the scenarios facing administrators in dealing with employees. Two solutions are provided for each ethical problem. Furnish additional answers to the 18 problems below by considering the sensitivity of ethics and the intensity of the response. Assessing how to act can also be illuminated by flowcharting and line drawing strategies.

Directions: After reading and analyzing Table 5.1, offer two additional solutions for each ethical dilemma:

1.

2.

3.

4.

5.

6.

7.

8.

9.

10.

11.

12.

13.

14.

15.

16.

17.

18.

Appendix 5.2
The Ethical Principles Approach

Cava, West, and Berman (1995) used this "series of questions" approach as shown in Appendix 5.1. These are categorized into groups focusing on principles of consequences, integrity, rights, and practicality, each of which is significant and sometimes conflicting when deciding how to resolve a dilemma.

To illustrate the application of this approach, consider the situation described in Case Study 5.2. The decision maker uses the ethical principles listed (along with the question prompts) to reason through the dilemma.

 CASE STUDY 5.2

Applying the Ethical Principles Approach: Playing Poker With a Vendor

Consider the following case.

Mario Rodriguez is a state-level purchasing agent who plays poker. He meets a vendor, Jay Roberts, who also enjoys poker. Jay gets Mario access to a prestigious private country club where Saturday night poker games are routinely played. Over time, stakes keep getting higher and higher. Money exchanges hands with Mario frequently winning. A membership to the country club and continued access to the poker game is also arranged by the vendor for the purchasing agent in the course of their relationship. As time goes on, Mario realizes that he is a much better poker player than Jay and that he has won quite a lot of money from him. He is also aware that he has a business relationship with the vendor on a daily basis. Should Mario continue socializing with Jay or not?

Mario can decide what action he wants to take, if any, by making assessments based on several different ethical principles from the list in Table 5.2:

Conventionalist ethic: "What action will further my self-interest without violating the law?"

Mario and Jay's relationship does not violate any law, and the relationship certainly benefits Mario: He has received membership at an exclusive club, money from Jay in the form of wagers, and new acquaintances and relations. This rather conventional principle supports Mario's continued social relationship with Jay:

Intuition ethic: "Which course of action feels right to me?"

Mario's awareness that he has a business relationship with Jay on a daily basis inevitably raises some questions in his mind about whether or not he should be allowing it to happen. His concern reveals that he knows that other vendors may argue that it is no longer a fair market and that his employer may believe he has stepped out of line. The application of this principle may not satisfy the "butterflies in the stomach" test:

Professional ethic: "Can my action be explained before a committee of peers?"

While Mario believes that he can explain that the relationship was harmless and consisted of just two new friends sharing a game they love, in reality, his peers may look at the relationship from another perspective. They may see the money and benefits being given to Mario, a state purchaser, from Jay, a vendor. Using this principle, it appears clear that continuing this relationship may compromise his professional standing, despite explanations that reveal no evil intent:

Proportionality ethic: "What are the good and bad results of this decision and do the good outweigh the bad?"

The good results revolve around Mario's self-interest. He receives membership at a country club, a group to play poker with, and the money from winning wagers. However, the bad results connect to his professional life. Mario may possibly lose his job, taint the integrity of his employer, and lose respect at work. On balance, it appears that the possible negative effects of continuing the relationship with Jay deserve greater weight than the beneficial results of continuing the relationship under these conditions:

Rights ethic: "Will my action deprive any person affected by it of a right that must be respected?"

Mario's relationship with Jay may deprive other vendors of their right to fair and free market trade. With money being exchanged and their relationship growing, Mario may feel indebted to Jay and the other contractors may unfairly lose out on business with Mario's company. The relationship is not advisable. Mario's decision is ultimately a personal one; guidance is obtained by using the principles of ethical decision making, cultivating critical thinking, and, as a consequence, improving decision making.

Exercise

Choose two other ethical principles from the list of 15 in Table 5.2 and use them to analyze Mario's decision.

Appendix 5.3

Line Drawing

To illustrate line drawing (Exercise 4), consider this government contracting case.

 CASE STUDY 5.3

Applying the Line Drawing Method: A Questionable Gift

You work for the XYZ Agency and are in charge of awarding a government contract for the production of solar panels to be installed on federal buildings. After a thorough review process, you decide that GREEN, Inc. can provide the highest quality panels for the best price, and will therefore be receiving the contract. Shortly after placing the order for the panels, a sales representative from GREEN, Inc. visits you and offers an all-expenses-paid trip to their factory in Hawaii, which includes a tour of their facilities as well as recreational excursions. Is this a bribe? Should you accept? (adapted from Harris et al., 2009, 81).

Case analysis includes identification of the negative paradigm and positive paradigm dimensions:

- Negative Paradigm: Bribery
  - Gift size: large
  - Timing: before decision
  - Reason: personal gain
  - Responsibility: sole
  - Product quality: worst in industry
  - Product cost: highest in market
- Positive Paradigm: Not Bribery
  - Gift size: small
  - Timing: after decision
  - Reason: educational
  - Responsibility: none

- Product quality: best in industry
- Product cost: lowest in market

Line plotting the features of the case result in this diagram:

Feature	Negative Paradigm (Bribery)	Test Case	Positive Paradigm (Not Bribery)
Gift size	Large	---X-----------	Small
Timing	Before decision	-----------X---	After decision
Reason	Personal gain	------X--------	Educational
Responsibility	Sole	--X------------	None
Product quality	Worst	-----------X--	Best
Product cost	Highest	-----------X--	Lowest

Although two out of the three most important factors (in bold) are closer to the NP, the timing criterion is close to the PP, and perhaps the fact that both product quality and cost fall closer to the PP outweighs the gift size and responsibility. Or maybe the fact that the decision maker bears sole responsibility for awarding contracts generates an overwhelming perception of impropriety, outweighing other factors. An important caution: Those who use this tool must consider all of the relevant factors, for failure to do so could distort the results.

6 Virtue Theory

An honest heart being the first blessing, a knowing head is the second.

—Thomas Jefferson

Cognitive ethics approaches, paradoxically, are both too precise in logic and too abstract to be easily applied. Importantly, an emphasis on results or rules can be seen as a cold rationalistic way to make decisions that ignore the person. The third and final individual-centered approach to ethics, accordingly, shifts the focus from cognitive philosophies to virtue theory—from "head" to "heart." The objectives of this chapter are to:

- contrast cognitive and virtue ethics,
- define key virtue ethics terms,
- understand how character is formed,
- apply virtue theory,
- assess the strengths and weakness of the theory, and
- determine the utility of virtue ethics for public managers.

COMPARING COGNITIVE AND VIRTUE ETHICS

Cognitive ethics holds that rationality can supply morality with a foundation by relying on a logical process to determine what to do in a given situation.[1] While helpful and illuminating, growing disillusionment with modernity leads to the realization that life is too complex to conform to a simple equation; cognitive ethics has undue confidence in the power of reason to recognize and pursue the good. Ethics involves more than following general norms like results or duty—the strength of cognitive ethics is its weakness. A preoccupation with the process of decisions cannot produce understanding about the actual content of an individual's morality. Indeed, a focus on process can be at the expense of substance.

Virtue ethics, then, is an alternative to endless debates between results and rules in cognitive ethics. Reason may be essential in carrying out moral decisions, but the source of morality is human sentiment. To whit, "The heart of the problem is the problem of the heart." That is, the formulation of a problem can never be a purely technical procedure; reason is usually greeted with indifference by the heart. Virtue theory is a framework, not a formula. As shown in earlier chapters, ethics can include questions about consequences and duties, but it also entails questions about what kind of person someone is. It concerns being considerate, helpful, and honest: being a good individual and taking responsibility for living a meaningful life. Ethics is about developing the right character more than following the right procedure. Behind every action is a person. This does not mean that results and rules are irrelevant, but rather that they are most effectively considered in the context of individual character. Stated differently, we cannot control circumstances, but we *can* control character. Virtue ethics is a branch of moral philosophy that emphasizes character rather than rules or results found in the rival cognitive strategies.

Virtue theory, accordingly, is more personal in approach than cognitive ethics. One's answer to "What to do?" has less to do with results and rules, and everything to do with what kind of person one is. Every action is measured in terms of character, one's internal moral compass. We must *be* before we can *do*; one must be good before one can do good (we are human beings, not human doings). Virtue ethics, it follows, is a way of life, not a mere method of analysis.[2]

The primary moral faculty is intuition and not intellect, because reason more easily leads to error. Many do not have the capacity or training for discursive reasoning. Cleopatra is said to have persuaded her people that twilight was dawn (consider, too, the convincing—and opposing—jury closings in television courtroom dramas such as "Law and Order" reruns). The intended role of theory in virtue ethics is not to get the decision maker out of a jam, but to help build her character. "Being virtuous is no precise science, (but) it is nonetheless a demanding art, whose mastery is vital to achieve human potential. Unfortunately . . . moral decision making lacks the conceptual clarity and compelling certainty of Euclidean geometry" (Anderson, 1996, 7).

THE VOCABULARY OF VIRTUE

If Socrates was right in saying that "the beginning of wisdom is the definition of terms," critical concepts—character, virtue, integrity, practical wisdom—require examination to comprehend the range of virtue ethics. As these terms are unpacked, beware that they are much more easily recognized than defined. *Character*, according to Anderson (1996, 5), is the sum of enduring dispositions—good or bad—that define the individual and are cultivated over a lifetime. Comprising a person's pattern of behavior, character is related to the moral qualities of individual self-discipline and collective social responsibility. An individual cannot be understood apart from the larger community in which he participates. "There is no such thing as a 'self-made man,'" asserts George Matthew Adams:

> We are made up of thousands of others. Everyone who has ever done a kind deed for us, or spoken one word of encouragement to us, has entered in the make-up of our character and of our thoughts, as well as our success (http://www.quoteworld.org/quotes/65).

Indeed, the polis is about learning how to live the good life. Character is developed experientially in communal relations through modelling significant others and by reflecting on important encounters (Preston, 2001).

Good character is not arrived at by accident. Developing strong moral fiber is a continuous process of self-discovery requiring commitment to ethical values and the cultivation of virtuous habits. Many people are clearer about how to build an external career than on how to build internal character. External success is gained through competition with others, while internal development occurs by confrontation with one's self. Character is one's moral center or "naked soul." What matters is not so much how long one lives, but how one lives. Franz (1998, 65) emphasizes the importance of personal identity:

> By character, I mean the internal resources, knowledge, and discipline to know one's own mind and the resolve to pursue its direction. Character is based on beliefs, nourished by knowledge, forged in experience, and committed to values. A person of character has the ability to make things happen, persevere through adversity, forgo alternatives, and alter course. Character implies a mastery over one's own will. Someone without such mastery would hardly be characterized as responsible . . . or a person of integrity. . . . This mastery is no accident. It is learned.

It is evident that citizens should care a great deal about their leaders' personality traits, apart from their policies, because no position is sufficiently prestigious to make a person of dubious character conduct themselves with honor.

One test of character is what one would do if one were invisible. Does the invisible person, in the modern vernacular, have the "right stuff" to do the right thing? Recall the Milgram experiments. Good people make moral choices. For them, the reply to "What is a good life for a human being?" is to create an ethical character, to achieve excellence in all aspects of life, to live virtuously with others—in brief, to become a "virtuoso." *Leadership*, in fact, can be defined as the practical application of character. In reciprocal fashion, virtuous citizens build moral communities that, in turn, encourage further character formation.

Virtue is a trait or excellence of individual and societal character. Virtues are principles of goodness and rightness in character and conduct that lead toward nobility and away from depravity. Common examples include justice, courage, truthfulness, and temperance. Woven into character, they are ingrained dispositions to act rightly, developed by practice, just as vices are tendencies to act wrongly. Not easily honed, virtues make people sensitive to ethical issues and shape how they think and act. One becomes prudent, for example, by repeatedly behaving in a prudent manner. Per the three perspectives on ethics (Chapter 2), an individual may be virtuous (micro-level ethics) through her personal character development, as can an organization (meso level) through integrity-based practices and a society (macro level) through upholding a pervasive culture of virtue.

Virtue (Greek: *arête*) is found between the vicious extremes of excess and deficiency—Aristotle's "golden mean" is between two vices (Confucius and the Buddha also endorse a concept of equilibrium). In every situation, a person of character will determine the mean—neither excessive nor deficient—based on reason and experience appropriate for that circumstance. Courage, to take one example, is the mean between the vices of foolhardiness and cowardice, an awareness of what to fear and what not to fear. Prudence, to offer another example, is the considered position between being overly cautious, on the one hand, and rash, on the other. What is reasonable in one situation may not be in another. Individuals of character are guided by their principles, not popularity or expedience.

Virtues, then, are more than habitual skills enabling right action—they promote the attainment of what it means to be human, to function well, to be moral. Virtues are character traits needed to live a flourishing life (*eudaimonia*). They are valuable for intrinsic, not instrumental, reasons. While there is no one, definitive list of virtues, seven cardinal virtues can be noted: prudence (wisdom), courage (fortitude), temperance (moderation, self-mastery), justice (rightness) (the "natural" virtues of ancient Greece philosophers), faith, hope, and love (from Christianity). These virtues are cardinal in the sense that all other moral virtues can be derived from them.

Integrity, a product or synthesis of virtues, is a predisposition to maintain one's virtues and act in accordance to character. In today's parlance, this consistency between belief and conduct, to make actions congruent with values, is to "walk the talk," to "have it all together." If a building has structural integrity, a person with integrity has "gravitas"—a sure sense of right from wrong; she knows what her core beliefs are, and what she will or will not do, no matter what. Integrity grows from internal values, experiences, and the ability to act thoughtfully. The individual must have a strong commitment to principles and self-discipline while continually striving to meet high ethical standards. Serving as one's "moral identity," integrity is the aptitude to contemplate one's roles and obligations, to nurture an ethical soundness both as an individual and as a member of the community. Compromising one's integrity is a profound mistake, as evidenced by officials when they are embroiled in scandal (Chapter 11).

To act thoughtfully requires *practical wisdom*. Such prudence, what Aristotle calls *phronesis*, is the capacity to distinguish right from wrong and take sensible action.[3] It is the ability to consider competing claims and to tolerate moral ambiguity. The reflective person recognizes the distinction between knowing and doing. Moral virtue directs one to the right end; practical wisdom directs one to the right means. It is not always enough to act with sincere intentions; behaving effectively demands discerning all the relevant factors leading to a fitting decision. Good judgment comes from the integrity of a well-developed character.

Practical wisdom enables one to grasp the golden mean in particular situations, a quality requiring experience that cannot be reduced to rules or consequences. The use of practical wisdom differs from analytical reasoning because formulating a judgment is circumstantial, personal, and steeped in wise counsel to do right for each member of one's community. It involves an understanding of what it means to be human, and the capacity to deliberate thoughtfully (thereby realizing virtuous ends) when confronted with dilemmas. For example, prudent rule following includes discerning the purpose of the measure, and when rule departure more effectively meets responsibilities than adhering to the rule.

Essential for an ethical life, practical wisdom engages and unifies the intellectual and the moral: Right action requires intellectual judgment, which itself requires virtue. Right action has no standard external to itself—to act rightly is to do what a good person would do in a particular circumstance. No pedestrian average, temperance is Greek for "the middle way," moderation, and balancing competing interests. One deliberates as long as necessary and then acts decisively with compassion, precision, and speed. One must see his duty and perform it. Virtuous action, founded on arduous practice, may be nearly spontaneous. A person cannot claim to be kind unless she is habitually kind—kindness is shown automatically, without thought of its being kind.

To summarize briefly, character (personal behavior patterns) is enriched by virtues (disposition to act). The synthesis of character and virtues constitutes integrity, something that can be achieved through the exercise of practical wisdom, a preeminent virtue. A good tree bears good fruit; good people make good decisions. As tennis champion Arthur Ashe observed, "You are really never playing an opponent. You are playing yourself, your own highest standards, and when you reach your limits; that is real joy."

Two sterling public officials, who display many of the virtues discussed in this chapter, are now profiled. The first shows how an appointed public servant, Donna Shalala, former secretary of Health and Human Service and current university president, has managed large organizations with honesty and integrity. The second demonstrates how an elected public servant, Cory Booker, former city council member and mayor of Newark, New Jersey, serves the public interest with integrity with a hands-on approach to addressing human problems. Both of these exemplary people have a blend of ethical, technical, and leadership competencies grounded in a virtue-based public service ethos.

Exemplar Profile: Donna Shalala

Donna Shalala is no stranger to major organizations: She holds the distinction of being the longest serving secretary of the Department of Health and Human Services (HHS), served as president of both Hunter College and the University of Wisconsin-Madison, and continued to make headlines as president of the University of Miami, which steadily ascended in academic ranking under her leadership. In 2015 she moved to New York to become chief executive officer of the Clinton Foundation. A few years later, she returned to the University of Miami to resume her status as a tenured faculty member. She has served on several corporate and civic boards of directors, and is the recipient of numerous awards including the Medal of Freedom, the Nelson Mandela Award for Health and Human Rights, and more than 50 honorary degrees.

While she is clearly a paragon of effective management, she is also an exemplar of the sort of virtue-oriented action that is the subject of this chapter. In fact, she is more than just a testament to virtuous leadership—she is also an outspoken advocate for it. In an article in *Public Integrity*, Shalala (2004, 350) shares 12 tips for "managing a large public sector organization with honesty and integrity," for she learned from experience that it is the cultivation of these virtues that makes an effective and ethical organization a reality. It is no coincidence that each of the 12 pointers is matched by an anecdote from her time at HHS. Examining some of these instructive snapshots of the career of a distinguished public servant should help you understand both why virtues are vital to an organization, as well as how they can be attained in practice.

One of Shalala's lessons speaks directly to the importance of character—but not simply the leader's character. Her advice is to "[c]hoose people based on both the content of their resume and their character" (351). She relates how it was crucial to resist pressure from the White House to appoint senior campaign officials to her HHS team, because the values of the staff were tantamount to favors owed: Without a team that shares your values and your vision, that is committed to "serv[ing] the public interest ethically" (355), the goal of an ethical organization could never be reached. Yet the resume is just as important as the individual's character, "because you can't make the right [ethical] decision if you don't have the necessary competence" (351). Thus, Shalala believes that competence and character feed into each other, and took care in selecting whom to work with.

Shalala also found that at the core of leading with integrity is "the courage of your convictions," which, in a government department, translates into refusing to "subordinate policy to politics." And the temptation to let politics take the wheel is always looming in the field of public health: While scientific facts cannot be disputed, unfavorable data can be swept under the rug and favorable information can be blown out of proportion. Yet when confronted with either, Shalala refused to yield to temptation. When HHS received a report from the nation's leading health officials indicating that a program to provide clean needles to drug addicts could reduce the rate of HIV infection, the department stood behind it, in spite of fierce opposition to needle exchange programs. Likewise, "the White House was told 'no' if they wanted to over-emphasize or distort the significance of a scientific finding" (353).

Integrity can also mean going above and beyond the merely required. At the meso-organizational level, this can mean being "concerned not just with the legal imperatives but the moral ones," as when the HHS inspector general issued criticism of the department's policy on the protection of human subjects in research. The report triggered an overhaul of the research-oversight process that went far beyond closing the gaps in legal compliance and properly reflected the importance of guaranteeing the safety of subjects (351).

Another more personal lesson of Shalala's is "It is your friends, not your enemies, who will often get you in trouble." She observes how even the most experienced official can unknowingly fall sway to the influence of a personal relationship, or simply be perceived as acting out of favoritism. As such, it is imperative to own up to the fact of one's own fallibility, and accept the need to avoid any signs of impropriety, real or imagined. It was for this reason that instead of self-righteously assuming that her actions were always beyond reproach, Shalala made sure there was always a witness to any meetings she had with individuals outside of HHS (354).

Shalala leads by example in the organizations she manages, an example useful in our discussion here. Virtues, while lofty, are not to be placed high up on a pedestal out of reach. They are, in conjunction with technical skills, the fuel that powers successful organizations. As Donna Shalala has proved in the course of a long career, demonstrating integrity, prudence, and humility in leadership "will never be easy, but it will always be right . . . it will never be effortless, but it will always be rewarding" (355).

Exemplar Profile: Cory Booker

In a crime-ridden city, a caped or costumed crusader fights for law, order, and justice. Gotham has Batman, New York City has Spider-Man, and Newark, New Jersey, for a time (2006–2013) had its mayor—Cory Booker. Booker is, *sans* the cape, the closest an American politician has come to being a superhero. Although his death-defying stunts—rescuing his neighbor from a burning building—had been sufficient to earn him the title "Savior of Newark" (Ripley, 2000), he also bears a superpower of a different sort: a virtuous character. Long before he was rushing into flaming buildings (Dixon, 2012) or tending to injured citizens on city streets (Associated Press, 2012), Booker was demonstrating what it means to serve the commonweal with integrity.

A crusader committed to ameliorating the plight of the inner city, Booker has proved time and time again that he has the courage of his convictions. For instance, as a city council member in the late 1990s, Booker sought to increase pressure on the police to crack down on drug-related crime. Aware that actions speak louder than words, he decided to go on a hunger strike for 10 days while living in a tent in the middle of his district, hoping to bring attention to the area's drug problem (Carbone, 2012). In his first year as mayor, Booker reprised this hands-on approach to crime by riding along with police officers on night patrols until the early morning hours. His message was one of solidarity: "I wanted to show people that I'm willing to work as hard or harder than anybody in city hall to get the word out to police officers that I was challenging them to show my level of commitment." This extraordinary commitment was a resounding success. In the years that followed Booker's acts of solidarity, Newark experienced an increase in police productivity and falling crime rates (Gilgoff, 2009).

While the turnaround in crime may suggest Booker's virtuous actions brought political success, he has incurred the costs of integrity as well. In an appearance on "Meet the Press," Booker made a comment about President Obama's negative political campaigning that triggered a severe backlash from fellow Democrats, who detected some suggestion of self-promotion. While he retracted his statement in light of this criticism, Booker still maintains his opposition to the corrosive political climate fostered by negative campaigning (Haddon, 2012). Indeed, Booker's true heroism is found in his desire to be a faithful public servant, acting out of good character regardless of whether it will be well or ill received. He sums up his own philosophy this way: "My mom used to say that who you are speaks so loudly that I can't hear what you say" (Gilgoff, 2009). Booker was elected to the U.S. Senate in 2013. His name has surfaced as a potential candidate for the 2020 presidential election, but he has publicly stated his preference to be a "person of purpose," devoting attention to his senatorial duties.

Both Shalala and Booker exemplify good character where right action became second nature based on habits cultivated over a lifetime of service. Ability may get someone to the top, but it takes character to stay there. The Good Men Project (https://goodmenproject.com/) and Bruce Weinstein's weekly high character leadership column in *Forbes* magazine offer regular profiles of praiseworthy individuals.

HABITUATION: THE FORMATION OF CHARACTER

How is character formed? Through habit. There are no instant habits—they must be repeatedly practiced. "Excellence," Aristotle believed:

> [I]s an act won by training and habituation. We do not act rightly because we have virtue or excellence, but rather we have those qualities because we have acted rightly. We are what we repeatedly do. Excellence, then, is not an act, but a habit. (In Durant, 1926/1991, 76)

Indeed, "we first make our habits," writes John Dryden, "and then our habits make us." Good habits (virtues) can be hard to form and easy to lose; cruelly, bad habits (vices) can be easy to form and hard to lose (Exhibit 6.1).

Habit shapes character, as improvement comes from repeatedly making good decisions that avoid extremes and aim at moderation. Like physical fitness, no one can transmute character to someone else; it cannot be bought, as it must be earned. "The highest reward for man's toil," writes John Ruskin, "is not what he gets for it but what he becomes by it." Moral behavior, rather than a product of cognition, is a product of habituation to virtuous conduct. It is quicker to act your way into right thinking than to think your way into right acting. Answers to life's questions are not found "in the back of the book," but rather inside one's self. You are the only person who can decide where you want to go in life and how you are going to get there. To cultivate virtues is required for the good life, the achievement of human purpose. As Eric Fromm said, "Man's main task in life is to give birth to himself." Every day and everything counts. Character is destiny. Success in life ultimately depends on what an individual knows, what she does, and what she becomes as a result. Your character will be what you yourself choose to make it.

Excellences of character find expression in action. The practice of virtues may not require deliberation; instead, it becomes ingrained in one's stature after years of performance. Benjamin Franklin describes in his autobiography how he consciously nurtured some dozen virtues he thought important to a meaningful life. A modern-day approach to such habituation is found in Stephen Covey's (1991) *Principle-Centered Leadership*. As a result of deliberate practice, virtue becomes natural, such that lying is not thought of as an option when confronted with a difficult issue. What we do will likely depend on what we already are, and what we will be in the future will be the result of ongoing self-discipline.

Because individuals and circumstances vary, no complete catalogue of virtues exists. More useful than a recitable slate is possession of the capacity (practical wisdom) to know when and how to exhibit the appropriate virtue. An individual with good character "knows" how to feel and act. Indeed, compiling a list misses the point, which is to get away from a formulaic way of thinking about ethics, and emphasize its personal nature and context sensitivity.

"The true test of character," according to John Holt, "is not how much we know how to do, but how we behave when we don't know what to do." Does the problem challenge or

| Exhibit 6.1 | **Managerial Work Habits** |

Since ethics is central to the professional identities of public officials (Chapter 1), they are responsible not only for acquainting themselves with the theories associated with a cognitive approach to ethics, but also for cultivating exemplary character traits. Thus, as habits (both good and bad) shape character, it is vital to understand how workplace habits are attained or lost, transformed or solidified. While developing an admirable character must take place at the individual level, the climate at the top sets the tone for those at the bottom and everywhere in between. It therefore behooves us to explore the work habits of managers.

West and Berman (2011) do just that, discussing the results of a national survey of senior officials in city governments with populations over 50,000 about the work habits of their subordinate managers. The reporting of managers on their employees and themselves represents the organizational or meso-level ethic. The institutional culture promoted by managers through the policies they implement is a feature of meso-level ethics. While managers are individuals with emotions and values, this may lead one to think they operate at the micro-personal level, but the role of the manager is typically to put the needs of the organization (meso) first. Although close to 90 percent of senior administrators report that their subordinates "regularly demonstrate civility, courtesy and decency," as well as "take a stand where issues of ethics are at stake" (69), the authors nevertheless stress the necessity of constant vigilance because of two unexpected discoveries.

First, 45 percent of those surveyed reported that one or more negative managerial habits (such as being overly judgmental, aggressive, passive, or defensive) were present alongside good habits (71). Second, while poor management habits can crowd out good habits, the converse relationship does not hold. "Managers cannot rely on the presence of good management work habits in order to reduce the presence of bad management work habits" (77). Officials must first work to elevate awareness of the presence of bad habits for training and incentives to be effective. Nevertheless, the findings also indicate that top management is least likely to concentrate on work practices when there are high levels of good managerial habits (and thus organizational performance). This contributes to a vicious cycle whereby "when things are going well, the possibility exists of giving insufficient attention to bad management work habits which, however minimal, sow the seeds of subsequent performance problems," and, it should be added, ethical problems, when ethical habits are at stake (79).

While these conclusions may seem discouraging, they only confirm that cultivating a virtuous professional character (where virtues of both competence and ethics converge) is a never ending process of habituation. At the individual level, this development requires engaging in "a difficult process that typically requires persistence, practice and, hence, considerable time" (67). However, employees do not have to set off alone on the long and winding road to virtue. Organizational policies can complement individual efforts by including certain positive behaviors as criteria in performance reviews or by establishing training, mentoring, and on-the-job coaching to help individuals identify good and bad work habits and strive toward reinforcing the former while weaning them off the latter (67).

Alternatively, and more in accordance with the personal nature of character development, Chun (2005, 281) sees the role of the manager as "to make sure the strategic virtues are . . . embedded in [a] member's cognition in everyday organizational life." Although this directive entails a cognitive component of identifying (with help from a manager) the virtues to be pursued, virtue ethics is still very much about the heart: It entails gaining, through experience, a practical knowledge of which actions lead one to virtue, and performing them routinely until they become second nature.

defeat us? While virtue ethics does not rely on methodical approaches to issues, some aids to thinking about the personal nature of decision making may nonetheless be helpful. Michael Rion (1996, 13–14) encourages managers to mull over the questions below when faced with a dilemma. Note that most of them directly or indirectly focus on the person as a decision maker:

1. Why is this bothering me? Is it really an issue? Am I genuinely perplexed, or am I afraid to do what I know is right?

2. Who else matters? Who are the stakeholders who may be affected by my decisions?

3. Is it my problem? Have I caused the problem or has someone else? How far should I go in resolving the issue?

4. What is the ethical concern—legal obligation, fairness, promise keeping, honesty, doing good work, and/or avoiding harm?

5. What do others think? Can I learn from those who disagree with my judgment?

6. Am I being true to myself? What kind of person or company would do what I am contemplating? Could I share my decision "in good conscience" with my family? With colleagues? With public officials?

A "defining moment" (Badaracco, 1997), one that reveals, tests, and shapes character, is portrayed in Case Study 6.1. A human being with good character, Aristotle believed, likely would be wise, temperate, courageous, and generous. The Greek admonition "know thyself" remains central to the study and practice of ethics in the 21st century.

VIRTUE THEORY STRENGTHS AND WEAKNESSES

Virtue theory attends realistically to the actual dynamics of moral life—what one feels comfortable with or what an admired person would do. Understanding virtue ethics is more intuitive than cognitive ethics. People cultivate ethics by living ethically and making every-day choices—not by studying isolated, dramatic cases of decision making. Blaise Pascal captures this distinction by saying, "The power of a man's virtue should not be measured by his special efforts, but by his ordinary doing." Indeed, developing virtues keeps us from finding ourselves in moral quandaries in the first place. We are not moral because of rules, but because of what we demand of ourselves in character—the capacity to recognize challenges and respond appropriately.

   Knowing the difference between right and wrong is necessary, but not sufficient; we must also care about the difference. If we ask the questions, "What is a moral life?" and "What is the right thing to do?" then cognitive ethics is a minimalist approach with an instrumental focus ("ethics without virtue"). Virtue ethics is a maximalist approach that demands ethics with virtue, deep reflection, and high ideals.

CASE STUDY 6.1

Applying Rion's Ethical Decision-Making Framework: Probing the Conscience

The following case concerns an ethical dilemma confronting an academic executive.

> You are the president of an elite public university and very much committed to fostering diversity within the student body. You have championed an affirmative action program that is widely popular throughout the university and has set an example for other high-ranking institutions. A wealthy alumnus has made a very generous donation, and the funds are desperately needed by the university. However, the alum is an outspoken opponent of affirmative action. (He attended the university when it was an all-white, male institution.) Should you accept the donation?

Rion's questions can be used as a guide to help the president in deciding whether or not to accept the donation:

1. *Why is this bothering me?* After a career spent supporting affirmative action programs and fostering diversity on campus, this decision has caused me many sleepless nights. In the short term, the funds are desperately needed, but I fear that in the long run, I will be tainting the school's character and my own. The face and integrity of the school, its financial stability, and its present and future students all play key roles in weighing this decision. I also must think of the colleges that have followed in our footsteps and view us as a role model. Making a prudent decision will require due diligence and the courage to explain my action to the wealthy alumnus.

2. *Is it my problem?* Yes, I cannot see how it is not my problem. After years of progress since the days of all-white, male graduating classes, I fear that my singular decision could eliminate that progress and take the university back decades. My own conscience and the well-being of the school I lead are on the line.

3. *What do others think?* This decision will certainly be accompanied by backlash either way: I will make headlines for ruining the school's progress or for denying it of essential funds. I risk losing major programs or polluting its character.

4. *Am I being true to myself?* To retain integrity, only one answer makes that possible. After defending and promoting student diversity, which I firmly believe in, I cannot be true to myself and accept a donation, no matter the size, from an opponent of everything we have stood for.

Yet virtue ethics lacks universality, as no general theory of human virtue exists. So-called cardinal virtues vary from time to time and place to place, and the same virtues may not apply to all individuals in a society. To illustrate, for centuries, a virtuous woman was considered to be quiet, servile, and industrious. Further, virtue ethics lacks a theory of action. Cognitive approaches have fewer problems precisely because they force decision, but virtue theory does not offer much direction about what people should do. Virtues may generate instructions for action (the virtue of justice, for instance, provides the motivation to act justly), but what does a just person do in a given dilemma? Finally, the theory—ironically—lacks integrity due to its ambiguity. One may be good, but may not know how to do good. Indeed, confusing being with doing can easily lead to self-righteousness—if one believes he is good, it is not hard for him to believe that what he does is good, even when it is not. To conclude, the revival of virtue ethics in contemporary times, despite its limitations, has resulted in a more complete portrait of morality in public affairs. The contemporary renaissance of virtue theory has both encouraged a scrutiny of other approaches and led to disagreements about the applicability of virtue theory for managers. This dichotomy is addressed below.

UTILITY OF VIRTUE ETHICS FOR MANAGERS: CHALLENGE AND RESPONSE

The literature on virtue theory includes critiques and rebuttals regarding its applicability to public administration. Alasdair MacIntyre (1985), among others, questions whether it can be imported into public administration because he sees the bureaucrat as a figure devoid of virtue: "[T]he bureaucratic manager relies on a system of knowledge that promotes efficiency and effectiveness—looks at controlling means rather than ends—and therefore leaves no room for moral debate" (in Macaulay & Lawton, 2006, 704). MacIntyre views administrators as operating solely within "the realms in which rational agreement is possible—that is, of course . . . to the realm of fact, the realm of means, the realm of measurable effectiveness" (30). If so, technical competence is the proper concern of bureaucrats, not perfection of character.

Bowman, West, and Beck (2010) contend, however, that technical skill is not the only element of good administration, as it must be complemented by ethical and leadership competence. Together, these three competencies provide the "edge" necessary for successful public service. Bowman et al. demonstrate that ethics is personally as well as professionally relevant. Officials encounter ethical issues at every level of bureaucracy—identifying and dealing with them are core responsibilities. The professional—whether in government, business, or nonprofit sector—must rely on ethical resources, including what constitutes a virtue, for guidance in addressing professionally perilous dilemmas.

Thus, technical, ethical, and leadership competencies are integrated and mutually reinforcing, evidenced by these observations:

- The competent administrator is technically adroit and ethically concerned, and takes the lead in performing his or her tasks with excellence.

- "[S]uch questions as 'What should I do?' and 'What kind of person am I?' are not separate questions, but come together to allow for individual flourishing."
- Competence is valued as a virtue, an excellence, of public service by employers. (Macaulay & Lawton, 2006, 709)

Macaulay and Lawton studied compliance officers in the United Kingdom and found no sharp distinction between competence and virtue in the perceptions of their knowledge, skills, and abilities (KSAs). Not only did officers cite a variety of virtue-based and competence-based KSAs, they also interpreted many in terms of both virtue and competence. The KSA of "ethical awareness," for instance, can be seen as invoking virtue (understanding morality and abiding by its dictates), as well as technically, in terms of "transparency, accountability, and the rights and wrongs of local authority systems and practices" (707–708).

Gilbert Harman (2003) and Miguel Alzola (2007) also contribute to the virtue ethics and public administration debate. Harman contends that "Aristotelian style virtue ethics [has] . . . a commitment to broad-based character traits of a sort that people simply do not have" (92). The argument maintains that although it may be possible to come to a conclusion about what characteristics constitute a virtuous person, individuals typically lack the "broad and stable dispositions corresponding to the sorts of character and personality traits" needed for virtue (92). Harman subscribes to the consensus of social psychology that the understanding of character presupposed by virtue ethics simply does not exist in human behavior. If he is correct, virtue ethics is misguided and cannot serve as a basis for bureaucratic ethics.

Harman's view is rooted in fundamental attribution error (Chapter 7), the erroneous tendency to attribute individual behavior to a person's character, not situational factors. Thus, he maintains that it is people's situation, and not just their character traits, that best explains what they do. It is a mistake to neglect the high susceptibility of public administrators to "subtle situational effects"—"minor and seemingly irrelevant differences in the perceived situation sometimes make significant differences to what people do" (90). Thus, even a morally upright person may make objectionable decisions under the pressures of the workplace to perform. Failure to do the so-called right thing does not mean an administrator is morally depraved, and that ethics therefore has no role at work—just as failure to obey street signs while in a rush to the hospital does not make one an inherently dangerous driver, or warrant the removal of street signs since "no one obeys them anyway." Circumstances matter.

For example, consider an experiment in which test subjects making a phone call in a telephone booth witness a passerby (a confederate of the experimenters) drop a folder full of papers, which scatter across the ground. Callers who found a coin planted in the return slot were far more likely to help than those who did not find a coin (Isen & Levin, 1972, cited in Harman, 2003). Just as the coins encouraged the subjects enough to perform an altruistic act (one that, ideally, they would have performed without the incentive), an administrator's willingness to do the "right thing" may vary with external factors—securing a grant or an argument at home—that make her more or less likely to ascribe to ethical behavior. The Milgram experiments (Chapter 4) also show the importance of situational factors in affecting ethical judgments. Although it is an oversimplification to impugn the character of those who (a) did not help pick up the papers (subject to subtle situational effects) or (b) administered shocks (the influence of authoritative figures), this is nevertheless what often happens because of the fundamental attribution error (i.e., the tendency to attribute events to individuals rather than situations).

Through rigorous analysis, Miguel Alzola (2007) demonstrates that the psychological studies cited by "situationalists" such as Harman are actually inconclusive: Many of the experimental conditions are unrealistic, and the evidence itself is inconsistent with the claim that situational factors determine behavior. Moreover, Alzola suggests that Harman draws the wrong conclusions from the psychological evidence, whether the evidence is accurate or not.

Alzola observes that the key lesson for virtue ethics from experimental psychology "is that human beings are morally weak," especially when confronted with an authority figure, a unanimous group, or an intense situation. He maintains that this pessimistic conclusion presents not just a cognitive weakness, in which the bearings of one's moral compass are lost to situational pressures, but also a motivational weakness. Most of humanity displays the unfortunate tendency, whether consciously or unconsciously, to subordinate the desire to be ethical to competing desires such as self-interest or obedience. Thus, "virtue ethics must account for the experimental evidence, but that does not lead to the abandonment of character and virtue" (354). To the contrary, this evidence that virtue is subverted to self-interest should compel people to strive harder to overcome the natural tendency toward vice that hinders, but does not foreclose, the attainment of a virtuous character.

The debate between Harman (the situationalist) and Alzola (the dispositionist)—as well as the controversy between MacIntyre (a partitionist, who sees a division between competence and virtue) and Macaulay and Lawton (integrationists, who reject the division)—over the contribution of virtue ethics to public administration testifies to the vibrancy of virtue ethics discourse.

CONCLUSION

Former U.S. secretary of Health and Human Services and past president of the University of Miami Donna Shalala's resistance to efforts by others to put politics ahead of policy provides a concrete example of integrity. Cory Booker's saving a woman from a fire is an ethical act because it shows courage. Integrity and courage are virtuous character traits reflected in the actions of these exemplary public servants. But it is not just the details of an event that are consequential—it is the virtuous life of the whole person over time that will be determinant of ethical evaluations. Ethical decision-making skills, as noted earlier, are nourished by consistently exercising practical wisdom. Aristotle makes the point, "We are what we repeatedly do. Excellence, then, is not an act, but a habit."

Virtue theory is both an alternative and a complement to other decision-making approaches. Unlike cognitive theories, virtue theory provides a more personal lens or basis for evaluating an ethical act by putting intuition and character front and center. Public servants have their character routinely tested, making prudent reflection, high ideals, and virtuous behavior essential to effective public service. While virtue theory does not come with precise instructions for right action, like cognitive theory, virtue theory can be helpful by raising questions to be considered when tested by a dilemma or judging the ethics of a decision.

As discussed, virtue theory has its advantages and disadvantages. It is not always clear why certain virtues are good or whether they are good in *all* situations. Anyone who has ever said "Yes, that outfit does make you look fat" has learned honesty is not always the best policy. It is critical to consider why certain virtues are good given the circumstances. In public service, however, honesty is a requirement, often legally, as on tax filings. It is also useful to ponder ways to cultivate virtues. One creative effort to nurture courage, for example, is the Seattle-based Giraffe Project, which has developed a character education curriculum that invites students to become "giraffes" who "stick their necks out for the common good" (Medlock, 2004, 338). This book provides examples of seasoned public servants who have displayed "giraffe-like" traits to advance the public interest. It also offers cases of rather ungiraffe-like employees who ran afoul of conflict-of-interest requirements, succumbed to bribery, deliberately mislead citizens and co-workers, and tarnished the image of public service by their actions.

The debates between situationalists and dispositionists, and partitionists and integrationists raise the question of the role of circumstance and character as well as competence and virtue in public administration. The contention here is that elements of both sides of the arguments are crucial components of a professional. As the Shalala profile shows, "competence and character can feed into each other," providing a useful guide to dealing with thorny moral quandaries and helping ensure a successful professional career as a leader in public service.

***

"I don't know what the best thing to do is" is a common statement, but rarely will someone say, "I don't know what the right thing to do is."[4]

—Laura Schlessinger

NOTES

1. This chapter is adapted from Bowman (2003). Used with permission.
2. In Biblical times, adults were named after their character (e.g., "Jacob" means deceiver; when asked his name, he answered by admitting that he was deceptive; Genesis 32:27).
3. In an insightful analysis, Kane and Patapan (2006) examine the loss of prudence as a result of the different values embodied by the New Public Management approach to government.
4. The distinction between knowing and doing can be illustrated by former Texas Governor Ann Richards, former Senator George Mitchell, and one-time Reagan White House Chief of Staff and former Senator, Howard Baker. In 1997, the tobacco industry hired them to lobby Congress. Each widely known for integrity, Richards (a recovering alcoholic familiar with the problem of addiction), Mitchell (a peace negotiator, could work for life in Ireland and death in America),

and Baker (whose sister died of lung cancer) earned huge sums of money for their efforts supporting an industry they knew to be harmful to the health of Americans. Unlike the elected officials-turned-lobbyists, Reagan's surgeon general, C. Everett Koop, on leaving office in 1989, refused millions of dollars in offers to endorse breakfast cereals and condoms—actions that were at least consistent with good health—because he did not want to erode the impartiality of his office by endorsing commercial products.

FOR DISCUSSION

1. Define virtue theory and evaluate its strengths and weaknesses.

2. Comment on these statements:

    - "Thoughts become words, words become actions, actions become character, and character is everything."—Anonymous.
    - "If you have integrity, nothing else matters. If you don't have integrity, nothing else matters."—Alan Simpson
    - "When you look for the good in others, you discover the best in yourself."—Martin Walsh
    - "You may find the worst enemy or best friend in yourself."—English aphorism
    - "Sometimes the heart sees what is invisible to the eye."—H. Jackson Browne

3. Produce a pithy, provocative proverb or submit an existing one to class discussion.

4. React to these claims:

    "Since virtues are the heart and soul of human existence, they must be cultivated. When people fail to do this, the results of the Milgram shock experiment (Chapter 4) should not be surprising."

    Milgram's and Zimbardo's experiments suggest that character does not matter as otherwise "good" people commit bad acts under certain circumstances.

5. "A leader of a value-intensive organization (especially, a nonprofit) is expected not only to adhere to, but also to create, morality in her unit by example." Examine this statement.

6. Widely respected Pennsylvania State University football coach, Joe Paterno, had his contract terminated in the wake of a sex scandal involving one of his assistant coaches (Chapter 2). In a provocative article, "The Devil and Joe Paterno," *New York Times* columnist Ross Douthat (2011) argued that a life of virtue became an excuse for extraordinary vice—good people, by their very goodness, their many duties and accomplishments, may overlook important responsibilities and duties. Discuss.

7. Explain this statement in light of virtue theory: "Learn the rules, so you know how to break them properly."

8. Weiner (2017, December 8) writes:

> Public and private virtue are not identical. Machiavelli showed that what is virtuous for the individual may be vicious in the prince. But that is fundamentally different from saying character does not matter at all or that policies may stand alone, disembodied from the human being who pursues them. Public virtue exists, and is separable from the character of the person who exercises it.

Discuss.

9. Regarding the debate between Harman (the situationalist) and Alzola (the dispositionist) on the contribution of virtue ethics to public administration, as well as the debate between MacIntyre (a partitionist who sees a division between competence and virtue) and Macaulay and Lawton (integrationists who reject the division), which point of view do you find most compelling? Why?

EXERCISES

1. Continue the journal/personal checklist assignment. As Michael Novak (1996, 159) notes, "Ethics . . . calls us to . . . ground ourselves in new habits . . . building our character, building up ourselves." It is never too late to make the most of your journal and checklist.

2. Vivian Buchan (1997) offers ideas about how to develop character:

   • Identify qualities you aspire to and admire in others; think of ways you can emulate those traits.
   • Recognize those qualities in other people and let them know how much you admire them.
   • Analyze and observe the actions of those individuals; let them serve as your guide.
   • Review your actions daily to ascertain if you are developing such qualities.
   • Visualize the virtuous person you want to be every day; if you can see that person, then others will start to see you in that manner too.

   Consider these suggestions in your journal with the goal of developing specific initiatives as part of your ethical effectiveness plan (Chapter 15, Exercise 2).

3. In a similar manner, Jacobs (2015, September 4) suggests that public administrators ask themselves, "do I" or "how to I do":

   • exercise integrity, courage, benevolence, and optimism?
   • maintain honesty and protect against the use of office for personal gain?
   • resist political, organizational, and personal pressures to compromise integrity—and support others subject to such pressures?
   • accept responsibility for my actions?
   • guard against the appearance and reality of conflict of interest?

- conduct business without partisanship or favoritism?
- ensure that others get credit for their contributions?

During the next week, record in your journal answers to as many of these questions as possible.

REFERENCES

Alzola, M. (2007). Character and environment: The status of virtues in organizations. *Journal of Business Ethics, 78,* 343–357.

Anderson, A. (1996). *Ethics for fundraisers.* Bloomington: University of Indiana Press.

Associated Press. (2012, June 23). Cory Booker again appears at scene of accident. Retrieved from http://www.politico.com/news/stories/0612/77753.html

Badaracco, J. L., Jr. (1997). *Defining moments: When managers must choose between right and right.* Boston, MA: Harvard Business School Press.

Bowman, J. (2003). Virtue ethics. In J. Rabin (Ed.), *Encyclopedia of public administration and policy* (pp. 1259–1263). New York: Marcel Dekker.

Bowman, J., West, J., & Beck, M. (2010). *Achieving competencies in public service: The professional edge* (2nd ed.). Armonk, NY: M. E. Sharpe.

Buchan, V. (1997). *Presentations with confidence* (2nd ed.). Hauppauge, NY: Barron's Educational Series.

Carbone, N. (2012, April 13). Cory Booker reminds us all he's still a superhero. *Time.* Retrieved from http://newsfeed.time.com/2012/04/13/cory-booker-reminds-us-all-hes-still-a-superhero/

Chun, R. (2005). Ethical character and virtue of organizations: An empirical assessment and strategic implications. *Journal of Business Ethics, 57,* 269–284.

Covey, S. (1991). *Principle-centered leadership.* New York: Summit Books.

Dixon, D. (2012, April 13). Mayor Booker saves woman in fire. *Politico.* Retrieved from http://www.politico.com/news/stories/0412/75097.html

Douthat, R. (2011, November 11). The devil and Joe Paterno. *New York Times.* Retrieved from http://newyorktime.com/2011/11/13/opinon/sunday/douthat-the-devel-and-joe-paterno.htm

Durant, W. (1991). *The story of philosophy: The lives and opinions of the world's greatest philosophers.* New York: Simon & Schuster/Pocket Books. [Original work published 1926]

Franz, R. (1998). Don't treat students like customers. *Journal of Management Education, 22,* 63–69.

Gilgoff, D. (2009, October 22). Cory Booker: Newark's mayor fights for a revival. *U.S. News & World Report.* Retrieved from http://www.usnews.com/news/best-leaders/articles/2009/10/22/cory-booker-newarks-mayor-fights-for-a-revival

Haddon, H. (2012, August 13). Q&A: Booker revisits role in Bain flap. *Wall Street Journal.* Retrieved from http://blogs.wsj.com/metropolis/2012/08/13/qa-booker-revisits-role-in-bain-flap/

Harman, G. (2003). No character or personality. *Business Ethics Quarterly, 13,* 87–94.

Isen, A. M., & Levin, P. F. (1972). Effect of feeling good on helping: Cookies and kindness. *Journal of Personality and Social Psychology, 21*, 384–388.

Jacobs, R. (2015, September 4). Leading by doing: Conducting a personal ethics audit. *PA Times*. Retrieved from http://patimes.org/leading-doing-conducting-personal-ethics-audit/

Kane, J., & Patapan, H. (2006). In search of prudence: The hidden problem of managerial reform. *Public Administration Review, 66*, 711–724.

Macaulay, M., & Lawton, A. (2006). From virtue to competence: Changing the principles of public service. *Public Administration Review, 66*, 702–710.

MacIntyre, A. (1985). *After virtue: A study in moral theory.* London: Duckworth.

Medlock, A. (2004). The courage to stick your neck out. In M. Josephson & W. Hanson (Eds.), *The power of character* (pp. 336–346) (2nd ed.). San Francisco: Jossey-Bass.

Novak, M. (1996). *Business as a calling: Work and the examined life.* New York: Free Press.

Preston, N. (2001). *Understanding ethics* (2nd ed.). Leichhardt: Federation Press.

Rion, M. (1996). *The responsible manager: Practical strategies for ethical decision making.* West Harford, CT: Resources for Ethics and Management.

Ripley, A. (2000, May 22). The savior of Newark? *Time.* Retrieved from http://www.time.com/time/magazine/article/0,9171,996967,00.html

Shalala, D. (2004). Managing large organizations with honesty and integrity. *Public Integrity, 6*, 349–356.

Weiner, G. (2017, December 8). The scoundrel theory of American politics. *New York Times.* Retrieved from https://nyt.com/.../roy-moore-scoundrel-politics-theory-politics.html

West, J. P., & Berman, E. M. (2011). The impact of management work habits on public sector performance: A study of local government managers. *Public Personnel Management, 40*, 63–86.

7 Conscious Deliberation and Subconscious Action

The Dishonesty of Honest People

Some folks are wise, and some are otherwise.

—T. Smollett

Consider this statement: Managers should be virtuous, but not only virtuous. If philosophers cannot agree on competing models, then why should managers? The reason is that managers must be able to defend their decisions—professionals are obligated to develop virtues, predict results, and adhere to rules. Unless a course of action can be justified on ethical grounds, it is not a responsible act. As a "knowledge worker" in today's economy, the duty of a professional is to provide her best thinking. While a good sense of right and wrong may be necessary, it is hardly sufficient in ethical decision making—a process that can be complex and complicated. If decisions are to be intentional and rational, then the procedure by which they are made must be more systematic.

There is little doubt that the use of various decision-making models can considerably enhance ethical discernment.[1] These approaches typically focus on step-by-step techniques, stages in decision making, or sets of principles (see Chapter 5). In so doing, the ethical dimensions of an issue can be explored and potential solutions identified. The seductiveness of such tools is evident—their use is superior to rigid rules, self-interest, and sheer opportunism. Indeed, this chapter employs one of these techniques, an ethics triad, to examine a case. Accordingly, the discussion encourages readers to embrace the complementarity and interdependence of both cognitive and virtue ethics. In so doing, it emphasizes that cognition without virtue is as insufficient as virtue without cognition. No single perspective is adequate, and no perspective should be neglected.

This same approach, however, is not without significant limitations. Philosophical ethics explains how rational people should act at the expense of how real human beings actually behave. Implicit in the traditional philosophical approach is the assumption that people will recognize ethical dilemmas and know how they should then act. Yet, if the goal of decision theory is to predict conduct, it is not always useful to ask people, or offer prescriptions about, what they might do. Instead, behavioral ethics, drawing from psychology, is less interested in prescriptions and more focused on descriptions of how individuals really act. With that knowledge, researchers will be better positioned to suggest ways to encourage ethical conduct.

This chapter, then, (1) consolidates the three individual-centered approaches to ethics into a tripartite framework and (2) examines the findings in the emerging field of behavioral ethics, with its focus on human conduct. Its objectives are to:

- understand that ethics requires not just the rectitude to refuse wrongdoing, but the resourcefulness to create a worthy alternative,
- analyze the strengths and weaknesses of the triad strategy and apply it to cases, and
- examine the behavioral ethics approach to understanding how people act.

The discussion begins by describing a comprehensive tool that encompasses results-based utilitarian ethics, rule-based duty ethics, and virtue-based character ethics. The technique is applied to a case to demonstrate its decision-making utility. A set of insights from behavioral ethics are then used to suggest that such models are problematic. The discussion and conclusion explores the implications of the findings of behavioral ethicists.

RESULTS, RULE, VIRTUE: DECISION MAKING WITH THE ETHICS TRIAD

While various frameworks shed light on how ethical issues might be considered, one is particularly helpful because its broad scope reduces the chances of an incomplete—and therefore potentially flawed—decision.[2] This tool, the ethics triad, triumvirate, or "triangle" (Svara, 1997, 2007), recognizes the value and utility of the imperatives in three schools of thought based on:

- results of an action (consequentialism or teleology),
- pertinent rules (duty ethics or deontology), and
- personal rectitude, integrity, or character (virtue ethics).

When considering results in decision making, the question is, "Which policy produces the greatest good for the greatest number?" (e.g., "Would I want my decision to be in the newspapers tomorrow?"). In contemplating rules, the issue is, "Would I want everyone else to make the same decision that I did?" (e.g., "What is good for one is good for all."). From the virtue ethics vantage point, one might ask, "What would a person of integrity do?" (e.g., seek the "golden mean" between the extremes of excess and deficiency). Accordingly, the ethics triad, comprehensive yet succinct, can help provide a defensible evaluation derived from consideration of results, rules, and virtues.

Although the synthesis developed from the analysis may not provide definitive solutions to an ethical dilemma, it offers guidance by teasing out the underlying logic by which decisions are justified. Importantly, an overreaching application of a single perspective, at the expense of the others, holds considerable dangers—expediency (results-based ethics), rigid rule application (rule-based ethics), and self-justification (virtue-based ethics). In light of the shortcomings of the individual vantage points, it is evident that this amalgamated technique can be helpful.

UTILIZING THE ETHICS TRIAD

Professionals should consider results, respect rules, and develop virtues to justify their decisions. Indeed, each philosophy represented in the trinity is attractive to decision makers:

- The results-based approach is useful for administrators seeking the common good for the majority of citizens.
- A rule-based strategy is appealing to managers obligated to follow the principles found in the Constitution, court cases, and laws and regulations.
- Virtue-based ethics is compelling for officials because it is a personal approach informed by one's character that nurtures individual and collective well-being.

Because credible arguments can be developed in support of each philosophy, deliberations stimulated by the ethics triad could provoke moral imagination in searching for a solution.

The triad is especially helpful in examining ethical issues wherein there is no clear sense of right and wrong. Public administrators may want to be good at what they do, but may not know how. Sincere intent and simple conviction are not enough. They may not recognize ethical issues or be able to articulate what is at stake in ethical terms. Whatever the situation might be, the strategy demands that it be examined in three different ways by using formal, abstract thinking to advance understanding of results, rules, and rectitude. It is not, however, a definitive tool; rather, it is a means to assess a policy from distinctive vantage points—impact (results), conduct (duty), and effort (virtue). Given the human genius for rationalization, a certain humility is necessary when employing the technique.

Note that each of the three components of the triumvirate does not necessarily attempt to argue what actions should be moral, but rather describes the underlying logic by which decisions are justified. Decisions are distinguished from one another based on the premises from which they are made. A better understanding of how judgments are made can produce ethically acceptable choices.

Each component of the tool provides a distinctive filter to reveal different aspects that clarify and reframe a situation. However, unduly emphasizing one component above others spells trouble. Full examination of all three viewpoints helps prevent the shortcomings of each one, since each acts as a limit on the others. Thus, the three perspectives may reinforce and inform one another. When they do not, then the decision should be guided by benevolence and the admonition "do no harm." The policymaker should exercise moral imagination and promote the public interest using an ethic of compromise and social integration—a moral tenet of democracy. However, do not assume there is some "objective reality" on which everyone agrees and set of evaluation criteria that all use. It is an imperfect world where no one gets all that one wants.

Encountering ethical issues—in both appearance and reality—is part of being a public servant.[3] To take a simple example of how the triad can be used, consider whether or not to run a red stop light when driving. From the results viewpoint, "the greatest good for the greatest number" is almost always achieved by not doing so (the ill consequences of not stopping are difficult to justify in the short and long run). Using a rules interpretation, the duty to honor an ethical law is also the right thing to do. To justify ignoring the rule would imply it is acceptable for everyone to run a red light ("what is good for one is good for all"), behavior difficult to defend. When an organizational policy or societal law conflicts with a universal ethical rule, the ethical rule predominates. Under virtue ethics—the third member of the trinity—excellence in individual and community character may be nourished by avoiding reckless driving (knowingly endangering one's self and others usually does not build good character).

Recognize that while the red light scenario is an elementary example, the findings do not suggest that running the light is never justified (Aristotle's "practical wisdom" could be carefully employed in specific circumstances; see Chapter 6). Ethics demands consideration of the social context, directing empathy with other people to ask, "What circumstances would account for his behavior?" Try the same three-part analysis for going considerably over—or under—the speed limit (e.g., for virtue ethics, to nurture character would be to avoid extremes of too fast or too slow driving).

Complex issues can be analyzed using the triad as well, producing more interesting—and often conflicting—findings. Unlike the stop light scenario, examining each school of thought in the approach may advise a different course of action (Case Study 7.1). In such circumstances, the policymaker at least has the satisfaction that the problem has been fully examined, balance has been sought, and the decision can be rationally defended.[4] She self-consciously weighed consequences, is familiar with ethical rules, and has considered what a virtuous person would do. Tough judgments, thereby, become easier (but not easy) than they might otherwise be. There are situations where "right-reason/wrong-action" and "wrong-reason/right-action" choices occur; using the triad may enhance the chances that "right-reason/right-action" decisions are made.

This approach cannot produce a final, perfect decision for all seasons. Instead, it attempts to reconcile conflicting values and highlights a key function of decision making: generating alternative viewpoints, systemically evaluating them, and crafting a considered judgment. The technique enables the management of ethical ambiguity and provides help in making the inevitable compromises. This eclectic, pluralistic method to adjudicate difficult ethical issues can be demanding, as it requires considerable discernment. Yet in light of the limitations of each part of the triad, there is little option given the complexity of the human condition.

The approach enables the user to learn to be ethical by developing well-rounded and well-grounded decisions.

CASE STUDY 7.1

The Ethics Triad: Applying the Rational Approach to a Birthday Invitation

Consider this case, a reprise from one in Chapter 5.

Mark and Frank Jordan have been close friends for years. They went to high school together and were college classmates. Each was the best man at the other's wedding. Their wives are good friends. For the past 10 years, Frank and his wife have taken Mark and his wife to dinner on Mark's birthday. It is something he insists on doing and has become something of a tradition. Frank can well afford it—he owns the largest plumbing supply business in the state and does more than $1,000,000 in business each year with the city.

Mark was recently hired as an aide to a councilman who chairs the committee that oversees procurement contracts, including plumbing supplies. His birthday is coming up in a couple of weeks. Frank has called to remind Mark that he and Mrs. Jordan have a special treat for his birthday dinner this year. Frank has made reservations at a fancy new restaurant that everyone is talking about.

Does Mark accept?

Results-Based Analysis. Thinking about the results part of the ethics triad, what is the greatest good for the greatest number? On the one hand, the most happiness and the least amount of harm may be achieved by accepting the invitation. After all, most people do not trade their integrity for gifts. There is no valid reason to avoid the party; indeed, the friendship may be put at risk if the invitation is declined—Frank may be insulted.

On the other hand, the greatest good could also be achieved by preventing erosion of public trust in governmental decision making. A key utilitarian guideline is "Would I feel comfortable if my action were on the front page tomorrow?" Clearly the greatest good extends well beyond personal acquaintances. Most individuals do not impugn their honor for gifts. But while the premise may be correct, the conclusion does not follow. As Paul Brest (2012, 490) suggests, "[W]e tend to accede to requests from people who have done favors for us—even when the favors were uninvited and trivial and the subsequent requests substantial." Thus, the counter-argument takes the form of a challenge: Name one good reason why an official should accept a gift presenting a conflict of interest. Corruption demands nothing as vulgar as a *quid pro quo*, because "business courtesies" introduce the potential for favoritism. Bribery is not the point. The value of dinner is not enough to sway a favor. Rather, the dinner secures access to the recipient, and influence. Wariness of inducements includes an understanding that individual presents can give rise to institutional corruption—the creation of a system that encourages decisions based not on the substance of issues, but on favoritism (see also Chapter 9).

Rule-Based Analysis. From the rules ethics angle, Mark asks, would I want everyone else to make the same decision that I did? Rules ethics dictates Mark's duty in this case is to cultivate friendship, something Aristotle believed should be universal practice in human relations to encourage ethical behavior. Rigidly applying rules when they are not germane is overreaching. So long as existing laws are followed, there is no basis for rejecting the invitation. Yet it is not clear that it would be acceptable if every civil servant routinely accepted such arrangements. One's responsibility as a public official is to help nurture citizen confidence in government. Participating in activities that arguably raise suspicions about decision making should not be a common practice.

Virtue-Based Analysis. From the virtue ethics vantage point, Mark asks, what would a person of integrity do? In this system, each person must continuously nurture his character and the character of the polity. By going to the dinner, deep friendships are maintained and enhanced. This helps nourish individual character and the strength of community ties. Turning down the invitation demonstrates pointless self-righteousness. Yet because it is not reasonable to expect citizens to delve into the particulars of specific cases, Mark should not attend. Taxpayers, after all, are more likely to be concerned that government employees use public monies effectively than whether they have friends. Thoughtlessly accepting the invitation—and ignoring other viewpoints—is simply expedient, hardly an ethical standard of decision making.

Summary. This case is based on a scenario presented to attendees at an International City and County Management Association (ICMA) convention in the early 1980s. There was no consensus among conferees, as they split almost evenly on whether or not to attend the party. ICMA's answer, in advising its membership on how to deal with the situation, does not directly allude to results, rules, or virtues. It does, however, indicate that "yes" the manager should go based on the following reasoning.

> Public service does not require that you give up previous acquaintances and friendships. What is required is that at any point in the future in which your friend's business is involved, i.e., contract negotiations, you disqualify yourself from influencing the decision in any way. If you decide not to go with Frank, you are still ethical, but probably overzealous ("Ethics," 1982) (see text on page 122).

By interpolation, the association does not think that everyone should attend the dinner, because it does not automatically serve the greatest good and would be unwise to universalize such practice. Also, and more directly, the case reveals sensitivity to the virtue of care and friendship. The golden mean would be to find a prudent course of action that lies between extremes of blissfully accepting and self-righteously rejecting the invitation—that is, Mark could pay his own way or recuse himself from any future committee actions involving Frank's business. A true friend would, after listening to Mark explain his new role in government, understand the situation and not take the decision personally.

Lessons from cases like those discussed here include an understanding that the manager is a moral agent responsible for her actions, doing right things is likely to be interpreted differently by others, appearances matter, ethical awareness may be accompanied by self-delusion, exemplary behavior is important, and ethics means engagement. The implications of these lessons include the need to have knowledge of ethical principles and codes, respect the rule of law, serve the public interest, and use ethical reasoning tools (Menzel, 2010, 225–231).

BEHAVIORAL ETHICS: WHAT PEOPLE DO VS. WHAT THEY SAY THEY DO

While rational decision-making models are certainly valuable, a relatively new school of thought—behavioral ethics—identifies significant shortcomings. One key criticism is the frequent failure to delineate a relationship between moral theorizing and ethical action. As Gazzaniga (2008, 148) observes, "It has been hard to find any correlation between moral reasoning and proactive moral behavior. In fact, in most studies, none has been found." Similarly, Haidt (2001, 817) contends that "moral reasoning is rarely the direct cause of moral judgment." This suggests that other factors—unconscious biases, moral emotions, personal intuitions—are likely to affect behavior (Shao, Aquino, & Freeman, 2008; also see Chapter 4). As Elder Shafir (2012, 2) observes, "People do not respond to objective experience; rather, stimuli are mentally construed, interpreted, and understood or misunderstood." Stated differently, behavioral findings offer an alternative view of the individual as a moral agent.

Behavioral ethics draws on work in psychology and focuses on the actual conduct of the individual. By examining psychological tendencies to explain human actions, this school of thought attempts to apply ethics to the real world. Not only does the rational model place considerable cognitive demands on people, it also devalues unconscious, emotional, and tacit elements in making judgments, elements that can subsume—or even be the basis of—reason. Moral claims motivate in ways that factual claims do not; factoring emotions into judgments explains much about them. The traditional approach is incomplete because it "fails to acknowledge our innate psychological responses when faced with ethical dilemmas" (Bazerman & Tenbrunsel, 2011, 4). Both the potency of passion and the limits of reason tend to be overlooked. We are not as good as we think we are, and we are apt to act unethically without being consciously aware of such behavior (Banaji, Bazerman, & Chugh, 2003; Bazerman & Banaji, 2004), as the Milgram and Zimbardo experiments demonstrated (Chapter 4). Further, people tend to overestimate how ethical they are and can fall into behavioral blind spots as a result.

This section identifies key propositions from behavioral ethics research.[5] Together, they highlight the underlying psychology behind unethical conduct, actions that may be unintentional and based on inadequate information, improper application of ethical principles, or lack of awareness of the moral dimension of problems. While these ideas are not necessarily new, what is new is the growing evidence that behavior is less under conscious control than believed. Instead of supposing people are rational, behavioral ethics investigates whether or not they act rationally in experimental or actual situations. The data suggest that humans are far less rational than assumed.[6]

Rather than "Star Trek"'s hyper-rational Mr. Spock, they can be more like "The Simpsons"' emotional and prejudiced Homer (Ariely, 2008; Bazerman & Tenbrunsel, 2011; Brooks, 2011). Feelings, intuition, and perception are at least as significant in affecting behavior as logic, rationality, and calculation. Indeed, emotion can be the foundation of reason. When making ostensibly conscious choices, the "architecture of the brain ensures that we feel first and think second" (Ropeik, 2012, 12); the linkages from emotional brain circuits to cognitive brain components are stronger than those from cognitive circuits to emotional systems. Modern neuroscience, then, suggests that people process information automatically and emotionally without reflection or even awareness—which leads them to misinterpret or dismiss objective evidence. The mind tends to refuse to engage the prefrontal cortex, the part of the brain needed to make sense of unfamiliar ideas.

Emotions, then, discolor what people otherwise see as their dispassionate, logical views. Reasoning is confused with rationalization. This does not mean that people are uninterested in accurate perception, but rather that there are objectives other than accuracy (Mooney, 2011). Humans prefer to believe that they are like judges, conscientiously deliberating over the issues and arriving at reasoned conclusions after examining all the evidence. Instead, people are more like lawyers, looking for anything that might help make their case (Seawright, 2013).

The field of behavioral economics employs controlled laboratory and field experiments in cognitive science, social psychology, and neuroimaging, and these have repeatedly shown how policymakers, average citizens, and students can be wrong about their motivations, justifications for their beliefs, and the accuracy of their memories. The choices they make may be unconscious because the brain is set on automatic pilot: Most of the stimuli it receives is processed instinctively, as a mere fraction of that information makes it into consciousness. This makes brains efficient (not everything need be attended to at once), but the effect is that judgments are made based on information of which there is not full awareness (Bennett, 2014, November 5).

Investigators have developed a set of complementary principles that help explain decision making. The resulting insights into systematic errors found in concealed biases, brain quirks, and behavioral traps highlight the underlying science behind dishonorable acts. Actions may be unintentional and based on inadequate knowledge, involve improper application of moral tenets, and/or simply miss the ethical dimension of issues. Just as people are tricked by visual illusions, they are fooled by illusions about how they make choices. The problem is that most individuals are often not rational actors (Ariely, 2008); they are fallible, normal human beings.

Pervasive and overlapping behavioral science claims are examined below. Primarily descriptive, rather than normative, the propositions show how cognitive heuristics, psychological tendencies, social and organizational pressures, and seemingly irrelevant situational factors can account for the dishonesty of otherwise honest people. These ubiquitous phenomena have serious consequences as they distort knowledge, corrupt public discourse, and conceal solutions to problems. The question may not be so much whether a decision maker is moral, but rather in what circumstances and to what degree. It is not only a matter of knowing what is right, but also about thinking of the meaning and relevance of rectitude in a given situation (Kaptein, 2013). Ethical issues are often embedded in decisions that appear to lack moral ramifications. Due to space limitations, the list of comparable behavioral science focal points that follows is simply illustrative of some of the most compelling ones (see Samson, 2017 for a fuller discussion). These include: (1) principles (bounded rationality/ethicality, System 1/System 2 thinking, motivated reasoning, and a set of biases), (2) monitoring and sanctions, (3) organizational context, and (4) debiasing techniques.

PRINCIPLES

Bounded Rationality/Bounded Ethicality

Bounded rationality, a term coined by Herbert Simon, describes a "behavioral model [in which] human rationality is very limited, very much bounded by the situation and by homo sapien computational powers" (1983, 34). Individuals often do not have complete and accurate information and, even if they did, they have a less-than-perfect capacity for information processing to reach an optimal choice.

Sub-optimization can overlook significant facts, omit stakeholders, or give insufficient attention to long-term consequences. Decision-maker rationality also may be affected by: self-interest, false assumptions, subliminal inclinations, innate responses to ethical circumstances, and failures in problem definition (Bazerman & Chugh, 2006). People can be blind to the obvious and blind to their blindness (Bazerman & Tenbrunsel, 2011; Kahneman, 2011). Bounded ethicality results in virtuous men and women making questionable decisions. The pressures and demands facing managers, for example, can cause them to depend on habit, instead of deliberation (Chugh, 2004), leading to a related principle: fast and slow thinking.

System 1/System 2 Thinking

System 1 is a rapid, intuitive way to process information and yields an instinctive response, or gut reaction, which can be a useful guide for many decisions. Indeed, Hoomans (2015, March 20) reports that adults make an incredible 35,000 conscious and non-conscious choices every day. In most situations there is just not enough time for another approach. System 1 is an effortless, decision-without-thought default process for arriving at routine judgments in a quick, visceral, and easy way.[7] Generally, the fast system is efficient and good enough—the immediate, obvious answer feels right—but it is also prone to prejudice and error. System 2 is a slow paced, thoughtful strategy that weighs the merits and demerits of an issue. Judgments made under stress might rely on System 1 when System 2 is warranted, because the linkages from emotional brain circuits to cognitive brain components are stronger than those from cognitive circuits to emotional systems. As Harvard's David Ropeik observes, the "architecture of the brain ensures that we feel first and think second" (2012, September 30, p. 12).

Haidt (2001) finds that intuitions like hunches are the primary source of moral judgments, as rational arguments are commonly used *post hoc* to justify determinations. And compromising those moral positions, unlike "split-the-difference" economic issues, is often unimaginable. Moreover, detecting error does not necessarily lead to change: The slow system's reasoning ability, in fact, may be invoked to generate rationalizations for decisions already made. Initial views are also strengthened by "confirmation bias," as people focus on data that reinforce their pre-existing opinions. Political scientist Emily Thorson (2016, January 8) points out that these "belief echoes" persist even when misinformation is corrected. Individuals have a built-in tendency to expect and see what they want to expect and see, so that fact checkers with their unwelcome facts are perceived as prejudiced. Falsehoods—like tax cuts increase revenue, health care death panels, voter fraud, Obama is a Muslim and/or is not a citizen, Iraqi–Al Qaeda 9/11 collaboration, and global warming denial—exemplify how System 1 thinking interacts with "motivated reasoning," a related supposition.

Motivated Reasoning

Facts mean little if someone ascribes to a belief different from what the facts dictate. Motivated reasoning indicates that individuals are psychologically geared to maintain their existing evaluations, independent of facts (Redlawsk, Civettini, & Emmerson, 2010). Opinions are based on beliefs. People feel what they think, as "emotion assigns value to things and reason can only make choices on the basis of those valuations" (Brooks, 2011, 21). As they become more informed, such viewpoints—despite their utter implausibility—make them more likely to be wrong, resulting in a kind of invincible ignorance.

This "smart idiot effect" explains why corrections to false information have a "backfire effect": When presented with documented facts, some people become *less* likely to believe them (Mooney, 2012; Mercier & Sperber, 2017; Sloman & Fernbach, 2017). Thus, if something or someone is disliked by the "true believer," contradictory information can be discounted to the point that the object of dislike will be loathed as much or more than before. When faith meets evidence, evidence does not have a chance.

The use of this defense mechanism is psychologically easier than to change beliefs and admit error. Once something is accepted as true, it is difficult to falsify the belief. If confidence is lost in society's institutions and its experts, then that may explain why many Americans are not affected by facts. This repudiation dangerously undermines the very idea of objective reality. The illogical denial of real existence, for example, puts both unvaccinated children and the community at risk. Motivated reasoning, like many behavioral principles, operates at the subconscious level. Sincere claims can be made that one is not influenced by prejudice, even though their "unbiased opinion" [sic] is self-serving—a process facilitated by decision framing.

Framing Effects

How issues are cast impact how people react to them (Kern & Chugh, 2009).[8] Many workplace decisions, for instance, have both a business and an ethical dimension, and decision makers may give primacy to one or the other. If the situation is seen as a business matter, it could lead to "ethical fading," and allow the emotional, impulsive "want" self to be dominant—especially since people tend to accept the frame that is provided. Improper behavior may occur instinctively without deliberation, as moral concerns are set aside in pursuit of other goals like efficiency. Tenbrunsel and Messick (2004, 22) use the term "ethical cleansing" to describe how individuals "unconsciously transform ethical decisions into ones that are ethically clean."

Further, "want" choices are made in the present, while "should" choices take place before and after the decision. Ironically, this "want–should theory" separation of the two selves—paralleling fast and slow thinking—can allow people to believe they are more virtuous than is actually the case. There is also a tendency to choose and then engage in faded, faux moral reasoning to justify the determination. Because human beings value morality, they are motivated to forget the details of their unjust actions in a kind of "ethical amnesia." In contrast, when the situation is interpreted primarily in ethical terms, the thoughtful, deliberative "should" self emerges, and fading and cleansing would not occur. Recognizing both the business side and the ethical side of judgments is crucial, then, if one seeks to do things right and do right things. In short, how a problem is framed affects susceptibility to the effects already noted as well as those discussed next.

Bias and Decision-Making Errors

In considering additional cognitive distortions, mental short cuts and unconscious presumptions, it is important to recognize that the brain interprets all experiences based on its model of the world. People hold certain beliefs because they fit the sense they have made of their environment. As already seen, this process can be inaccurate—and convincing—in part, because of unacknowledged competing emotions and conflicting intuitions. Subliminal predispositions, described below, materialize in differing circumstances, appear in many guises, interact in pernicious ways to impair judgment, and are not readily susceptible to reasoned debate and negotiation.

First, "status quo bias" takes place when someone is faced with choices, and the default option operates (deciding not to decide) to live in the moment. This occurs: (a) by taking the path of least resistance ("effort aversion"), (b) by valuing what one has ("present preference") because she owns it ("endowment effect" or "loss aversion") and (c) by staying the course, the person can hope to capitalize on "sunk costs" (Schmidt, 2016). It would be a serious error to underestimate the difficulty in changing lifetime habits: the 600,000 patients who have heart bypasses each year are told their lifestyle (diet, exercise, smoking) must change because surgery is a temporary fix. Change or die? The answer is not a question of awareness or knowledge. Instead, the reaction is the "deaf effect": Over 90 percent of patients choose death, as immediate pleasures override long-term survival (Rainer & Geiger, 2011; see also Cotteleer & Murphy, 2015). Applied to management of organizational change, likely losers will fight a lot harder against reforms than potential winners, due to loss aversion.

Second, "preference falsification," happens when someone suppresses what they think to agree with what others think—"private truths, but public lies" (Kuran, 1997). This phenomenon may prop up social stability; however when norms erode, otherwise puzzling events occur, such as the seemingly widespread surprise endorsement of gay marriage, abrupt condemnation (and support) of the Confederate battle flag and monuments, and unexpected enthusiasm for nativism in recent years.

Third, "overconfidence bias" assumes comprehension when comprehension does not exist. This well-documented tendency shows individuals believe that they know far more than they actually do. In fact, the least proficient often overestimate their abilities, as cupidity begets confidence. The greatest enemy of knowledge is not ignorance, but the illusion of knowledge (Sloman & Fernbach, 2017). Overstating one's talents, for instance, famously clouds drivers' judgments: most rate themselves better than average (the "Lake Wobegon effect"). The vast majority of the population believes that it cannot multitask well enough to drive safely, yet many drivers admit to regular texting (Hogan Assessment Systems, 2017). It is not just that they do not know what they do not know, but that they do not factor their limitations into their decisions: they are quite certain about uncertainty. The problem is that the incompetent cannot know they are incompetent—a dangerous phenomenon in management decision making.

Fourth, when faced with a dilemma, people may predict that they will make an honorable choice, but when actually faced with the dilemma, they do not. Overestimating their moral capacity, they nonetheless still consider themselves to be ethical ("ethicality bias") (Bazerman & Tenbrunsel, 2011). They are not only wrong, but are confident that they are right. In fact, humans recall their unethical behavior with less-than-vivid clarity—increasing the likelihood of similar decisions in the future. Those who set aside moral concerns in pursuit of other goals can be quite creative in the rationalization of behavior and may not even be aware that this process is occurring.

Professionals, for instance, tend to believe in their work and to view themselves as persons of integrity in control of their lives. However, overconfidence in one's own ability (and the arrogance that can accompany it) affects decisions. Eventually a "new normal," an adjustment of what is defined as proper, emerges. These cognitive distortions help justify and forget questionable behavior, and reconcile it with the self-image as a righteous person. Eisenberger and Lieberman (2009) suggest that high intelligence often corresponds with low self-awareness: Neural networks involved in cognitive problem solving reside in the lateral portions of the brain, whereas the middle regions support self-awareness. These individuals may have ill-contrived views, but they are seldom in doubt (see Jones-Lee & Aven, 2017 for data on this point).

Fifth, a similar phenomenon is the "moral equilibrium scorecard," wherein individuals keep a mental ledger that compares the type of person they believe themselves to be with their actual behavior (Prentice, 2015, 45). If they do something worthwhile, the account is then in surplus, giving them license to do something dubious. If they then make a poor judgment, they may compensate by doing something positive to balance the record. This kind of "moral licensing" makes it possible for moral actors to do bad things, while thinking of themselves as good.

Among the many other tendencies (see Samson, 2017, 82–114), "naïve idealism" is the belief that one's own views reflect reality and that they are shared by neutral parties. The "availability effect" bases a decision simply on immediately available information. "Action bias" is the felt pressure to do something, anything to reduce anxiety. The "forbidden fruit" effect is the temptation to react to rules and regulations by breaking them ("reactance bias"). Thus, desiring to maintain control, employees rebel against being distrusted and told what to do. An organization that focuses on controls and sanctions may very well result in lower compliance with procedures than one that encourages personal integrity and responsibility (Bowles, 2017).

As already seen, these cognitive dispositions (and others not discussed here due to page constraints) can combine in powerful ways. They can also culminate in a self-limiting manner; no one knows less than the individual who knows it all. Once someone begins to feel that they have mastered their biases, they may be experiencing the "bias blind spot": seeing shortcomings in other people but not in their own (Bradberry & Greaves, 2012), as they consider others to be more unreasonable than themselves.

The product of all these stubborn biases—as well as bounded ethicality, System 1 thinking, motivated reasoning, and decision framing—can be unethical behavior that may occur slowly, incrementally and unconsciously, rather than in an abrupt shift. Ariely (2008) finds that individuals have an inclination to cheat a little (a "personal fudge factor") without the inconvenience of changing their honest self-image. This erosion of ethics might begin as a trivial infraction (the "peanuts effect") with the seriousness of the wrong doing growing as time passes, leading the wrongdoer to alter her definition of appropriate standards. Moral seduction theory (Moore, Tetlock, Tanlu, & Bazerman, 2006) posits that decision makers can become compromised over time, a development facilitated by nonconscious habits, ingrained motives, and deeply seated thought patterns.

In short, behavioral science concepts, both obvious and subtle, are not necessarily new, but they are important and interesting. What *is* new is the mounting evidence that ethical behavior is less under conscious control than commonly believed. The science of decisions has demonstrated that the faith in the power of pure reason is unwarranted; people are susceptible to subliminal beliefs, emotional reactions, and mental shortcuts that help explain deviations from a rational norm. Questionable behavior is not necessarily a function of bad character, but a consequence of shared *homo sapien* cognitive inheritance.

Preconceived ideas, to summarize, can trump better judgment and good intention; the brain relies on personal convictions over hard fact. These relatively unacknowledged predilections are often so strong that they are inconsistent with logic and reason and personal motives and ethics. Intuition tends to involve certainty about uncertainty, and it is usually followed by an inability to accept one's determination as wrong (Hogan Assessment Systems, 2017). Like the allegory of Plato's cave, humans are bound by the images received through the senses. Men and women have, accordingly, a distorted view of reality because they cannot observe reality objectively (Kaptein, 2013). "Decisions are not based on the objective state of the world," according to Rogerson et al. (2011, 616), "but rather on our subjective experience with it." Such cognitive distortions help justify questionable behavior, and reconcile it with her self-image as a praiseworthy person. As Elder Shafir (2012, 5) argues, it is difficult to know when to expect bias as well as when to anticipate clear judgment: "Things that ought not to matter . . . often do, and things that ought to matter often fail to have an impact." Yet while there may be no sure way to take into account biases, they can be identified and techniques can be employed to limit their impact.

Monitoring and Sanctions

This behavioral ethics tenet includes the counterintuitive role of sanctions and the nature of those sanctions. "Common sense" approaches to monitoring and penalties intended to promote exemplary behavior may be ineffective or dysfunctional. "There is a charm," Mark Twain said, "about the forbidden that makes it unspeakably desirable." Compliance systems, then, can have a "forbidden fruit" effect—that is, noncompliance may become attractive simply because it is prohibited (Bazerman & Tenbrunsel, 2011, 113). As discussed, when decisions are framed in business terms (rather than ethical terms)—and the existence of a sanctioning system notwithstanding—the decision maker might view wrongdoing as a cost of doing business, allowing ethical concerns to recede from consideration.

Implementing sanctions can lead to calculations of the likelihood of being caught or punished—rather than reflective thought questioning whether the action is the proper thing to do. By relabeling situations as "business decisions," ethical implications may be hidden, discounted, or disregarded, making it more likely that dubious behavior will result. In the dinner case, it would be expedient to downplay the importance of appearance. Mark calculated the risk of being caught out to dinner to be low and accepted, rather than ask himself if accepting were a violation of a professional ethic. Similarly, with both principals and teachers involved in erasing answers, rationalizing the behavior may have been relatively easy. A teacher could figure the risk of being caught by his principal to be low, given that the principal was in on the scheme, too!

Gneezy and Rustichini (2000) confirmed the connection between framing, sanctions, and behavior with a practical case evaluating a new fine imposed on parents by a daycare center when they arrived late to pick up their children. Unexpectedly, the number of parents arriving late increased rather than decreased. The explanation is that the payment led parents to view the matter as a business calculation. A harried parent determined the cost of arriving late, and decided to pay the money—rather than viewing on-time arrival as right behavior. A sanctioning system can produce less cooperative behavior if intrinsic motivation to cooperate is replaced by extrinsic motivation to respond to penalties. Tenbrunsel and Messick (1999) suggest that when a no-punishment procedure exists, people are more likely to see the decision as a moral one.

Organizational Context and Ethical Infrastructure

The penultimate behavioral ethics tenet, organizational context, can influence behavior in many ways, including job pressures to behave unethically, unrealistic organizational goals, rewards or incentives to act improperly, and weak sanctions for questionable behavior and organizational cultures that normalize unethical conduct (Treviño, Weaver, & Reynolds 2006). The ethical infrastructure, designed to counteract these factors and encourage right behavior in the workplace, includes robust formal and informal systems (Tenbrunsel, Smith-Crowe, & Umphress, 2003; also see Chapter 8).

The formal infrastructure includes communication (codes, mission statements, performance standards, training), surveillance (performance monitoring, hotlines, ethics ombudspersons), and management systems (evaluations, salaries, promotions, bonuses). Informal information systems also include communication (hallway conversations, unofficial training, stories), surveillance (personal observation and relationships, extra-organizational sources), and sanctions (group pressure, whistleblowing). Together with the organizational climate, formal and informal systems can influence conduct. The "morning moral" effect (Kouchaki & Smith, 2013) suggests that ethical awareness and self-control decline during the day; accordingly, important meetings and decisions should be scheduled before noon. Thus, while systems and organizational climate may foster proper behavior, under certain circumstances, they can be counterproductive. In both the dinner and school cases, weak formal penalties and a permissive informal ethical climate could easily suggest that dubious behavior would be tolerated.

Given the findings from the behavioral ethics literature summarized above, what strategies might be used to mitigate the dishonesty of otherwise honest people? While there may be no sure way to take into account biases, they can be identified and techniques can be employed to limit their impact. "De-biasing" requires determination to deal with unconscious biases and to make an effort to correct them, as discussed below.

Countering Biases

In recognizing that more information alone is insufficient to solve problems, behavioral science looks for ways to help the prefrontal cortex make better choices. After all, as the epigram above the chapter introduction implies, people have the ability to change behavior by thinking about thinking. In point of fact, the same psychological tendencies that induce irrational behavior can be used to encourage better choices; it is better to work with human nature than against it. What a classical philosopher and neoclassical economist might regard as an irrelevant situational factor, a behaviorist might see as a useful tool. But do not underestimate the mind's ability to sabotage good intentions.

Using behaviorally informed activities and prompts, organizations and their employees can change the "choice environment" to override blind spots and improve decisions, by:

1. practicing narratives to plan ahead, and write out, how to respond to issues (role play exercises, for example; Gentile, 2010) in order to narrow the intention-action gap,

2. setting self-binding pledges in advance to specific courses of action with an implementation procedure to overcome bounded will power (bank vacation savings clubs, predetermined stock price buying/selling plans, advanced medical directives),

3. utilizing checklists, fact checks, and moral reminders ("priming" per Gawande, 2011) to encourage awareness and foster compliance with best practices by exposing employees to ethics stimuli such as placing a conduct code, a mirror, or surveillance cameras in strategic places or enclosing citizen-comparison, moral-appeal letters with tax bills (Bott et al., 2017),

4. forming diverse teams to reach a fuller understanding (by taking advantage of knowledge aggregation and error reduction) to counter "group think,"

5. implementing training programs showing how vulnerable employees are to mental shortcuts and how simple tactics such as those here can reduce their influence,

6. engaging in critical reflection to legitimize and incentivize doubt (e.g., by challenging assumptions and prevailing norms, developing alternatives, employing dialectical problem solving, dialoguing between System 1 and 2, playing "devil's advocate," referring to one's self in the third person to gain psychological distance from the issue, holding a "pre-mortem" by imagining the plan failed and seeking to understand why),

7. creating "cooling off" time (anxiety and fatigue—cognitive depletion—impede thoughtful decisions) to monitor emotions, encourage self-reflection, and consult with disinterested parties,

8. being wary of rationalizations ("it's legal," "I had no choice," "everyone does it"),

9. considering if the pending option appeared on the front page tomorrow, and

10. contemplating one's own eulogy.

There are many obstacles in behavior; individuals and organizations should not allow themselves to become one of them. Indeed, there is evidence that social biases also may be reduced when sleeping, through subliminal reinforcement and brain training (Varazzani, 2017, June 20).

The toolset above can encourage decision makers to thoughtfully consider dilemmas by developing methods that enhance the ability to make sound decisions. It should also be recalled that heuristics can be efficient; accordingly, the use of cognitive expedients resulting in seemingly irrational decisions can actually be quite sensible under select circumstances. In any case, the behavioral approach offers insights to understand conduct, counterfactuals to mitigate error, and evidence-based management strategies.

In brief, it is simply not sufficient to assume that men and women are good, and that the ethical issues they encounter will take care of themselves. Behavioral science cannot tell individuals what they ought to do. However, as this review of its components suggests, it can help explain how and why people act, something of great value to practitioners and academicians alike. As Varazzani (2017, June 20) reports, for example, "neuroscience can lend insight into when a bias will manifest and how to design an effective intervention to counteract it." When it is understood why mistakes are made, steps can be taken to minimize them by using behaviorally informed policies.

The shift in approach from philosophical to psychological decision making portends an important implication for thinking about ethics: The focus should be understanding psychological factors that lead to unethical behavior rather than just emphasizing how people should behave. Because good people unwittingly contribute to unethical action, change in the practice of ethics needs to emphasize hidden, unconscious influences on behavior. For Bazerman and Tenbrunsel (2011), the goal is to become prepared for unrecognized psychological forces that occur during decision making—that is, to learn to think in a thoughtful manner to help ensure that self-interest does not smother self-integrity. This usually involves correcting System 1 intuitions with System 2 analysis by becoming aware of biases and using formal procedures that require consideration of opposing viewpoints.

In addition, creating time for reflection in the face of a superior's demand for a quick decision may be helpful, as shown in Exhibit 7.1. Finally, because fatigue and sleep deprivation reduce clear thinking and moral engagement, organizational cultures that demand overwork and long hours need re-examination.

EXHIBIT 7.1   **Avoiding Poor Judgments With Confidence**

In the crush of everyday business, managers confront demands to respond to difficult questions without delay. If pressured to make a quick decision, consider these guidelines:

- Ask for time to think it over. Most decisions do not, in fact, have to be made immediately. Bargaining for time ("Let me think about it, and I'll get back to you by 2:00 today.") should provide space to confer with others and to use systematic decision–making techniques.
- Ask if your organization has a policy relevant to the situation.
- Turn the demand around and ask your boss for his advice or ask if you and she can take a minute to consult with the department's legal staff or her superior.
- Use the disclosure test—that is, if you would be embarrassed to have the decision reported in the newspaper, then defer until a proper judgment can be rendered.
- Trust yourself and value intuition. If your "heart" suggests that something is not quite right, then consider it a warning siren (adapted from Treviño & Nelson, 1995, 77).

Impatience breeds anxiety, fear, and failure. Patience creates confidence, deliberation, and decisiveness.

Prudent decision makers prepare for uncertainty by having premeditated processes and behavioral ethics frameworks for finding answers. The response, then, to challenges becomes not to provide solutions immediately but to use reliable procedures in the pursuit of answers.

Skilled decision makers know that confidence and certainty are not synonymous—the latter emphasizes outcomes that can seldom be predicted and the former focuses on known procedures to deal with the issue. Confidence comes not from always being right, but from not fearing mistakes—a deliberate, rational decision-making process, including consulting with others, will limit the magnitude of error. Throughout an ethical crisis, the confident administrator remains calm, asks hard questions, and rejects an elusive perfect result for the quest for the good. Such managers act as a morally conscious person would act in any setting, and set the example for the workplace. Slow down. No one is in a hurry for a bad decision.

Exercises like those listed in Exhibit 7.1 can assist in problem framing, interfering with the "want" self and System 1 thinking, and moderating biases and errors (also see Banaji et al., 2003, esp. 61–63). In the dinner case, the "front page" caution may have been useful to Mark; in the test-tampering case, a pre-commitment by teachers and school administrators to hold independent audits would likely have identified problems. Thus, a variety of concerns that are examples of decision mistakes (e.g., action bias, self-serving bias) can be exploited to help individuals accomplish their ethical objectives.

CONCLUSION

Obviously, people make decisions deviant from the classical rational model and its prescriptions. Often the expression "I'm only human" is offered as a tenuous defense of a less-than-rational decision. Many factors, including situational context, can help explain the dishonesty of honest people. The heroic assumptions made by the traditional approach—that individuals are ostensibly and universally logical, possess full information, have the willpower to use it, and act in their self-interest—often do not hold in real life. Thus, for instance, if the goal is to persuade someone to change her views, then do not lead with evidence and facts that are likely to provoke defense mechanisms such as the backfire effect discussed above. Rather, ethical thinkers from Plato to St. Augustine to Thomas Hobbes understand "that human beings are fundamentally passionate creatures and that reason alone is too weak to contain their drives" (Lilla, 2010, December 17). Political controversies are often really debates about values, not facts. Seeking common ground, lead with values in a context within which she is familiar to engage emotions; introducing new information in that psychologically safe environment may be effective.

The various irrational behaviors explored in this chapter must be taken into account when choices are made. Hypocrisy is part of the human comedy. In so doing, behavioral ethics is transforming the way conduct is understood when ethics matters most—individuals actually making judgments. The limited applicability of traditional ethics does not warrant casting it off altogether—upholding ideals under stress is the very reason for the classical study of ethics. One is unlikely to carry out an action in pursuit of a principle to which he has never given thought. As Paul Moloney (2011) observes, "What gives meaning to behavior is purpose." For this reason philosophy examines thought, not behavior.

Tools like the ethics triad nudge decision makers to thoughtfully consider perplexing moral dilemmas. Accordingly, each of the chapters that follow will include one or more cases that are briefly analyzed using the lens of the trinity. Readers should keep in mind, however, the insights from behavioral ethics when relying on such cognitive approaches. If the prescriptions characteristic of the orthodox triune decision-making model and the descriptions of conduct in the behavioral model are viewed as mutually reinforcing, rather than inimical, a more complete understanding of the human condition may result in the workplace. They both ask to think about thinking. The incorporation of such a synthesis into organizational cultures promises that the quality of ethical decision making will improve in the future.

***

One way to find out if a man is honest is to ask him. If he says "yes," you know he is crooked.

—Groucho Marx

NOTES

1. With permission, the following discussion draws on Bowman and West (2013). Copyright © 2013 by M. E. Sharpe, Inc. Used by permission. All Rights Reserved. Not for reproduction.
2. Parts of this and the next section are drawn from Bowman, West, and Beck (2010). Copyright © M. E. Sharpe, Inc. Used by permission. All Rights Reserved. Not for reproduction.
3. Some decision situations may be "easy" to analyze since they are right vs. wrong "problems" (there is a clear ethically correct answer), and others more convoluted, as in right vs. right dilemmas (there may be several "right" solutions, all of which nonetheless may be problematic). Simplicity does not imply ease of solution—even in dilemmas wherein the right answer is evident, for nonethical reasons, the dilemma may remain difficult to resolve. In both simple and complex cases, ethics requires not just the rectitude to support the proper decision and refuse wrongdoing, but also the resourcefulness to devise honorable ways to deal with the issue. Scores of public sphere cases providing testimony from administrators have been gathered by Menzel (2010). Among the many issues discussed are those dealing with the ethics of commercializing a city's website (139–142) and the hiring of a supervisor's highly qualified friend (193–194).
4. Beware the pitfalls risked when just one school of thought is emphasized at the expense of the others. For example, reliance on the results approach alone may be problematic because it is difficult to anticipate all possible consequences of a decision, and because limiting the focus to results may lead to imprudent, expedient action.
5. Parts of this section are adapted from Bowman (2018).
6. Similarly, exclusive use of rule-based ethics may lack compassion (Svara, 1997), as when truth telling produces cold and inconsiderate behaviors. The benevolence of virtue ethics, combined with the greater good—emphasis of results-oriented ethics, might humanize the hard objectivity of a rule-based approach. Last, the potential of virtue theory to be self-serving can be

counterbalanced with results and rules ethics thinking. An integrated approach produces a defensible decision that takes into account results, rules, and virtues. To battle a dilemma, an administrator must choose wisely from the armory of ethics, and choose more than one weapon. An important tool is used in behavioral ethics: human subject laboratory experiments. Although college students are often participants in these trials, some experiments are conducted using business professionals with similar results (e.g., Bazerman & Tenbrunsel, 2011).

7. Joshua Greene (2010) employs a camera metaphor (recounted in Brooks, 2011, 290) that helps to explain the role of intuition in System 1. Automatic settings on the camera quickly and efficiently regulate the focus and shutter speed, but sometimes the settings need to be overridden to allow for manual adjustment. While manual adjustment is more time consuming, it enables the photographer to accomplish things that could not otherwise be done. Similarly, a person may experience automatic ethical concerns, but then override them and fine-tune them through a slower, in-depth reasoning.

8. Also see Thaler and Sunstein (2009), who argue that people's behavior can be influenced in predictable ways without their realizing it. The key is the "architecture" of a decision.

9. A link between the want/should self-theory and ethical fading (as well as bounded ethicality) is evident. As Tenbrunsel et al. (2009) point out, when the ethical dimensions of a decision fade away, it enables the "want" self to appear.

FOR DISCUSSION

1. It is said the biggest problem is not ignorance, but the illusion of knowledge. Examine this claim in the context of the assumptions of rational ethical decision making.

2. Identify the strengths and weaknesses of the classical rationalism and psychological realism approaches to understanding ethics.

3. Examine at least one of the major findings of behavioral ethics. Critique it.

4. Thomas Jefferson wrote, "In matters of style, swim with the current. In matters of principle, stand like a rock." Consider how this insight is germane to both the classical and psychological schools of ethical decision making. Discuss.

5. It is said that morality both binds and blinds. Comment.

EXERCISES

1. Several cases (Bowman & Knox, 2008; Svara, 1997) can be used to illustrate the interactive nature of the three-fold decision-making approach described in this chapter; for each one that follows, examine the decision using the three viewpoints and explain what the individual should do. (Note: There is always incomplete information; if there were complete information, the case would be a foregone conclusion, not a dilemma.)

Recognize that some of the "ethical pickles" below should be fairly easy to analyze since they are right vs. wrong "problems," not right vs. right "dilemmas." For both problems and dilemmas, the best way out is through. Note that ethics requires not just the rectitude to support the proper decision and refuse wrongdoing, but also the resourcefulness to devise possible noble ways to deal with the problem:

The Candidate. A candidate for a city manager position is asked by the city council to agree to fire the public works director and is told that the other finalist for the job has agreed, if hired, to fire the public works director.

The Sting. A properly conducted law enforcement sting operation nets some criminals.

The Analyst. A data analyst for a community college finds that enrollment figures are being padded to increase state funding.

The Boss. Your boss tells you your organization may be downsized next month and pledges you to secrecy. One of your subordinates, about to purchase a house with his expecting wife, later asks you about downsizing rumors that are going around.

Each school of thought is represented by a shorthand question that corresponds to results, rules, or rectitude. Some illustrative prompts may be helpful in puzzling through what to do:

- Results approach: "What's the greatest good for the greatest number of people?" "What are the short- and long-run consequences of the proposed decision?
- Duty-based approach: "Is what's right for one, right for all?" "What if everyone did that?" "Is this action universally acceptable?" (Note: Assume that specific organizational rules are trumped by universal ethical rules reflected in the prompts immediately above.)
- Virtue ethics: "Does the proposed decision make me a better person in my community?" "Which choice is most true to my character?"

For each case, answer the question raised by each school of thought. Then explain what would you do and why. Be alert to the human capacity (yours!) for self-deception.

Avoid talking about results, rules, and virtues without a clear reference point. Discuss each philosophy separately using the prompts above as a starting point. Resist the temptation to let other philosophies obstruct the analysis as illustrated below. They will get their turn; the overall assessment at the end will provide a synthesis. For a critique of some student case analyses, see Appendix 7.1, which shows (a) how students reacted, using the three-fold decision-making procedure, to a complex classroom dishonesty case; and (b) why their responses were understandable, but an incorrect application of the procedure.

2. Continue condensing your notes (made in the page margins of the text or a notebook) after reading each chapter to establish links between chapter and course objectives. While doing this, create sentence stems (see Chapter 1) to identify insights and questions.

3. In light of bias and common decision-making errors, do facts actually work to change minds—or do inertia and denial predominate? Provide examples.

4. Examine criticisms of behavioral ethics (e.g., Bubb & Pildes, 2014) and assess their validity.

5. Retrieve David Brooks' (2015, January 13), "Child in the Basement" in the *New York Times* at www.nytimes.com/2015/01/13/opinion/david-brooks-the-child-in-the-basement.html. This riveting story compels readers to confront the tragic compromises that are built into society (don't miss it!).

6. View Michael Sandel's "Justice," Episode 01 (15 minutes)" in YouTube to further enrich this chapter's discussion by reinforcing the distinction between utilitarian and deontological arguments (includes the trolley case and organ replacement).

REFERENCES

Ariely, D. (2008). *Predictably irrational.* New York: HarperCollins.

Banaji, M., Bazerman, M., & Chugh, D. (2003). How (un)ethical are you? *Harvard Business Review, 81,* 56–63.

Bazerman, M., & Banaji, M. R. (2004). The social psychology of ordinary ethical failures. *Social Justice Research, 17*(2), 111–115.

Bazerman, M., & Chugh, D. (2006). Bounded awareness: Focusing failures in negotiation. In L. L. Thompson (Ed.), *Negotiation theory and research* (pp. 7–26). New York: Psychology Press.

Bazerman, M., & Tenbrunsel, A. (2011). *Blind spots: Why we fail to do what's right and what to do about it.* Princeton, NJ: Princeton University Press.

Bennett, D. (2014, November 5). How to take control of your brain and make better decisions. *Washington Post.* Retrieved from https://www.washingtonpost.com/posteverything/wp/2014/11/05/how-to-take-control-of-your-brain-and-make-better-decisions/?utm_term=.344e25176145

Bott, K., Cappelen, A., Sorensen, E., & Tungodden, B. (2017). Research: Moral appeals can help reduce tax evasion. *Harvard Business Review.* Retrieved from https://hbr.org/2017/07/research-moral-appeals-can-help-reduce-tax-evasion

Bowles, S. (2017). *Moral economy: Why good incentives are no substitute for good citizens.* New Haven, CT: Yale University Press.

Bowman, J. (2018). Thinking about thinking. Beyond decision-making rationalism and the emergence of behavioral ethics. *Public Integrity* (in press).

Bowman, J., & Knox, C. (2008). Ethics in government: No matter how long and dark the night, *Public Administration Review, 68,* 625–637.

Bowman, J., & West, J. (2013). From classical rationalism to psychological realism in ethical decision-making. In R. Ghere & H. G. Frederickson (Eds.), *Ethics and public management* (pp. 155–171) (2nd ed.). Armonk, NY: M. E. Sharpe.

Bowman, J., West, J., & Beck, M. (2010). *Competencies in public service: The professional edge* (2nd ed.). Armonk, NY: M. E. Sharpe.

Bradberry, T., & Greaves, J. (2012). *Emotional intelligence 2.0.* San Diego, CA: Talent Smart.

Brest, P. (2012). Quis custodiet ipsos custodes? In E. Shafir (Ed.), *Behavioral foundations of public policy* (pp. 481–493). Princeton, NJ: Princeton University Press.

Brooks, D. (2011). *The social animal: The hidden sources of love, character, and achievement.* New York: Random House.

Bubb, R., & Pildes, R. (2014). How behavioral economics trims its sails and why." *Harvard Law Review, 127,* 1593–1678.

Chugh, D. (2004). Why milliseconds matter: Societal and managerial implications of implicit social cognition. *Social Justice Research, 17,* 203–222.

Cotteleer, M., & Murphy, T. (2015). *Ignoring bad news* (Paper, Series on Behavioral Economics and Management). West Lake, TX: DeLoitte Consulting, LLP.

Eisenberger, N., & Lieberman, M. (2009). The pains and pleasures of social life. *Science, 323*(5916), 890–891.

Gawande, A. (2011). *Checklist manifesto.* New York: Picador.

Gazzaniga, M. (2008). *Human: The science behind what makes us unique.* New York: Harper Perennial.

Gentile, M. (2010). *Giving voice to values.* New Haven, CT: Yale University Press.

Gneezy, U., & Rustichini, A. (2000). A fine is a price. *Journal of Legal Studies, 29,* 1–17.

Greene, J. (2010). Does moral action depend on reasoning? Less than it should. Retrieved from https://www.ethics-based-on-science.com/uploads/2/8/5/1/28516163/mjm-notes-moral-reasoning_bq_spring_2010.pdf

Haidt, J. (2001). The emotional dog and its rational tail: A social intuitionist approach to moral judgment. *Psychological Review, 108,* 814–834.

Hogan Assessment Systems. (2017). Hey, your biases are showing. Tulsa, OK: Author.

Hoomans, J. (2015, March 20). 35,000 decisions: The great choices of strategic leaders. *Leading Edge Journal.* Retrieved from https://go.roberts.edu/leadingedge/the-great-choices-of-strategic-leaders

Jones-Lee, M., & Aven, T. (2017). Weighing private preferences in public sector safety decisions. *Behavioral Public Policy, 1*(1), 122–142.

Kahneman, D. (2011). *Thinking, fast and slow.* New York: Farrer, Straus, & Giroux.

Kaptein, M. (2013). *Workplace morality: Behavioral ethics in organizations.* Bingley: Emerald.

Kern, M., & Chugh, D. (2009). Bounded ethicality: The perils of loss framing. *Psychological Science, 20,* 378–384.

Kouchaki, M., & Smith, I. (2013). The morning effect: The influence of time of day on unethical behavior. *Psychological Science, 25*(1), 95–102.

Kuran, T. (1997). *Private truth, public lies.* Cambridge, MA: Harvard University Press.

Lilla, M. (2010, December 17). The president and the passions. *New York Times.* Retrieved from http://www.nytimes.com/2010/12/19/magazine/19Fob-WWLN-t.html.

Menzel, D. (2010). *Ethics moments in government: Cases and controversies.* Boca Raton, FL: CRC Press.

Mercier, H., & Sperber, D. (2017). *Enigma of reason.* Cambridge, MA: Harvard University Press.

Moloney, P. (2011, April 2). Comments. *Philosophy on the Mesa.* Retrieved from http://philosophyonthemesa.com/2011/03/30/behavioral-ethics-explanation-or-excuse/

Mooney, C. (2011, April 18). The science of why we don't believe in science. *Mother Jones*. Retrieved from http://www.motherjones.com/politics/2011/03/denial-science-chris-mooney

Mooney, C. (2012). *The Republican brain*. Hoboken, NJ: Wiley.

Moore, D., Tetlock, P., Tanlu, L., & Bazerman, M. (2006). Conflict of interest and the case of auditor independence: Moral seduction and strategic issue cycling. *Academy of Management Review*, *31*, 10–49.

Prentice, R. (2015). Behavioral ethics. *Notre Dame Journal of Law, Ethics, and Public Policy*, *29*(1), 36–85.

Rainer, T., & Geiger, E. (2011). *Simple church*. Nashville, TN: B&H Publishing.

Redlawsk, D. P., Civettini, A. W., & Emmerson, K. M. (2010). The affective tipping point: Do motivated reasoners ever "get it"? *Political Psychology*, *31*, 563–593.

Rogerson, M., Gottlieb, M., Handelsman, M., Knapp, S., & Younggren, J. (2011). Nonrational processes in ethical decision making. *American Psychologist*, *66*(7), 614–623.

Ropeik, D. (2012, September 30). Inside the mind of worry. *New York Times*, p. SR12.

Samson, A. (Ed.). (2017). *The behavioural economics guide*. London: Behavioral Science Solutions Ltd. Retrieved from http://www.behavioraleconomics.com

Schmidt, R. (2016). *Frozen: Using behavioral design to overcome decision making paralysis*. (Paper, Series on Behavioral Economics and Management). West Lake, TX: DeLoitte Consulting, LLP.

Seawright, R. (2013, March 10). The narrative opportunity [Web log comment]. Retrieved from http://rpseawright.wordpress.com/2013/03/10/the-narrative-opportunity/

Shafir, E. (2012). Introduction. In E. Shafir (Ed.), *Behavioral foundations of public policy* (pp. 1–12). Princeton, NJ: Princeton University Press.

Shao, R., Aquino, K., & Freeman, D. (2008). Beyond moral reasoning: A review of moral identity research and its implications for business research. *Business Ethics Quarterly*, *18*, 513–540.

Simon, H. (1983). *Reason in human affairs*. Stanford, CA: Stanford University Press.

Sloman, S., & Fernbach, P. (2017). *The knowledge illusion*. New York: Riverhead.

Svara, J. (1997). The ethical triangle: Synthesizing the bases of administrative ethics. In J. Bowman (Ed.), *Public integrity annual* (pp. 33–41). Lexington, KY: Council of State Governments.

Svara, J. (2007). *The ethics primer for public administrators in government and nonprofit organizations*. Sudbury, MA: Jones & Bartlett.

Tenbrunsel, A., & Messick, D. (1999). Sanctioning systems, decision frames, and cooperation. *Administrative Science Quarterly*, *44*, 684–707.

Tenbrunsel, A., & Messick, D. (2004). Ethical fading: The role of self deception in unethical behavior. *Social Justice Research*, *17*, 223–236.

Tenbrunsel, A., Smith-Crowe, K., & Umphress, E. (2003). Building houses on rocks: The role of ethical infrastructure in the ethical effectiveness of organizations. *Social Justice Research*, *16*, 285–307.

Tenbrunsel, A., Diekmann, K., Wade-Benzoni, K., & Bazerman, M. (2009). The ethical mirage: A temporal explanation as to why we aren't as ethical as we think we are. *Research in Organizational Behavior*, *30*, 153–173.

Thaler, R., & Sunstein, C. (2009). *Nudge*. Delmar, NY: Caravan Books.

Thorson, E. (2016, January 8). Debunking Donald Trump won't work if you repeat what he got wrong. *Washington Post.* Retrieved from https://www.washingtonpost.com/opinions/why-correcting-donald-trump--or-anyone-else--doesnt-work/2016/01/08/9e5ef5d4-b57d-11e5-a842-0feb51d1d124_story.html?utm_term=.57f7bd2d35f7

Treviño, L., & Nelson, K. (1995). *Managing business ethics.* New York: Wiley.

Treviño, L., Weaver, G., & Reynolds, S. (2006). Behavioral ethics in organizations: A review. *Journal of Management, 32,* 951–990.

Varazzani, C. (2017, June 20). The risks of ignoring the brain. *Behavioral Scientist.* Retrieved from http://behavioralscientist.org/risks-ignoring-brain/

Appendix 7.1

Critiquing Student Case Analyses

Below are responses from graduate students in a professional ethics course to a complex classroom dishonesty case. The reactions show how they tried to apply the decision-making procedure discussed in this chapter. The italicized sentences note the shortcomings in their analyses. The argument offered may function logically, but does not address the issue at hand (Aristotle's *ignoratio elenchi*, or ignoring the issue).

"In this cheating case, the ethics trinity may not lead to an easy determination."

This is a reasonable statement, as that is to be expected when dealing with true dilemmas; the tool is not likely to produce facile answers; it will provide a comprehensive analysis of the issue.

"From the rules viewpoint, it would clearly be determined that academic dishonesty is against school policy and any moral code that lists honesty as an essential value."

This comment does not speak to the rules prompt: What is good for one is good for all. School rules are secondary to ethical rules.

"The results perspective may point to either the results the accused is aiming for in getting a good grade, which would say cheating is alright to achieve the best results, or it may say that the activity is still wrong because it does not make him a better person."

This view misconstrues the results prompt by converting the greatest good for the greatest number to the best result for one person by emphasizing the short run. It then focuses on virtue theory, which, by definition, cannot be part of the results theory.

"The virtue approach is likely to disallow disgraceful behavior because it does nothing productive for society as a whole and does not contribute to the greater good."

This response includes results thinking ("does nothing productive" and the "greater good"), ignoring the virtue prompt: How does the decision affect my character and that of my community?

As noted in the chapter, the case should be examined by each of the three philosophies, one by one, using their respective question prompt. When searching for insights from one approach, the other approaches should not interfere with the one under analysis. When all three philosophies are considered, it will provide a synthesis, or at least a conclusion, of sorts. Don't jump to confusions (!). Indeed, recall the behavioral ethics tenets that might be useful in formulating a final judgment. Beware anyone, including yourself, who seems to know all the answers but none of the right questions.

PART III

Institutional Approaches to Ethics

8 Organizational Ethics

Nothing is possible without individuals; nothing is lasting without institutions.

—Jean Monnet

Mastery of individual-centered, micro-level ethics is necessary, but not sufficient, for understanding the full scope of ethics, as it revolves around both individuals and organizations (recall the Greek perspective on ethics in Chapter 1). Cognitive and virtue ethics by themselves may not produce ethical behavior, as people remain susceptible to meso-level workplace influences. Recall from Chapter 2 that the organizational level of ethics interacts with both the narrower and broader levels of ethics—micro (individual) and macro (societal), respectively. As Milgram demonstrated so shockingly with his laboratory experiments (Chapter 4), it is faulty to assume that people are ethical no matter what the context because ethics are revealed in social situations. Good intentions may not be enough when employees are overwhelmed by pressures to conform to improper organizational behaviors that conflict with their good intentions.

As observed in earlier chapters, individual ethical judgment is an ability to be developed through practice. People must be given opportunity, autonomy, power, and encouragement to gain a new skill. In the workplace, some kind of collective basis for professional conduct is necessary. Employees may make decisions based on personal standards, but institutions define and govern the situations in which decisions are made. Individual responsibility is often discharged through organizations. Consider the possibilities if Milgram had designed an experiment to encourage praiseworthy behavior. Stated differently, the ethical health of a society and its members is significantly affected by the institutions that employ them.

Organizations represent major agencies of social control. Ethical behavior is not only an individual psychological phenomenon, but also collective and sociological. Disreputable conduct is not just committed by a few "bad apples," but also by ordinary people doing extraordinary things under certain circumstances. Some people refuse to acknowledge organizational factors contributing to wrong behavior for fear of diluting personal moral responsibility. Yet this concern is based on a false dichotomy—recognizing the role of organization does not exculpate individual wrongdoers. Personal responsibility is by no means identical to sole responsibility. Individual blame (the "rotten apple") and institutional innocence ("the barrel") is an unwarranted double standard.

This chapter—which commences Part III of the book—begins the shift from cognitive ("head") and virtue ("heart") individual-centered ethics to organization-centered ("body") approaches. Examining organizational ethics will be followed in subsequent chapters on corruption control and whistleblowing. The discussion here encompasses:

- the recognition that individual-centered cognitive and virtue ethics is an important but inadequate basis for a comprehensive understanding of management ethics,
- the delineation of types of organization and the strategies that they use to nurture ethics,
- a critique of compliance-based and integrity-based ethics strategies, and
- the elements of an ethical infrastructure.

Organizations put people in environments where they have discretion, and it may be difficult to ascertain what appropriate behavior is. Employers are responsible, therefore, for the conduct of employees, as it would be imprudent to leave this important management function to chance. Creating an admirable institution is no mean task, yet it is easier—and more controllable—than attempting to directly affect individual behavior.

TYPES OF ORGANIZATIONAL STRATEGY

Approaches to ethics—immoral, amoral, moral—that may be used by organizations (Carroll, 1987, 12) are shown in Table 8.1. For the immoral unit, the norms, motives, goals, orientation toward law, and overall ethical strategy emphasize doing whatever is necessary to achieve its goals. Amoral institutions, by definition, are neither unethical nor ethical, as a minimalist stance toward ethical behaviors and laws prevails so as to avoid unnecessary trouble and do what needs to be done. Moral management defines success within professional (ethical) and legal standards of conduct.

Recall Kohlberg's stages of individual moral development (Chapter 4), a framework that also can be applied to organizations. Thus, Stage 1 organizations focus on financial survival as their moral beacon. Characteristic of this simplest level is preservation—any strategy is employed to protect against extinction. Stage 2 institutions stress the exclusive pursuit of self-interest, success justifying the tactics used. The two stages are not unlike Carroll's immoral organizations. Stage 3 companies, nonprofits, and public agencies conform to the practices of peer institutions—the vogue of rival organizations dictates what is right and wrong. This stage corresponds to Carroll's amoral organization, especially if the nature of the sister organizations are amoral. Stage 4 organizations take direction from institutional authority to determine their standards. Their moral compass is based on society's legal structure. This stage, and the following one, characterize moral management in increasing degrees of substance. Stage 5 departments rely on participatory management and democratic decision

TABLE 8.1	Approaches to Management Ethics		
	Immoral Management	**Amoral Management**	**Moral Management**
Ethical Norms	Management decisions, actions, and behavior imply a positive and active opposition to what is moral (ethical)	Management is neither moral nor immoral, but decisions lie outside the sphere to which moral judgments apply Management activity is outside or beyond the moral order of a particular code	Management activity conforms to a standard of ethical, or right, behavior Conforms to accepted professional standards of conduct Ethical leadership is commonplace on the part of management
Motives	Selfish Management cares only about its or the organization's gains	Well-intentioned but selfish (impact on others is not considered)	Good Management wants to succeed but only within the confines of sound ethical precepts (fairness, justice, due process) Success within the confines of legal obedience and ethical standards
Goals	Organizational success at any price	Success; other goals are not considered	Success within the confines of legal obedience and ethical standards
Orientation Toward Law	Legal standards are barriers that management must overcome to accomplish what it wants	Law is the ethical guide, preferably the letter of the law The central question is what can be done legally	Obedience toward letter and spirit of the law Law is a minimal ethical behaviour Prefer to operate well above what law mandates
Strategy	Exploit opportunities for organizational gain Cut corners when it appears useful	Give managers free reign Personal ethics may apply but only if managers choose Respond to legal mandates if caught and required to do so	Live by sound ethical standards Assume leadership position when ethical dilemmas arise Enlightened self-interest

Source: Carroll (1987, 12).

making—majority rule becomes the standard. Stage 6 businesses, not-for-profits, and governmental offices value moral ideals such as justice and individual rights, balancing judgment among competing interests, based on universal principles, to determine right behavior.

With these types of approaches to moral management and organizational development, what is the best way to manage a diversity of values that emphasizes service to the commonweal? The aim of an ethically grounded system of management is to build and sustain a set of shared values that will be beneficial to the organization, its members, and the public (Berman & West, 1994). Maintaining the health of the system requires continuous communication and education that reaches beyond mere compliance with laws and rules, and involves communicating a vision of the organization and cultivating trust among its members and stakeholders.

Achieving consensus on values raises this puzzle: Do top officials designate a set of values that determine subordinate behavior and performance, or do the values of employees determine outcomes? The two directions of causality can be described as two institutional models of ethics (Table 8.2). The personal, negative, punitive, "low-road" compliance strategy is clearly important, for without it, an ethics program may lack credibility. Yet it focuses on individuals, defines ethics as avoiding problems, emphasizes "symptom solving," fosters the view that ethical practices are best regulated from the outside rather than from within, and often uses ethics to control behavior instead of encouraging reflection.

TABLE 8.2	**Comparing Low- and High-Road Compliance Strategies**	
	Low-Road Compliance	**High-Road Compliance**
Ethos	Conformity with external standards	Self-governance according to chosen standards
Objective	Prevent criminal conduct	Enable responsible conduct
Leadership	Lawyer driven	Management driven
Methods	Training, limited discretion, controls, penalties	Education, leadership, accountability
Assumption	People driven by material self-interest	People guided by humanistic ideals

Source: Adapted from Paine (1994, 113).

The structural, affirmative, "high-road," integrity commitment system is aimed at deterring—rather than merely detecting—problems by emphasizing right behavior. Rather than blame and punishment, it focuses on reform and improvement. It is easy to manipulate an organization's policies and procedures relative to trying to change individual behavior. Programs focused on inspiring positive conduct are more effective than those limited to requiring compliance with minimal legal standards (Anechiarico & Jacobs, 1996; Hoekstra, Belling, & van der Heide, 2008; Rohr, 1988). Yet to the extent that the high road relies on the more mature levels of moral development theory, the approach, while laudable, may not be readily attainable.

The Organisation for Economic Co-operation and Development (OECD) (1996) examined values management systems in nine countries and plotted them using a two-dimensional classification scheme with an integrity–compliance dimension and a public administration–managerialism dimension (Figure 8.1). The report concluded that a balance is needed, avoiding too much control (where nothing gets done) and too little control (where

FIGURE 8.1	**Classification by Integrity–Compliance Dimension and Public Administration–Managerialism Dimension**

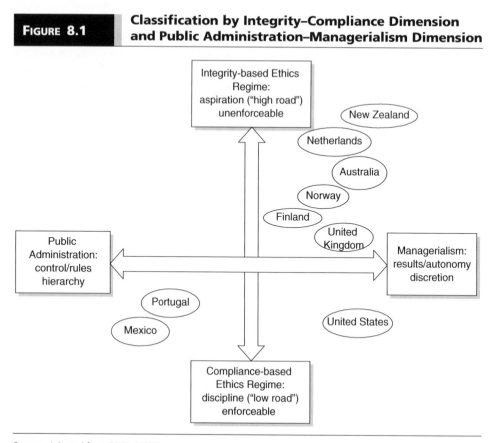

Source: Adapted from OECD (1996).

wrong things occur), and recognizes that each nation's ethics infrastructure must be based on local political and bureaucratic traditions.

One dimension, a low-road strategy based on strict centralized compliance, emphasizes staying out of trouble; a high-road integrity approach relies on self-governance and personal responsibility for engaging in ethical behavior (Bowman, West, & Beck, 2010; Paine, 1994). The other dimension—a rule-based system built on hierarchy and control—differs from the results-oriented, flexible managerialist system. Tradeoffs must be finely calibrated for both dimensions between decentralization and control. In like measure, values management strategies must weigh the diverse values public servants bring to their work against the unity of purpose in government organizations needed to realize common goals.

A complete ethics strategy, then, should include all elements, and involve a plan for what to do when something goes wrong. Overall, such programs are intended not mainly to prevent crimes (the purpose of law) and not simply to promote favorable public relations (the goal of public affairs staff). Their objective, instead, is to create and sustain confidence in government, nonprofit, and business arenas (Thompson, 2009). Precisely because people are not saints, ethical institutions, standards, and programs seek to channel human behavior in productive ways (Heclo, 2008, 25). That is, organizations have an opportunity to affect the moral agency of their employees, to reinforce their ethical identity. Although an effective system will not produce perfect people, an inadequate system will produce wrongdoers. Many of the organizations mired in scandal had rules in place and even won ethics awards. What they lacked was a proactive strategy—an ethical infrastructure—that relied more heavily on commitment than compliance.

Challenges arise when individual ethics clash with organizational ethics. The organizational ethos is often reflected in policies and procedures. An employee who possesses an affirmative, high-road personal ethic will resist a low-road compliance strategy she finds demeaning. The employee may express her concerns to management or resist the approach by ignoring it or meeting the minimum compliance requirement. Even a policy that reflects the high-road method may cause internal disagreements, because of differing positions on the appropriateness of implementing a policy. Someone who objects to a policy may recognize its ethics "on paper" but still feel the policy will produce unethical results in practice. The ethics triad presented in the previous chapter can be applied to resolve tensions between individual and organization ethics, and help decide whether the individual ought to resist a policy. (See Case Study 8.1).

ETHICAL INFRASTRUCTURE: BUILDING BLOCKS IN ETHICS MANAGEMENT

Managers, as moral custodians of collective goals, are strategically placed to recognize factors that promote and inhibit laudatory behavior. Accordingly, they are responsible for providing a foundation for professional conduct. An ethical infrastructure includes the building blocks discussed in the next section: organizational structure, values statements, psychological contracts, oaths and codes, managing institutional ethics, and creating ethical competency. In developing this approach to ethical action, the following assumptions are made:

- The maintenance of a high level of trust and confidence between the public and its government is essential in democracy.
- Since each group in society is governed by a written or unwritten code of behavior, effort to encourage ethical action must be "culture based," and germane to the performance of public service.
- Humans are at least partially knowing beings, and while knowing is not an automatic process, the potential for learning exists. Modifying behavior, however, is a difficult task, and transformations should not be expected in the short run.
- Any significant organizational activity must be integrated into the mainstream of operations or it does not get done; ethical programs must be infused into the everyday life of the agency.
- In an institution where ethics is taken seriously, an atmosphere of trust, mutuality, and credibility will exist.

- Under appropriate circumstances, ethical programs can result in a different standard of conduct than would be achieved by the spontaneous development of group norms. (Bowman, 1983)

Stated differently, public confidence cannot be left to chance. The citizenry deserves assurance that government can be depended on to conduct the people's business according to high standards. Likewise, the public is entitled to socially responsible practices in the nonprofit and business areas.

CASE STUDY 8.1

Applying Philosophical and Behavioral Ethics Approaches: To Follow or Not to Follow Government Hiring Policy

The Human Resource Management Department of Metropolitan County government receives background checks on job applicants from the State Bureau of Investigation. The job in question is a supervisory position in a politically popular preschool summer program operated by the Parks and Recreation Department. Public policies state that hiring should not be biased against those with arrest (not conviction) records, because consideration of arrests may adversely affect some minority groups with higher than average arrest rates. Even convicted felons could be hired under certain circumstances, such as the nature of the offense and rehabilitation efforts. Patricia Cobb, a county human resource specialist, is concerned about two applicants. One has a deferred sentence for child molestation, the other a suspended sentence for domestic violence. While there was no legal conviction in either case, Patricia decided not to pass these files to the hiring authority in the Parks and Recreation Department, and indicated instead that the other candidates "were a better fit" for the job. Now she is having second thoughts and wonders if she behaved unethically.

Results-Based Analysis. Both philosophical rationalism and psychological realism approaches, discussed in the last chapter, provide insight into thinking about this case. Classical philosophy prescribes how people should act using the three schools of thought below. From a results perspective, Patricia believes she has minimized any risk to the student participants in the program by excluding the two applicants: the greatest good for the greatest number. She knows that any harm that may come to a child while in the care of the county would put the program in jeopardy. She realizes that a deferred or suspended sentence does not necessarily mean that the applicant would be technically "unqualified," but she did not want to take a chance that could result in danger to children.

Patricia is also aware that employees who disregard policy may be putting themselves at risk. If the two applicants learned that their files were not seriously considered, they might challenge the hiring process and question the grounds for their exclusion. The prior deferred and suspended sentences should not have been the basis for any action regarding their application. An appeal on these grounds would put the spotlight on Patricia and force her to explain actions difficult to justify.

Rule-Based Analysis. From a rules or principles perspective, Patricia's decision can be both supported and criticized. She violated organizational policy, which clearly states that the deferred and suspended sentences are not relevant criteria in hiring decisions. Employees who disregard policy can face adverse personnel actions. Patricia normally complies with policy; she views this as an exceptional circumstance. The moral minimum to "avoid and correct social injury" could be used in her defense. However, the "what is good for one is good for all" triad guideline mandates that applicants be reviewed according to the same screening standards.

All public employees should consider law and policy when making a decision. Substituting one's own judgment for policies that have been approved by legitimate bodies is typically ill-advised. Patricia could have consulted with her superiors before excluding the two candidates from the applicant pool. She failed to do so and violated the rights of the applicants by excluding them, putting them at an unfair disadvantage in the selection process. This is inconsistent with her role as a human resource management specialist. Any bias in the selection process is a breach of the merit system. Her professional obligation is to minimize any preferential treatment of applicants and to rule out criteria that are not strictly job related.

Virtue-Based Analysis. Considering virtue ethics, she must ask, "Does this decision represent what a virtuous person would do?" Honesty, integrity, and fairness are important virtues, and when Patricia indicates that other applicants were a "better fit for the job," she is not being entirely honest with the preschool's hiring department about her motivations in passing over these two candidates. While she may initially believe that she is preserving the preschool's integrity by excluding these applicants, she is also compromising integrity by rejecting two qualified applicants, denying them a chance at a job even though neither of them was legally convicted. This violates the preschool's integrity because the program has pledged not to consider arrest reports in its hiring process. Denying these two applicants was unfair to them when they did not legally do anything wrong, and organizational policy says arrest records are not legitimate grounds for such denials.

Caring, prudence, and empathy are three other important virtues that help her to see another side of the dilemma. Patricia did mull over her decision and did not act in an arbitrary and capricious manner. She prides herself on her character traits of empathy and commitment to the best interests of children. She could not live with herself if harm were to come to a child because of a decision she made. It would violate her personal code to put children at risk. However, she also sees virtue in evenhanded treatment and policy compliance, recognizing that willingness to substitute one's personal judgment for established standard operating procedures can become a character flaw if taken too far or too often. She values her good judgment and believes she displayed practical wisdom, but she also knows of cases of wrongdoing when public administrators disregard organizational norms and act in any way they see fit.

Behavioral Ethics-Based Analysis. While the cognitive and virtue theories focusing on results, rules, and virtues help Patricia reason through her decision, the psychological realism approach embodied in behavioral ethics suggests that something else is needed for a complete analysis. The case, accordingly, can also be considered drawing on concepts such as bounded rationality, inadequate information, and ethical fading (Chapter 7). Recall that reason may be well intended—but also unreliable—due to unacknowledged, emotional effects on conduct (e.g., people tend to believe what they want to believe).

Bounded rationality suggests that decision makers often lack complete and accurate information, and even when they have it, they may not process it in a way that yields the best decision. Patricia did not discuss this issue with the appointing authority, neither did she dig deeper through fact finding beyond what was on the applications.

She did not conduct an interview with the two excluded applicants to determine the details about prior arrests and whether they were just misunderstandings with no bearing on the position. Her focal concern on protecting the children might have blinded her to the unfairness to the two unsuccessful applicants. This is a framing issue indicating that ethical fading may have occurred. Clearly, Patricia must be alert to the possibilities of various irrational, unconscious influences by, for instance, consulting with others, setting aside time for reflection, and considering what might happen if her decision appeared on the front page of tomorrow's newspaper.

Source: Case adapted from Sharp, Aguirre, and Kickham (2010, Case 48).

ORGANIZATIONAL STRUCTURE

The evolution from the "old" to the "new" public service has resulted in flatter organizational structures that are increasingly modifying or replacing hierarchical models. The former public service emerged from industrial-era government typified by centralized bureaucracies, routine standard operating procedures, and limited decision-making discretion. The new public service is defined as a postindustrial model typified by horizontal networks rather than vertical hierarchy, "flattened" agencies, cross-sector service delivery, and shared leadership structures. These changes bring managers into closer contact with employees, thereby potentially facilitating the communication of values. Networked organizations can enhance communication among different sections of the enterprise and foster employee interaction, even if they are not part of the same team. The resulting interactions should help managers and leaders align organizational values with diverse employee values, and encourage personnel to develop behaviors integral to the organizational mission that may not flow from their existing value orientations.

Only by understanding the motivations and behavior of colleagues, and the different norms on which these are based, can values be synthesized or prioritized in ways that correspond to the agency's overall goals. Decentralization measures used to enhance organizational performance also can be used to produce a culture that helps translate varied values into a unified public service mission (Barrett, 2006, 199–200).

An organization can complement the new public service by encouraging honorable public service as compared to traditional civil service administration. As shown in Table 8.3, such a shift is animated by citizen-like commitments instead of bureaucratic administration.

	TABLE 8.3	Comparing Honorable Public Service With Civil Service Administration

	Public Service as Responsible Citizenship	Civil Service as Program Administration
Guiding Documents	Declaration of Independence and the U.S. Constitution	Agency-specific law and regulation
Ethical Touchstone	Oath of Office (moral obligation)	Code of Ethics (regulatory and legal observance)
Orientation to Public Service	Public service as a calling Public servant as trustee	Government employment as a job Government employee as a delegate
Orientation to the U.S. Constitution	A work in progress, toward the achievement of the Preamble's promise	A rulebook and a guide to permissible action
Goal	The success of the "American experiment" in republican government	Program effectiveness/efficiency
Justice Achieved Through	Benevolence, charity, love	Adherence to law and program success
Key Metaphor	The public as a commons	Government as a business
Time Orientation	Past, present and future	The short-term present
Key Audience	Citizens	Customers
Key Expectation of the Public	Responsible and engaged citizenship	Consumer of government goods and services
Approach to the Public	Engage and learn	Serve and guide
Engagement in Political Management	High—in service to the common good and regime values	Low—in service to neutral competence
Focus for Education of the Public Servant	Constitutional thinking, regime values, ethical behavior	Professional expertise and administrative excellence
Risk from Failure	Shame	Loss of power, pay, and perquisites

Source: Adapted from Newell (2016, December 13).

VALUES STATEMENTS

Kenneth Kernaghan (2003) identifies the values statement as the centerpiece for integrating values into public service. His analysis focuses on ways to embed values into organizational structures, processes, and systems. Statements alone do not promote value integration—efforts must be made to align values with actions—but they can furnish general guidance to aid in the creation of ethics codes and more detailed provisions customized to particular units. The challenge begins with identifying public service values and then assimilating them into the institutional culture, management processes, and practices. Christopher Bauer

(2016) suggests six essentials when creating a values statement: make it organization wide, keep it brief (four to eight values), write it with as few words as possible, identify only the most important values, vet the statement with everyone in the organization, and take the time to do it right. Thus, human resource management strategies can be designed to implement agency values through hiring, promotion, performance appraisal, training, and termination. During a job interview, commitment to the value of "meeting citizen needs," for instance, can be strengthened by asking applicants to provide examples of how their past actions support the goal of responding effectively to the general public (Berman & West, 2012).

Values integration requires leaders to set the tone in the organization and promote, protect, and manage the desired norms. Managers can hone moral insight and teach personnel how to translate values into praiseworthy behavior by emphasizing priorities, highlighting the role and importance of ethics, and providing feedback on behavior. An illustration of feedback a manager could provide to an employee might be, "I appreciate your telling me that you are related to a candidate for the job we are seeking to fill." Dynamic interaction between leaders and employees is central to the process of aligning values with the organizational mission.

PSYCHOLOGICAL CONTRACTS

The psychological contract is another device that helps both parties in the employment relationship—the agency leadership and the individual employee—to understand reciprocal obligations. These contracts are typically informal agreements that seek to increase commitment to the organization and its mission by clarifying expectations, addressing ambiguity, and establishing a balance between expectations and contributions (Berman & West, 2003; Guest, 2000). Once consensus is reached on core organizational values, managers work with individuals to develop a contract that translates values into performance-specific obligations (e.g., more timely response to citizens' service requests).

Psychological contracts enhance personal well-being by fostering a sense of security through "mutual commitment on the part of managers and employees to shared ideals and values, and shared organizational identity" (Bruce, 2000, 136). By emphasizing the multifaceted components of spiritual and professional development, these agreements help employees "bring their whole selves" to work, while concurrently communicating departmental values and reinforcing organizational culture in daily work (Selden, 2009, 63–64, 87). Verbal contracts promote ethical behavior and prevent devolution into "anti-ethics," while also making personnel accountable to each other, as well as to management (Barrett, 2006, 114; Bruce, 2000).

OATHS AND CODES

An oath of office may share similarities with codes of ethics, a core element of a profession and a key component in an ethics program. Both raise the question of what difference such promises or commitments might make when taken seriously. An example of a government oath follows:

> Federal Oath of Office
> I, [name], do solemnly swear (or affirm) that I will support and defend the Constitution of the United States against all enemies, foreign and domestic; that I will bear true faith and allegiance to the same; that I take this obligation freely, without any mental reservation or purpose of evasion; and that I will well and faithfully discharge the duties of office on which I am about to enter. So help me God. (5 U.S.C. & 3331)

No shallow legalism, an oath of office is profound moral commitment that "binds the conscience" and appeals to a higher authority (Rohr, 1986, Ch. 4). It is what distinguishes the public servant from those in other organizations.

In the private arena, Harvard Business School students, with the support of their dean, developed the MBA Oath (www.mbaoath.org). The testament includes statements such as, "I will understand and uphold, in letter and spirit, the laws and contracts governing my conduct and that of my enterprise." While it may be valid to question the efficacy of oaths, it is also fair to ask if circumstances can be created in which they are effective. For example, what might have happened if oaths were taken at the start of meetings? Would they be more impactful then? Are oaths often dismissed because they are ineffective, or are they ineffective because they are dismissed? Scott Eblin (2010) answers, "Who knows? One thing I do know, however, is what doesn't get said, doesn't get heard." In sum, an oath is one way organizations instill and reinforce core values in their members and they serve as useful reminders of obligations such as faithful discharge of duties.

There are two types of code: conduct codes (Exhibit 8.1) and ethics codes (Exhibit 8.2). The former delineates—often in considerable detail—legislative and executive legal restraints placed on employees that typically prohibit use of public position for private gain, gifts, conflicts of interest, nepotism, and political activity. Sanctions are levied for violations of conduct codes. Ethics codes may be promulgated by governments or professional associations, and, typically, are aspirational in nature (Bruce, 1996). These codes, relatively brief and general, represent a collective recognition of professional responsibilities to nurture an environment wherein ethical behavior is the norm. Such canons are controversial, as opinions of them range from pointless and unnecessary to useful and important. What might be said is that codes are more likely to have indirect, rather than direct, effects as they can serve as a "signpost," leading employees to consult other employees and organizational policies; a "shield," allowing personnel to better challenge dubious actions; and an "alarm," encouraging individuals to report wrongdoing (Schwartz, 2011, 280). While codes cannot "solve" ethical conundrums, they do set standards, identify duties, and provide principles against which to assess behavior.

To be taken seriously, managers need to translate code generalities into guidance for specific situations. Codes in government agencies, nonprofit and philanthropic organizations, and professional organizations, such as the American Society of Public Administration

EXHIBIT 8.1	**Code of Conduct Sample**

United Nations (1996) Principles of the International Code for Public Officials

I. General Principles

1. A public office, as defined by national law, is a position of trust, implying a duty to act in the public interest. Therefore, the ultimate loyalty of public officials shall be to the public interests of their country as expressed through democratic institutions of government.

2. Public officials shall ensure that they perform their duties and functions efficiently, effectively and with integrity, in accordance with laws or administrative practices. They shall at all times seek to ensure that the public resources for which they are responsible are administered in the most effective and efficient manner.

3. Public officials shall be attentive, fair, and impartial in the performance of their functions and, in particular, in their relations with the public. They shall at no time afford any undue preferential treatment to any group or individual or improperly discriminate against any group or individual, or otherwise abuse the power and authority vested in them.

II. Conflict of Interest and Disqualification

1. Public officials shall not use their official authority for the improper advancement of their own or their family's personal or financial interest. They shall not engage in any transaction, acquire any position or function or have any financial, commercial or other comparable interest that is incompatible with their office, functions and duties or the discharge thereof.

2. Public officials, to the extent required by their position, shall, in accordance with laws or administrative policies, declare business, commercial and financial interests or activities undertaken for financial gain that may raise a possible conflict of interest. In situations of possible or perceived conflict of interest between the duties and private interests of public officials, they shall comply with the measures established to reduce or eliminate such conflict of interest.

3. Public officials shall at no time improperly use public moneys, property, services or information that is acquired in the performance of, or as a result of, their official duties for activities not related to their official work.

4. Public officials shall comply with measures established by law or by administrative policies in order that after leaving their official positions they will not take improper advantage of their previous office.

III. Disclosure of Assets

1. Public officials shall, in accord with their position and as permitted or required by law and administrative policies, comply with requirements to declare or to disclose personal assets and liabilities, as well as, if possible, those of their spouses and/or dependants.

IV. Acceptance of Gifts or other Favours

1. Public officials shall not solicit or receive directly or indirectly any gift or other favour that may influence the exercise of their functions, the performance of their duties or their judgment.

V. Confidential Information

1. Matters of a confidential nature in the possession of public officials shall be kept confidential unless national legislation, the performance of duty or the needs of justice strictly require otherwise. Such restrictions shall also apply after separation from service.

VI. Political Activity

1. The political or other activity of public officials outside the scope of their office shall, in accordance with laws and administrative policies, not be such as to impair public confidence in the impartial performance of their functions and duties.

Source: United Nations (1996).

Exhibit 8.2	**Code of Ethics Sample**
	Code of Ethics for U.S. Government Service

Adopted July 11, 1958 Resolved by the House of Representatives {the Senate concurring}, that it is the sense of the Congress that the following Code of Ethics should be adhered to by all Government employees, including officeholders.

Code of Ethics for Government Service

Any person in Government service should:

1. Put loyalty to the highest moral principles and to country above loyalty to Government persons, party, or department.

2. Uphold the Constitution, laws, and legal regulations of the United States and of all governments therein and never be a party to their evasion.

3. Give a full day's labor for a full day's pay; giving to the performance of his duties his earnest effort and best thought.

4. Seek to find and employ more efficient and economical ways of getting tasks accomplished.

5. Never discriminate unfairly by the dispensing of special favors or privileges to anyone, whether for remuneration or not; and never accept for himself or his family, favors or benefits under circumstances which might be construed by reasonable persons as influencing the performance of his governmental duties.

6. Make no private promises of any kind binding upon the duties of office, since a Government employee has no private word which can be binding on public duty.

7. Engage in no business with the Government, either directly or indirectly which is inconsistent with the conscientious performance of his governmental duties.

8. Never use any information coming to him confidentially in the performance of governmental duties as a means for making private profit.

9. Expose corruption wherever discovered.

10. Uphold these principles, ever conscious that public office is a public trust.

Source: *House Ethics Manual* (n.d.).

(ASPA) and the International City/County Management Association (ICMA), all state that it is essential to be impartial, not to unfairly favor (or appear to favor) anyone in the performance of duties, and to avoid conflicts of interest or their appearance. These provisions, however, are often vague and open to interpretation. The ICMA code, to illustrate, states, "Members should disclose any personal relationship to the governing body in any instance where there could be the appearance of a conflict of interest." The language leaves the types ("instances") and nature ("appearance of conflict of interest") of specific encounters vulnerable to a variety of interpretations. Other expressed values, such as loyalty, honesty, promise keeping, and privacy, are also susceptible to different definitions. Exhibit 8.3 compares the theory and practice of codes in the auditing profession.

While less than everything, codes are more than nothing, as oaths and codes provide a standard against which behavior can be assessed. Indeed, arguments against them fail when asked for the philosophical grounds for rejection and for practical alternatives. Few observers suffer from the delusion that oaths and codes will dramatically improve conduct. These documents do, however, function as enabling devices to strive for high ideals and as record of professional consensus.

INSTITUTIONALIZING ETHICS CULTURAL COMPETENCY

A more valuable question than efficacy is how oaths and codes are developed and what developmental activities accompany them. They should be a part of a larger effort to nourish the organizational culture by offering incentives, reducing opportunities for corruption, and increasing risk of unethical behavior. The strategy, designed and implemented by a

| EXHIBIT 8.3 | **Organizational Ethics and the Case of Auditing** |

Auditing standards and procedures, George Lowenstein believes, virtually guarantee unethical behavior:

> In theory, auditors are supposed to represent the interests of external users of financial statements. They are paid by the company they audit ... who can hire or fire them ... Moreover, auditors often socialize with company management. The American Institute of Certified Public Accountants acknowledges the pressures on auditors, but argues that personal integrity is sufficient for objectivity, ... maintaining that "members should accept the obligation to act in a way that will serve the public interest ... and demonstrate commitment to professionalism." (1996: 225–226)

Lowenstein thinks this standard is entirely unattainable for most auditors because those affected by misrepresentation are statistical in contrast to organization executives who would be personally impacted by a negative opinion. And, such an opinion would likely mean immediate loss of business. Further, financial records are inherently ambiguous, so it is easy to rationalize departures from standards.

Sam McCall, the past national president of the Association of Government Accountants, recognized by the AICPA as Outstanding CPA in Government for Career Contributions, and member of The Institute of Internal Auditor's American Hall of Distinguished Audit Practitioners responded:

> The public's desire for reliable financial statements is the reason an independent auditing profession exists. It is made up of dedicated individuals, who have demonstrated their knowledge of accounting and auditing standards by passing the national Certified Public Accountant examination and who are licensed by state Boards of Accountancy. There is additional oversight audit by the Securities and Exchange Commission, the Public Company Accounting Oversight Board, the Government Accountability Office, the U.S. Department of Labor, and other federal, state, and local authorities.
>
> As to Lowenstein's assertions, it is true that an auditor is unlikely to issue a qualified opinion when minor monetary losses occur. The auditor's opinion is based on whether the financial statements are "fairly stated" and presented in accordance with Generally Accepted Accounting Principles (GAAP). The auditor is responsible for providing reasonable, not absolute, assurance that the statements are free of material misstatement, whether caused by error or fraud.
>
> As to loss of friendship, a contract, or unemployment, no auditor would knowingly jeopardize their license and career because of such factors. The profession is clear that auditors should honor the public trust, perform work with integrity, and be independent in fact and appearance.
>
> The author also states that auditors may adapt to gradual changes in the company's financial condition and arrive at judgments consistent with self-interest rather than actual figures. The profession provides guidance when there are threats to independence caused by familiarity, undue influence, and self-interest. When these occur, the auditor is required to address and document them in the working papers by identifying safeguards (actions to eliminate or reduce the threat) or consider resignation from the audit.
>
> Nonetheless, there have been audit failures that have tarnished the profession. These incidents lend support to the view that it is difficult for the auditor to be independent and

think of the public interest at the same time the auditor is paid by the organization they audit.

For internal auditors, maintaining integrity and objectivity is challenging because the Chief Audit Executive (CAE) often has a dual reporting responsibility to both the Chief Executive Officer (CEO) and to the Board of Trustees. Since the CEO is the one that normally recommends raises and promotions, some have asserted the CAE may be less likely to report issues that cast the CEO in a bad light. A 2015 IIA survey found that 49 percent of CAE's were told not to perform work in high-risk areas and 32 percent were told to work in low-risk areas. Should the auditor succumb to such direction and undue influence, that would be a reflection on the auditor and not on the standards the auditor is professionally bound to follow. A company's Board of Trustees and audit committee should want to know about unacceptable risk posing a threat to operations and should fully expect the auditor to report those risks.

Most audit failures occur because the auditors lacked independence, placed firm profit ahead of their responsibility, or did not follow GAAS (Generally Accepted Auditing Standards). When company and auditor actions have been determined to be egregious, there have been significant consequences. Companies of note include Enron, WorldCom, and Bernard L. Madoff Investment Securities. Affected audit firms include Arthur Andersen (Enron and WorldCom) and Friehling & Horowitz (Madoff Securities). Firms convicted of wrongdoing lost their ability to file financial statements with the SEC and the privilege to practice. Individual independent auditors associated with the firms were sanctioned by their respective State Boards of Accountancy.

What is clear is that government cannot regulate greed or prevent persons or companies from committing fraud. Yet, Lowenstein offered little in the way of a better system of independent auditing. To be fair, since Lowenstein's comments, there has been a movement toward establishing Board appointed audit committees made up of financially literate members, requiring audit committee charters, and tasking the committee with selecting the external audit firm. Audit Committees have also addressed auditor independence when an audit firm has a multiple year contract by requiring a change in audit partners at least once every five years.

CPAs do not produce tangible products such as manufacturing goods. They provide a service which is an independent opinion on the accuracy of financial statements. The acceptance of the opinion is dependent on the public trusting the audit was conducted with integrity. For an auditor or firm to commit dishonorable acts is to jeopardize the accountants' license, public confidence, and the profession itself. That is why the word "Public" is so prominent in the CPA, Certified Public Accountant, designation. (McCall, personal communication, November 24, 2017)

Behavioral ethics research (Chapter 7) demonstrates that people tend to be overconfident in their ethicality; indeed, there is some evidence that the mere exposure to money increases unethical activity. Unaware of or doubting the effect of blind spots, such as motivated reasoning and ethical fading, those exposed to such phenomena usually believe they are immune to their influence. When there is a conflict of interest, it is especially difficult for well-meaning individuals to see things objectively. This was poignantly noted by Upton Sinclair who observed, "It is difficult to get a man to understand something, when his salary depends on his not understanding it."

In the end, do you think Lowenstein's or McCall's claims are the more illuminating? Why?

Source: Lowenstein (1996).

representative task force of employees, is to conduct a self-generated needs assessment. Depending on the results of the task force efforts, initiatives could include:

- decision-making mechanisms (e.g., use of an ethics board, an "angel's" advocate, or an ombudsperson),
- promotional activities (e.g., posting the code and reprinting it in agency reports; establishing an awards program), and
- personnel system changes (e.g., recruitment, training [see below], performance evaluation processes including a specification of the ethical dimensions of tasks in job descriptions, independent grievance processes, whistleblower protections, and sanctions).

Periodic ethics audits—document reviews, interviews, vulnerability assessments, survey data, and evaluation of existing systems—provide an ongoing appraisal of the effectiveness of the program. Indeed, the Program Effectiveness Index could be used to assess ethical decision making, organizational justice, and freedom of expression (Jacobs, 2017, July 28).

Stated differently, leaders should "ask for trouble." If the old rule was never surprise the boss, then the new rule should be to tell her about the problem to foster learning and accountability. The focus, then, is on prevention and solutions, not blame and consequences. When dealing with issues is a natural part of daily work, not something to be feared or avoided, people become more confident and competent (Mabry, 2017, September 6). To address small problems before they become big ones, the "bad-news-never-travels-up" norm should be discarded; instead, agency leadership should clearly support those identifying issues, ensure the problems are investigated, visibly protect and reward the employees, and take them and their colleagues to lunch (Behn, 2017).

Several more types of institutionalization merit notice. First, Lewis and Gilman (2012) recommend the use of Ethical Impact Statements. This tool, modeled after environmental impact statements (prepared prior to major federal decisions affecting the natural environment), can "assist in setting priorities and realistic objectives, identify early on the problems and needed corrections in policy or regulation, pinpoint unsettled issues and unanticipated effects . . . and inform decision makers and the public" (267–268). Second, the U.S. State Department has a longstanding, effective Dissent Channel that permits Foreign Service Officers to directly contest policy with senior executives. The Secretary of State and his staff reply to messages within 60 days and employees are shielded from retaliation.

Various forms of institutionalization, then, can enhance organizational life. An example from history is the 20th-century adoption of the merit system in federal government. Yet that transformation can be a slow, frustrating process (e.g., torture of alleged terrorists, and who is and who is not honored for their roles, as shown in Exhibit 8.4; also, consult Bowman et al., 2010, Ch. 5).

All of these initiatives can help employees translate values into honorable behavior. Training, in particular, can focus on making all personnel aware of their responsibilities by understanding ethical principles, behavioral standards, and legal requirements—not merely

| EXHIBIT 8.4 | **Honoring Those Who Said No to Torture** |

Thus far, only those public officials who approved torture, not those who vigorously protested against it as an abandonment of the rule of law and morality, have been honored. In 2004, President George W. Bush awarded the nation's highest civilian honor, the Presidential Medal of Freedom, to the former Central Intelligence Agency director who had authorized "enhanced" interrogation. In 2006, the Army general responsible for prisoners at Guantánamo was given the Distinguished Service Medal. One of the lawyers responsible for the Bush administration's "torture memos" received awards from the Justice Department, the Defense Department, and the National Security Agency.

President Barack Obama has since (a) prohibited cruelty as official American policy, (b) retained illegal rendition and detention practices in modified form, (c) opposed an official inquiry into the efficacy and legality interrogation methods, and (d) resisted investigation and prosecution of those responsible. Maintaining that the country should look forward, not back, the president appears to consider torture to be an unfortunate policy choice instead of war crimes in violation of U.S. laws and international treaties.

While it may be impossible to prove that degrading and inhumane treatment never works, there is a great deal of evidence suggesting that it is an ineffective way to gather reliable intelligence. In 2006, for example, the Defense Department's Intelligence Science Board found that there is no scientific evidence to demonstrate that cruelty produces valid information (see Case Study 11.4). But framing the controversy in terms of the efficiency of torture misses the point: "This is," as Senator John McCain (2011) indicates, "a moral debate. It is about who we are." The only way to resolve such a dispute is on the basis of principle. It is noteworthy that most of those who are willing to accept painfully excruciating methods are unwilling, on the grounds of national security, to document cases that they argue justified extreme techniques; they are also not prepared to state that, as a matter of principle, they favor torture (Neier, 2011):

> A refusal to torture, like a refusal to use terrorism, is a basic dividing line between civilized and uncivilized peoples. . . . The American republic rests upon the centrality of human liberty and dignity. . . . We must secure our principles as we secure our nation. (Bandow, 2011)

One way to do that is to recognize that those civil and military public servants who stayed true to American values, and stood up against cruelty, are worthy of a wide range of civilian and military commendations. Honoring them is a way of encouraging the best in our public servants, now and in the future. It is a way of honoring the best in ourselves, a nation and people worthy of Jefferson, Washington, and Madison.

Note: In February 2011, George W. Bush cancelled a trip to Switzerland where alleged victims of torture intended to file a criminal complaint against him.

Sources: Adapted from Bandow (2011), Jaffer and Siems (2011), McCain (2011), and Neier (2011).

as just another organizational routine, but rather as integral to the core of the organization. To be effective, the program should engender recognition of critical values and how they may be interpreted in different contexts. One creative Federal Bureau of Investigation educational program, designed to ensure that trainees keep morality in mind, includes a visit to the Washington, D.C., Holocaust Museum. Trainees must learn not only how to follow policies, but also how to make decisions that speak to their spirit in situations not addressed by value statements, oaths, and codes. In addition to training, outreach activities—having personnel at all levels meet those who they serve, staff call-in public information and help lines, monitor social media, conduct web chats—will bring employees into contact with those affected by agency decisions (Newell, 2015, 161–162).

Overall, a self-governance approach to ethical competency is needed. Beyond understanding policies and statutes, de las Fuentes, Willmuth, and Yarrow (2005) recommend that the workforce should learn to (a) develop moral reasoning skills, (b) appreciate the cultural contexts from which beliefs derive, and (c) comprehend the values on which codes are built. Rest's (1983) model is a useful guide for honing reasoning abilities, recognizing a dilemma, employing a cognitive understanding of the issues involved, deciding on a course of action, and implementing an appropriate response. Recognizing the principles on which codes are written—duty, justice, equity, utility, public interest—can provide the basis for critically evaluating or justifying actions, when simply referring to a code is not sufficient. Assessments of ethical competency can be conducted using "360-degree" evaluations, whereby all of those in the learning environment provide feedback to the trainee. Critical incident methodology can also be useful in noting whether, or in what ways, the individual has recognized a dilemma and responded in an ethical manner using appropriate (or inappropriate) sensitivity. Finally, case studies, role plays, and vignettes based on ethics codes allow trainees to demonstrate logic and decision making, and help reveal the thought processes used in code interpretation.

Another ethical infrastructure dimension is the cultivation of cultural competency. Organizational values are not always understood by employees, even when managers attempt to communicate them in a variety of ways (Paarlberg & Perry, 2007). Further, organizational values, as determined by leaders and managers, are most effectively operationalized when they correspond to employees' existing values. This receptivity requires skillful values management within a rapidly changing public service. The intent is to develop cultural competency among organizational members given the multiple identities of the public workforce, including race, culture, ethnicity, gender, age, religion, disability, and sexual orientation. Additional differences in communication style, education, work style, organizational role, sectorial location, economic status, national/geographic origin, and conceptions of work (as a job, a career, or a calling) further complicate implementation of values management initiatives. What are some of the strategies and issues involved in cultivating shared organizational values in a diverse workforce and linking those with employees' existing values? How can ethical and cultural competency be promoted given system reforms and increased workforce heterogeneity?

A model based on the work of Arredondo et al. (1996, 11–27) is helpful in understanding how cultural competency contributes to ethical competency. Multicultural competency encompasses an acknowledgment of one's personal assumptions, values, and biases; an understanding of the different orientation of diverse colleagues; and the skill to think creatively. Arredondo and colleagues identify characteristics of culturally skilled personnel: (a) recognition of how personal cultural background and experiences shape attitudes, values, and biases; (b) knowledge about personal racial and cultural heritage and how these affect perspectives and behavior; and (c) skills acquired through educational, consultative, and training experiences to improve working with culturally diverse populations.

To comprehend the worldview of diverse co-workers, Arrendondo et al. (1996) point out that culturally skilled staff must be aware of prevailing stereotypes; discern how race, culture, ethnicity, and religion may influence attitudes and behaviors; and become involved with minority individuals outside the workplace. Their objective is to respect co-workers' values, recognize how convictions may affect work habits, be alert that the beliefs of cultural groups may clash, and be capable of promoting accurate and appropriate verbal and nonverbal communication among various groups.

Cultural competency alone is not sufficient in establishing norms that form the basis for individual and organizational ethical behavior. Recognition of cultural differences must be matched by an attempt to reach consensus on a set of universal values that transcend particular belief systems, create value links among different groups, and thus lead to a higher form of value formation (Barrett, 2006). Cultural competency and value formation must take place within the context of the overall mission, for organizations cannot simply reflect the sum total of the beliefs of their employees. Without a clear mission based on a cohesive set of values, there is the danger that organizational fragmentation and empire building lead to self-interest prevailing over the common good (116).

Diversity management plays a critical role in combining cultural competency with the integration of organizational values necessary to enhance performance. It is the process by which employee diversity is turned into a creative force by producing a synergy of values through workshops and activities that challenge "the way things are usually done." Diversity by itself may not be productive; in fact, without the proper management, it may result in poor morale, personnel problems, and decreased work unit effectiveness (Choi, 2009; Dobbin, Kalev, & Kelly, 2007; Pitts, 2005; Pitts & Jarry, 2007). Unmanaged diversity on company boards, for instance, has proved to be divisive and unproductive (Manzoni, Strebel, & Barsoux, 2010). Only through concerted management techniques can the creative potential of a multicultural workforce be fulfilled to contribute to the organizational mission (Collins, 2010, 107). Possible methods include sensitivity training, team building, mentoring programs, and discussion of communication styles.

Managing ethics in institutions is not just about implementing specific initiatives. Rather, the ethical context or climate of the organization is at least as important. That context includes such elements as leadership, reward systems, perceived "fairness" of the organization, and ethics as a topic of daily conversation (Weaver, Treviño, & Cochran, 1999). Ethics programs can help maintain a moral course in organizations and support employee growth. While they have many benefits, they should be established not simply for instrumental reasons, but because it is the right thing to do (McNamara, 1998). A viable infrastructure includes exemplary officials, meaningful oaths and codes, a legal framework, accountability mechanisms,

| EXHIBIT 8.5 | Ethics Training |

Ethics instruction is a central component of any meaningful strategy for promoting an organizational environment. While both the tangible controls and the intangible nudges that constitute an organization's ethical infrastructure are essential, training is the key complement to both. It can provide realistic simulations of "the ways things are done around here," thereby increasing the probability of compliance. The resultant sharpening of ethical awareness and problem solving can bolster proper behavior. Yet not all instructional programs are created equal.

West and Berman (2004) found that although ethics training initiatives are widespread in city governments, they vary widely in both purpose and form. Following Paine's (1994) high-road/low-road distinction, training can either take the low road, serving "defensive" purposes such as avoiding embarrassment or adverse legal action, or it can take the high road, furthering "aspirational purposes" like contributing to a positive organizational culture or developing employees' critical thinking skills.

These differing approaches are far from merely symbolic—their divergent emphases influence the content of instruction. Organizations that "take the high road" are more likely to delve into topics such as transparency and the importance of ethics, whereas those that opt for the low road focus on technical understandings of issues such as conflict of interest. The form that programs take is also important. Live instruction that is "reality based" and "practical"—exercises that include hypothetical scenarios and case studies and provide opportunities to practice decision–making skills—is the most effective pedagogical approach (West & Berman, 2004, 195–197).

Through the use of statistical models that suggest causality, it was found that "training is associated with fostering organizational cultures of openness, accountability, and performance that, in turn, are associated with increased employee productivity" (West & Berman, 2004, 202). This is not an all-too-surprising conclusion; a recurring theme of this book is that acting ethically and acting effectively often go hand in hand. The finding is nevertheless worthy of careful attention, as approximately 85 percent of city governments use training for at least some defensive purposes (195). They frequently pass up opportunities to enhance their strategies by employing such techniques as incorporating ethics training into new-employee orientation (197; for an account of similar shortcomings in state government, see Menzel, 2012, 82–86). Carefully crafting an instructional program should therefore be a primary concern of any manager seeking to grow an ethically oriented organization.

effective human resource systems, and a supportive citizenry. In many ways, as Exhibit 8.5 demonstrates, training opportunities serve as a centerpiece of an ethics program. Yet, to the extent that such initiatives rely on untested assumptions and models about rationality—at the expense of understanding why people behave unethically—they have very real limitations in affecting change (see Chapter 7 for a discussion of behavioral ethics).

No strategy will be without criticism, but if all proposals are rejected until perfection is guaranteed, then improvement is unlikely. In the meantime, agencies should plant and cultivate standards by which an individual can measure his or her activities, encourage the correction of deficiencies, and aid in the identification and minimization of those institutional conditions that lead to unethical actions. This effort should establish a culture that encourages the asking of right questions to facilitate discussion. Most problems, including ethical ones, are more easily prevented than they are corrected. Effective prevention is an initiative that includes instruction, celebrates exemplary employees, holds wrongdoers accountable, and integrates ethics into the routines of the department. The issue is not whether norms of conduct will be communicated, but rather what they are, how they are disseminated, and whether all personnel are fully conscious of the ethical dimensions of work. Such a program can provide a point of departure (like the top of a jigsaw puzzle box), offer guidance to know what to do in the absence of a specific rule, and serve as an empowering device to strive for high ideals. Not failure, but low aim is a tragedy.

CONCLUSION

Ethics provides coherence to organizational policies and individual behavior. Without consistent behavior, there would be no working together (Bowman, 1981). It is imperative to develop a widely shared vocabulary of ethics in institutions. Men and women in workplaces that value and nurture a reputation for integrity are the surest safeguard against corruption. If ethics, the cornerstone of organizational practice, is not explicit to each person, then the prospects of making praiseworthy decisions and accepting responsibility are diminished.

The steps detailed in this chapter will not by themselves build a moral community. The system cannot operate without leaders with formal authority, but what really makes it work is moral authority (Freidman, 2017, June 21). Ethics programs can only reinforce a moral climate, but they cannot create it—that remains the function of leadership. Ethics initiatives are difficult to establish and maintain (Gilman, 2005). Those involved must embed moral imperatives into the work of the agency. Underlying formal systems are influential informal norms that teach employees behaviors that are really expected at work. It is the task of leadership to align formal obligations with informal practices. In the absence of such an approach, expediency is likely to dominate. If organizations do not take action to prevent unethical conduct, it is an abdication of responsibility and they should be held responsible for the misconduct that occurs within them.

***

Mostly, we are good when it makes sense. A good society is one that makes sense of being good.

—Ian McEwan

FOR DISCUSSION

1. Describe differences between immoral, amoral, and moral management. Identify examples of organizations that appear to be representative of each type, including those of which you are or have been a member (e.g., clubs; colleges; or business, nonprofit, or governmental organizations).

2. While an organizational ethics infrastructure can enhance individual judgment, it is not a substitute for it. Examine this claim.

3. The nonprofit sector is sometimes referred to as "America's conscience." Indeed, the sector historically has escaped the kind of scrutiny directed at government and business. Ironically, however, not-for-profit agencies have not generally developed ethical infrastructures common in the other sectors. This is especially surprising because their work often involves society's most vulnerable members. Discuss.

4. Discuss some ways that the informal ethics behaviors (e.g., hallway conversations, peer reporting, social rewards or punishment based on work-group approval) may reinforce or be in conflict with formal ethics structures (e.g., codes of conduct, core value statements, ethics training).

EXERCISES

1. Complete:

   • Analyze the code of ethics used by your university or place of employment using the ethics trinity (Chapter 7). Is the code largely based on results, rules, or rectitude? How could it be enhanced?
   • Visit http://www.aspanet.org/public/ and go to the "Resources" tab, then click "Code of Ethics" to view the American Society for Public Administration ethics code. Critique it.
   • Provide brief general background information on the organizational size, sector, and geographic location of an organization familiar to you. Compare and contrast the ethical infrastructure of the organization with the material in this chapter.

2. You have a friend from a foreign country who is returning home to attend medical school. Unfortunately, admissions officials expect bribes. Your friend has asked for your help. What do you say and why? (This scenario is based on Randy Cohen's 2004 column in the *New York Times*.) Your response could employ materials in this chapter, the ethics triad and behavioral ethics (Chapter 7), or Kohlberg's moral development theory (Chapter 4).

3. Vienna subways, inexpensive and efficient, work on the honor system. There are no ticket turnstiles at stations and no routine ticket checks. However purchasing a ticket is a good idea, as undercover agents randomly ask to see tickets. Riders with no tickets are fined $100.

   Comment on this system in light of compliance-based and integrity-based organizational ethics systems. Consider these points:

   • You can have an ethical organization but not a quality organization; you cannot have a quality organization without being ethical.

- Does removing turnstiles encourage passenger integrity or does it do more harm than good?
- Does random checking without warning constitute integrity-based practice?

4. Respond to these claims:

- "If you think you can get away with it, don't do it." Texas senator Carl Parker
- "To be the best, you must be able to handle the worst." Wilson Kanadi

5. Summarize your notes and establish links between chapter and course objectives. Continue to do this as self-study exercise. While doing this, create sentence stems (see Chapter 1) for use in discussion.

6. Access and view "The Ghosts of Abu Ghraib" on YouTube.

REFERENCES

Anechiarico, F., & Jacobs, J. (1996). *The pursuit of absolute integrity: How corruption control makes government ineffective.* Chicago: University of Chicago Press.

Arrendondo, P., Toporek, R., Brown, S., Jones, J., Lock, D., Sanchez, J. et al. (1996). *Operationalization of the multicultural counseling competencies.* Alexandria, VA: American Counseling Association.

Bandow, D. (2011, June 13). Getting Osama Bin Laden: The case against torture. *Huffington Post.* Retrieved from http://huffingtonpost.com/doug-bandow/getting-osama-bin-laden-t_b_861451.html

Barrett, R. (2006). *Building a values-driven organization: A whole system approach to cultural transformation.* Burlington, MA: Butterworth-Heinemann.

Bauer, C. (2016). *An ethics thought—Six values statement essentials.* Nashville, TN: the author.

Behn, B. (2017). Take a whistleblower to lunch. *Performance Leadership Report.* Retrieved from https://thebehnreport.hks.harvard.edu/files/thebehnreport/files/behnreport_2017-8_aug.pdf

Berman, E., & West, J. (1994). Values management in local government. *Review of Public Personnel Administration, 14,* 6–23.

Berman, E., & West, J. (2003). Psychological contracts in local government: A preliminary survey. *Review of Public Personnel Administration, 23,* 267–285.

Berman, E., & West, J. (2012). Public values in special districts: A survey of managerial commitment. *Public Administration Review, 72,* 43–54.

Bowman, J. (1981). The management of ethics: Codes of ethics in organizations. *Public Personnel Management, 10,* 67–76.

Bowman, J. (1983). Ethical issues for the public manager. In W. Eddy (Ed.), *Handbook of organizational management* (pp. 69–89). New York: Marcel Dekker.

Bowman, J., West, J., & Beck, M. (2010). *The professional edge: Competencies in public service* (2nd ed.). Armonk, NY: M. E. Sharpe.

Bruce, W. (1996). Codes of ethics and codes of conduct. In J. Bowman (Ed.), *Public integrity annual* (pp. 23–30). Lexington, KY: Council of State Governments.

Bruce, W. (2000). Breaking the psychological contract: An act of anti-ethics. *Global Virtue Ethics Review, 2*(2), 134–174.

Carroll, A. (1987). In search of the moral manager. *Business Horizons, 30*, 7–15.

Choi, S. (2009). Diversity in the US federal government: Diversity management and employee turnover in federal agencies. *Journal of Public Administration Research and Theory, 19*, 603–630.

Cohen, R. (2004, October 10). Acceptable bribe. *New York Times*. Retrieved from http://www.nytimes.com/2004/10/10/magazine/10ETHICIST.html?n=Top%2fFeatures%2fMagazine%2fColumns%2fThe%20Ethicist&_r=0

Collins, D. (2010). Designing ethical organizations for spiritual growth and superior performance: An organization systems approach. *Journal of Management, Spirituality, and Religion, 7*, 95–117.

Dobbin, F., Kalev, A., & Kelly, E. (2007) Diversity management in corporate America. *Contexts, 6*(4), 21–28. Retrieved from https://scholar.harvard.edu/dobbin/files/2007_contexts_dobbin_kalev_kelly.pdf

Eblin, S. (2010, May 24). Why we need an MBA oath. *Government Executive*. Retrieved from http://www.govexec.com/excellence/executive-coach/2010/05/why-we-need-an-mba-oath/39874/

Freidman, T. (2017, June 21). Where did we the people go? *New York Times*. Retrieved from https://www.nytimes.com/2017/06/21/opinion/where-did-we-the-people-go.html

de las Fuentes, C., Willmuth, M., & Yarrow, C. (2005). Competency training in ethics education and practice. *Professional Psychology: Research and Practice, 36*, 362–366.

Gilman, S. (2005). *Ethics codes and codes of conduct as tools for promoting ethical and professional public service: Comparative successes and lessons*. PREM paper, Winter. Washington, DC: World Bank.

Guest, D. (2000). *The psychological contract in the public sector*. London: Chartered Institute of Personnel Development.

Heclo, H. (2008). *On thinking institutionally*. St. Paul, MN: Paradigm.

Hoekstra, A., Belling, A., & van der Heide, E. (2008). A paradigmatic shift in ethics and integrity management within the Dutch public sector? Beyond compliance—A practitioners' view. In L. Huberts, J. Maesschalck, & C. Jurkiewicz (Eds.), *Ethics and integrity of governance: Perspectives across frontiers* (pp. 143–158). Cheltenham: Edward Elgar.

House Ethics Manual: Code of Ethics for Government Service. (n.d.). Retrieved from http://www.house.gov/ethicsreform/Appendix_Code_of_Ethics.html

Jacobs, R. (2017, July 28). Building a 'core' culture: The public administrator as ethical leader and chief learning officer. *PA Times*. Retrieved from http://patimes.org/building-core-culture-public-administrator-ethical-leader-chief-learning-officer/

Jaffer, J., & Siems, L. (2011, April 17). Honoring those who said no. *New York Times*. Retrieved from http://www.nytimes.com/2011/04/28/opinion/28jaffer.html

Kernaghan, K. (2003). Integrating values into public service: The values statement as centerpiece. *Public Administration Review, 63*, 711–718.

Lewis, C., & Gilman, S. (2012). *The ethics challenge in public service* (3rd ed.). San Francisco: Jossey-Bass.

Lowenstein, G. (1996). Behavioral decision theory and business ethics: Skewed trade-offs between self and other. In Messick, D. & Tensbrunsel, A. (Eds.), *Codes of conduct: Behavioral research into business ethics* (pp.214–229). New York: Russell Sage Foundation.

Mabry, S. (2017, September 6). Why you should be asking for trouble. *Soul2Work*. Retrieved from https://soul2work.com/2017/09/why-you-should-be-asking-for-trouble/

Manzoni, J., Strebel, P., & Barsoux, J. (2010, January 25). Why diversity can backfire on company boards. *Wall Street Journal*, p. R3.

McCain, J. (2011, May 11). Bin Laden's death and the debate over torture. *Washington Post*. Retrieved from http://www.washintonpost.com/opinions/bin-ladens-death-and-the-debate-over-torture/2011/05/11

McNamara, C. (1998). *Complete guide to ethics management: An ethics toolkit for managers.* Retrieved from http://www.managementhelp.org/ethics/ethxgde.htm

Menzel, D. C. (2012). *Ethics management for public administrators: Leading and building organizations of integrity* (2nd ed.). Armonk, NY: M. E. Sharpe.

Neier, A. (2011, May 14). "Enhanced" to the point of torture. *Washington Post*. Retrieved from http://www.washintonpost.com/opinions/enhanced-to-the-pointof-torture/2011/05/013/AFQhDz2G

Newell, T. (2015). *To serve with honor: Doing the right thing in government*. Crozet, VA: Loftlands Press.

Newell, T. (2016, December 13). Beyond ethics: Honor and public service. *PA Times*. Retrieved from http://patimes.org/ethics-honor-public-service/

Organisation for Economic Co-operation and Development (OECD). (1996). *Ethics in the public service: Current issues and practice* (Public Management Occasional Papers No. 14).

Paarlberg, L., & Perry, J. (2007). Values management: Aligning employee values and organizational goals. *American Review of Public Administration, 37*, 387–408.

Paine, L. (1994). Managing for organizational integrity. *Harvard Business Review, 72*, 106–117.

Pitts, D. (2005). Diversity management, job satisfaction, and organizational performance: Evidence from federal agencies. *Public Administration Review, 69*, 328–338.

Pitts, D., & Jarry, E. (2007). Ethnic diversity and organizational performance: Assessing diversity effects at the managerial and street levels. *International Public Management Journal, 10*, 233–254.

Rest, J. R. (1983). Morality. In J. H. Flavell & E. M. Markman (Eds.), *Handbook of child psychology: Vol. 3: Cognitive Development* (pp. 556–629) (4th ed.). New York: John Wiley.

Rohr, J. (1986). *To run a constitution: Legitimacy of the administrative state*. Lawrence: University of Kansas Press.

Rohr, J. (1988). *Ethics for bureaucrats* (2nd ed.). New York: Marcel Dekker.

Schwartz, M. (2011). How to minimize corruption in business organizations: Developing and sustaining an ethical corporate culture. In R. Burke, E. Tomlinson, & C. Cooper (Eds.), *Crime and corruption in organizations: Why it occurs and what to do about it* (pp. 273–296). Farnham: Gower.

Selden, S. (2009). *Human capital: Tools and strategy for the public sector*. Washington, DC: CQ Press.

Sharp, B., Aguirre, G., & Kickham, K. (2010). *Managing in the public sector: A casebook in ethics and leadership*. New York: Pearson.

Thompson, D. (2009). Obama's ethics agenda: The challenge of coordinated change. *The Forum*, *7*, Article 8.

United Nations. (1996). *General Assembly Resolution 51/59: Action against corruption*. Retrieved from http://www.un.org/documents/ga/res/51/a51r059.htm

Wagner, B. (2016, March 29). Simple reasons why torture is still wrong. *Huffington Post*. Retrieved from http://www.huffingtonpost.com/brian-wagner/3-simple-reasons-why-tort_b_9557438.html

Weaver, G. R., Treviño, L. K., & Cochran, P. L. (1999). Integrated and decoupled corporate social performance: Management commitments, external pressures, and corporate ethics practices. *Academy of Management Journal*, *42*, 539–552.

West, J., & Berman, E. (2004). Ethics training in U.S. cities: Content, pedagogy, and impact. *Public Integrity*, *6*, 189–206.

9 Corruption Control

A people that values its privileges above its principles soon loses both.
—Dwight Eisenhower

One indication of failure to develop a robust ethics infrastructure in institutions is the presence of corruption. Because most of it is clandestine, no one really knows the magnitude of corruption—it is only possible to discuss the actual exposure of corruption. This secrecy makes it difficult to accurately gauge overall severity and trends; corruption may not be known to exist and, if discovered, may not be reported. Still, media coverage is more intensive (the sheer quantity of information) and extensive (the geographic spread of information) today than ever before, as pervasive corruption seems to be a common reality in the life of institutions. The previous chapter was an affirmative attempt to construct an ethical infrastructure in organizations; this one targets the absence of ethics by examining corruption and ways to deal with it. Objectives include an understanding of:

- the scope and definition of corruption,
- root causes of corruption in human nature and American history,
- individual and organizational ethical failure,
- moral hazards and gift giving,
- the role of scandals in civic life,
- reform efforts, and
- invalid reasons for not dealing with corruption.

An administrator can be lulled into a false sense of security if she assumes that organizational "right-doing" programs discussed in the last chapter will prevent wrongdoing. Given human frailty and institutional dysfunctions, there will always be the potential for corruption. That does not, however, relieve individuals and institutions of the obligation to mitigate it.

SCOPE AND MAGNITUDE OF CORRUPTION TODAY

The greatest evil is not now done in those sordid dens of crime that Dickens loved to paint . . . but is conceived and ordered . . . in clear, carpeted, warmed, well-lighted offices, by quiet men with white collars and cut fingernails and smooth-shaven cheeks who do not need to raise their voices.

—C. S. Lewis

Public and private organizations in the United States lose at least 6 percent of annual revenue (over $994 billion/year) to corruption, according to the Association of Certified Fraud Examiners (2016). One in four businesses loses more than $1 million annually; 76 percent of companies believe the problem is getting worse, and 76 percent believe the worst fraud could be prevented through adequate controls. In government, much of the public believes that government wastes nearly half of its tax dollars; expert estimates of spending lost to waste, fraud, or abuse range from 2 to 7 percent (Cooper, 2009; Nye, Zelikow, & King, 1997). Yet, looking just at the Pentagon, a 2015 internal study revealed that nearly one-fourth of its $580 billion budget was spent on administrative waste (Whitlock & Woodward, 2016, December 5).

Simple dollar losses in direct expenditures are an inadequate measure of total costs of corruption. For example, related expenses include legal fees, internal investigations and remedial actions, lost time and productivity, training, recruitment, and opportunities forgone due to damaged credibility. Burke, Tomlinson, and Cooper (2011, 16) argue that the price of corruption is "huge and includes less organizational and country growth, lower levels of public spending on education and healthcare, less revenue from taxes, greater political instability, and lower levels of direct foreign investment."

Globally, corruption is key to understanding many problems. Refugees drowning in the Mediterranean are fleeing corrupt states. International efforts to address to poverty are frequently undermined by corrupt governments. Corruption damages the global economy; the World Economic Forum estimates that it adds 10 percent to business costs, while the World Bank believes some $1 trillion is paid in bribes every year. Corruption threatens not only prosperity; it also threatens security. For instance, kidnapping of children and tourists for ransom as well as recruitment of fighters by extremist groups is facilitated by governmental oppression and corruption (Cameron, 2015, June 6).

The levy paid by society is not evenly distributed, as wrongdoing (a) harms the poor severely (by diverting services from those who need them the most), (b) strangles commercial growth (by driving legitimate companies out of business), and (c) saps support for public initiatives (by creating the perception that all programs are corrupt). Stated differently, when competent government and business—which provide the basis for economic development—are eroded, the only winners are the corrupt; the gains from corruption are specific and immediate, while the harms are diffuse and long-lasting.

While overall crime rates in the United States have flattened in recent years, there has been a marked increase in white-collar crime according to federal and state officials.[1] Despite the fact that corporate crime costs easily dwarf those of ordinary street crime, the federal government does not track the incidence and magnitude of the damage corporate crime causes—there is no national database for these crimes and their disposition. Even when enforcement of relevant anticorruption laws occurs, the penalties are often so low that they are easily absorbed as a cost of doing business.[2, 3] Not surprisingly, there is no shortage of problems, as news reports revealed "breathtaking" corruption in the wake of Hurricane Katrina in 2006 and that "pandemic" corruption occurred during the attempted reconstruction of Iraq (Rich, 2007). One in-depth study (Ashforth & Anand, 2003), in fact, examined how easily corruption becomes institutionalized—and normalized—in organizations to the point that it not only can neutralize the stigma of deviant conduct, but also can rationalize wrongdoing in socially desirable terms.

Other recent indicators of ignoble behavior in public and private sectors include the following:

- Every year the Multinational Monitor (http://multinationalmonitor.org) publishes its "Ten Worst Corporations of the Year," complete with a detailed analysis. A recent listing included AOL-Time Warner, Bank of America, Coca-Cola, General Electric, Wal-Mart, Merck, Monsanto, Nestle, News Corporation (owner of Fox News), Hardee's, Abbott Laboratories, Dow, Xerox, and numerous others that engaged in civil and criminal wrongdoing (many enterprises are repeat offenders).
- A study of the *Fortune* 100 found that 40 of the firms engaged in unethical behavior, suggesting that "the level of misconduct . . . is the highest in American history" (Clement, 2006, 317). As if to update that finding, Bank Whistleblowers United announced its Financial Fraud Lemons of the Week award was presented to the U.S. Department of Justice (Black, 2016, February 12).
- The Governmental Accountability Project (http://www.whistleblower.org) publishes an annual "Hall of Fame" and a "Hall of Shame," consisting of business and governmental organizations.
- Citizens for Responsibility and Ethics monitors government ethics, bringing egregious conduct to light and holding officials accountable for their misconduct (http://www.citizensforethics.org/); it also maintains an annual list of the top 10 scandals.
- The "Political Graveyard" (http://politicalgraveyard.com) is an extensive catalogue of transgressions by politicians.
- Transparency International (http://www.transparency.org) compiles a yearly "Global Corruption Barometer" and the "Corruption Perception Index."
- Global Integrity (http://www.globalintegrity.org) publishes an annual report and index that tracks governance and corruption trends.
- The Association of Certified Fraud Examiners sponsors an annual International Fraud Awareness Week.

The need for watchdog programs was dramatically illustrated by a 2010 U.S. Inspector General for Iraq Reconstruction report. It found not only that 96 percent of the $9 billion reconstruction monies were unaccounted for by the Defense Department, but also that the expenditures resulted in few successful reconstruction projects (Spoth, 2010). At the state level of government, a recent study measured the risks of corruption, as reflected in the strength of laws and policies designed to ensure transparency and accountability in government. It revealed that most states avoid public scrutiny; do not enact or enforce ethics laws; cut, consolidate, or eliminate auditing agencies; and allow corporate interests to dominate policy (Center for Public Integrity, Global Integrity, & Public Radio International, 2012). A state-by-state assessment of their vulnerability to corruption is shown in Figure 9.1. Such initiatives challenge the idea that corruption is someone else's problem and instead document the need for change. To that end, the discussion continues with a definition of corruption.

DEFINING CORRUPTION

Corruption is the abuse of position or power—a violation of public trust—often for personal gain by an individual or institution in the public or private sector. Government or business employees can be corrupt and organizations can be systemically corrupt.[4] The term is derived from the Latin *corrumpere* for "distort." The word appeared in English medicine during the 14th century in reference to decomposition of the body, and has subsequently referred to moral decay. Government is often an accessory to corporate corruption—and vice versa (Gitlow, 2005), as the public and private spheres are deeply intertwined and can collude for mutual benefit. Regulatory negligence, for instance, can enable corporate malfeasance, and the latter can reveal the former.

There are many kinds of corruption such as bribery, nepotism, misappropriation of funds, kickbacks, extortion, spoils, and conflict of interest. Incidences differ in scale (small vs. large) and duration (isolated vs. repeated incidences). Thus small-scale corruption could range from a single $50 bribe to routine payments of such amounts, whereas large-scale corruption could be either rare (a one-time $50,000 bribe) or repeated (systemic corruption). Reaction to each of these types—and their impact on business and government—can vary, from indifference to outrage (Thompson, 2000).

Corruption at the individual level can also be understood using role theory (Dobel, 1999). Thus, role distortion—the use of position for personal gain—may or may not involve massive greed. Whatever the form of wrongdoing, corruption violates public trust and generates unnecessary costs. Role failure occurs when an individual assumes office with laudatory goals, but either loses sight of them or confuses them with his own views. Ethical violations may stem not only from failure, but also from success (e.g., in the biblical "Bathsheba Syndrome," the highly regarded King David seduced Bathsheba with disastrous results including failed cover-ups, deaths, and dishonor with extreme personal misery). Senior executives feel invulnerable, control resources, and believe they are entitled to make up their own rules ("The fish rots," the saying goes, "from the head."). But rank-and-file employees also engage in dubious behaviors to rationalize and compensate for low salaries. Both the powerful *and* the powerless can be corrupted (Bowman & West, 2007).

FIGURE 9.1   State Vulnerability to Corruption

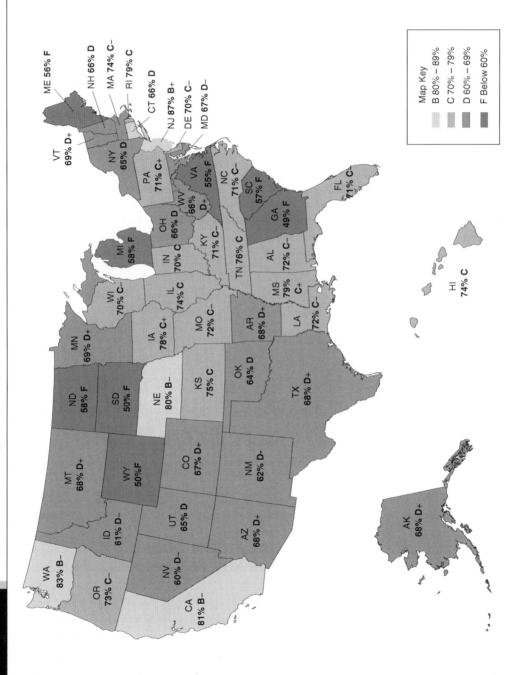

Map Key
B 80% – 89%
C 70% – 79%
D 60% – 69%
F Below 60%

Source: Center for Public Integrity, Global Integrity, & Public Radio International (2012).

Note: The numbers represent each state's integrity score. A high score (and letter grade) corresponds with a low vulnerability to corruption; a low score corresponds with a high vulnerability to corruption.

Finally, role rejection occurs when officials disdain public stewardship. Such people consider the workplace an extension of private life. They take advantage of the trust society places in institutions by exploiting opportunities for self-enrichment and rewarding friends. At the extremes of corruption, those with specific skills and access to valuable information become vulnerable to organized crime as it expands operations (Camilleri, 2011). Indeed, criminal networks overlap and cooperate with terrorists, a synergy that is growing because similar conditions give rise to both and because both depend on mutually beneficial relationships with well-known banks to launder their monies (Perri & Brody, 2011; Saviano, 2012).

There is no employee perpetrator profile, as wrongdoers may be very much like most people (Albrecht, Sanders, Holland, & Albrecht, 2011). Some analysts find the "20–60–20" rule to be useful. At the two ends of the spectrum, 20 percent of employees will always do the right thing and 20 percent will always be involved in wrongdoing when there is opportunity, high reward, and low risk. The remaining 60 percent may or may not be unethical depending on organizational culture (Brooks & Dunn, 2010) and which 20 percent component is the more influential. Corruption incurs the loss of legitimacy and effectiveness, adds to taxpayer burden, and increases openings for organized crime. Exacerbated by an "epidemic of infallibility," powerful officials never admit making a mistake. "No error is ever admitted, there is nothing to apologize for: 9-11, the bungled occupation of Iraq, the botched response to hurricane Katrina" (Krugman, 2017, March 17). Given the implications, the causes of corruption demand attention.

CAUSES OF CORRUPTION AND EVOLUTION OF ANTICORRUPTION STRATEGIES

Give a man a gun and he can rob a bank. Give a man a bank and he can rob the world.

—Anonymous

Root causes of corruption, according to Mahatma Gandhi, include wealth without work, pleasure without conscience, knowledge without character, commerce without morality, science without humanity, worship without sacrifice, rights without responsibilities, and politics without principles. Gandhi's causes often explain corruption in the worlds of government, business, and nonprofit organizations.

Government

In the public arena, the incubus of corruption provided much of the impetus for modern administration, which sought to address corruption by improving the quality of both personnel (via the merit system) and procedures (e.g., lowest bid, audits, council-manager government, and conflict of interest regulation). The evolution of corruption control can be depicted in stages with overlapping legacies, shown in Table 9.1. For each stage—the legacies of which remain today—the strategy, causes, prescriptions, and implications are outlined.

For example, the strategy of the Progressive Movement at the turn of the 19th century was emphasis on professionalism to replace amateur, partisan administration. Important reforms included the creation of independent regulatory commissions and nonpartisan elections. Largely a response to scandal, however, the focus on corruption can come at the expense of effectiveness and efficiency when reforms become so burdensome as to defy common sense (Anechiarico & Jacobs, 1994). Thus, while the changes in each era were well meaning, they can lead to counterproductive actions in which the public good was not served. Regulations designed to prevent corruption, for instance, can be so annoying that they may actually encourage more corruption.

The interplay between government and business is illustrated by the 2016 Morgan Stanley bank settlement with the Department of Justice. The Financial Crisis Inquiry Commission repeatedly documented that the bank was one of the largest criminal enterprises in the world. Yet, like in other settlements with Wall Street, the Department refused to prosecute the executives responsible, did not require that they return the monies they received from fraud, did not ask that they be terminated, or even require that they be named. It did not, in short, apply the rule of law (Black, 2016, February 12).

Business

In the private sphere, revelations of slush funds and secret payments were regarded as a detriment to foreign policy, the image of American society, and citizen confidence, and led to the 1977 Foreign Corrupt Practices Act. Intended to prevent bribery of foreign officials, the law requires that firms maintain a responsible internal accounting control system. As of 2012, 78 corporations were under investigation for possible violations of the Act (Wayne, 2012).

Corruption also led to the following 1991 U.S. Federal Sentencing Guidelines:

1. The firm's standards must be tailored to its business operations.

2. Top leadership must be personally involved in the program.

3. Corporations must not delegate significant discretion to those who have shown themselves inclined to deviant conduct.

4. The policy must be effectively communicated throughout the company.

5. Businesses must have compliance standards and reporting systems.

6. There must be disciplinary procedures in place to address problems.

7. Companies must respond to offenses, report them to the government, and seek to deter future issues.

The statute mandates that firms develop programs that can then be used both as a deterrent to wrongdoing and as a means to limit corporate liability. Organizations are expected to create an ethical climate, develop an active oversight program, identify risk factors and offer

TABLE 9.1 Visions of Corruption Control: Strategies, Causes, Prescriptions, and Implications

Corruption Control Vision	Anti-patronage (1870–1900)	Progressive (1900–1933)	Scientific Management (1933–1970)	Panoptic (1970–1990s)	Revisionist (1990s–Present)
Strategy	Credential and competence testing	Professionalism	External control	Law enforcement	Public entrepreneurship
Perceived causes of corruption problem	Partisan control of personnel	Partisan, unprofessional administration	Inadequate organizational controls	Inadequate monitoring	Bureaucratic pathology
Key policy prescription	Merit system	Electoral reform, independent regulatory commissions, administrative expertise, apolitical administration	Government reorganization and centralization	Surveillance, investigation, fiscal controls	Market privatization
Implications for public administration	Peer enforcement of norms, personal controls	Enforced standards of efficiency	Oversight of agencies and appropriate span of control	Strong investigative and auditing agencies	Decentralized debureaucratized structures, deemphasize corruption control

Source: Anechiarico and Jacobs (1994, 466).

training, and reduce the opportunities for, and increase the risks of, malfeasance. Often, the provision of a proper climate includes the creation of codes of ethics, ethics audits, ethics officers, and other components of an infrastructure discussed in the previous chapter. One reason why corporations might encourage whistleblowers (Chapter 10) to report problems internally may be so that they can turn themselves in and qualify for leniency.

Another technique is the use of "honest services" fraud and conflict-of-interest legislation (18 U.S.C. & 1346). It requires that public and corporate officials act in the best interests of their constituents or employers by criminalizing schemes to defraud victims of "the intangible right of honest services," including the right to good government (Schwartz, 2009). Thus, a decision maker can be charged with depriving others of that right, if she puts her own interest or those of another person above the interests of citizens or shareholders.

David Brooks (2010) noted that after the controversial Vietnam War and the Watergate scandal, an "ethos of exposure" swept American culture. According to this view, the political and corporate elite, while appearing to be upstanding, are actually corrupt. The private lives of officials, once considered inconsequential, became at least as prominent as their performance. In many cases, the exposure ethos elevated the trivial above the significant while simultaneously corroding faith in the nation. Transparency has been dramatically magnified in the last generation by the development of the Internet and the proliferation of media outlets. As web-based public information sharing portals become more common (Chapter 11), scandals once revealed by employees may be teased out from aggregate data by citizens. The historically low rate of waste in the 2009 federal stimulus package, for example, has been credited to Recovery.Gov: Track the Money (www.recovery.gov), an official website that provides public access to Recovery Act spending and allows for reporting of potential corruption (Exhibit 9.1).

Exhibit 9.1	**The 2009 Federal Stimulus Bailout Program**

The New New Deal: The Hidden Story of Change in the Obama Era, by Michael Grunwald (2012), argues that the "unprecedented $800 billion package of spending and tax cuts" was fraud free and exceptionally well managed. The Recovery Act prevented the economy from total collapse by providing funds for electronic health care records, information technology, green energy, and high-speed rail infrastructure projects. Yet "more Americans think Elvis Presley is still alive than think that the stimulus was a success"—even Obama seldom mentions it (Clark, 2012).

Observers predicted that government would lose over 5 percent of the funds to fraud, but just 0.0001 percent consisted of questionable payments. The sources of the conventional wisdom about the failure of the stimulus law include, according to Grunwald, incompetent White House communication, political opposition to the bailout, an unquestioning media, and bad timing (the act was passed when the country was losing hundreds of thousands of jobs a month). Examples of the misuse of funds reported by the credulous media—a train to Disneyland, millions for government furniture, honeybee insurance, sod for the National Mall—were found to be false.

Source: Clark (2012).

Nonprofit Organizations

The nonprofit sector is not immune from issues of corruption, asset manipulation, and fraudulent accounting (see, e.g., the end-of-the-chapter Exercise 5, the "Bad Boss"). Headline stories have exposed conflicts of interest, bribery, unlawful gratuities, economic extortion, as well as illegal financial and nonfinancial statements with growing frequency. Given the size and scope of the sector with its $665 billion in revenues, 12 million employees (Stephens and Flaherty, 2013), and 65 million service recipients (Greenlee, Fischer, Gordon, & Keating, 2007), it is a ripe target for wrongdoers. Using data from the Association of Certified Fraud Examiners (2016), it can be estimated that fraud losses in the nonprofit arena amount to around $40 billion annually.

The United Way, Boy Scouts of America, and other high-profile organizations have been embarrassed by disclosures of corruption in recent years. The Red Cross comes under repeated criticism for poor performance ("How to help the neediest Harvey victims," 2017, August 31). Congressionally charted, the charity is a monopoly provider of national first responder services; no other organization has a similar stature or scope. Its failures during 9/11 and Katrina compelled Congress to demand governance changes, but better results were not forthcoming for the 2010 Haiti earthquake or for Super Storm Sandy and Hurricane Isaac, both in 2012. ARC's 2015 response to California fires was so bad that residents shunned the organization. In 2017, a Red Cross executive was asked what percentage of funds donated in the wake of Hurricane Harvey would be devoted to relief; he did not know. One local official begged residents, "not to give a penny" to the Red Cross and others simply said they did not trust it (Madry, 2017, September 8).

Additional examples abound both here and abroad:

- Potential donors seeking to provide assistance to Hurricane Katrina victims were likely deceived by more than 2,000 fraudulent Internet sites soliciting contributions (Aviv, 2005).
- The former CEO of the National Kidney Foundation Singapore was charged with corruption and jailed for questionable business practices, ranging from conflicts of interest to misrepresentations of organizational performance and wasteful spending (see Rowe & Dato-on, 2013, 94–107).
- The Association of Community Organizations for Reform Now (ACORN) was busted for voter registration fraud and for employees caught on videotape facilitating tax fraud and covering up a child sex slavery ring (McRay, 2009).
- The bankruptcy filing of the Miami-area James E. Scott Community Association listed $3.4 million in liabilities and only $1.7 million in assets after it lost government contracts over fears about its financial management. The charity had been administering programs for infants, teenagers, and the elderly in the city's poorest neighborhoods (Grimm, 2010; "Miami-Area Social-Service Charity," 2009).
- Another nonprofit, the MDHA Development Corporation, received $16 million from Miami Dade County as well as land and other assets, but finished just one affordable

housing project, a failed effort with months of delay and building breakdowns (Cenziper, 2006).

How can nonprofits curb corruption and preserve both their reputations and funding base? Greenlee and her colleagues (2007, 688–691) provide numerous strategies. Some suggestions include (a) establishing clear lines of authority, (b) creating proper procedures for authorizing transactions, (c) auditing monthly financial transactions in addition to an annual audit, (d) training volunteers about theft risks, (e) recruiting quality, independent board members, (f) creating an audit committee to detect or deter financial mismanagement, (g) completing background checks on employees with access to cash or assets, and (h) providing whistleblower protection.

Beyond root causes of corruption as manifested in government and in business and nonprofit organizations, how else can individual and collective moral failure be explained?

INDIVIDUAL AND INSTITUTIONAL MORAL FAILURE

There is no right way to do a wrong thing.

—Howard S. Kushner

Individuals

Personal moral lapses can stem from the human genius for self-serving rationalization. Because there is often a grain of truth in rationalizations, it is easy to understand, and hard to deny, their seductive nature. Anand, Ashford, and Joshi (2004) highlight seven rationalization techniques and provide examples of each (Table 9.2). Most of these psychological defense mechanisms—used to mask the true reasons for behavior—cannot withstand the "front-page test" ("Would you be willing to see your actions in the newspaper?"), but two additional common excuses not included in the table warrant comment: contingent necessity ("If I don't do it, someone else will") and ignorance ("I didn't know").

First, conduct must be judged on its merit, not on a vague possibility of what a nameless "someone else" may or may not do. That is, ethics is about personal responsibility. One individual may not be able to do everything that needs to be done, but she can improve conditions around her by avoiding unethical behavior, setting an honorable example, and strengthening her character (Chapter 6). Second, what executives do not know may not be their fault, but it is their responsibility—they are accountable for organizational climate and due diligence. The official's obligation is not fulfilled unless everything possible is done to ensure proper standards of practice.

Looking at sexual harassment as a case study of rationalization, Bauer (2017, June 19) points out common, but toxic, claims by managers, colleagues, and victims:

- "The individual is being too sensitive" (blaming the victim is never an appropriate response).

TABLE 9.2		Rationalization Techniques: Description and Summary	
Category	**Rationalization Technique**	**Description**	**Examples**
Justification	Appeal to higher loyalties Denial of injury	The actors argue that their violation of norms is due to their attempt to realize a higher-order value The actors believe that no one is harmed by their actions; so the actions aren't corrupt	"We answered to a more important cause" "I wouldn't report it due to loyalty" "No one was really harmed" "It could have been worse"
Social Excuses	Denial of victim Social weighting	The actors counter blame for their actions by arguing that the violated party deserved it The actors assume a practice that moderates the salience of corrupt behavior: condemn or compare	"They deserved it" "They chose to participate" "You have no right to criticize us" "Others are worse than we are"
Contextual Excuses	Denial of responsibility Denial of illegality Metaphor of the ledger	The actors engaged in corrupt behavior perceive that they have no choice but to participate Actors excuse corrupt practices on the basis that their actions are not illegal The actors rationalize that they're entitled to indulge in deviant behavior because of their accrued credits	"What can I do?" "It is none of my business what the corporation does overseas" "There's no law against it" "We've earned the right"

Source: Adapted from Anand et al. (2004, 11).

- "The perpetrator is such a good person that this allegation is difficult to believe" (many caring people do untoward things).
- "If I endure this, others won't need to" (this self-destructive response ignores other past, current, and future victims).
- "This too will pass" (this condones the offensive conduct).
- "Complaining will only lead to retaliation" (while this may be true, it "kicks the problem down the road").

Establishment of an ethical infrastructure (Chapter 8), ethical audits, consultations with legal and human resource professionals, and "management by walking around"—and listening—can help protect against corruption. Not only do ordinary people populate the ranks of the corrupt, but many organizations are also prone to criminality (Ashforth & Anand, 2003). Recent incidents—the Flint, Michigan water crisis and the Wells Fargo scandal—implicating individuals as well as institutions are examined below.

Flint, Michigan Water Crisis. Water supplies, roads, bridges, airports, and dams are in a precarious state. The significance of maintenance and upkeep is not only unappreciated, but also it is taken for granted by the general public. The result is the failure of physical and human infrastructure (Veruil, 2017). The American Society of Civil Engineers grades the nation's water system as a "D," requiring at least $400 billion to modernize (Leber, 2017, July 19; Russell & Vinsel, 2017, July 3). Taxpayers also fail to support blue- and white-collar maintenance workers with recognition and competitive salaries.

To save money and "run government like a business," in 2014 a state-appointed emergency manager switched Flint's water supply from a lake to the Flint River, and unqualified technical personnel were hired to oversee the change. For over a year, local and state managers denied the resulting contamination problems—even though General Motors and a Flint hospital stopped using the water because it was damaging metal automobile parts and medical instruments.

In mid-2017, the Michigan Attorney General, in an ongoing investigation, charged 15 officials with neglect of duty, including the state's health department's secretary (involuntary manslaughter) as well chief medical officer (obstruction of justice). His report found that the solution to pollution problem could have been handled easily at the outset by the use of common anti-corrosion chemicals costing $200 per day (Atkins & Davey, 2017, June 14). Later that year, reduced fertility rates, increased miscarriages, and more fetal deaths were linked to the crisis (Delaney, 2017, September 21).

People may assume that by now the problem is fixed, but residents point out that thousands of lead pipes need to be replaced (a process that will take years), citizens may lose their homes if they do not pay dramatically escalating water bills, and they fear tap water will continue to make them sick. Flint, a town of nearly 100,000, is a majority Black community with 40 percent of residents living below the poverty line; it is doubtful that this crisis would have emerged in a white, wealthy community. The Environmental Protection Agency, at this writing, is posed to repeal the federal clean water rule which protects waterways that provide drinking water. The Flint physical infrastructure tragedy demonstrates the need for human infrastructure—technically and ethically competent professionals as well as responsible elected officials—to provide basic services to the citizenry.

Elsewhere, there were more than 12,000 health violations in 5,000 community water systems, as 19 million Americans are stricken each year after drinking contaminated water (Baptiste, 2017, May 8). Desperate to raise money to address the problem, communities across the country have gotten entangled in risky Wall Street transactions that endanger the local economy in pursuit of corporate gain at the expense of the public. Known as "disaster capitalism" (Klein, 2007), banks use their political power to persuade elected officials to cut local taxes resulting in reductions of revenue necessary to maintain infrastructure. City officials then seek ways to fund projects, and are readily exploited by too-big-to-fail banks offering opaque, high-risk Wall Street financial deals. "When the deals fail and those responsible have collected their payday, there's always another profiteering company ready with more promises of 'cost savings' and 'efficiencies'" (Sloan, 2016, March 14).

Wells Fargo Scandal. In 2016, Wells Fargo, the nation's most profitable bank, announced that it would pay $185 million in fines to regulators; the action would settle allegations that its employees created 2.1 million fraudulent credit card and checking accounts since 2002 without their customers' knowledge or permission. Hoping to put the issue behind them, the bank's decision sparked a firestorm instead. The predatory fraud was something people could easily understand and was done in the context of dozens of fines for other abusive practices in recent years, costing the bank $10 billion.

A management-created sales pressure scheme and unrealistic quotas drove employees to falsify documents and game the system to meet sales goals. Failure to do so met with disciplinary action. This large-scale, brazen, systematic institutionalized program led a Republican congressman to charge that the bank was running a criminal enterprise and a Democratic legislator to call it a "school for scoundrels" (Merle, 2016, September 29).

Wells Fargo admitted no wrongdoing in the settlement and no high-level officials were singled out for prosecution. The fines are a "rounding error" compared to the company's 2016 second quarter profits of $5.6 billion ("Wells Fargo fined $185 million," 2016, September 9). In connection with the scandal, 5,300 personnel were discharged over a period of five years (apparently including those who reported misconduct) with one exception: the executives in charge.

But is it reasonable to blame them for the actions of a relatively small number of employees in a huge institution with branches throughout the nation? The illicit behavior involving thousands of staff and millions of phony accounts cannot be dismissed as the work of a few bad apples. Systemic problems like this is *exactly* the responsibility of top executives (Ochs, 2016, September 15). A profit-over-people organizational culture lead to gross mismanagement, according to the chair of the U.S. House of Representatives Financial Services Committee.

For a supposedly well-run bank—Wells Fargo's John Stump was named "CEO of the Year in 2015—it is inconceivable that senior management could miss the creation of millions of bogus accounts. Executives were either complicit or should have been terminated for gross incompetence. Indeed, they repeatedly certified the accuracy of financial reports and the adequacy of quality controls. Stump, who would resign with a $130 million payout, is no longer at Wells; while it made some personnel and procedural changes, the bank feels no obligation to honor his reform commitments made when the scandal broke.

A year later more than 1.4 million additional fake accounts were identified (Cowley, 2017, August 31). As if to demonstrate that white-collar crime defendants do not limit their dishonest activity to just one crime (Warren Buffett observed, "There's never just one cockroach in the kitchen"), a broader bank review revealed that hundreds of thousands of customers were affected by: (a) unauthorized enrollments in the bank's online bill payment service, (b) unrequested auto insurance, (c) secret changes to mortgage repayments, and (d) improper withholding of refunds to car loan customers. Department of Justice, Securities and Exchange Commission, and the Federal Reserve investigations are continuing. At the same time, however, the U.S. Senate is considering limiting the powers of the Consumer Financial Protection Bureau and the Bureau's new leadership stopped: payments to victimized customers, hiring, new rule making, and ongoing investigations.

It is evident that years of tighter rules from legislators have done nothing to fix the "me-first" cultures that afflict large financial firms. It is also plain that bankers are not willing to institute a system of self-regulation and personal liability. Despite the scandal, Wells remains as a large, profitable institution. Customers are vulnerable to fraud due to the complexity of many financial products, the opacity of fine print, and the lack of genuine recourse. Without real reform, people can continue to be victimized (Ramirez & Ramirez, 2017). Among the ironies are that mega banks tend to underperform inclining them to criminality that, in turn, undermines capitalism.

Institutions

As the above cases suggest, failure on the part of the organization to avoid corruption may originate from the nature of work itself, groupthink, management-induced fear, or retaliation. Awareness of individual and institutional pressures is the initial step toward addressing them. Consider two cases, one focusing on the private sector and one on the public: moral hazard and gift giving.

Moral hazard refers to undue risks that organizations and people are likely to take if they are not responsible for the consequences (as when financial firms make high-risk investments with federally insured taxpayer money and are subsequently bailed out). Shirking fiduciary responsibilities, and saved from failure by government, such conditions increase moral hazard, inhibit trust in institutions, and permit failed capitalists to become corporate socialists.[5] Eduardo Porter (2012) puts it this way:

> Bigger markets allow bigger frauds. Bigger companies, with more complex balance sheets, have more places to hide them. And banks, when they get big enough that no government will let them fail, have the biggest incentive of all. A 20-year-old study by the economists Paul Romer and George Akerloff pointed out that the most lucrative strategy for executives at too-big-to-fail banks would be to loot them to pay themselves vast rewards—knowing full well that the government would save them from bankruptcy.

A defense against moral hazard constitutes a system of controls that prevents firms from taking risks with other people's money—and at their expense—in the first place. The New Deal stock market regulations are an iconic anticorruption system. Yet those provisions were repealed in the late 1990s. In their place, Congress deregulated the financial sector and allowed Wall Street to self-regulate, abandoning the idea that markets need oversight: The result was one of the biggest crime waves the country has ever experienced.

Turning to gift giving in public service, the practice is often regulated—unlike business norms wherein such goodwill courtesies are common. These prohibitions, however, are frequently criticized as ineffective, on the grounds that most individuals do not sacrifice their honor for gifts.[6] The premise of this contention—predicated on valorizing self-interest and invalidating moral concern—may be correct: many officials are not "for sale." As legendary California Assembly Speaker Jesse Unruh used to say of lobbyists, "If you can't eat their food, drink their booze and [expletive deleted] their women, and then vote against them, you have no business being up here."[7]

Yet as discussed in Chapter 7, the conclusion—that inducements are acceptable—must be rejected as pernicious for three reasons. First, it is difficult to discern a defensible reason (as opposed to an expedient or self-serving reason) why an official should expect gratuities. Next, corruption requires nothing so crass as a *quid pro quo*, because such offerings introduce the possibility of favoritism. Bribing is generally not the issue; rather, it is access and the attendant appearance of impropriety, conflict of interest, entitlement, influence peddling, and self-dealing. The challenge for administrators to avoid corruption intensifies when the ethics of an action are unclear, as in the case of transition from public to private employment (Case Study 9.1).

Individual gifts, third, can help create organizational corruption—the creation of a system that encourages decisions based not on the substance of issues, but rather on friendships and cronyism among the political and financial officialdom. Immersed in a culture of the comfortable:

> [T]he process of influence doesn't have to involve raw corruption (although that happens too). All that it requires is the tendency to assume that what's good for the people (those who you associate with the most), must be good for the economy as a whole. (Krugman, 2011)

As Dan Ariely (2012) points out, people are social creatures. Someone gives a person a present—even, or perhaps especially, a small one—and the recipient tends to feel a debt of gratitude. That sense of indebtedness subtly influences perceptions and behavior by the need to clear a perceived debt. Gifting, in short, is a technique of power exercised by one party over the other. Lobbyists spend a small part of their time with politicians on official business and most of the time "trying to implant a feeling of obligation and reciprocity in politicians who they hope will repay them by voting with their interest in mind" (78).

The financial industry, for instance, creates conflicts of interest, nurtures them, and the banking and political elite benefits from a shared ideology—a belief system that the continued existence of Wall Street firms, and business as usual, is in the best interest of the economy. It is not necessary for the wealthy to buy a lawmaker's vote. Rather, they "buy his mind" (Reich, 2011, 110). The most recent financial debacle—the third in 20 years after the Savings and Loan disaster and the Enron Era—is, at heart, a political crisis. Financiers elicit cooperation from elected officials who depend on them in the form of gifts, campaign donations, and future employment.

Gifts are, in short, one manifestation of a deep culture of corruption as suggested by one state employee:

If corruption is defined as the abuse of position or power, this could be anything. Using your position to receive gifts is an example. I work for the Department of Economic Opportunity. Our gift policy (http://www.ethics.state.fl.us/publications/gifts%20info_2007_web.pdf) requires filling out forms when receiving gifts valued at over $100. It was created to deal with corruption or the appearance of corruption. The forms are public record.

The problem is that the policy relies on self-reporting: the individual must act ethically to determine if any wrongdoing has occurred. It is very difficult to catch someone accepting presents and not reporting it unless the giver reports the receiver. I think that the $100 amount is arbitrary; the amount is not all that relevant. Taking gifts gives the appearance of bias and corruption, regardless of how much they cost. (Anonymous personal communication, November 1, 2016)

Jurisdictions lacking workable gift regulations and tax-supported campaigns for office should consider them. The imperative of serving citizens before self ought to be enough for a public official. Why should presents, cash donations, and promises of impending jobs be routinely anticipated? Does anyone really think that they are offered in the name of "good government"? Perhaps Plato said it best, "The servants of the nation are to render their services without any presents. The disobedient shall, if convicted, die without ceremony." Admittedly, prohibiting inducements may not be the preeminent issue—as long as privately funded political campaigns continue, the biggest source of corruption is legal—but it is a good place to begin.

Individual and institutional moral failure stems from a variety of sources, many of which are manifested in moral hazards and gift giving. When corruption is revealed, the dishonor it produces may have serious and long-lasting effects. The next section examines such *contretemps* with particular attention to government and corporate roles in recent events.

SCANDALS: TYPES AND IMPACTS

Corruptio optimi pessimum (The corruption of the best is the worst).

—Latin proverb

Types of Scandal

Scandals reveal opportunities for the public to obtain information not otherwise available. As they occur in public service, these issues often have shared characteristics:

- There is no clear connection between the gravity of misdeed and the controversy.
- Their impact may depend on electoral cycle, partisan balance, presidential or gubernatorial approval ratings.
- Good journalism is bad business (expensive investigatory journalism), and bad journalism is good business (sensationalized coverage of sex peccadilloes).

- Republican scandals reinforce the conservative claim that government is corrupt, while Democratic scandal undercuts the liberal view that government can be trusted to do good. (Brooks, 2012)

A scandal refers to actions or events involving transgressions that become known and are perceived to be sufficiently serious to merit a public response (Thompson, 2000).

Several types of revelation combust in spectacular ways and are based on the fatal attraction of sex, money, and/or power (Thompson, 2000, 122). Sex incidents may or may not involve criminal offenses, but generally reflect actions that are regarded as hypocritical or unseemly. The more citizens have to rely on the character and discretion of officials, the more significance is given to personal weaknesses—especially if they affect broader issues of public concern. Financial scandals, second, disclose improper linkages between economic and political powerbrokers, and often involve violations of law because there is a well-developed set of statutes that cover them (this does not mean that such cases are easily resolved; see Case 9.1). Yet the mere presence of legislation means little, if laws are ignored or if ongoing investigations confront statutes of limitations.

There has been, for example, a stunning lack of accountability for the crimes that helped create the gravest economic crisis since the Great Depression. In a mockery of the rule of law, there has not been a single prosecution of a major Wall Street bank or executive for what the FBI termed "an epidemic of fraud" that blew up the entire economy (Dwyer, 2013; Morgenson & Story, 2011; "No Fault Corporate Crime," 2012). The same can be said for the 2001 terrorist attacks, the torture of detainees during the Iraq War, and the 2010 BP Deep Water Horizon oil spill. No one was terminated, no one resigned, and no one took responsibility. There has been, in other words, a *de facto* decriminalization of unethical behavior by banks that are above the law and beyond the discipline of the market. One of the world's largest banking groups, HSBC, for example, admitted to laundering billions for drug cartels and violating critical bank laws, including the Bank Security Act and the Trading With the Enemy Act (Protess & Silver-Greenberg, 2012).

Abuses of power, third, often do not involve extraneous factors such as sex and money, but the illicit use of power itself. As Teddy Roosevelt observed, "You cannot give an official power to do right, without at the same time giving him the power to do wrong." Scandals reveal activities that transgress the rules of governance in the acquisition and exercise of power. The preemptive war against Iraq as a response to the 9/11 terrorist attacks, for instance, was described by the chief official in the White House situation room on 9/11 as making as much sense as "invading Mexico after the Japanese attacked us at Pearl Harbor" (Clarke, 2004, 30–31).

Finally, the miasma of scandals can stem from power but entangle money and sex—or just plain waste. An imbroglio involving sex, money, and power occurred in the Department of Interior's Minerals Management Service, a unit responsible for collecting $10 billion in royalties (one of the federal government's largest sources of non-tax revenues). Regulators accepted bribes, negotiated for industry jobs, engaged in illicit drug use and sex with oil company employees, falsified reports, and waived regulatory requirements. In the wake of the

2010 Deep Water Horizon blowout, the agency was renamed and reorganized. An instance of waste, in a time of fiscal austerity, was revealed by the General Services Administration (GSA) Inspector General in 2012—a lavish 2010 Las Vegas conference at a cost of $823,000. The convention featured mind readers, magicians, clowns, souvenirs, and expensive dinners. Some of those involved received bonuses. The agency head resigned, all travel expenditures and conferences were suspended, and a thorough review of personnel and planning practices was undertaken. Ironically, the U.S. Office of Government Ethics evaluated the GSA during the time it was planning the convention, and praised it for using exemplary practices, while failing to address known risk factors that could have prevented the problem (Epstein, 2012).

Impacts on the Government Service, Business, and Nonprofit Sectors

If our civilization is destroyed, disaster will not be by . . . barbarians from below. Our barbarians come from the top.

—Henry Lloyd, Wealth Against Commonwealth

Government Service. Sex, financial, and power scandals belie the idea of public service: These abuses are problematic for democracies as they subvert governmental legitimacy and obstruct the rule of law.[8] It should be noted, however, that such events have a Janus-faced nature about them (Garment, 1991). On the bright side, they can be seen as actually stabilizing the political system. The contention is that it needs pathologies for purification purposes, as exposures take the abstract values of democracy (such as due process and equal protection) and make them tangible. As a result, it is said that "the process works," and the system deserves support. What began as abuse of self-government culminates in a celebration of its values. Scandals also satisfy the need for the citizenry to participate, albeit vicariously, in public affairs. On the dark side of the Janus face, revelations may not have the claimed beneficial effects. The lesson of the Watergate affair in the Nixon administration was not so much that the rule of law was effective, but that few citizens since then wanted to experience a failed presidency again (Pierce, 2012). Worse, scandals can become an alternative to dealing with important societal issues: the politics of scandal replaces the politics of democracy. Perversely, public attention can be diverted away from debate and discourse to fake scandals, which, in turn, spawn faux outrage obscuring actual, less easily reported problems. Such non-incidents (e.g., rejecting documentation of Barack Obama's birthplace) create a culture of mistrust and undermine the polity.

The result of real and specious scandals is that it is more difficult to govern. Ethics can even be used as a weapon to discredit reformers—all that may be necessary is a well-financed misinformation campaign aimed at their personal and professional lives to frustrate reform. Instead of stabilizing the system, Garment (1991) argues, scandals destabilize it as they are morally repugnant, economically distorting, and politically de-legitimating. Each round of revelations and allegations weakens the system and diminishes public trust. As a consequence, we feel "perpetually dirty," have contempt for everyday politics, and believe that the system is dishonorable. Instead of eliminating corruption, even those incidents that are "successfully" resolved damage faith in government.

Business. In every era marked by rapid technological change, entrepreneurial zeal is apt to be attracted to the lure of quick riches. The cavalcade of corporate scandals since the turn of the 21st century should not be surprising. Yet merely pointing out that dishonesty is not the norm in business is insufficient. For all the attention to the Wall Street crime wave, significant audit and accounting issues persist. The federal government's response to the crisis—to re-establish the status quo as soon as possible—is also not unexpected, given that the officials responsible for financial law enforcement are the same people who played important roles in the financial sector when it imploded. "There is an awful lot to do in the world of corporate fraud," according to the FBI (Johnson, 2006).

Further, there are ongoing lobbying efforts to thwart the landmark 2002 Sarbanes-Oxley Act (intended to curb accounting abuses) and the 2010 Dodd-Frank legislation (designed to prevent another 2008-style meltdown of the financial system) (Chapter 10). As irresponsible stewards of the power surrendered to them through deregulation, investment firm CEOs wrecked the economy, received bailouts from the federal government, and are richer than ever (Dionne, 2010). "The dogma of 'free markets,'" Bill Black (2012) points out, "turned into an anti-regulatory creed that produces an environment so criminogenic that it drives our recurrent, intensifying financial crises." Ironically "the spectacular failure of financial markets," writes Michael Sandel (2012, 12), "did little to dampen the faith in markets generally," as public opinion polls showed that Americans blamed the government more than Wall Street for the scandal.

It is doubtful, in any case, that recent reforms have been institutionalized as the nation has yet to grasp the depth of the problem. There is a big difference between being accountable and being held to account. Examples of "failing upward" include:

- State and federal changes made in the early part of this century did little to prevent the 2007–2010 credit crisis (Chapter 1). In fact, investigations into banking practices—including widespread fraudulent documentation of mortgage loans—have not yet come to closure—although the statutes of limitations are set to expire (Note: Mortgage-backed securities are the biggest asset class in the world.)
- White-collar crime federal sentencing guidelines (www.ussc.gov/orgguide.htm) discussed above, which place responsibility for establishing an ethical organizational culture on top executives, were recently changed from mandatory to advisory in nature (also see Chapter 10).
- The epic corruption by military contractors reached twice the amount of money (adjusted for inflation) expended to rebuild Iraq as it did to rebuild Japan—"an industrialized nation three times the size, two of whose cities had been incinerated by atomic bombs" (Rich, 2007).
- In contrast to the Savings and Loan scandal and the Enron Era, there have been very few investigations and many fewer prosecutions during the Great Recession, as miscreant financiers avoided jail, made sweetheart deals, paid modest fines (often

covered by corporate insurance policies), and collected millions in bonuses (evaluation of executive performance typically excludes legal settlement costs) while many citizens lost much of their life savings, their jobs, and even their homes.

- The longstanding practice of permitting an organization or individual to neither admit nor deny wrongdoing ("no-fault" corruption) might encourage compliance, but also enables widespread recidivism; it overlooks, in addition, that guilty pleas make it easier for victims to recover damages and take advantage of law that treats past offenders differently than one-time perpetrators.

- An emblematic case of these problems is the Federal Deposit Insurance Corporation that allowed the most notorious executives to walk away wealthy, proving itself to be lacking in integrity and courage and unfit to represent the nation (Black, 2013, March 12).

- Major investment banks are "dismissive, even defiant" when criticized for "business as usual" investment and compensation practices supported by bailout money (Anderson, 2009); "they were embarrassed for about 15 minutes," grew bigger than ever, and worked to block or repeal reforms (Clark, 2013). The current administration has made it clear that Wall Street need have no concern about any remaining reforms as it seeks to dilute or ignore them ("Why the return of bigger banks means more risks for everyone else," 2017, September 8).

At issue is not merely honest bookkeeping, but the fact that governance of corporations and capitalism as a whole becomes increasingly predatory (Ferguson, 2012). Free markets are supposed to allocate capital efficiently to the benefit of everyone, but only if subject to meaningful oversight. Many corporations no longer exist to produce goods; rather, they are owned by global speculators and institutional investors who demand short-term profits, often achieved by eliminating jobs and slashing wages. Instead of building industrial capacity and public works infrastructure, investment banking created financial innovations for the sake of profit at the expense of social value. Indeed, much of the problem is what is legal when firms are rewarded for lobbying clout rather than contributing to the economic health of the nation. As Senator Richard Durbin (D-Ill.) said in 2009, despite having caused the crisis, the same financial firms "are still the most powerful lobby on Capitol Hill. And they, frankly, own the place" (quoted in Friedman, 2011).

Perhaps the best illustration of this is the "shadow banking system"—unregulated, dangerous, speculative credit derivative markets that changed the way Wall Street made money—that played a key role in creating the 2007–2009 recession and its continuing aftereffects. Shadow banking accounts for more assets than those held by the traditional banking system (Cowen, 2013). A particularly destructive form of capitalism, these opaque markets offer little or no social or economic purpose, while tying up billions of dollars that could otherwise be used to finance businesses to create jobs and produce goods and services. Much more of the system's assets are devoted to trading corporate securities than to supporting long-term investment in productive assets. Derivatives—what Warren Buffet called "weapons of mass financial destruction"—were devised to distribute risk broadly so that they made the system safe. But "they interlocked risk so completely that they brought the system down" (Meyerson, 2011) to the point that Wall Street banks stopped lending even to one another.

This is an example of the financial industry detached from the real economy it is supposed to serve (Brady, 2011; Pearlstein, 2012). Until reforms address "a financial system that really serves society, rather than just trying to stay ahead of misdeeds of the one that doesn't, we'll struggle in vain to bridge the gaps between Wall Street and Main Street" (Foroohar, 2017, September 27). In short, the impact of scandals makes it difficult to govern, to hold public and corporate officials accountable, and to chart reform.

Nonprofits. Not-for-profit organizations are also adversely impacted by scandals. Stories of the misdeeds tarnish the reputation not only of those smeared with the taint of corruption, but also legitimate programs that might lose favor with the public. Damaged reputation can sour potential donors who may withhold cash because of real or actual misdoings. Not-for-profits are especially susceptible to fraudsters because of their characteristics such as a trusting atmosphere, revenue streams that are hard to verify, insufficient knowledge and experience in business and financial matters, and unpaid volunteer boards of directors (Douglas & Mills, 2000). Add to this the legal system's inconsistent approach to pursuit of white-collar criminals in the nonprofit setting (Croall, 2003) and problems may escape detection and be allowed to fester. Because of these vulnerabilities it is important for nonprofits to defend themselves by fortifying their ethical infrastructure (Chapter 8) and by standing up for integrity.

AVENUES FOR REFORM

Power concedes nothing without a demand.

—Frederick Douglass

A more successful, less crisis-prone financial system would include initiatives such as:

- establishing a national commission on corporate crime,
- restricting the use off-shore tax havens,
- strengthening conflict of interest rules,
- limiting stock options,
- using the authority federal and state law enforcement agencies already have,
- acknowledging that fines and court settlements, "which don't even rise to the level of a minor inconvenience" (Gongloff, 2012), are meaningless unless coupled with executive exposure to criminal and civil liability,
- improving business accountability to not only company stockholders, but also societal stakeholders by enacting legislation that prohibits making a profit at the expense of the environment, human rights, public safety, the welfare of the community in which the corporation operates, or the dignity of employees (several large cities have passed a Code for Corporate Citizenship or "responsible banking" ordinances that require

banks to reveal their impact on the community and/or require city officials to only do business with banks that are responsive to local needs),

- forbidding corporate law breakers the right to bid on governmental contracts that are a significant source of business for most major companies,
- establishing a reparations fund—like the BP fund to reimburse 2010 Gulf oil spill victims—for Main Street victims of Wall Street avarice—the source of revenues would be a "Robin Hood" tax (Exhibit 9.2), and
- enacting a corporate "death penalty" by revoking the firm's charter after three criminal convictions (Exhibit 9.3).[9]

Reforms specifically targeting banks include capital requirements, standardized and transparent derivatives, and independent auditing. Absent regulation, "capitalism's most dangerous enemies are capitalists" (Samuelson, 2008), not unlike the communists who destroyed communism. A "criminogenic" environment is created by speculation, chicanery, and outright fraudulent behavior. Analogous to Gresham's Law (counterfeit money drives legal currency out of circulation), regulatory negligence and corporate excess permit bad behavior, allowing honesty to wither.

Indeed, banks, according to U.S. Representative Maxine Waters (D-Calif.) (2012), "will fight against regulation even when it is in their own best interest." Thus, the head of JP Morgan acknowledged before Congress that reckless trading fueled by "greed, arrogance, hubris, and lack of attention to detail" continues, even as the industry resists rules to curb its toxic practices ("Mr. Dimon," 2012). Leading financial firms have been caught committing fraud, financing terrorists, and laundering money. For example, transgressions include the 2012 LIBOR (London Interbank Offered Rate) interest-rate rigging scandal (which affects the cost of borrowing for corporations and consumers), JP Morgan Chase's 2013 $6.2 billion

---

EXHIBIT 9.2   Robin Hood Tax

The "Robin Hood" tax would offset the cost of the financial sector-caused recession, suppress high-risk and high-speed trading that caused the crash, and limit the casino culture of Wall Street. The United States not only had this tax in the past (1914–1966), but also doubled it during the Great Depression to help pay for recovery. Revenues would be collected on financial transactions detailed in the proposed Wall Street Trading and Speculator Tax Act. The tiny levy, 0.03 percent of each transaction, is able to generate significant funds due to high frequency of billion-dollar trades (Gerard, 2012; van Gelder, 2002). The nation charges sales taxes on many consumer goods, but nothing on the sale of stocks, bonds, and derivatives—at a time when many other nations use the Robin Hood tax. Added impetus for this reform was provided by the May 2012 $5 billion loss sustained by JPMorgan and the credit downgrades of 15 major banks the next month. This was followed by the global Libor interest rate exposé. Even after being bailed out by the taxpayer in 2008, it was evident that banks continued to speculate and fail to protect themselves from future crashes. Critics maintain that banks need adult supervision.

| **EXHIBIT 9.3** | **Corporate Charters** |

I believe . . . that banking institutions are more dangerous than standing armies.

—Thomas Jefferson

A potential reform strategy is to reinvigorate corporate charters, the legal instruments by which state governments incorporate businesses (Kelly, 2001). Historically, corporations were creatures of, and subordinate to, state governments. The Founders understood that "we the people" would be sovereign over not only the political, but also the economic system. Since corporations were seen as a threat to democracy—the American Revolution was a reaction to British trading companies—citizens determined whether corporations had the right to exist. Indeed, Thomas Jefferson wanted an Eleventh Amendment to prevent companies from dominating entire industries or having power to influence government. He saw this as necessary because the Bill of Rights does not protect people against private institutions (employees, for instance, have no powers of free speech). The main reason it was not incorporated into the Constitution was that it was deemed unnecessary given the state-chartering process.

Corporations possessed no authority, as legislatures set the terms of their existence—public corporations were not private enterprises and not run to maximize shareholder value. It was a privilege to serve the commonweal. The public governed corporations by detailing rules and defining operating conditions in charters (few were granted, and then only after legislative debate). In short:

- corporations had to serve a public purpose,
- they were limited to what business they could pursue (they could not buy other businesses) and could amass only certain amounts of wealth,
- there was a 15- to 20-year limit to the charter, subject to renewal,
- corporations were prohibited from lobbying,
- the penalty for abuse was not a fine or plea bargain, but charter revocation, and
- stakeholders were to be treated responsibly by corporations. (Hightower, 2003)

In 1886, however, a Supreme Court ruling—*Santa Clara vs. Southern Pacific Railroad Co.*— was widely misinterpreted to mean that corporations were "persons" with the same inherent, inalienable rights, freedom, and mobility as human beings (Hartmann, 2010). In subsequent years, courts established new doctrines (freedom of contract, managerial prerogative) to weaken state laws and citizen sovereignty over corporations, as they bestowed on corporations authority over investment, production, and organization of work (Grossman, 2001). The result: Shareholder primacy over public interest was established and the role of government changed from defining corporations to attempting to regulate them. Corporations, accordingly, have claimed such rights as the Fourteenth Amendment right to stop cities from favoring local businesses over chain stores, the Fourth Amendment right against search and seizure to prevent surprise inspections of companies, and the First Amendment right to free exercise to spend unlimited monies in political campaigns. Many states, nonetheless, still retain formal charter revocation authority, and some businesses— notably those that are small with little political power—may lose their charters.

In 1976, a Supreme Court decision equated free speech with spending, resulting in corporations having the biggest, wealthiest, and most undemocratic voice in electoral process. This was dramatically reinforced by the Court's 2010 *Citizens United vs. Federal Election Commission* decision, which removed limits on corporate contributions to political campaigns. Businesses are now able to tell employees which politicians they support, in effect, campaigning and collecting donations in the workplace. The implication is that "the rich and powerful transform free speech—our most important tool of bottom-up self-government—into a means of allowing top-down control" (Epps, 2012). Revisiting the origins of corporate charters, in brief, may hold promise as a reform strategy, one that might merit national standards for large corporations—the issuance of federal charters.

trading fiasco (Morgenson, 2013), and the Wells Fargo fake customer accounts discussed above. There is, in brief, no shortage of ideas to reform the system; what is missing is political will. Failing to confront lawlessness contributes to citizen feelings of alienation and powerlessness that feeds corruption.[10]

An indicator of the validity of reform is the inability of opponents to make an honest case against them. The implacable, tenacious power of existing stakeholders cannot be underestimated. An important consideration in enacting change is what may happen when and if they are implemented. Many white-collar crimes are extraordinarily complex, and public service frequently does not have the necessary expertise and funding to pursue them in court. In addition, resource-poor government prosecutors typically face well-financed corporate defense teams (e.g., Enron's Kenneth Lay and Jeffery Skilling's legal defense cost at least $70 million). Business corruption in recent years is not just a corporate failure, but also a failure of governmental oversight eviscerated by deregulation. Indeed, the sheer volume of cases simply overwhelms prosecutors (Ramirez & Ramirez, 2017).

The inability or unwillingness to employ anticorruption approaches amounts to the institutionalization of corruption that not only degrades democracy and the rule of law, but also imperils the future of the nation. Even the most egregious failures do not seem to be consequential to policymakers or banking officials. Evidence matters much less than a narrative that supports their interests. In a fact-free environment, unaffected by conventional understandings of facts, no one pays the price for disinformation. Reality-based governing is at risk. In many respects, America has become a society that cannot self-correct. Edward Wyatt (2012) says this about the Securities and Exchange Commission:

> Critics of the agency have raised concerns about its settlement practices over the last decade. According to the *New York Times* analysis of enforcement cases, nearly all of the biggest Wall Street firms have settled fraud cases by promising never to violate the law that they had already promised not to break, usually multiple times. In addition . . . those settlements also repeatedly granted exemptions to the biggest Wall Street

firms from punishments intended by Congress and regulators to act as a deterrent to multiple fraud violations.

The 2011 Financial Crisis Inquiry Commission faulted two administrations and regulators with permitting fraudulent lending practices, bundling of toxic loans for sale to investors, and risky bets on securities backed by the loans. One commentator explained the importance of this finding, saying, "The greatest tragedy would be to accept the refrain that no one could have seen this coming and thus nothing could have been done. If we accept this notion, it will happen again." (Chan, 2011)

 CASE STUDY 9.1

Applying Philosophical and Behavioral Ethics Approaches: Public to Private Employment on Similar Work

Craig Weatherford has worked for many years in Metropolitan County government. Trained as an engineer, his job is to conduct evaluations for the county zoning board regarding engineering features of filed petitions. Weatherford decides to retire. He then opens a consulting business and does similar work in the private sector. Given his prior experience in government, he is approached by a fellow engineer from a development firm who is petitioning the county zoning board for a variance. Weatherford agrees to represent the client and is slated to offer expert testimony before the board regarding the technical soundness of a large water system and the ecological consequences for surrounding jurisdictions. Previously, while employed by the county, Weatherford had completed preliminary assessments of this petition. His status as an expert witness for the company was challenged by citizen groups who opposed approval of the zoning variance. They questioned Weatherford's involvement in this issue. Now, he is uncertain about whether to continue to testify and represent his client.

Results-Based Analysis. Like the case in the last chapter, this case study can be examined using both philosophical theory and behavioral ethics. Beginning with the former, a results-based analysis focuses on the greatest good for the greatest number. Thinking broadly about the case, it is hard to argue that allowing one side of a dispute to use insider knowledge not available to the other side serves the greater good, especially when it creates an unlevel and unfair playing field. More narrowly, Weatherford may be viewing results differently. He thinks his experience will likely enable him to be successful in persuading the board to approve the variance. Weatherford's clients would be pleased if he prevailed and his business would likely flourish as a result. He doubts that there would be any mistakes in his testimony because he has intimate knowledge not only about board policies and procedures, but also regarding the nuances of the case based on his preliminary review. Nonetheless, the advocates opposing the variance will question the legitimacy of the process if the board relies on testimony from someone with the unfair advantage of inside information.

Weatherford is aware of his vulnerability to the charge of trading on insider knowledge, which undoubtedly will be emphasized by those opposing the variance. He is concerned that this allegation might be effective and undercut his credibility. Failure to win the variance for his client could damage his reputation for competence and lead people to question his integrity. He worries: Is he putting the end of achieving the variance ahead of the ethics of his profession regarding "avoiding the appearance of impropriety"? He realizes that there may be legitimate concerns regarding the ethical permissibility of his private employment following public service, but he is unwilling to withdraw.

Rule-Based Analysis. A rule- or principle-based analysis considers what is good for one is good for all. The privileged information is not available to all stakeholders. Weatherford does not seem willing to recognize that he may resent it if everyone was allowed to use the information in the way he intends to use it. Is giving an unfair advantage to one side of a dispute a practice he would want to universalize? Probably not, but he may feel that while the rules regarding conflict of interest and inside information are found in the relevant provisions of professional ethics codes, these provisions are vague and subject to interpretation. Further, he knows he is qualified professionally to evaluate the proposal objectively.

Weatherford recognizes he has an edge in this dispute because of his prior experience, but he also knows he will confront charges that he is violating standards. Despite fears that the citizen group would approach the media and publicly criticize his role, he is convinced that he can defend the variance on the merits and that the facts are on his side. The professional ethic requires him to represent his client to the best of his ability. Withdrawal from the case means failure.

Virtue-Based Analysis. A virtue ethics approach focuses on whether the decision makes him and his community better. Weatherford has promised to represent his client and to appear before the board; he is convinced that the variance will advance the community's interest and is loath to renege on this promise. Does he walk away from his client and give up midway through the case? Does he wither in the face of criticism? He thinks it is important to stand up and to be an effective advocate for those who are paying for his services. He owes them his best effort. He would not deny that his prior experience is an asset, but he would not apologize for using his skills acquired in civil service.

Yet does he have an unfair advantage over his opponents? Would the decision to continue pursuing the case reflect the actions of a person of good character? Can he look himself in the mirror and comfortably conclude he could live with himself if he continued to pursue the case? If not, he should withdraw. He wants to be prudent by carefully weighing the pros and contras of the case and consulting colleagues for advice before deciding definitively.

Behavioral Ethics-Based Analysis. Prior to a decision, however, it is important to consider insights from behavioral ethics that lead to consideration of other possible, sometimes unconscious, motivations and intuitions at play in Weatherford's actions. Recall that it is a universal human condition that people think that they are better than they really are. Self-serving bias, thus, can often influence decisions; Weatherford is likely making judgments based on what would advance his self-interest. The "want" and "should" selves might have been at odds with each other: He may have failed to distinguish between his emotional and impulsive "want" choice to take the case and the more thoughtful and deliberative "should" choice. This bounded ethical awareness could help account for the acceptance of the case and agreement to testify without giving sufficient attention to the possible appearance of impropriety. He may have framed the situation as one that he could win rather than considering the ethical implications, rationalizing that the rules on conflict of interest were vague and inapplicable. Upton Sinclair's famous line, "It is difficult to get a man to understand something, when his salary depends on his not understanding it," comes to mind.

Source: Online Ethics Center for Engineering (2006).

Indeed, years after the Wall Street debacle, several self-serving rationalizations—that no one saw it coming and bailing out the banks was the only responsible choice—attempted to provide exoneration of those responsible (Prasch, 2013). To the contrary, it was predicted by many analysts and economists (none of whom was later elevated to responsible positions in government or business). An alternative choice to subsidizing bankrupt investment firms would have been to follow the 1984 Continental Illinois bank collapse (one of the nation's largest banks), which was taken over by the Federal Deposit Insurance Corporation, the agency with extensive experience with resolving failed financial institutions.

Except for these widely overlooked studies, there have been no other authoritative examinations of the role that financial institutions played in the worst recession since the 1930s, no financial settlements proportionate to the crisis, and no criminal indictments of megabank executives. Stanford University economist Anat Admati (2013) wrote that huge banks "take enormous risks that endanger the economy. . . . We will never have a safe and healthy global financial system until banks are forced to rely much more on money from their owners and shareholders to finance their loans and investments."

Wall Street firms, whose resources easily surpass those of state and federal governments, may not only be too big to fail, but also too big to investigate, prosecute, and jail (Eisinger, 2017).[11] Operating with impunity, the banking industry continues to imperil American society as crime without punishment prevails. Prosecutorial passivity in the face of overwhelming evidence remains, but there are several isolated exceptions. Federal criminal charges were levelled against the major hedge firm SAC Capital Advisors, and the nation's largest bank, JPMorgan, confronted multiple investigations by the U.S. Justice Department, the Securities and Exchange Commission, and the Commodity Futures Trading Commission (Douglas, 2013; Lattman & Protess, 2013). SAC plead guilty to insider trading and paid a $1.23 billion fine, and JP Morgan settled for $13 billion, the largest fine ever levied by the government (it represents one-half of the bank's 2012 profits). No individuals at either institution were held accountable ("JP Morgan Pays," 2013).

CONCLUSION

Only they deserve power who justify its use daily.

—Dag Hammarskjold

No organization is corruption proof. Dishonorable behavior is often easy, it pays, and getting caught is improbable. However, ignoble conduct cannot be minimized, as the costs of corruption are intolerably high in a democracy. Paradoxically, Daniel Kaufmann (2005) argues, "You don't fight corruption by fighting corruption." Most jurisdictions do not need more politically expedient studies, anticorruption campaigns, laws, and agencies to serve as a scapegoat for lack of progress or a wall behind which to shield wrongdoing. What is needed is to (a) use the authority already present to pursue fundamental, systemic reforms; (b) end the deliberate underfunding of law enforcement and the judicial system; and (c) fortify a merit-based public service to deter and detect corruption.

For example, while the Securities and Exchange Commission charged 100 firms and 545 executive officers in connection to the 2008 economic collapse, the commission's budget is a fraction of those found in Wall Street firms. Further, federal regulations restrict the size of fines—most of which, in any case, are covered by corporate insurance policies. Investigations of institutions at the center of the debacle—Goldman Sachs, Lehman Brothers, Countrywide Financial, American International Group—have been dropped. Stated differently, the financial crisis was exacerbated by a violation of the fundamental principles that make democracy and capitalism work: accountability and equal justice (Judson, 2011).

In the meantime, it is useful to respond to common reasons for not dealing with corruption:

1. "Corruption is everywhere." The statement is not only self-defeating, but also makes an assumption that is contestable. Poor health is worldwide, but no one concludes that treating it is a bad idea.

2. "Corruption is culturally determined." While cultural diversity is a fact, there are some practices condoned by none. No culture, for example, condones outright bribery. Exaggerating the importance of culture is often a facade for practices grounded in self-interest. When this happens, it may preempt policies to change culture and save it from itself (Chapter 3).

3. "Cleansing society of corruption requires vast change taking many years." While evil has been present for centuries, so has honor. There is no time like the present to close loopholes, create incentives and deterrents, and augment accountability. The objective is to change the perception of corruption from a low-risk, high-profit enterprise to one that is a high-risk, low-profit peril.

4. "Worrying about corruption is pointless; with free markets, corruption will disappear." Corruption can easily inflict serious harm on free markets, as today's Wall

Street scandals, like the Enron Era and Savings and Loan disasters before it clearly demonstrate. Widespread misdoings have been exposed, annihilating the myth of self-regulating markets. Yet that does not stop many decision makers from fighting for the continuation of the same failed policies that caused the disaster. Markets, as imperfect human-created constructions of reality, eventually may be self-correcting, but not without considerable damage to society (adapted from Klitgaard, MacLean-Abaroa, & Parris, 2000).

In brief, the beginning and end of wrongdoing starts with each person. It is important to be aware of the types of circumstances likely to disorient one's moral compass and the rationalizations used to excuse dubious behavior. If corruption problems are ignored, we will not be able to deal with them—they will deal with us.

To combat corruption, a strong civil society (legitimacy of open debate, reform movements, institutions designed to serve the commonweal), clear vision for reform, vigorous political leadership, and rigorous monitoring of progress are necessary. Unfortunately, these critical elements seldom emerge simply because they are needed. The combination of circumstances necessary to attract national attention occurs so rarely that once reforms pass, it is unlikely that such issues will gain widespread attention for some time to come. It has been years since the near-collapse of the economy, and the problems that caused it remain.

The spreading scourge of corruption and the resulting systemic failures on Wall Street should mandate active, disinterested governmental regulation rooted in a "sober, conservative assessment of the human capacity of mistake and self-delusion, not to mention avarice and chicanery" (Meyerson, 2011). The economy should be a servant, not a master, of human needs. As James Madison famously said, "if men were angels, no government would be necessary." But the greed of an unchecked market system calls for regulation of corporate conduct that denigrates human worth and stifles social justice. Government is not a necessary evil, but a necessary good. Yet, until genuine reform is achieved, major scandals can be expected in the years ahead. The indelible lesson to date is that perpetrators can act with impunity. If there are limits to corruption, perpetrators are still trying to find them.

Discredited financial firms are transforming themselves into a larger, more centralized, and more virulent form, as they continue to corrupt the political system through campaign donations. At some point, a choice will have to be made: rescue investment banks or civil society.

***

The disposition to admire and almost worship the rich and the powerful is the great and most universal cause of the corruption of moral sentiments.

—Adam Smith

NOTES

1. Actual data are difficult to obtain for the reasons already noted and because statistics are ambiguous due to definitional issues. At the same time, Kaufmann, Kraay, and Mastruzzi (2006, 3–4) argue that imperfect proxies—informed stakeholder perceptions, institutional practices, project audits—furnish useful measures of corruption. In fact, "there should be no presumption that objective data is necessarily more informative than data that relies on survey responses from firms and citizens about the reality (of corruption) on the ground."

2. For a running commentary on these matters, see http://www.corporatecrimereporter.com. An interesting group of articles on white-collar crime can be found in the June 6, 2004, *New York Times Magazine*.

3. Mark Warren (2006) argues that the focus on corruption should be on how it undermines the processes of democracy. It does so by limiting the capability of governments to be responsive to the people when it excludes citizens from decisions that affect them.

4. Moral hazard is most often applied to individual consumers rather than too-big-to-fail institutions. "A lot of energy has gone into arguing that higher workers' comp payments, for example, make workers careless," writes Shaila Dewan (2012). "Far less is said about how lower workers' comp invites moral hazard for employers, making them less attentive to workplace safety."

5. See gift giving "point-counterpoint" feature in *Public Integrity*, 4(1) (Winter 2002); also examine Schultz (2010).

6. As noted in Lou Cannon, *Governor Reagan: His Rise to Power* (New York: Public Affairs, 2003).

7. The citizenry may have a pragmatic view toward many transgressions, overlooked so long as the elected official does not lie about them and can still be effective by providing for constituency needs. As one politico said, "[P]eople love a titillating story, but they care much more about who can deliver for them"—a fall from grace, followed by redemption, is the classic religious model of salvation. After reviewing the numerous sex scandals and the growing tolerance of some behavior, columnist Lenore Skenazy (2008) observed, "We are officially adults now, just like the French people but without the delicious pastries and nude first lady."

8. Charles Pierce (2012) writes that "if the lessons of Watergate really were that 'the system' worked and that 'the people' triumphed," then Ronald Reagan would have been impeached for the Iran-Contra affair, George W. Bush would not have gotten away with what his 2000 campaign did in Florida (to say nothing of what was done once in office), and Barack Obama would have been under much more pressure than he was for continuing many of the Bush–Cheney civil liberties policies. "The lasting lesson of Watergate," Pierce writes, "is that self-government was too dangerous."

9. For additional ideas dealing with corporate disclosure, citizen rights, employee participation, and related issues, see Kelly (2001) as well as http://multinationalmonitor.org (click on archived issues, July/August 2002, Corporate Reform After Enron, especially the "Introduction"), www.citizensforethics.org, www.corporatecrimereporter.com, and www.corpwatch.org. Also refer to "USA: 12 Things to Do Now About Corporations" (van Gelder, 2002). On a lighter note, defense attorney Edward W. Hayes created several measurements for gauging the ups and downs of Wall Street: the HEGI and the HESI (the High End Girlfriend Index and the High End Stripper Index). When the financial sector's business is good, traders and bankers spend enormous sums of money on high-end girlfriends and in the VIP rooms of Manhattan's pricey strip clubs (Richberg, 2008).

10. Yet citizens do not have to wait for politicians to act; they can be imaginative when the need arises. In the classical Greek play *Lysistrata*, the women of Athens go on strike, refusing to have sex until war ended. Peace negotiations were quickly concluded (also see Miller, 2005). Likewise Liberia's women used the same strategy in 2003 to campaign for peace, as did women in Togo

to demand the resignation of the country's president (Associated Press, 2012). In addition, as part of a 2012 Spanish national strike protesting austerity measures, the executive-class escorts refused bankers until they opened up credit lines to middle-class families and small businesses. Madrid's largest prostitute trade association (Moran, 2012), said, "We are the only ones with real ability to pressure [bankers]." Apparently, the idea for the strike came after one of its members pressured a bank employee to grant a loan to a struggling citizen by withholding her services.

11. Nonetheless, in 2007, the Justice Department decided to prosecute baseball star Roger Clemens for lying to Congress about steroid use (he was acquitted in 2012), while failing to prosecute government torturers and white-collar criminals.

FOR DISCUSSION

1. To the extent that people tend to think of themselves as more ethical than others, they may overestimate the degree of improper conduct in organizations. They then might modify their own behavior accordingly, with the result that corrupt behavior expands. Critique.

2. Comment:

   - "Behind every fortune lies a crime."—Balzac
   - "Behind the ostensible government sits enthroned an invisible government owing no allegiance and acknowledging no responsibility to the people. To destroy this invisible government, to befoul the unholy alliance between corrupt business and corrupt politics is the first task of the statesmanship of the day."—Theodore Roosevelt
   - "One of the most important duties of government is to put rings in the noses of hogs."—William Jennings Bryan
   - "It is easy to get into trouble and hard to get out."—Anonymous
   - "You can count on Americans to do the right thing—after they have tried everything else." —Winston Churchill

3. Choose at least one of the topics below for examination.

   - The nation's nonprofit groups were held in high esteem immediately after September 11, 2001. In the months that followed, however, questions about the practices of the United Way, the American Red Cross, and others caused public confidence in not-for-profits to plummet. A survey conducted several years later by Paul Light (Brookings Institution) found public trust in nonprofit organizations had not been regained. Assuming that attitudes are slow to change, how can high esteem and confidence be restored?
   - It is said the major banking institutions are "too big to fail." How does this explain (if it does) the failure to indict individual bank executives—an action that would not endanger the economy?
   - Corruption tends to prevail when the state is captured by elites who use it for their own purposes. Comment on this claim in the context of such concerns as campaign finance, low voter turnout, millionaires winning office, lack of competition for many

congressional seats, absence of political attention to major issues affecting the average voter, and so forth.

- "In government, there is no comparison private sector; there is no escape route—you can't declare bankruptcy."
- The military dictator of the Democratic Republic of Congo built a palace in his native village. The air conditioning had to run continuously so the jungle heat would not tarnish the gold leaf on the chandeliers. (Kingsolver, 2008, 547)

4. React to the statements below:

- "We have a formidable ethics program—we always catch and punish violators."
- "We have a very effective ethics program—we have 100 percent compliance; no one has ever been caught doing something wrong."
- "Without effective societal institutions—government and business transparency, checks and balances, a free press, independent judiciary—corruption control will be significantly hampered."

5. Populist Jim Hightower (2013, 2) writes, "Wall Street's super-rich speculators are now making millions of super-fast, robotic financial transactions per second, generating trillions of dollars a year from them—but producing nothing of real value for us, which is distorting and endangering markets." Discuss.

EXERCISES

1. Check with the secretary of state in your state or a local corporation; ask for a copy of a corporation's state charter. Examine its content and critique.

2. Consult these websites for updates on corruption: www.corpwatch.org, www.corporate policy.org, and www.citizensworks.org (which contains 12 reforms to crack down on white-collar crime).

3. Ralph Nader (2013) suggests that corporate CEOs should recite the Pledge of Allegiance at shareholder meetings because:

   [I]t is our country that chartered (their corporations) into existence and helped insure their success. . . . And these corporations now wield immense power in our elections, in our economy, over our military and foreign policies, and even in how we spend time with our friends and families. [This] is an ideal time to call out these runaway corporate giants who exploit the patriotic sensibilities of Americans for profit and, in wars, for profiteering, but decline to be held to any patriotic expectations or standards of their own.

   Contact businesspeople in your community for their views on this claim.

4. Examine the detailed investigation of corruption in nonprofit organizations by the *Washington Post* https://www.washingtonpost.com/investigations/inside-the-hidden-

world-of-thefts-scams-and-phantom-purchases-at-the-nations-nonprofits/2013/10/26/
825a82ca-0c26-11e3-9941-6711ed662e71_story.html?utm_term=.45c546ebec16.

5. **Bad Actor Tabletop Exercise 3:** The Bad Boss (see instructions in Chapter 3, Exercise 5)

Mark Sandsburg is the Director of Finance for Be a Friend, a local nonprofit organization that serves at-risk youth in the community. Most of his experience has been with for-profit organizations, and he has only recently become involved with the charity. He has a reputation of being good with numbers, but his methods are not completely sound. Mark has been shuffling funds between accounts to balance the budget and reporting some individual donations as unrestricted when they were collected for a specific cause. His methods, while shady, have lightened the financial burden the organization had been facing for the past year, but there is a chance that, if audited, his underhanded practices could come to light. The organization has recently cancelled its annual voluntary audit.

Role 1: Executive Director

You are the Executive Director of Be a Friend. With no expertise in finance, Mark's practices have evaded you until recently. You have temporarily cancelled your annual audit until you can resolve this issue. Mark assures you that no audit would uncover his practices and that you should continue business as usual. You can't be sure that's the right thing to do, but you do know Mark has improved the financial situation. There is a board meeting next week, and they expect an explanation as to why the audit was canceled. What do you do? Consider your obligations, ethical and otherwise. To whom are you accountable as the Executive Director of a nonprofit? What factors impact your decision?

Role 2: Chairman of the Board

You are the Chairman of the Board of Directors for Be a Friend. After finding out that the audit has been canceled, you decide to review this year's financial documents before the next meeting. In reviewing the documents, you find that Mark has been finagling the balance sheet. Despite the impropriety of these tactics, he has been able to free up funds for use on new initiatives. Do you bring this issue to the board for punitive action against Mark? Why or why not? Consider your obligations, ethical and otherwise. To whom are you accountable as a board member? What factors impact your decision?

Role 3: Donor

You are a representative for a private trust that funds Be a Friend. You know that it typically releases its annual audit in June, and it is nearly August. You have not been able to get a straight answer from anyone regarding the holdup. You become suspicious knowing that it recently replaced its Director of Finance and started several new initiatives. It is within your power to impose an independent audit to ensure your funds are being used as stipulated, but this organization is well connected within the community, and its events provide opportunities for your business to grow. What do you do? Consider your obligations, ethical and otherwise. To whom are you accountable as an investor? What factors impact your decision?

Role 4: Independent Auditor

You are an independent auditor. Be a Friend has hired your company to complete an audit. While reviewing their finances, you notice that funds have been changed around rather frequently, and are unsure whether you should investigate further. With the knowledge you have now, there appears to be no definitive wrongdoing, but if you continue your investigation, that may become an issue. Do you investigate the issue further, or clear the audit? Consider your obligations, ethical and otherwise. To whom are you accountable as an auditor? What factors impact your decision?

REFERENCES

Admati, A. (2013, August 25). We're all still hostages to the big banks. *New York Times*. Retrieved from http://www.nytimes.com/2013/08/25/

Albrecht, C., Sanders, M., Holland, D., & Albrecht, C. A. (2011). The debilitating effects of fraud in organizations. In R. Burke, E. Tomlinson, & C. Cooper (Eds.), *Crime and corruption in organizations: Why it occurs and what to do about it* (pp. 163–185). Guildford: Gower.

Anand, V., Ashford, B., & Joshi, M. (2004). Business as usual: Acceptance and perpetuation of corruption in organizations. *Academy of Management Executive*, *19*, 9–23.

Anderson, J. (2009, August 6). Despite bailouts, business as usual at Goldman. *New York Times*. Retrieved from http://www.nytimes.com/2009/08/06/business/06goldman.html? pagewanted=all&gwh=7C3735518D2FCA44B002654FF16B628F

Anechiarico, F., & Jacobs, J. (1994). Visions of corruption control and the evolution of American public administration. *Public Administration Review*, *54*, 465–773.

Ariely, D. (2012). *The (honest) truth about dishonesty: How we lie to everyone—especially to ourselves*. New York: Harper.

Ashforth, B., & Anand, V. (2003). The normalization of corruption in organizations. *Research in Organizational Behavior*, *25*, 1–52.

Associated Press. (2012, August 27). Togo sex strike: Women's group plans to withhold sex in effort to unseat president Faure Gnassingbe. *Huffington Post*. Retrieved from http://www.huffingtonpost.com/2012/08/27/togo-sex-strike-against-president-faure-gnassingbe_n_1832575.html

Association of Certified Fraud Examiners. (2008, July 14). New report estimates U.S. organizations lose 7 percent of revenues to fraud. Retrieved from http://www.acfe.com/press-release.aspx?id=4294968565&terms=(occupational)

Association of Certified Fraud Examiners. (2016). *2016 report to the nation on occupational fraud and abuse*. Austin, TX. Author. Retrieved from http://www.acfe.com/fraud/report.asp

Atkins, S. & Davey, M. (2017, June 14). 5 charged with involuntary manslaughter in Flint water crisis. *New York Times*. Retrieved from https://www.nytimes.com/2017/06.14/us/flint-water-crisis-manslaughter

Aviv, D. (2005, September 28). *Testimony to the U.S. Senate Finance Committee, hearing on Hurricane Katrina: Community rebuilding needs and effectiveness of past proposals*. Retrieved from http://www.senate.gov/~finance/hearings/testimony/2005test/092805datest.pdf

Baptiste, N. (2017, May 8). Millions of Americans are drinking contaminated water—and don't even know it. *Mother Jones*. Retrieved from http://www.motherjones.com/environment/2017/05/millions-drinking-contaminated-water/

Bauer, C. (2017, June 19). The five most toxic reasons for not confronting harassment. Retrieved from Christopher Bauer: chris=bauerethicsseminars.com@ send.aweber.com; on behalf of Christopher Bauer chris@bauerethicsseminars.com

Black, B. (2012, August 9). Eduardo Porter's "folly"—Why we must end the "race to the bottom." *New Economic Perspectives*. Retrieved from http://neweconomicperspectives.org/2012/08/eduardo-porters-folly-why-we-must-end-the-race-to-the-bottom.html

Black, B. (2016, February 12). The inaugural financial fraud lemons of the week award goes to DOJ. Retrieved from https://www.nakedcapitalism.com/2016/02/bill-black-the-inaugural-financial-fraud-lemons-of-the-week-award-goes-to-doj.html

Black, W. (2013, March 12). Which aspect of the FDIC's litigation failure is the most embarrassing and damaging? Naked Capitalism. Retrieved from https://www.nakedcapitalism.com/2013/03/bill-black-which-aspect-of-the-fdics-litigation

Bowman, J., & West, J. (2007). Lord Acton and employment doctrines: Absolute power and the spread of at-will employment. *Journal of Business Ethics, 74*, 119–130.

Brady, N. (2011, October 28). What, if anything, to do about Wall Street's wealth. *Washington Post*. Retrieved from http://www.washingtonpost.com/opinions/what-if-anything-to-do-about-wall-streets-wealth/2011/10/26/gIQASfYNNM_story.html

Brooks, D. (2010, June 24). The culture of exposure. *New York Times*. Retrieved from http://www.nytimes.com/2010/06/25/opinion/25brooks.html

Brooks, D. (2012, January 9). Where are the liberals? *New York Times*. Retrieved from http://www.nytimes.com/2012/01/10/opinion/brooks-where-are-the-liberals.html

Brooks, L., & Dunn, P. (2010). *Business and professional ethics* (5th ed.). Mason, OH: South Western Cengage Learning.

Burke, R., Tomlinson, E., & Cooper, C. (Eds.). (2011). *Crime and corruption in organizations: Why it occurs and what to do about it*. Farnham: Gower.

Cameron, D. (2015, June 6). Corruption is the cancer at the heart of so many of the problems we face around the world. *Huffington Post*. Retrieved from https://www.huffingtonpost.co.uk/david-cameron/david-cameron-fifa-corruption_b_7524550.html

Camilleri, J. (Ed.). (2011). *Organized crime: Challenges, trends, and reduction strategies*. New York: Nova Science.

Center for Public Integrity, Global Integrity, & Public Radio International. (2012). *State integrity investigation: Keeping government honest*. Washington, DC: Authors.

Cenziper, D. (2006). House of lies: Nonprofit's connections, performance raises questions. *Miami*

Herald. Retrieved from http://www.miamiherald.com/multimedia/news/houseoflies/part2/index.html

Chan, S. (2011, January 25). Financial crisis was avoidable, inquiry finds. *New York Times*. Retrieved from http://www.nytimes.com/2011/01/26/business/economy/26inquiry.html

Clark, C. (2012, August 16). Agency handling of Recovery Act praised in new book. *Government Executive*. Retrieved from http://www.govexec.com/technology/2012/08/agency-handling-recovery-act-praised-new-book/57481/

Clark, C. (2013, April 4). "Cassandras" of financial crisis blast Justice, Treasury departments. *Government Executive*. Retrieved from http://www.govexec.com/management/2013/04/cassandras-financial-crisis-blast-justice-treasury-departments/62298/

Clarke, R. (2004). *Against all enemies: Inside America's war on terror*. New York: Free Press.

Clement, R. (2006). Just how unethical is American business? *Business Horizons*, *49*, 313–327.

Cooper, M. (2009, September 18). On the lookout for stimulus fraud. *New York Times*. Retrieved from http://www.nytimes.com/2009/09/18/us/18fraud.html

Cowen, T. (2013, September 5). The age of the shadow bank run. *New York Times*. Retrieved from http://www.nytimes.com/2012/03/25/business/the-ban-run-updated.html

Cowley, S. (2017, August 31). Wells Fargo review finds 1.4 million more suspect accounts. *New York Times*. Retrieved from https://www.nytimes.com/2017/08/31/business/dealbook/wells-fargo-accounts.html

Croall, H. (2003). Combating financial crime: Regulatory versus Crime-control approaches. *Journal of Financial Crime*, *11*(1), 45–55.

Delaney, A. (2017, September 21) Flint water crisis likely increased fetal deaths, Study shows another hint that the U.S. ought to quit using lead pipes for water. *Huffington Post*. Retrieved from https://www.huffingtonpost.com/entry/flint-water-fetal-deaths_us_59c2ae5ee4b06f93538bf1ce

Dewan, S. (2012, February 26). Moral hazard: A tempest-tossed idea. *New York Times*, pp. 1B, 7B.

Dionne, E. (2010, December 19). Even progressives need CEOs. *Washington Post*. Retrieved from http://www.washingtonpost.com/wpdyn/content/article/2010/12/19AR2010121903017.html

Dobel, P. (1999). *Integrity*. Baltimore, MD: Johns Hopkins University Press.

Douglas, D. (2013, August 20). Legal troubles mount at JP Morgan. *Washington Post*. Retrieved from http://articles.washingtonpost.com/2013–08–20/business/41429476_1_jpmorgan-chase-biggest-bank-jamie-dimon

Douglas, S., & Mills, K. (2000, August 16). Nonprofit fraud: What are the key indicators? *Canadian Fundraiser*. Retrieved from http://www.charityvillage.com/cv/research/rlega116.html

Dwyer, P. (2013, November 17). Why no bankers go to jail. *Bloomberg*. Retrieved November 17, 2013 from http://www.bloomberg.com/news/2013-11-17/why-no-bankers-go-to-jail.html

Eisinger, J. (2017). *The chickenshit club: Why the justice department fails to prosecute executives*. New York: Simon & Schuster.

Epps, G. (2012, April 16). Don't blame corporate "personhood." *American Prospect*. Retrieved from http://prospect.org/article/dont-blame-corporate-personhood

Epstein, D. (2012, August 13). Ethics office audit of GSA fell far short. *Federal Times*. Retrieved from http://www.federaltimes.com/article/20120812/ADOP06/308120001/Ethics-office-aud it-GSA-fell-far-short

Ferguson, C. (2012). *The predator nation: Corporate criminals, political corruption, and the hijacking of America*. New York: Crown.

Foroohar, R. (2017, September 27). How big banks became our masters. *New York Times*. Retrieved from https://www.nytimes.com/2017/09/27/opinion/how-big-banks-became-our-masters.html

Friedman, T. (2011). Did you hear the one about the bankers? *New York Times*. Retrieved from http://www.nytimes.com/2011/10/30/opinion/sunday/friedman-did-you-hear-the-one-about-the-bankers.html

Garment, S. (1991). *Scandal*. New York: Crown.

Gerard, L. W. (2012, June 25). Robin Hood tax: Economic justice. *Huffington Post*. Retrieved from http://www.huffingtonpost.com/leo-w-gerard/robin-hood-tax_b_1622176.html

Gitlow, A. (2005). *Corruption in corporate America*. Lanham, MD: University Press of America.

Gongloff, M. (2012, September 6). Risky business pays off for Wall Street: Financial crisis penalties pale compared to profits. *Huffington Post*. Retrieved from http://www.huffingtonpost.com/2012/09/06/wall-street-financial-crisis-penalties_n_1858738.html

Greenlee, J., Fischer, M., Gordon, T., & Keating, E. (2007). An investigation of fraud in nonprofit organizations; Occurrences and deterrents. *Nonprofit and Voluntary Sector Quarterly*, *36*, 676–694.

Grimm, F. (2010, July). A conspiracy of silence killed JESCA. *Miami Herald*. Retrieved from http://miamiherald.typepad.com/grimm_truth/2010/07/a-conspiracy-of-silence-killed-jesca.html

Grossman, R. (2001). Taking care of business: citizenship and the charter of incorporation. In D. Ritz (Ed.), *Defying corporations, defining democracy: A book of history and strategies* (pp. 59–72). Lanham, MD: Apex Press.

Grunwald, M. (2012). *The new New Deal: The hidden story of change in the Obama era*. New York: Simon & Schuster.

Hartmann, T. (2010). *Unequal protection: How corporations became "people" and how to fight back* (2nd ed.). San Francisco: Barrett-Koehler.

Hightower, J. (2003). How a clerical error made corporations "people." *Hightower LowDown*, *5*(4). Retrieved from http://www.hightowerlowdown.org/node/664/

Hightower, J. (2013, Autumn). A modest proposal on student debt. *Hightower LowDown*, p. 2.

"How to help the neediest Harvey victims" (2017, August 31). *Naked Capitalism*. Retrieved from https://www.nakedcapitalism.com/2017/08/help-neediest-harvey

Johnson, C. (2006, October 25). End of Enron's saga brings era to a close. *Washington Post*. Retrieved from http://www.washingtonpost.com/wp-dyn/content/article/2006/10/24/AR2006102401246.html

JP Morgan pays. (20 November, 2013). *New York Times*. Retrieved November 20, 2013 from http://www.nytimes.com/2013/11/21/opinion/jpmorgan-pays.html?_r=0

Judson, B. (2011, December 2). Restoring capitalism: Occupy our homes shines a light on our great failure. *Huffington Post*. Retrieved from http://www.huffingtonpost.com/bruce-judson/restoring-capitalism-occu_b_1124841.html

Kaufmann, D. (2005). Back to basics: 10 myths about governance and corruption. *Finance and Development*, *42*(3). Retrieved from http://www.imf.org/external/pubs/ft/fandd/2005/09/basics.htm

Kaufmann, D., Kraay, A., & Mastruzzi, M. (2006). Measuring corruption: Myths and realities (Working paper). Retrieved from http://www1.worldbank.org/publicsector/anticorrupt/corecourse2007/Myths.pdf

Kelly, M. (2001). *Divine right of capital*. San Francisco: Barrett-Koehler.

Kingsolver, B. (2008). *The poisonwood bible*. New York: Harper Perennial.

Klein, N. (2007). *The shock doctrine: The rise of disaster capitalism*. New York: Picador.

Klitgaard, R., MacLean-Abaroa, R., & Parris, H. L. (2000). *Corrupt cities: A practical guide to cure and prevention*. Washington, DC: World Bank.

Krugman, P. (2011, June 11). Rule by rentiers. *New York Times*. Retrieved from http://www.nytimes.com/2011/06/10/opinion/10krugman.html/

Krugman, P. (2017, March 20). America's epidemic of infallibility. *New York Times*. Retrieved from https://www.nytimes.com/2017/03/20/opinion/americas-epidemic-of-infallibility.html

Lattman, P., & Protess, B. (2013, July 25). SAC Capital is indicated and called a magnet for cheating. *New York Times*. Retrieved from http://www.nytimes.com/2013/07/25sac-capital-is-indicted?pagewanted=print

Leber, R. (2017, July 19). Trump's big plan for EPA is already dead. *Mother Jones*. Retrieved from www.motherjones.com/environment/2017/07/trumps-big-plan-for-a-tiny-epa-is-already-dead/

Lloyd, H. (2009). *Wealth against the commonwealth*. Ithaca, NY: Cornell University Library Press. [Original work published 1894]

Madry, K. (2017, September 8). Calling Red Cross "inept"; Houston councilman urges Harvey donors to send money elsewhere. *Dallas News*. Retrieved from https://www.dallasnews.com/news/texas/2017/09/08/houston-councilman-tells-residents-donate-inept-red-cross

McRay, G. (2009, September 16). Bad seeds—Why the ACORN scandal matters to other nonprofits. *Foundation Group*. Retrieved from http://www.501c3.0rg/blog/acorn-scandal-matters-to-nonprofits

Merle, R. (2016, September 29). Lawmakers to Wells Fargo CEO: "Why shouldn't you be in jail?" *Washington Post*. Retrieved from https://www.washingtonpost.com/news/wonk/wp/2016/09/29/wells-fargo...

Meyerson, H. (2011, March 15). From Japan's devastation, our Lisbon moment? *Washington Post*. Retrieved from http://www.washingtonpost.com/opinions/from-japans-devastation-our-lisbon-moment/2011/03/15/ABPH0yZ_story.html

Miami-area social-service charity files for bankruptcy. (2009). *Philanthropy Today*. Retrieved from http://philanthropy.com/blogPost/Miami-Area-Social-Service-c/18013

Miller, M. (2005, May 25). Listen to my wife. *New York Times*. Retrieved from http://www.nytimes.com/2005/05/25/opinion/25miller.html

Moran, L. (2012, March 27). A national sex strike! *Daily Mail Online*. Retrieved from http://www.

dailymail.co.uk/news/article-2120984/Spains-high-class-hookers-ban-sex-bankers-provide-credit-cash-strapped-economy.html

Morgenson, G. (2013, March 17). JP Morgan's follies for all to see. *New York Times*, BU, p. 1.

Morgenson, G., & Story, L. (2011, April 14). In financial crisis, no prosecutions of top figures. *New York Times*. Retrieved from http://www.nytimes.com/2011/04/14/business/14prosecute.html?pagewanted=all

Mr. Dimon on the hill. (2012, June 13). *New York Times*. Retrieved from http://www.nytimes.com/2012/06/14/opinion/jamie-dimon-on-the-hill.html

Nader, R. (2013, July 3). To big US corporations: What about some patriotism for America? *Huffington Post*. Retrieved from http://www.huffingtonpost.com/ralph-nader/corporate-patriotism

No fault corporate crime. (2012, April 3). *Corporate Crime Reporter*. Retrieved from http://www.corporatecrimereporter.com/news/200/no-fault-corporate-crime/

Nye, J., Zelikow, P., & King, D. (1997). *Why people don't trust government*. Cambridge, MA: Harvard University Press.

Ochs, M. (2016, September 15). In Wells Fargo scandal, the buck stopped well short. *New York Times*. Retrieved from https://www.nytimes.com/2016/09/15/opinion/in-wells-fargo-scandal-the-buck-stopped-well-short.html

Online Ethics Center for Engineering. (2006, June 10). *Related work done by a private party following public employment (adapted from NSPE Case No. 78–10)*. Retrieved from http://www.onlineethics.org/Resources/Cases/ec78–10.aspx

Pearlstein, S. (2012, May 20). JP Morgan's soap opera makes clear that Wall Street is detached from reality. *Washington Post*. Retrieved from http://www.washingtonpost.com/jpmorgans-soap-opera-makes-clear-that-wall-street-is-detached-from-reality/2012/05/18/gIQAIJwvbU_story.html

Perri, F., & Brody, R. (2011). The dark triad: Organized crime, terror, and fraud. *Journal of Money Laundering Control*, *14*, 44–59.

Pierce, C. P. (2012). The lessons of Watergate do not belong to us. *Esquire*. Retrieved from http://www.esquire.com/print-this/watergate-40-years-later-9747335?page=all

Porter, E. (2012, July 11). The spreading scourge of corporate corruption. *New York Times*. Retrieved from http://www.nytimes.com/2012/07/11/business/economy/the-spreading-scourge-of-corporate-corruption.html

Prasch, R. (2013, September 22). The "lessons" that Wall Street, Treasury, and the White House need you to believe about the Lehman Collapse. *Huffington Post*. Retrieved from http://www.huffingtonpost.com/robert-e-prasch/the-lessons-that-wall-str_b_3953321.html?view=print&comm_ref=false

Protess, B., & Silver-Greenberg, J. (2012, December 10). HSBC to pay $1.92 billion to settle charges of money laundering. *New York Times*. Retrieved from http://dealbook.nytimes.com/2012/12/10/hsbc-said-to-near-1–9-billion-settlement-over-money-laundering/?_r=0

Ramirez, M., & Ramirez, S. (2017). *The case for the corporate death penalty: Restoring law and order on Wall Street*. New York: New York University Press.

Reich, R. (2011). *Aftershock*. New York: Knopf.

Rich, F. (2007, October 21). Suicide is not painless. *New York Times*. Retrieved from http://www.nytimes.com/2007/10/21/opinion/21rich.html

Richberg, K. (2008, September 28). Power shifts from N.Y. to D.C. *Washington Post*. Retrieved from http:www.washingtonpost.com/wp-dyn/content/article/2008/09/27/ArR200909027021.html

Rowe, W., & Dato-on, M. C. (Eds.). (2013). *Introduction to nonprofit management*. Thousand Oaks, CA: Sage.

Russell, A., & Vinsel, L. (2017, July 3). Let's get excited about maintenance. *New York Times*, SR 3.

Samuelson, R. J. (2008, January 23). Capitalism's enemies within. *Washington Post*. Retrieved from http://www.washingtonpost.com/wp-dyn/content/article/2008/01/22/AR2008012202615.html

Sandel, M. (2012). *What money can't buy: The moral limits of markets*. New York: Farrar, Straus, & Giroux.

Saviano, R. (2012, August 25). Where the mob keeps its money. *New York Times*. Retrieved from http://www.nytimes.com/2012/08/26/opinion/sunday/where-the-mob-keeps-its-money.html

Schultz, D. (2010). Ethics regulations across the professions: The problem of gifting. *Public Integrity*, *12*, 161–172.

Schwartz, J. (2009, December 7). Justices to weigh honest-services law. *New York Times*. Retrieved from http://www.nytimes.com/2009/12/07/us/07honest.html

Skenazy, L. (2008, August 12). A mistress, a baby, a men's room. *New York Sun*. Retrieved from http://www.nysun.com/opinion/a-mistress-a-baby-a-mens-room/83674/

Sloan, C. (2016, March 14). Wall Street is causing the water crises in American cities. *Whistleblow Wall Street*. Retrieved from https://whistleblowwallstreet.com/wall-street-is-causing-the-water-crises-in-american-cities/

Smith, Y. (2012, May 22). Earth to Dimon: Banks don't have a right to profit. *New York Times*. Retrieved from http://www.nytimes.com/roomfordebate/2012/05/21/what-could-have-prevented-the-jpmorgan-chase-disaster/for-starters-reinstate-glass-steagall

Spoth, T. (2010, July 27). IG: DoD can't account for almost 9 billion in Iraq funds. *Federal Times*. Retrieved from http://www.federaltimes.com/article/20100727/DEPARTMENTS01/7270304/IG-DoD-can-t-account-almost-9-billion-Iraq-funds

Stephens, J., & Flaherty, M. (2013, October 13). Inside the hidden world of thefts, scams and phantom purchases at the nation's nonprofits. *Washington Post*. Retrieved from www.washingtonpost.com/investigations/inside-the-hidden-world-of-thefts-scams-and-phantom-purchases-at-the-nations-nonprofits/2013/10/26/825a82ca-0c26-11e-9941-6711ed662e71_story.html

Thompson, J. (2000). *Political scandal*. London: Blackwell.

U.S. Senate Permanent Committee on Investigations, Committee on Homeland Security and Governmental Affairs. (2011). *Wall Street and the financial crisis: Anatomy of a financial collapse*. Retrieved from http://www.hsgac.senate.gov//imo/media/doc/Financial_Crisis/FinancialCrisisReport.pdf?attempt=2

van Gelder, S. (2002, September 30). 12 things to do now about corporations. *Yes! Magazine*.

Retrieved from http://www.yesmagazine.org/issues/living-economies/12-things-to-do-now-about-corporations

Veruil, P. (2017). *Valuing bureaucracy: The case for progressive* government. New York: Cambridge University Press.

Warren, M. (2006). Political corruption as duplicitous exclusion. *PS: Political Science and Politics, 37*, 803–807.

Waters, M. (2012, May 22). Wall Street should stop trying to gut financial reform. *The Hill.* Retrieved from http://thehill.com/blogs/congress-blog/economy-a-budget/228597-wall-street-should-stop-trying-to-gut-financial-reform

Wayne, L. (2012, March 21). Hits and misses in war on bribery. *New York Times.* Retrieved from http://www.nytimes.com/2012/03/11/business/corporate-bribery-war-has-hits-and-a-few-misses.html?_r=1&pagewanted=all&gwh=0FBC2847B1A3A6E7AD0870C37 3627B5E

"Wells Fargo fined $185 million" (2016, September 9.) *Naked Capitalism.* Retrieved from https://www.nakedcapitalism.com/2016/09/wells-fargo-fined-185-million-for-opening-phony-customer-accounts-charging-fees-without-consent-executives-go-scot-free.html

Whitlock, C. & Woodward, B. (2016, December 5). Pentagon buries evidence of $125 billion in bureaucratic waste. *Washington Post.* Retrieved from https://www.washingtonpost.com/investigations/pentagon-buries-evidence-of-125-billion-in-bureaucratic-waste/2016/12/05/e0668c76-9af6-11e6-a0ed-ab0774c1eaa5_story.html?utm_term=.1ebf7b981e71

"Why can't Red Cross say how much of your donation goes to Harvey relief?" (2017, September 4). *Des Moines Register.* Retrieved from https://www.desmoinesregister.com/story/opinion/editorials/2017/09/04/red-cross-donation-harvey-relief-grassley/626028001/

Why the return of bigger banks means bigger risks for everyone else. (2017, September 8) *New York Times.* Retrieved from https://www.nytimes.com/2017/09/08/opinion/why-the-return-of-bigger-banks-means-bigger-risks-for-everyone-else.html

Wyatt, E. (2012, February 22). Responding to critics: S.E.C. defends "no wrongdoing" settlements. *New York Times.* Retrieved from http://dealbook.nytimes.com/2012/02/22/s-e-c-chairwoman-defends-settlement-practices/

10 Whistleblowing in Organizations

The ultimate measure of a man or woman is not where he stands in moments of comfort and convenience, but where he stands at times of challenge and controversy.

—Martin Luther King

The last chapter demonstrated that corruption is a significant problem in society. Indeed, many scandals are revealed by "whistleblowers," those who disclose organizational misconduct. Whistleblowing is a manifestation of serious issues; as long as fraud, waste, and abuse exist, so will the need to expose them. Consistent with legal usage, blowing the whistle is a process, as external reports of wrongdoing typically start with internal reports. Although dissent on the job is at least as old as the republic—the 1778 Continental Congress voted unanimously for the first U.S. whistleblower legislation—it only crystallized into a social movement in the late 1970s as public interest groups formed, professional associations sponsored symposia, universities encouraged research, unions protected members, national conferences convened, and legislatures held hearings and passed laws. The importance of the whistleblower in responsible administration—an individual who reveals information about illegal, immoral, or inefficient organizational action that endangers the health, safety, or freedom of the public—is undeniable.[1] The U.S. Senate, in fact, unanimously passed the National Whistleblower Appreciation Day resolution on July 14, 2014 celebrating the 236th anniversary of the initial whistleblower law.

Among the many examples since the start of the new century are the following:

- Whistleblowers won *Time* magazine's Persons of the Year Award for their role in exposing problems at Enron, Worldcom, and the Federal Bureau of Investigation.
- University of Massachusetts student J. Stone Laraway, in the face of a national cheating epidemic, blew the whistle on "crime in the classroom," saying that "this is my school, and I will not tolerate it."
- An Army general questioned administration projections about needed troop strength in Iraq.

- The chief of the U.S. Park Service was terminated for voicing concerns about staffing shortages (she was reinstated).
- A prominent climate change official complained that misleading statistics were being used by the White House.
- A soldier exposed torture of inmates in Iraq's Abu Ghraib prison.
- "Alumni" whistleblowers—such as a past White House terrorism chief, a former Treasury secretary, and numerous retired generals—renounced the Iraq War.
- The official who managed the Pentagon's largest contract in Iraq was discharged when he refused to pay $1 billion in questionable charges to a contracting firm (the bill was later paid and the company was awarded performance bonuses, plus a new $150 billion contract).
- An Army enlisted man was charged with the largest military leak in history, and remained in custody for nearly four years before being convicted and sentenced.
- A National Security Agency official—who blew the whistle on massive fraud, waste, and abuse—was indicted on espionage charges for allegedly making unauthorized contact with a newspaper (the court proceedings collapsed in 2011 when the judge ruled that the government had no case).
- A Marine Corps whistleblower, estimating that one in every four combat deaths in Iraq could have been prevented by timely shipping of mine-resistant vehicles, was stripped of his job duties and security clearance (he was reinstated).
- Whistleblowers revealed that BP and the federal government made long-term public health and environmental effects of the Gulf oil spill worse by using a chemical to disperse oil that was more toxic than the crude oil alone.
- A Veterans Administration employee blew the whistle on poor care for mental-health patients at the Phoenix VA hospital—the same facility involved in the agency's wait-time scandal (see Chapter 12); he faced retaliation in 2015, but was recently assigned to the new VA Office of Accountability and Whistleblower Protection.
- A U.S. Environmental Protection Agency and Justice Department employee team won a Service to America medal for exposing a scheme by Volkswagen to rig over half a million vehicles to circumvent auto emission standards (for an extensive list of whistleblowers since 1773, see https://www.whistleblower.org/timeline-us-whistleblowers).

There are numerous cases in the business and nonprofit sectors as well involving, for example, "liar loans" and "robo signings" in home mortgage approvals, the use of beef trimmings known as "pink slime" in the meat-packing industry, widely reported misdoings in pharmaceutical firms and tobacco corporations, and scandals at the Red Cross, United Way, and Boy and Girl Scouts. While not all disclosures become headline news, these "moral sentinels," "truth tellers," or "insider threats" have been responsible for revealing problems in such areas as regulatory corruption, merit system abuses, dangers to public health, and conflict of interest irregularities. Common to all incidents is the realization that organizations can be held to account by those willing to put principles into practice by "speaking truth to power." Yet the majority of ethical rebels exist in obscurity and never receive vindication as lionized persons of conscience. Those who are vindicated "are the rare exception, and even most of them pay a horrible price with lifelong scars" (Devine & Maassarani, 2011, 18; for a more optimistic, albeit cautious, assessment, see Hesch, 2008).

In light of such events, the chapter objectives are to:

- understand the importance of conscientious employees in contemporary affairs,
- describe relevant statutes,
- analyze cases,
- comprehend the pervasiveness of organizational power, and
- evaluate current trends in whistleblowing.

The overall challenge is not only to achieve new civil rights for those who speak out, but also to reduce the need to blow the whistle.

SIGNIFICANCE OF WHISTLEBLOWING

Whistleblowing occurs when micro-level personal ethics compel a person to bring meso-level organizational wrongdoing to light sometimes for macro-level reform. Employee efforts to detect and correct fraud or waste committed by an employer demonstrate the permeable nature of the boundaries between the three levels of ethics.

As insiders, employees are well positioned to uncover—and help control—waste and fraud in the workplace. Given the low public visibility and high technical complexity of organizational activities, detection of abuse rests in large part with the workforce. In fact, it is amply documented that public and private sector whistleblowers are the single most important source for detecting and preventing crime—more than government regulators, law enforcement personnel, and professional auditors combined (Association of Certified Fraud Examiners, 2016; PricewaterhouseCoopers, 2007; U.S. Department of Justice, 2010). The federal government, for instance, recovers $7 for every $1 spent fighting fraud, much of which comes from such insider information (Kennedy, 2012; Ventriss & Barney, 2003).

Rothschild and Miethe (1999) estimate that while one-third of employees have seen unethical conduct, over half of them remain silent probably from either a fear of consequences or a sense of futility ("Why bother?"). Revelations in 2011, for instance, revealed that Pennsylvania State University administrators and football coaches knew of criminal sexual conduct for years, but failed to report it to police (see Case Study 2.1). Silence, while understandable, is ethically problematic from results, rules, and rectitude perspectives (Chapter 7). Nondisclosure does not represent the greatest good for the greatest number; it is a form of deceit that causes harm and compromises personal integrity. Rates of disclosure are highest in the public service when compared to business and nonprofit sectors (Brewer & Selden, 1998). There are a variety of reasons for this; one is the oath of office that obligates civil servants to uphold the constitution, not necessarily one's supervisors. Corporate America, in contrast, often requires employees to sign a non-disparagement, nondisclosure, or mandatory company-dominated arbitration agreements in case of disputes.

Nonetheless, "[t]he wave of corruption," one observer noted, "has been the catalyst for a public mandate to protect whistleblowers. There's been more raw material ... than at any time since Watergate" (Beutler, 2007), a statement that continues to be true in a social media era. An audit by the U.S. Department of Treasury found that in just one year, tipsters reported $65 billion in unpaid taxes (Kocieniewski, 2010). In 2011, the federal government broke all records, bringing nearly $2.3 billion in whistleblower settlements and judgments. Yet complaints that contractors have defrauded taxpayers out of billions of dollars languish at the U.S. Department of Justice because of case backlog—by 2012, over 3,500 fraud cases had not been investigated due to lack of resources (Kennedy, 2012), a problem yet to be fully rectified. By 2016, however, over $37 billion had been collected since 1986 as a direct result of whistleblower information (Kohn, 2017, 12).

The larger, more systemic, and more institutional nature of the problem, the greater the managerial effort is to punish the truth teller. It is unusual for employees to be victims of adverse personnel actions when they report behavior of subordinates. It is when superiors are implicated that retaliation occurs. Workers are also more likely to blow the whistle when wrongdoing is serious, frequent, or widespread—but under these conditions, they are also less likely to persuade management to correct the problem and more apt to suffer reprisal (Near & Miceli, 2008, 277).

Organizations create a self-contained, self-serving worldview wherein dissent is seen as a challenge to the legitimacy of the leadership. Ironically, ethical resisters are often competent professionals who possess the attributes that employers claim they desire—in reporting one's superior, the ultimate act of loyalty becomes an act of betrayal (Matt & Shahinpoor, 2011). Conscientious employees usually believe their organizations will be gratified that they reported misconduct, instead of recognizing that their unwelcome allegations can make their superiors' life—and their own—far more difficult. Nonetheless, as shown in Case Study 10.1, blowing the whistle may be protected by law, but only when certain conditions are fulfilled.

The act of whistleblowing can be justified when:

- it is done with an appropriate moral motive,
- internal channels of dissent have been judiciously considered,
- it is based on evidence that would persuade a reasonable person,
- analysis has been made of the seriousness, immediacy, and specificity of the problem,
- possible solutions to the issue are offered,
- it is commensurate with the employee's responsibility,
- it has some chance of success, and
- the employee is ready to accept the personal and professional consequences that accompany the decision (adapted from Bowman, 1983, 91; also see Bauer, 2015, August 24).

It is common for personnel to work within the system. But when superiors do not do anything about illegal conduct or when individuals experience retaliation, the employee may feel the only ethical choice is to go public. Stated differently, can information be turned into power? Can disclosure make a difference? Did intelligence analyst Edward Snowden fulfill the elements of justified whistleblowing (Exhibit 10.1)?

A valid concern is no defense from organizational revenge. Thus, while one survey of civil servants reports that employees claiming direct knowledge of waste and fraud decreased during the last two decades, a significant number of those who reported problems experienced either threats of reprisal or reprisal (U.S. Merit Systems Protection Board, 2011). Retaliation can be subtle and occur without witnesses or happen for otherwise routine administrative reasons (changed duties, job transfers, performance evaluations, and otherwise marginalized). In many other instances, employees also often lose their jobs, their family, their careers, their retirements and their savings, as employers find it more expedient to "shoot the messenger."[2] Being right is no protection from revenge, as organizations transform whistleblower issues into employee subordination. The truth teller has the burden of proof to show that he was a victim of retaliation.

CASE STUDY 10.1

Problem Solver or Trouble Maker?

Vera English worked in a laboratory at the General Electric (GE) plant in Wilmington, North Carolina, as a quality control specialist responsible for the handling of radioactive materials. Dangerous practices and resulting hazards—contamination, defective equipment, leaks, and employee exposure—were common to everyday work conflicting with Vera's personal, micro ethic of employee safety at work. Her complaints led to work stoppages and caused the Nuclear Regulatory Commission to cite GE for safety violations.

The company, espousing a starkly different meso-level ethic of allowing lax safety standards, barred her from the lab and gave her 90 days to find another position at the facility; when that failed, she was terminated. Under the federal law at the time, she filed a wrongful discharge claim within 30 days of her firing. In court, GE was found guilty of illegal retaliation. English was reinstated and awarded damages.

The company, however, "was not finished. . . . [It] fought English's case every step of the way. . . . Numerous legal technicalities were raised, and they finally found one that would stick: failure to file a timely complaint. . . . GE argued that because she was told that she had 90 days to find a new position within the company, her 30-day filing period commenced to run even before her last day of work. The courts agreed, and her case was thrown out."

QUESTIONS TO CONSIDER

1. What, if anything, should English have done differently?

2. What lessons can be drawn from this case?

Source: Adapted from Kohn (2017, 68–69, 258–260).

| **Exhibit 10.1** | **Is Edward Snowden a Whistleblower? Turncoat or Patriot?** |

Revelations by National Security Agency (NSA) contract employee Edward Snowden sparked a global firestorm of controversy over surveillance and privacy. What are people entitled to know about their government, and what is government entitled to know about its people (Clark, 2013; also see Chapter 14)? A free society requires an informed citizenry to protect both national security and personal privacy. Appropriate measures of transparency and accountability are essential components of that goal.

In June 2013, intelligence analyst Snowden revealed to the *Washington Post* and *The Guardian* (UK) illegal NSA surveillance, done under the mantle of national security, of hundreds of millions of Americans and foreigners through a secret data-mining program. The disclosure of thousands of secret, heavily encrypted documents in the release confirmed what advocacy organizations have known or suspected.

Is Snowden a traitor or a profile in courage? A naïf or a hero? A spy or a whistleblower? Some officials, including the Speaker of the U.S. House of Representatives, found him guilty of espionage for taking top-secret records out of the country to China and Russia (Thiessen, 2013). Others pointed out that leaking classified information, and ignoring internal procedures to address problems, is against the law; in contrast, whistleblowers often engage in lawful disclosures and use approved channels for raising concerns (Hicks, 2013). Perhaps Snowden is more of a conscientious objector than a whistleblower, according to R. Scott Osward of the Employment Law Group (as cited in McElhatton, 2013), although some practitioners of civil disobedience believe that they should accept punishment for violating the law. Still others see Snowden as a "classic" whistleblower because he disclosed information about a rogue program and was then subjected to derogatory characterizations by the government in an effort to shift attention from the message to the messenger (Jesslyn Radack, as quoted in Wemple, 2013).

While Snowden is criticized for releasing classified information:

> [P]ervasive surveillance does not meet the standard for classified information. Documents are properly classified only if they reveal sources or methods of intelligence gathering used to protect the US from its enemies. Information on domestic surveillance cannot be classified unless the US government deems its own population as an enemy. ("GAP stands with Snowden," 2013)

The public has a constitutional right to know how and why the government is conducting domestic surveillance. Like Wall Street (Chapter 9), the intelligence community exercises vast powers and lacks genuine accountability. Tellingly, the Obama administration did not label Snowden a spy. Even though he was indicted under the Espionage Act, the charges are theft of government property and unauthorized communication of national defense data.

Danah Boyd (2013) argues that what it means to protest may be changing in today's information age. Traditional forms of dissent and civil disobedience no longer create iconic narratives, and increasing secrecy since the 2001 terrorist attacks has made the rule of law ineffective as a check on power. Instead, Snowden created a new model of how to expose information (Rosen, 2013), at least so long as the Snowden "effect" (public attention to secret surveillance) outlasts the Snowden "saga" (his personal story in seeking asylum). While claiming a moral motive for his actions, Snowden left the country because, in the words of Project on Government Oversight executive director Danielle Brian, "there are very weak protections for intelligence whistleblowers and none at all for intelligence contractors" (quoted in Davidson, 2013).

When *The Guardian* asked if there was evidence that Snowden had cooperated with any intelligence service or American adversary, the administration and Congress declined to provide any (Ackerman, 2013). For now, Snowden's remaining stockpile of stolen documents is designed to automatically become public knowledge should something happen to him (Publius, 2013). Instead of just divulging information and being forgotten, his approach may be a more effective form of opposition because it threatens the authority of the state and invites "the American people to consider . . . less militaristic and more democratic approaches to national security" (Bacevich, 2013). In the meantime, a government that employs massive secrecy, paradoxically, makes it harder to keep genuine secrets. "When far too much information gets classified, nothing is really classified" (Sanger, 2013) as much of what is secret is misclassified and publically available.

Sources: Ackerman (2013); Bacevich (2013); Boyd (2013); Clark (2013); Davidson (2013); "GAP stands with Snowden" (2013); Hicks (2013); McElhatton (2013); Publius (2013); Rosen (2013); Sanger (2013); Theissen (2013); Wemple (2013).

In light of the economic, emotional, and psychological risks, the existence of whistle-blowing in organizations is remarkable. The pressure to hide bad news is often intense—efforts to discredit and remove the employee are equally intense. The irony is that the bias against dissenters is counterproductive: Silencing complaints does not solve the problem, and when the cover-up is revealed, the institution is discredited. According to a landmark empirical study, organizations that react in a responsible manner to whistleblowing benefit themselves and society as a whole by reducing corruption (Micheli, Near, & Dworkin, 2008). Further, Wilde (2017) finds that whistleblowing has an important deterrent effect on firm financial misreporting: Using a large sample of cases, companies subject to whistleblowing allegations are substantially less likely to engage in "creative accounting" for at least two years. Moreover, he and his colleagues (Call, Martin, Sharp, & Wilde, 2017) reveal that whistleblower involvement is a key source of information for officials who investigate and prosecute wrongdoing that results in higher penalties for companies and longer prison sentences for executives.

WHISTLEBLOWER LAWS

Unlike other areas of employment law (such as antidiscrimination policy), there is no uniform national whistleblowing law. Instead, there are over 50 separate federal statutes and literally hundreds of state statutory or common law protections. This body of law consists foremost of legislation in specific policy areas (which includes reprisal protection measures) and, second, legislation designed to encourage whistleblowing. Under law, the dissenter does not have to be right to receive protection, but must reasonably believe that a violation occurred. Legal safeguards, however, are denied for bad-faith whistleblowing.

The complex patchwork of legislation may safeguard the jobs of staff, forbid adverse personnel actions, allow employees to sue for back pay and legal fees, or award the critic a percentage of the money recovered in fraud cases—but only under specific circumstances and depending on the jurisdiction, the industry, and the issue in question. Although the numerous statutes are too diverse to summarize here (cf. Kohn, 2017, Chapter 4), some of the most important are described below.

The landmark 2002 Sarbanes-Oxley Public Corporation Accounting Reform and Investor Protection Act (SOX) was enacted in response to Enron Era scandals at the beginning of the century. It broadened whistleblower protections, for the first time, to include employees of publically traded private companies and their contractors. SOX also mandates that companies establish processes to handle employee claims. Further, the most significant pieces of legislation passed in the 111th Congress (2009–2011) contain whistleblower safeguards—the economic stimulus bill, health care reform, as well as financial reform. Those improvements, the Dodd-Frank 2010 Wall Street Reform, and the Consumer Protection Act defend workers against retaliation, while also providing substantial financial inducements to blow the whistle on securities fraud. Under Dodd-Frank, the Securities and Exchange Commission's whistle-blower program has paid out more than $160 million dollars over seven years to informants, a low and declining amount according to critics (Scofield, 2017, November 20; cf., Kohn, 2017, 114).

The classic example of laws that support dissent through the use of incentives, the False Claims Act of 1863 covers fraud in federal procurement and contracting. Originally used against war profiteers during the Civil War, it authorizes citizens, acting as "private attorney generals," to file charges on behalf of the taxpayer and receive a percentage of the financial penalties collected by government. In 1986, the law was amended in response to the failed whistleblower effort to stop the launch of the space shuttle *Challenger*, as well as contracting scandals over $435 hammers and $600 toilet seats. Since then, these *qui tam* whistleblower suits have enabled the federal government to recover $20 billion (www.whistleblowerlaws.com). Whistleblowing by business contractors in 2010, for instance, saved the federal government $3 billion (Reilly, 2010) as the False Claims Act (FCA) has become the premier whistleblowing tool (Lipton, 2012). The Department of Justice program under the statute has been so successful that many states have similar programs (see Micheli et al., 2008, 178–181, on the content of state FCA laws). Rather than publicly calling attention to wrongdoing, the act encourages personnel to quietly inform the government so that investigations may take place before culprits hide their misdeeds (Kohn, 2017, pp. 21ff.). Tipsters benefit only if their charges result in a fine of at least $1 million (thereby minimizing baseless complaints).

The Internal Revenue Code (Section 406) was enacted in 2006 to resolve the difficulty of detecting large-scale tax fraud and underpayment in offshore accounts when there were few incentives—and many disincentives—for bankers and accountants to expose illegality. The Internal Revenue Service has long received tips from informants, but now with the payouts in its Whistleblower Reward Program, the number of cases and payments has dramatically increased (U.S. Governmental Accountability Office, 2015; Internal Revenue Service, 2017). Corporate Sentencing Guidelines (Chapter 9) also use incentives to benefit employers, encouraging them to have an ethics code and to establish reporting channels for whistleblowers. Doing so reduces fines and penalties if the organization is convicted of crimes.

For reasons to be discussed, much of this legislative activity functions as little more than a "mirage of protection" for dissenters, because much of it lacks due process and adequate remedies. The laws are not only confusing and riddled with loopholes, but also they are not comprehensive or consistently enforced by government agencies and the courts. For example, according to Devine and Maassarani (2011, 197), "SOX is a pioneering reform because it systemically extends corporate freedom of speech in principle, solidifies modern legal burdens of proof, and creates the right to seek justice from a jury." However, "it has helped few actually achieve justice," as just 1.4 percent of over 2,000 claims resulted in whistleblower victories (166). Explanations for the state of affairs include procedural complexity in bringing a claim, short statutes of limitations, inadequate agency staffing, and narrow or incorrect interpretations of the law (Micheli et al., 2008, 169–170).

A best practice standard, based on national laws and international organization policies, contains 20 specific criteria organized by:

- the definition scope of whistleblowing coverage (the presences or absence of loopholes),
- the forum for whistleblower cases (adjudication bodies that provide fair process),
- rules needed to prevail (realistic burdens of proof and statutes of limitations),
- scope of relief (victim obtains benefit and wrongdoer is held accountable), and
- making a difference (positive results for not only the employee but also society) (Devine & Maassarani, 2011, 256ff).

The Whistleblower Protection Enhancement Act of 2012 (S743), reflective of many of these standards, was over 12 years in the making. Among the provisions are an increased protection of disclosures and retaliatory actions taken against them (both generally and for defense contractors), inclusion of Transportation Security Administration baggage handlers, expanded appeal rights in federal courts, provision of economic reparations for whistleblowers, and creation of an ombudsman office to train employees on their rights. The new law does not provide jury trial rights for federal employees, cover national security whistleblowers who disclose information within their agencies, or cover nondefense contractors. Recommendations to improve the law include: whistleblower jury trials, fortified protection against reprisals, financial relief during long cases (which often go on for five years and leave employees without income), each Inspector General to have a whistleblower ombudsman, and formal disciplinary system for superiors who harass dissenters (Burleigh, 2017, July 27).

As noted, many states have whistleblower laws (for a summary, see Kohn, 2017, Chapter 5), which vary considerably. Like federal legislation, these state laws often protect a narrow range of speech, impose burdensome procedures on employees, and provide weak remedies. The most robust laws are found in California, Florida, Michigan, New Jersey, and the District of Columbia, but it is difficult to receive protection under most state statutes. Patrick (2010) examined a random sample of statewide cases between 1994 and 2009 and found that 74 percent of whistleblowers were terminated, 6 percent suspended, 5 per cent transferred, and 15 per cent were given poor evaluations.

Since 2013, over half of the states have introduced legislation that seeks to ban videotaping of animal, environmental, and food safety abuses—a critical form of evidence to substantiate claims by moral sentinels. These "ag gag" bills would criminalize agricultural whistleblowers, instead of holding those responsible for wrongdoing accountable (see Update: Civil service whistleblower laws, 2017). Many of these bills were thwarted, and those that became law have lawsuits pending. Arkansas passed a bill that also makes it a crime to report patient abuse, elder abuse, and puppy mills (Broad Ag-Gag bill becomes law in Arkansas, 2017).

Overall, federal and state legislative initiatives imply it is prudent for organizations to have meaningful internal compliance programs (see Chapter 8). In the wake of the 2012 U.S. General Services Administration (GSA) Las Vegas conference scandal (Chapter 9), the public interest group Cause of Action requested that the U.S. Office of Management and Budget conduct a government-wide audit to verify whether agencies are following whistleblower protection laws (no such audit was conducted). It also asked that the Office of Government Ethics disclose information on GSA's compliance with the 1989 Standards for Ethical Conduct for Employees of the Executive Branch (the Office of Government Ethics found GSA to be in compliance, but did not audit the agency).

Blowing the whistle on whistleblowing protections, six reports have documented widespread problems. The U.S. Office of Special Counsel, the small bureau created to protect dissenters, found that just 5 percent of its clients were satisfied with the treatment their cases received (Sandler, 2007). More recently, and in response to a surge of disclosures, the agency reported favorable outcomes in 75 percent of retaliation cases (Tully, 2013). The U.S. Government Accountability Office (2010), second, examined the Labor Department's Occupational Health and Safety Administration (OSHA), the department which investigates retaliation against employees under more than 20 federal laws. It criticized OSHA for ineffective whistleblower protections that have persisted for 20 years after the accountability office first reported weaknesses. Another study, this one looking at 27,298 claims under all whistleblower laws between 1994 and 2008, reported that OSHA found merit in 3.2 percent of the cases (cited in Devine & Maassarani, 2011, 166). Next, the agency's Inspector General established that OSHA failed 80 percent of the time to meet all elements essential to the investigative process (U.S. Department of Labor, 2010). The report further revealed that OSHA dismissed 1,066 claims of business fraud and upheld only 25 claims under SOX.

The U.S. Merit Systems Protection Board, an appeals panel for federal civil servants, rules against whistleblowers in 95 percent of cases (Davidson, 2010). The research arm of the same agency, however, documented how the treatment of dissenters has deteriorated since 1992. Whistleblowers are substantially more likely to be terminated, suspended, demoted, reassigned, or denied a promotion (U.S. Merit Systems Protection Board, 2011). Finally, the 1994–2012 record of the Federal Circuit Court of Appeals (the only review body for all 1989 Whistleblower Protection Act cases) was 3–220 against employees (Devine & Clark, 2012,

21). There are many factors to explain the results reported here—poor management, meager funding, inconsistent interpretation of laws, lengthy processing time, lack of training, and insufficient staff are among them (for a discussion of OSHA's problems, see Kohn, 2017, 57–60).

To be covered by the relevant statutes, the concerned employee must act in good faith—the disclosures are to be objectively reasonable, specifying what misconduct is unlawful. A general claim is not sufficient. The majority of whistleblowers—at least once those making frivolous claims are excluded—are not malcontents, misfits, neurotics, crusaders, crackpots, or radicals. Typically, they are middle managers or professional staff persons, knowledgeable individuals able to observe problems, but may not have a vested interest in ensuring they are never made public. Most whistleblowers are normal people with no record of animosity toward the organization. They are "just doing their job," not considering themselves to be dissenters, and expecting problems to be addressed when brought to the attention of those in authority (see Case Study 10.2). When problems are not rectified, and corruption goes unchallenged, conscientious employees expose the issue. Nonetheless, it is important not to romanticize such individuals—they may speak out for selfish as well as altruistic motives.[3] While some dissenters may have mixed motives, this does not mean that they are wrong. The ideal case—where the cause is just, where all administrative appeals have been tried, where responsibility is openly accepted, and where the employee is above reproach—may not always emerge.

CASE STUDY 10.2

Applying Rational and Behavioral Ethics Approaches: Cooking the Books

Grant monies for Program X in nonprofit agency MNO are insufficient to cover client needs. The chief executive officer authorized expenditures for the program from grant monies awarded to unrelated Program Y. She would change line items in the budget and modify supporting documentation (e.g., purchase orders, travel expenses, supplies) to make it appear that Program Y made purchases which in reality applied to Program X. These expenditures sometimes amounted to thousands of dollars, occasionally for questionable items. Sophia Rasmussen, a senior staffer, was disturbed by this practice. When she mentioned this to her superiors, she was told, "This is the way things are done around here." Sophia's dilemma is whether to press the issue further.

Following the approach described in Chapter 7 and used in case studies in the previous two chapters, this dilemma can be explored from the perspective of rational decision-making theory as well as the behavioral ethics approach.

Results-Based Analysis. Starting with philosophical theory, consider the issue by centering on results—the greatest good for the greatest number—she can see that Program Y's resources are being depleted to augment funds in Program X. She knows that both programs provide valuable services that together benefit the entire community, but denial of services to Program Y recipients narrows the impact by depriving deserving service recipients. She could report this to the external auditors or, if the government agency is the funding source, to appropriate authorities. Doing so would potentially satisfy those benefiting from Program Y's services and possibly advance the greater good.

The result for Sophia may not be positive. While she will feel better about herself for acting on her convictions, she will undoubtedly anger the CEO and those assisted by Program X. She may also find that blowing the whistle may not solve the problem. If the lax attitude reflected by her superiors is one permeating the organization, her objection falls on deaf ears. If she goes outside the organization, the external entity she contacts may not be empowered to correct the situation. It is unlikely that an aroused public would apply sufficient pressure to force a change to this practice, unless some dramatic event (e.g., media coverage) prompted the need for drastic action.

Rule-Based Analysis. Second, focusing on rules and principles, Sophia is aware that federal law mandates that nonprofits have reporting channels for whistleblowers and protects them from retaliation. As an astute observer of organizational behavior, she also knows that her organization is often noncompliant and lax in enforcing legal strictures. If funds are being misallocated, this could lead to criminal charges against the CEO. If the funds are coming from a person whose intent for the use of the monies was made explicit, then the use of Program Y funds to cover Program X's expenses is a clear contravention of donor intent. The criterion "what is good for one is good for all" is being violated; one also would not want to universalize the deceptive modification of documents and disregard of donors' intentions.

Sophia sees the misallocation of funds as a form of lying and wonders if she can live with herself knowing that she has not pursued every avenue to correct this wrongdoing. She prides herself on her honesty; one of the reasons she decided on a career in nonprofit organizations is her commitment to public service, which she sees as being subverted and harming innocent clients of Program Y. She thinks those higher up need to be held accountable for their behavior and pay the penalty for their actions.

Virtue-Based Analysis. Third, from a virtue ethics perspective, excellence in individual and community character is not promoted by the CEO's actions. Sophia believes that moral courage is required to stand up for ethical principles. She does not like to back down from a fight when a principle is at stake. She feels her views were discounted and disregarded, but is convinced that she is right. Her individual responsibility requires her to act to correct what she knows to be improper behavior, but prudence requires her to carefully weigh the costs and benefits of ways to resolve the issue.

She also is concerned about the damage to her self-esteem and character if she remains silent on this issue and she wonders whether she has the moral courage to pursue this matter outside the organization. She has a well-deserved reputation as a principled, cooperative, and competent member of the senior staff team. By going outside, she risks alienating not only her superiors but also her co-workers whose friendship and support she values. Her reputation is important to her, as is her character; she is torn between wanting to do the right thing and hoping to avoid being branded as a troublemaker.

Behavioral Ethics-Based Analysis. Behavioral ethics concepts can be used to help explain actions of the CEO and Sophia in this case; recall that many of the behavioral phenomena occur at the unconscious level—that is, decision makers may well believe that they are rationally addressing the issue at hand. Yet feelings and perceptions are at least as important in understanding why people do what they do. The CEO is likely confident that he has the discretion to move funds from one program to another, and could be annoyed by the suggestion that his behavior was inappropriate. His moral blindness is most evident in his modification of documents, which his "want" self might think is OK, but his "should" self may later regret. Ethical fading happens when one is so focused on a specific matter to the exclusion of other matters that may occur at the same time. His single-mindedness in pursuing Program X may have led him to discount the importance of Program Y, and to believe that no one would care about the diversion. Sophia cares, but she needs to be mindful of the tendency she may have to be overly optimistic and overconfident that her whistleblowing will result in the successful resolution of the problem and elimination of wrongdoing.

As in other cases (e.g., Case Study 8.1), decision makers would do well to take steps to ensure that easily overlooked behavioral ethics phenomena receive attention (Chapter 7). Believing in something is not the same as knowing the correct judgment to make; the basis of a decision may not stem from moral reasoning, but rather from an after-the-fact rationalization for a dubious decision already made. Referring to Chapter 7, specify other behavioral ethics tenets that are likely to be present in this scenario.

DISSENT IN ORGANIZATIONS

A milestone book by C. Fred Alford (2000) presents a dark, chilling, sobering account of institutional power and employee character. The grim contention of the rich, complex analysis is that the organization is a feudal institution dedicated to the neutralization of its members' moral individuality—the ability to think seriously about what one is doing (recall the Milgram experiment in Chapter 4). Public, nonprofit, and private bureaucracies resemble authoritarian states that do not permit legitimate opposition. The same organizational DNA appears everywhere as whistleblowers are seen as a threat to be exterminated (Taibbi, 2012, May 10). Anyone questioning the organization is seen as a disloyal defector to be dealt with severely. The institution's greatest fear is not corruption, but rather that its most competent people will blow the whistle on misdoings. Echoing Jackall (1988), what matters most to the organization is that the person be subservient.

The employee need not go outside the workplace to get in trouble—as a whistleblower, she is one who remembers that there *is* a world outside the organization. Alford (2000) argues that when a person comes forward to protest malfeasance, the institution is inherently unable to properly deal with the challenge because of its imperative for survival. When six experts on a National Space and Aeronautics Administration safety panel, for example, issued warnings prior to the 2003 *Columbia* space shuttle explosion, they were discharged. In contemporary times, it seems that admiring moral bravery is far less common than is admiring physical bravery; indeed, there is often suspicion toward those who expose problems (for a commentary on this worldwide problem, see Rushdie, 2013).

In such an environment, according to one whistleblower, the chances of success can be characterized as, "If you have God, the law, the press, and the facts on your side, you have a 50–50 chance of victory." In Alford's view, the organization simply cannot—and will not—tolerate individuality. Eventually insiders with outsider values are branded as "nuts or sluts"—or both. When the subordinate confronts the employer he must make a "choiceless choice," risking career and family in order to stay true to self. The biggest shock comes when he realizes that nothing he believed is true, including that:

- the individual matters,
- law and justice can be relied on,
- government is of laws, not people,
- one's friends will remain loyal even if one's colleagues do not,
- the organization is fundamentally moral,
- it makes sense to stand up and do the right thing,
- someone, somewhere who is in charge knows, cares, and will do what is right, and
- the truth matters, and someone will want to know it. (Alford, 2000, 49)

As Martin Luther King said, "Our lives begin to end the day that we become silent about things that matter." The protester blows the whistle because the dread of living with a corrupted self outweighs the risk of recrimination. These persons do not take the easy way out. They are not good at "doubling," living morally compartmentalized lives, one at work and one at home. However, most employees, as suggested below, can do so. Particularly insidious, Alford believes, is the way the organization uses someone's personal responsibility to her family to justify behavior at work up to and including doing nearly anything for her superiors.

This may explain failures to speak out. For instance, scores of personnel at Enron and Arthur Andersen, as well as Ford and Firestone at the beginning of the century, knew about dubious accounting practices and tire safety concerns for years and said nothing. The same phenomenon was true of Tyco, Worldcom, General Electric, Halliburton, and hundreds of other organizations, private, nonprofit, or public, as well as leading banks that facilitated duplicitous transitions during the Enron Era (Bowman, West, & Beck, 2010, 150). Further, there were numerous people in the nation's vast civilian and military intelligence bureaucracy who knew that pre-Iraq War intelligence was being misused, but did little. It is likely also that conscientious employees could have helped avert the 2008 financial crisis. Case Study 10.3 portrays a case when the whistle was silent, and Case Study 10.4 reports an incident when sounding the alarm was successfully accomplished.

If a person knows what his values are (Chapter 3), difficult decisions to speak out become easier to make. In the face of institutional power and pressure, it is critical to understand where the organization ends and the individual begins. It is ethically suspect to remain silent because harm could occur. Silence is a type of deceit; failure to protest likely is self-compromising. Consequences of inaction, duty, and virtue should be part of decision making in organizations that strive for integrity (Chapter 7; Verhezen, 2010).

As 18th-century philosopher and statesman Edmund Burke observed, "All that is necessary for the triumph of evil is for good men to do nothing." Passive complicity is a far bigger, more telling concern than whatever catalyst finally brought scandals to light. Too often, when the dissenter makes a commitment and is seemingly alone, there are others who want to make a like commitment but will not (also see Reed, 2015). It is advisable, in any event, to have professional liability insurance that provides legal defense protection when contending with agency investigations and/or disciplinary proceedings.

CASE STUDY 10.3

The Silent Whistle

In 2008, sickness and death were caused by contaminated peanut butter sold by the Peanut Corporation of America in Blakely, Georgia. Eight people died, and an estimated 19,000 people were sickened in 43 states. No employees had attempted to blow the whistle to the public or government agency in an effort to stop shipments of the product. They not only knew of conditions that contributed to contamination (water leaks, rats and roaches, failure to clean the facility), but they also knew that the peanut butter tested positive for salmonella. Some expressed concern within the company, but most remained silent. Knowing the delay caused by stopping shipments cost money, managers and owners did nothing.

If a worker had spoken to an attorney, would he have been protected under state or federal law from retaliation? No, he would have been on his own. Because there was no food safety whistleblower law in Georgia, the employer could terminate the employee. There are many federal whistleblowing protection laws, but none covers food safety. The most germane law was the 2002 Sarbanes-Oxley Act. However, that statute covers fraud in publicly traded companies and the peanut firm was a family-owned business. Had the lawyer asked if any public organization purchased the peanut butter, he would have learned that federal agencies and the state of California, as well as their contractors, did. The worker, accordingly, would be protected by national and California laws aimed at preventing fraud in government procurement and contracting. The key in this case, then, was not merely the sale of poisoned product, but that taxpayer-supported agencies had paid for it.

QUESTIONS TO CONSIDER

1. Review the behavioral ethics discussion in Chapter 7 to help explain why employees did not speak out (one starting point: bounded ethicality).

2. Use the ethics triad in the same chapter to determine what you might have done. What might have stopped you from taking action?

Source: Adapted from Kohn (2017, 51–52).

While some organizations say they welcome criticism, common techniques—such as suggestion boxes, hotlines, and "open door" policies—not only lack the power to compel officials to examine criticisms they are reluctant to deal with, but also could turn out to be a trap for the employee. Since he is objecting to policy, it is not reasonable to expect an unbiased review of the compliant—or the person. For example, internal hotline programs have no responsibility to assist callers or inform them of their legal rights; they exist for the benefit of the organization, not the individual. In one case, a major corporation assumed that callers were a potential litigation risk, and forwarded concerns to in-house attorneys. "While the worker was manipulated into thinking he or she was doing a good job, the company . . . started to build a case that could justify disciplinary action (Kohn, 2011, 18).

More systematic procedures, both internal and external to the institution, may not entirely deal with these problems, but they can have a deterrent effect if employers know that their actions are subject to review. Indeed, how agencies handle ethical resisters can be seen as an indicator of its level of moral development (Chapter 8). Organizations could, for instance, provide their staff with independent disclosure systems that genuinely aim to uncover and correct problems. Bok (1980, 292) suggests that the organization develop and specify conditions, perhaps in a code of ethics, under which the whistle *must* be blown. The absence of such provisions virtually guarantees that the issue will develop into a confrontation between management and the subordinate. In light of the significance of whistleblowing, and the development of current law, and the nature of large bureaucracies, what does the future hold?

CASE STUDY 10.4

Successful Whistleblowing

The contract in this case was a sole-source bid, and no one really knew how much it would cost to build something that had not been done before. The military asked FlyX to come up with its best estimate of costs. Based on the estimation, the military would negotiate a fair contract price. The concerned employee possessed evidence revealing the "financial program plan" cost compared to the "contract value" cost given to the government. At the bottom of a key document was a line labeled "risk/reserve," a $700,000 difference between the financial plan and contract value. This figure was the extra amount the company built into the contract price. The practice was not limited to one contract; the risk/reserve was part of all their sole-source contracts, meaning that they cheated by some $100 million. The U.S. Department of Justice and the FBI agreed to pursue the case, creating an investigative strategy that included hiring more auditors and attorneys. After the preliminary investigation was completed in four months' time, agents went to the homes of six FlyX employees to gather additional information for corroboration.

Several months later, subpoenas were served at the corporation seeking documents. It took five months for the company to produce the materials, at which time the case became public information. The employee was no longer invited to business meetings, lost his administrative assistant in a reorganization, and was assigned complex tasks that could not be completed by non-negotiable, unrealistic deadlines. When the company produced the requested information, it provided 40 boxes of papers. This was viewed as an attempt to bury the government in paper. Months passed, but it became increasingly evident that FlyX could not escape the fact that it failed to report its true best estimates in violation of the Truth in Negotiation Act. Still, it refused to repay any funds.

Instead, it counterattacked through fierce litigation, filing numerous motions to dismiss the suit and attempting to disqualify the whistleblower from receiving any payments from the government's reward program should the case go forward. In the meantime, the employee received poor performance evaluations for the first time in his career, was demoted, and was moved to a small storage area in the building basement with a desk, but with no telephone or computer. After a year of active ligation, the judge denied the corporation's motions. Under the False Claims Act, FlyX would have to pay triple the amount of loss, a liability of $210 million. It filed for bankruptcy.

It was uncertain whether this action was part of a strategy aimed at reducing the amount it would pay in a settlement or if the expenses incurred from hiring outside law firms to defend itself was weighing heavily on the company. It was clear that it would not be able to pay the full amount of the judgment. The question became, "What could the company afford and still keep its doors open?" After weeks of negotiation, the parties settled for $70 million. FlyX changed its bidding practices and continued providing much needed equipment to the military. The government, which earned millions for taxpayers in this case, would not have known about it had the person not blown the whistle. The employee was awarded $13 million three and a half years after he first alerted the government of his suspicions.

QUESTIONS TO CONSIDER

1. Make a case that all parties to the settlement were "winners."

2. Make an argument that, in some sense, all parties were "losers."

Source: Based on and adapted from Hesch (2008, 23–29).

TRENDS IN BLOWING THE WHISTLE

Since the September 11, 2001, terrorist attacks, conditions may have become worse for dissenters. Growing corporate power, as well as congressional and judicial deference to the executive branch (regarding suppression of information or punishment of nonconforming employees), illuminate three trends: the fate of recent reforms, whistleblowing case disposition data, and treatment of dissenters during the Obama and Trump administrations.

As noted above, the 2002 Sarbanes-Oxley Act (passed to reform corporate practices and protect those who report wrongdoing) has been criticized as costly, overreaching, and unnecessary. Some say the "swagger" of American business is back, suggesting the changes, rather than being embedded into corporate practices, have simply been undermined and unenforced (Moberly, 2008). Similar concerns exist for the 2010 Dodd-Frank Act enacted to restore selected Depression Era banking regulations, regulate new financial instruments that contributed to the 2008 crash, safeguard consumers, and avoid future bailouts. The act is being systematically exploited for loopholes, litigated against, and delayed or disregarded (Taibbi, 2012). As a result, employees may simply quit. The abuse of both laws clearly demonstrates that a legislative victory is just the start, not the end, of a policy battle.

Second, data from the U.S. Office of Special Counsel, the department charged with whistleblower protection, reported that in 2003 it received 535 cases. It determined that 11 merited investigation and sent them back to the agency where the problem originated. While the Office became much more effective during the Obama years, it remained under-resourced, operated "at a molasses pace," and hesitated to take legal action against agencies that violated whistleblower rights (Davidson, 2017, June 7). Similar findings occurred at the Internal Revenue Service. Although there have been recent improvements (discussed earlier), the trend for most of the last decade shows that from 2003 to 2008, it received over 500 tips per year, but pursued just 20 cases, netting $20 million in penalties (Kocieniewski, 2010). Likewise, as indicated above, the U.S. Government Accountability Office (2010) audited the Occupational Safety and Health Administration with comparable results. Also consider the experience of Eileen Foster (Exhibit 10.2) who blew the whistle, but no one heard it. The evidence here is hardly surprising in light of Alford's thesis.

The final trend concerns an apparent change on the part of Barack Obama when he was president, who as a private attorney defended a moral sentinel and, later as a Senator, voted for the then-pending Whistleblower Protection Enhancement Act. On assuming office, the president ordered departments to be responsive to freedom-of-information requests, banned them from altering scientific findings for political purposes, and appointed whistleblower advocates to key positions. And in 2012, he issued a presidential directive that prohibited retribution against intelligence community employees who reveal abuse when it became evident that they would not be included in the new reform law.

Yet during the Obama administration, there was an historic increase in the "criminalization" of whistleblowers, as officials attacked the news media and initiated prosecutions against WikiLeaks, Army private Bradley Manning, and Edward Snowden. As stated earlier, it also indicted a national security agent under the 1917 Espionage Act, a law intended for prosecution of spies, not whistleblowers. The agent was the sixth official so indicted by the administration, more than all other presidencies combined. Finally, the administration supported a reform act provision that permits agencies to bypass due process and whistleblower rights in the name of national security. In a related development, the U.S. Court of Appeals issued a ruling—a "sensitive jobs loophole"—that "openly backed a proposed administration rule to declare virtually any job as national-security sensitive." Critics point out that this would mean agencies could retaliate against whistleblowers (Hicks, 2013).

The current administration reflects its predecessor's equivocal position in at least two ways. During the campaign, Mr. Trump enthusiastically supported WikiLeaks, but once in office he has regularly denounced leaks, creating a chilling effect among employees. And like

EXHIBIT 10.2	Sounding the Alarm, No One Is Listening

Whistleblower Eileen Foster asks, "Why, four years after large banks brought our economy to the brink of disaster, are we still reading about fraud, deceit, and reckless gambling by leading banks?" An important part of the answer is that the U.S. Department of Justice (DoJ) has failed to use evidence provided to them by whistleblowers.

Foster supervised Countrywide Home Loans internal fraud investigators and reported to federal regulators and the company's board of directors. In 2007, the investigations showed that commission-hungry loan officers routinely forged borrowers' signatures and falsified income statements. With detailed evidence of fraud, she reported the findings to her superiors. "At that point I became a target. Countrywide managers went after my job and reputation, intimidating witnesses and altering statements to produce derogatory—and entirely phony—'findings,' which they passed on to Bank of America (BofA)," then in the process of buying out Countrywide. Both Countrywide and BofA worked "to silence employees, using weapons like blacklisting, hush money and confidentiality agreements. The upper echelons at BofA attempted to buy my silence with more than $200,000," which she rejected.

Three years later, she offered evidence of systemic fraud to the Financial Crisis Inquiry Commission. The commission's final report found widespread fraudulent actions in financial institutions and referred their findings to DOJ. Yet no successful criminal prosecutions have resulted. DOJ says it cannot indict and convict company officials just because they behaved badly; greed, they point out, is not a crime. "Together with other Commission witnesses," Foster writes, "I alleged *fraud*, not greed, and that *is* a crime."

Foster concludes:

Today, millions of Americans are paying more on their mortgages than their homes are worth, and millions more are facing foreclosure. Meanwhile, those who cashed in while ordinary Americans lost their homes and their jobs remain at large. . . . Whistleblowers like me know who they are. . . . Why won't the government listen?

Source: Adapted from Foster (2012).

Mr. Obama, he has made well-regarded appointments to oversight offices. In addition, many dissenting individuals believe in Trump because they see him as a whistleblower himself (Burleigh, 2017, July 27).

The President signed a 2017 Veterans Administration law containing important whistleblower reforms, notably agency employees now have unique anti-retaliation rights. Yet, unprecedented challenges regarding censorship of information and employees, ethical norms and rules, those who question the administration (including other branches of government) suggest reports of misconduct may rise as a way to counterbalance understaffed oversight functions. The time may be ripe for persons of conscience to step forward as today's workforce is said to be more willing to buck the system, and voice discontent than may have been the case in the past (Conway-Hatcher & Bourelly, 2017, January 30).

In summary, the uncertain destiny of corporate reform, troublesome handling of cases, and government proceedings against its employees suggest the tensions between individual democratic rights and organizational authoritarianism in American life are likely to continue.

Nonetheless, it is also true that there has been a "revolution" in whistleblower rights (Kohn, 2017), suggesting that a new era (Hertsgaard, 2016) may be emerging in the attitudes about, and the actions by, whistleblowers. Not only do large majorities of the public support them, but they favor increased protections for conscientious employees because they can get results (National Whistleblowers Center, 2007). In law, a complex framework has been developed in recent decades to facilitate blowing the whistle and to protect those who do. In reality, employees and employers are not generally aware of their rights and obligations—those that speak out continue to assume the best outcome only to be victimized in the end. Although whistleblower law has arguably matured, it nonetheless confronts deep-seated cultural biases in organizations. They seldom acknowledge that disclosures are in their long-run best interest. The legal framework for changing administrative cultures exists, but the risks facing dissenting employees remain—even advocates agree that strong, well-documented whistleblower cases are hard to win (e.g., Devine & Maassarani, 2011; Hesch, 2008; Kohn, 2017).

CONCLUSION

Whistleblowing is a compelling and problematic aspect of organizational life. On the frontlines in the fight against corruption, responsible personnel confront a bleak choice between becoming self-compromised by not acting ethically or being vilified for acting ethically. It remains to be seen whether the 2012 Whistleblower Protection Enhancement Act will be any more effective than earlier legislation—although it includes most provisions advocates deemed necessary. Further, during the Obama tenure, the Office of Special Counsel changed from a "whistleblower graveyard" to "a formidable force for good government" (Davidson, 2012). It is also evident that judicious officials—as ethical agents—can act strategically to protect organizational reputations, deter wrongdoing, avoid lawsuits, retain thoughtful employees, and reduce regulatory intervention. This can be accomplished by creating an ethical infrastructure (Chapter 8) to heighten transparency and encourage sound decision making.

Despite promising signs of change, little can be expected from whistleblower programs and offices plagued by lack of resources and case backlogs if internal checks (such as reporting procedures) are treated as little more than window dressing and external checks (like statutes) are ignored or turned into management tools. But without them, society risks one scandal after another. Whistleblowing can and does make a difference. Reforms must become ingrained in a process that deals with the substance of dissent. If the daily interactions among employees and employers do not provide for the exercise of integrity, whistleblowing will remain a dangerous, if essential, task.

***

To see what is right and not do it is cowardice.

—Confucius

NOTES

1. Small parts of this chapter are adapted from Bowman (1980).
2. One study of 27,000 whistleblowers from 1994 to 2008 who filed retaliation complaints with the Occupational Safety and Health Administration found that 78 percent struggled financially for the first five years after blowing the whistle, 83 percent found it "extremely difficult to impossible" to find a new job in their field, 66 percent found it "extremely difficult to impossible" to find a new job after changing professions, and 54 percent could not find work until they changed profession (cited in Devine & Maassarani, 2011, 31). According to Micheli, Near, and Dworkin (2008, 25–26), there exists substantial variation among organizations regarding the incidence of whistleblowing, the frequency of retribution, and the impact of dissent. Such differences result from not only operational differences from organization to organization, but also difficult, perhaps inherent, methodological problems in data collection.
3. Heumann et al. (2013–2014) developed a tentative typology of whistleblowers: The Altruist who acts as the conscience of the organization by fighting for justice in the public interest; the Organization Man who interprets the organization's action from his perspective and issues a warning to superiors. If ignored, the public will never hear from him; if the problem becomes known, he exposes management's cover-up; the Avenger who, for selfish and dishonorable reasons, seeks retribution against the organization; the Alarmist who repeatedly, and wrongly, predicts dire consequences of a policy; the Bounty Hunter who demands financial gain by suing the organization (the odds for which are akin to winning the lottery, according to Devine & Maassarani, 2011, 43).

    Heumann et al. (2013–2014), contrary to nearly all existing literature, claim that there is insufficient evidence to demonstrate whether protection laws are "failing spectacularly" to care for employees ("the whistleblower-as-hero") or are working well to screen out malcontents ("the dissenter-as-false accuser"). There is little controlled research on the proportion of whistleblower complaints judged to have merit. Governmental watchdog agencies typically report that most cases fail, while anonymous employee surveys suggest that wrongdoing is widespread. Micheli et al. (2008, 21–22) believe that employee perceptions may sometimes be erroneous, but point out that most have no incentive to distort their perceptions on confidential questionnaires. Such data imply that the validity of estimates offered by official compliant recipients are too low.

FOR DISCUSSION

1. Critically evaluate these statements and questions:

    -   Organizations create whistleblowers.
    -   The biggest shock to dissenting employees: Nothing they believed in is true.
    -   Is whistleblowing on the increase or decrease? Why?
    -   How well an organization treats whistleblowers is an indication of how ethical it is.
    -   "Here I stand. I can do no other." Max Weber
    -   What lessons, if any, have been learned by government and business as a result of recent scandals?

2. In 2010, U.S. Army private Bradley (now Chelsea) Manning released hundreds of thousands of classified documents and was found guilty in largely secret military court

proceedings. Over 80,000 people signed a petition nominating him for the Nobel Peace Prize. Discuss.

3. Less sensational cases of ethical incidents are useful to understanding whistleblowing. To take a classroom dishonesty example, have you or anyone you know had an opportunity to blow the whistle on cheating (an obligation common in university honor codes)? Was it blown or not? Why? What, if anything, happened as a result?

4. Discuss a relevant incident in the news or from your own organization or experience.

5. Analyze the implications of these queries:

   - Alford's work calls into question ethics laws and organizational ethics programs. What good, if any, do they do? What limitations do they have?
   - After the 9/11 attacks, airport screeners (n = 76,000) originally were exempted from federal civil service and whistleblower protections. Assuming that tipsters can play an important role in bringing problems to light, how does this action relate to Alford's thesis?
   - What does it mean to be a professional? Who is the "traitor"—the dissenter or the non-dissenter? What is the lesson(s) that might be drawn from Alford's views?
   - Doing the right thing does not mean right things will happen to you.

6. America does not have a tradition of "resignation in protest," an honorable practice in England—that is, when a high appointee cannot support a policy, she resigns and clearly states why, which might have an effect on policy. In the United States, rather than regarding speaking out as a public duty, whistleblowers are often seen as "troublemakers" or "squealers" and endure the consequences. Accordingly, most officials tend to remain "loyal" by staying in office, resigning quietly, and then waiting for their book to be published before telling the citizenry about their concerns. Discuss.

7. Technology is a double-edged sword for concerned employees: it is both easier to leak information and to trace the source of the leak.

8. Many whistleblowers who see fraud, waste, and abuse may initially believe that *res ipas loquitur* ("the thing speaks for itself"). Explain why this may be the case and why the moral sentinel may find it is simply not true.

EXERCISES

1. Explore these websites:

   - The Project on Governmental Oversight (http://www.pogo.org) and the Government Accountability Project (http://www.whistleblower.org) are independent watchdogs who investigate fraud, waste, and abuse and assist dissenters. They publish newsletters, blogs, or reports, and their activities can be followed on Facebook and Twitter.
   - The National Whistleblowers Center (http://www.whistleblowers.org) is a nonprofit

advocacy organization that deals with corporate issues, cases, historical information, and legislation. The National Whistleblower Legal Defense and Education Fund independently manages the legal programs supported by the Center.

- The mission of the Office of Special Counsel (http://www.osc.gov) is to assist federal personnel who report fraud, waste, and abuse.
- The law firm Labaton Sucharow (http://www.labaton.com/), sponsors a whistleblower program and a corporate ethics clearinghouse; it is a comprehensive resource to assist individuals and organizations in building cultures of integrity.
- The Securities and Exchange Commission maintains a comprehensive website (http://www.secwhistlebloweradvocate.com) that includes an insider's guide, a whistleblower handbook, a legal primer, videos, webinars, and podcasts.
- Whistleblow Wall Street (htttps:www.whistleblowwallstreet.com) provides a secure platform and attorneys to help employees to anonymously expose the worst practices of the financial industry.
- ExposeFacts.org encourages secure, anonymous disclosure of information which examines the material and, if appropriate, arrange for release of information to the media.
- Whistleblower Aid (https://whistlebloweraid.org) offers a legal alternative to illicit leaking without exposure to criminal liability by helping federal investigators gather evidence, file complaints, and meet with officials.

2. For a compelling documentary on the plight of conscientious federal employees, view "War on Whistleblowers: Free Press and the National Security State" (Brave New Foundation, 2013, 66 mins.), available for purchase or rental from Amazon, iTunes, Netflix, or Hulu.

3. In addition to dramatic incidents that make the front page of the newspaper, there are many less publicized instances of fraud, waste, and abuse that occur in everyday management, such as the one below (adapted from Cohen, 2009):

> "I am an employee of a large contractor working on a small government office restoration project with a $800,000 construction budget. Because of poor work by a subcontractor (an old friend of my boss's), the paint was not properly applied and will fade and peel in the near future. The project is almost finished. The boss will not inform the government and we were clearly told to say nothing. What should I do?"

Randy Cohen, the *New York Times* "ethicist," replies:

> Your boss's actions are, of course, also unethical. Declining to report others' misdeeds is one thing; committing your own is quite another (e.g., if you act to disguise the bungled paint job).
>
> My guideline for duty-to-report questions is this: You must come forward when doing so will prevent imminent harm; that is not the case here, and ethics does not

require you to sacrifice your job. Yet, informing the government is desirable. How much jeopardy should you shoulder? That depends on your tolerance for risk (and the advice of an attorney), the quality of the evidence you have in hand to prove the case, the likelihood that the problem will be corrected, and other factors.

Apply the ethical schools of thought found in the three-pronged decision-making approach (Chapter 7) to the problem to achieve a more fully considered judgment about what to do. Using the prompts representing each approach—the greatest good for the greatest number, what is good for one is good for all, excellence in individual and community character—will help ensure that all dimensions of the issue are explored, especially when tempered by the insights from behavioral ethics. Consider also the levels of ethics interacting in the dilemma (the individual, the manager, the subcontractor) and how they affect the decision.

REFERENCES

Ackerman, S. (2013, July 5). Edward Snowden is a whistleblower, not a spy—But do our leaders care? *The Guardian*. Retrieved from http://www.guardian.co.uk/world/2013/jul/05/edward-snowden-nsa-whistleblower-spy

Alford, C. (2000). *Whistleblowers: Broken lives and organizational power*. Ithaca, NY: Cornell.

Association of Certified Fraud Examiners. (2016). *Report to the nations on occupational fraud and abuse: 2016 global fraud study*. Retrieved from http://www.acfe.com/rttn2016.aspx

Bacevich, A. (2013, August 6). Are Manning and Snowden patriots? That depends on what we do next. *Washington Post*. Retrieved from http://www.washingtonpost.com/opinions/are-manning-and-snowden-patriots-that depends

Bauer, C. (2015, August 24). An ethics thought before you get to "enough is enough." Retrieved from www.aahamwesternregion.org/docs/ethicsthought-enough2.pdf

Beutler, B. (2007, October 12). Short arm of the law. *American Prospect*. Retrieved from http://prospect.org/article/short-arm-law

Bok, S. (1980). Whistleblowing and professional responsibility. In D. Callahan & S. Bok (Eds.), *Teaching ethics in higher education* (pp. 277–295). New York: Plenum.

Bowman, J. (1980). Whistle-blowing in the public service: An overview of the issues. *Review of Public Personnel Administration, 1*, 15–27.

Bowman, J. (1983). Ethical issues for the public manager. In W. Eddy (Ed.), *Handbook of organization management* (pp. 69–103). New York: Dekker.

Bowman, J., West, J., & Beck, M. (2010). *Achieving competencies in public service: The professional edge* (2nd ed.). Armonk, NY: M. E. Sharpe.

Boyd, D. (2013, September 2). Whistleblowing is the new civil disobedience: Why Edward Snowden matters [Web log post]. Retrieved from http://www.zephoria.org/thoughts/archives/2013/07/19/edward-snowden-whistleblower.html

Brewer, G., & Selden, S. (1998). Whistle-blowers in federal civil service: New evidence of the public service ethic. *Journal of Public Administration and Theory, 8*, 413–439.

"Broad Ag-Gag bill becomes law in Arkansas." (2017, Spring). *Whistleblower.org*. Retrieved from https://www.whistleblower.org

Burleigh, N. (2017, July 27). Trump hates leaks, but some federal whistleblowers love him. *Newsweek*. Retrieved from www.newsweek.com/trump-scaramucci-tsa-whistleblowers-leaks-642866

Call, A., Martin, G., Sharp, N., & Wilde, J. (2017). Whistleblowers and Outcomes of Financial Misrepresentation Enforcement Actions (April). Available at https://ssrn.com/abstract= 2506418 or http://dx.doi.org/10.2139/ssrn.2506418

Clark, L. (2013, August 1). Whistleblowers and the national security state. *Government Accountability Project*. Retrieved from http://www.whistleblower.org/press/gap-op-eds/ 2941-washington-spectator-whistleblowers-and-the-national-security-state

Cohen, R. (2009, March 15). Painted into a corner. *New York Times Sunday Magazine*. Retrieved from http://www.nytimes.com/2009/03/15/magazine/15wwln-ethicist-t.html

Conway-Hatcher, A., & Bourelly, A. (2017, January 30). Today's whistleblower realities: Learning to expect and effectively respond to the unexpected. *Corporate Law & Accountability Report*. Retrieved from https://www.bna.com/todays-whistleblower-realities-n57982083035

Davidson, J. (2010, August 27). Nod to national security advances whistleblower protection bill. *Washington Post*. Retrieved from http://www.washingtonpost.com/wp-dyn/content/ article/2010/08/26/AR2010082606569.html

Davidson, J. (2012, June 28). Under Carol Lerner, Office of Special Counsel is doing its job now, observers say. *Washington Post*. Retrieved from http://www.washingtonpost.com/politics/ under-carolyn-lerner-special-counsel-office-is-doing-its-job-now-observers-say/2012/06/28/ gJQApX229V_story.html

Davidson, J. (2013, June 25). How do whistleblower advocates deal with Edward Snowden's case? *Washington Post*. Retrieved from http://www.washingtonpost.com/politics/ federal_government/how-do-whistleblower-advocates-deal-with-edward-snowdens-case/2013/06/24/180df296-dd03-11e2-9218-bc2ac7cd44e2_story.html

Davidson, J. (2017, June 7). Special counsel Lerner leaves office as Trump rejects highly praised whistleblower advocate. *Washington Post*. Retrieved from https://www.washingtonpost. com/news/powerpost/wp/2017/06/07/lerner-leaves-office-of-special-counsel-as-trumps-rejects-highly-praised-whistleblower-advocate/

Devine, T., & Clark, L. (2012, May 21). Now more than ever, stronger whistleblower protections essential. *Federal Times*, p. 21.

Devine, T., & Maassarani, T. (2011). *The corporate whistleblowers' survival guide: A handbook for committing the truth*. San Francisco: Barrett-Koehler.

Foster, E. (2012, August 9). Obama administration needs to tap, not stiff-arm Wall Street whistleblowers. *Rolling Stone*. Retrieved from http://www.rollingstone.com/politics/blogs/ national-affairs/the-obama-administration-needs-to-tap-not-stiff-arm-wall-street-whistle blowers-20120809?print=true

GAP stands with Snowden. (2013, Autumn). *Bridging the Gap*, pp. 1, 3, 4, 6.

Hertsgaard, M. (2016). *Bravehearts: Whistleblowing in the age of Snowden*. New York: Hot Books.

Hesch, J. (2008). *Whistleblowing: A guide to government reward programs*. Lynchburg, VA: Goshen Press.

Heumann, M., Friedes, A., Cassak, L., Wright, W., & Joshi, E. (2013–2014). The world of whistle-blowing: From the Altruist to the avenger. *Public Integrity, 16*, 25–52.

Hicks, J. (2013, September 6). Grassley calls on Obama to ensure protections for federal whistleblowers. *Washington Post*. Retrieved from http://www.washingtonpost.com/blogs/federal-eye/wp/2013/09/06/grassley-calls-on-obama-to-ensure-protections-for-federal-whistle blowers/

Internal Revenue Service. (2017). *IRS whistleblower program: Fiscal Year 2016 Annual Report to Congress*. Washington, DC: IRS.

Jackall, J. (1988). *Moral mazes: The world of corporate managers*. New York: Oxford University Press.

Kennedy, K. (2012, February 23). Whistleblowers key in health care fraud fight. *USA Today*. Retrieved from http://www.usatoday.com/news/washington/story/2012–02–22/health-care-fraud-whistleblowers/53212468/1

Kocieniewski, D. (2010, May 19). Whistleblowers become investment option for hedge funds. *New York Times*. Retrieved from http://www.nytimes.com/2010/05/20/business/20whistle blower.html?pagewanted=all

Kohn, S. (2017). *The new whistleblower handbook: A step-by-step guide to doing what's right and protecting yourself*. Guilford, CT: Lyons Press.

Kohn, S. (2011). *The whistleblower handbook: A step-by-step guide to doing what's right and protecting yourself*. Guilford, CT: Lyons Press.

Lipton, E. (2012, October 1). A legal circle reached deep to aid Obama. *New York Times*. Retrieved from http://www.nytimes.com/2012/10/02/us/politics/whistle-blower-lawyers-don ate-to-obama-campaign.html

Matt, B., & Shahinpoor, N. (2011). Speaking truth to power: The courageous organizational dissenter. In D. Comer & G. Vega (Eds.), *Moral courage in organizations: Doing the right thing at work* (pp. 157–171). Armonk, NY: M. E. Sharpe.

McElhatton, J. (2013, June 11). Snowden the whistleblower? Not exactly. *Federal Times*. Retrieved from http://blogs.federaltimes.com/federal-times-blog/2013/06/11/snowden-the-whistleblow er-not-exactly/

Micheli, M., Near, J., & Dworkin, T. (2008). *Whistleblowing in organizations*. New York: Routledge.

Moberly, R. (2008). Protecting whistleblowers by contract. *University of Colorado Law Review, 79*, 975–1042.

National Whistleblowers Center. (2007). http://www.whistleblowers.com, author

Near, J., & Miceli, M. (2008). Wrongdoing, whistle-blowing, and retaliation in the U.S. government: What have researchers learned from the Merit System Protection Board (MSPB) survey results? *Review of Public Personnel Administration, 28*, 263–281.

Patrick, P. (2010). Be prepared before you blow the whistle: Protection under state whistleblowing laws. *Fraud Magazine*. September/October. Retrieved from www.fraud-magazine.com/article.aspx?id=4294968656

PricewaterhouseCoopers Investigations and Forensic Services. (2007). *Economic crime: People, culture and controls: The 4th biennial global economic crime survey*. Retrieved from http://www.pwc.com/gx/en/economic-crime-survey/pdf/powc-20078gecs.pdf

Publius, G. (2013, August 16). Whistleblowing is the new civil disobedience: Why Snowden matters [Comment]. Retrieved from http://americablog.com/2013/08/whistleblowing-is-the-new-civil-disobedience-why-snowden-matters.html

Reed, G. (2015). Expressing loyal dissent: Moral considerations from literature on followership. *Public Integrity, 17*(1), 5–18.

Reilly, S. (2010, November 23). $385M is whistleblowers' share of 2010 False Claims Act recoveries. *Federal Times*. Retrieved from http://www.federaltimes.com/article/20101123/AGENCY02/11230301/-385M-whistleblowers-share-2010-False-Claims-Act-recoveries

Rosen, J. (2013, July 5). The Snowden effect: definition and examples [Web log post]. Retrieved from http://pressthink.org/2013/07/the-snowden-effect-definition-and-examples/

Rothschild, J., & Miethe, T. (1999). Whistle-blower disclosures and management retaliation: The battle to control information about organization corruption. *Work and Occupations, 26*, 107–128.

Rushdie, S. (2013, April 28). Whither moral courage? *New York Times*, p. SR 5.

Sandler, J. (2007, November 1). The war on whistle-blowers. *Salon*. Retrieved from http://www.salon.com/2007/11/01/whistleblowers/

Sanger, D. (2013, August 3). A Washington riddle: What is "top secret"? *New York Times*. Retrieved from http://www.nytimes.com/2013/08/04/sunday-review/a-washington-riddle-what-is-top-secret.html?_r=0

Scofield, J. (2017, November 20, 2017). SEC continues to tout performance of underwhelming whistleblower program. *Naked Capitalism*. Retrieved from https://macro.economicblogs.org/naked-capitalism/2017/11/scofield-sec-continues-tout-performance-underwhelming-whistle-blower/

Taibbi, M. (2012, May 10). How Wall Street killed financial reform. *Rolling Stone*. Retrieved from http://www.rollingstone.com/politics/news/how-wall-street-killed-financial-reform-201 20510

Thiessen, M. (2013, July 1). The danger of what Edward Snowden has not revealed. *Washington Post*. www.washingtonpost.com/opinions

Tully, M. (2013, July 14). OSC: Whistleblower disclosures "skyrocketed." *Fedsmith*. Retrieved from http://www.fedsmith.com/2013/07/14/osc-whistleblower-disclosures-skyrocketed/

Update: Civil service whistleblower laws (2017). *Whistleblower*, Spring, 5–6.

U.S. Department of Justice, Civil Division, Commercial Litigation Branch. (2010). *Fraud statistics—Overview: Oct. 1, 1987–Sept. 30, 2010*. Retrieved from http://www.taf.org/FCA-stats-2010.pdf

U.S. Department of Labor, Office of Inspector General. (2010, September 30). *Complaints did not always receive appropriate investigation under the Whistleblower Protection Program* (Report No: 02-10-202-10-105). Retrieved from http://www.oig.dol.gov/public/reports/oa/2010/02-10-202-10-105.pdf

U.S. Government Accountability Office. (2010). *Whistleblower protection: Sustained man-*

agement attention needed to address long-standing program weaknesses (GAO-10-722). Retrieved from http://www.gao.gov/assets/310/308767.pdf

U.S. Governmental Accountability Office (2015). IRS whistleblower program: Billions collected, but timeliness and communication concerns may discourage whistleblowers. Washington, DC: GAO-113-318, March.

U.S. Merit Systems Protection Board. (2011). *Blowing the whistle: Barriers to federal employees making disclosures.* Retrieved from http://www.mspb.gov/netsearch/viewdocs.aspx?doc number=662503&version=664475&application=ACROBAT

Ventriss, C., & Barney, S. (2003). The making of a whistleblower and the importance of ethical autonomy: James F. Alderson. *Public Integrity, 5*, 366–368.

Verhezen, P. (2010). Giving voice in a culture of silence: From a culture of compliance to a culture of integrity. *Journal of Business Ethics, 96*, 187–206.

Wemple, E. (2013, June 10). Edward Snowden: "Leaker," "source," or "whistleblower"? *Washington Post.* Retrieved from http://www.washingtonpost.com/blogs/erik-wemple/wp/2013/06/10/edward-snowden-leaker-source-or-whistleblower/

Wilde, J. (2017) The Deterrent Effect of Employee Whistleblowing on Firms' Financial Misreporting and Tax Aggressiveness. *The Accounting Review, 92*(5), 247–280.

PART IV

Issues in Public Service Ethics

11 Ethics and Elected Officials

Art, like morality, consists of drawing the line somewhere.

—G. K. Chesterton

This chapter represents the first of four chapters in Part IV of the book, Issues in Public Service Ethics. Here, attention is turned from ethical issues confronting appointed public servants who implement programs to those faced by elected officials who seek to reach agreement with other policy-makers to advance a particular agenda. Some may conclude that "political ethics" is an oxymoron, assuming a bright line distinguishing ethical from unethical behavior that is routinely crossed by politicians. The reality of politics is not that simple—the line between right and wrong is often indistinct and vague.

Chapter objectives are to:

- understand the ethical obligations of elected officeholders and their appointees,
- examine the character of these public servants,
- analyze the influence of partisanship, publicity, and polarization on congressional ethics,
- consider questions of ethics in presidential decisions, and
- explore citizen and media ethics when dealing with officials.

The sources and types of ethical obligation of civil servants include broad duties to protect the constitution, law, nation or country, and even democracy. Narrower responsibilities include adherence to organizational norms and professional standards, as well as obligations to family, friends, self, and "mid-range collectivities" (e.g., party, socioeconomic class, ethnicity) (Waldo, 2009). More general responsibilities shared by both appointed career civil servants and elected officials or their political appointees serve as guides to action to promote the public interest. However, contradictions or dilemmas arise because of conflicts between and among these duties. For example, a decision may pit an official's partisan concerns against the public interest he has been elected or appointed to serve. Reconciling such conflicts is an ongoing challenge to conscientious public servants. Failure to adequately consider these duties can lead to misconduct. (See Exhibit 11.1

EXHIBIT 11.1	**Need for Bridge-Building Leaders**

How political appointees and career civil servants view each other?		What can be done to bridge the gap?	
Political Appointees	*Civil Servants*	*Political Appointees*	*Civil Servants*
The Commissar: In charge of enforcing fidelity to the cause of power	**The Troll** : The career staffer with the reflexive, "we're already doing that"	Leap No.1: **Seek out the mavens:** The true federal experts with deep knowledge and experience	Leap No.1: **Put your fixer forward:** Counsel the political team to articulate the desired outcomes while the fixers work with the career staff to make it happen
The Hack: Sole interest in their own advancement	**The Turtle**: Withdraws into his shell and waits for better times	Leap No.2: **Don't ignore the trolls:** This will reveal the legislative, regulatory, budget and policy constraints that could get in the way	Leap No.2: **Make the political calendar work for you:** The career staff needs to understand the best time to float new ideas. It's vital to understand the importance of quick wins in any long -term effort
The Closer: Possesses the juice to work the bureaucracy, and puts the agency's mission over personal advancement	**The Maven**: Subject matter experts. Treasure trove of expertise and institutional knowledge	Leap No.3: **Play fair**: Fairness, integrity, competence and predictability are the bedrock behaviors for promoting organizational trust	
The Wonk: Honest effort to advance the work of the department	**The Translator**: Provides both the context for the latest initiative as well as the winning turn of phrase that conveys the career staff's view in a language that can win over balky political appointees	Leap No.4: **Have the conversation:** Leaders on both sides need to figure out how to discuss issues where political leadership can clearly articulate their needs and expectations Career folks need to think how they might reframe old and new problems to release the talents and reduce bureaucratic restraints	
The Visionary: Seeks alignment of mission and talent, inspires passion	**The Fixer**: The seasoned federal manager requires technical knowledge and bureaucratic savvy to solve		

Source: Adapted from Levine (2017).

to contrast the perspectives of political appointees and career staff and how to bridge the gap.) Two ethical problems elected incumbents encounter, especially members of Congress, also confront civil servants: conflict of interest and insider trading. An ethical choice the U.S. president faces is between truth telling and deception when dealing with national security.

Elected officials in both the legislative and executive arenas are influenced by their obligations, their roles, their character, institutional constraints, partisanship, and circumstances. The chapter begins with two recent congressional cases highlighting issues of conflict of interest and insider trading. That discussion is followed by a broader discussion of ethics and legislative decision making.

The first congressional incident presents a situation in which one person's perception of constituent service can be another's perception of conflict of interest or public corruption; the second case shows how privileged access to nonpublic knowledge can lead to charges of insider trading.

CASE STUDY 11.1

Congressional Conflict of Interest

Congresswoman Shelley Berkley (D-NV) has been walking a fine line between constituent service and public corruption for several years. Representing Nevada's first district in the House of Representatives, Berkley has fought hard against federal termination of Medicare programs that allow for kidney transplants in her state.

In recent years, Nevada's University Medical Center—the only medical center for kidney transplants in the state—experienced a decline in the effectiveness of its transplants. A large number of patients died or experienced transplant failure following their operations—a rate far above the norm. In its wake, the federal government began taking steps to shut down the center's kidney transplant programs, which are almost fully covered by Medicare, regardless of the patient's age or the severity of the chronic illness. Berkley took a stand against government intervention and kept the government from terminating the program.

While Berkley's actions surely benefitted some of her constituents and patients, it also privileged another group of individuals—including Berkley's husband, Dr. Lawrence Lehrner, who is a well-known nephrologist. He owns 11 dialysis centers throughout the state and was instrumental in making a lucrative deal with University Medical Center. Not only is his profession directly connected with the political issue at hand, but Lehrner himself is also the leader of a political action committee that he created on behalf of renal physicians, making him an unofficial lobbyist. He also co-owns his dialysis centers with DaVita, Inc., which contributes large sums to Berkley's campaigns, including her 2012 campaign for Nevada's vacant Senate seat.

The possibility of conflict of interest and corrupt activity was brought to the attention of the House Ethics Committee in March 2012. While the Committee chose to delay weighing in on the issue until after the fall election, Berkley's support for her husband's industry and agenda was a key point throughout the race between her and Senator Dean Heller. Heller's campaign, as well as members of the Republican Party, accused Shelley of directly profiting from her political actions at the expense of federal dollars.

According to legislative acts, as well as reports from the House of Representatives, a conflict of interest is generally defined as "a situation in which an official's private financial interests conflict or appear to conflict with the public interest." While it seems as though Berkley's actions are not in conflict with her constituents' interests, another rule obscures the fine line. According to House ethics policies, a conflict of interest "becomes corruption when an official uses his position of influence to enhance his personal financial interests," which is what many accused Berkley of doing. The problem before the Ethics Committee lies between these two rules. The ambiguity and leeway in between these statements is where corruption certainly lies, and it is up to the committee to decipher on what side of the line Shelley Berkley's actions fall. No decision had been rendered up to the time of the 2012 election. However, Berkley's fate was determined by her electoral defeat in a close contest that centered on the ethics charges she was facing.

QUESTIONS TO CONSIDER

1. Is this primarily a case of constituency service or political corruption? Why?

2. If it is political corruption, what is the appropriate penalty?

Sources: Lipton (2011); U.S. House of Representatives Committee on Ethics (n.d.); 5 USC. app. 4 §§ 101–111.

The initial case contrasts the imperative legislators have to serve their constituents with the tendency to serve their own personal and financial interests at the expense of taxpayers. The subsequent scenario illustrates the privileged access to information available to members of Congress. The House Ethics Committee must decide at what point their colleagues depart from acceptable to unethical behavior, not always an easy task. Punishment has typically been slow in coming and weak in consequences, except for the most egregious violations. This mild response is also typical of Senate Ethics Committee action (see Appendix 11.1 for a brief history of congressional ethics committees). Reforms with clearer standards and stronger sanctions, together with greater public and media scrutiny, are prerequisite to reduce wrongdoing and increase citizen confidence. This raises a broader question: What is the role of ethics in legislative decision making?

CASE STUDY 11.2

Congressional Insider Trading

While the supremacy clause of the U.S. Constitution subjects all elected officials to the laws of the nation, some officeholders question whether certain laws truly apply to them. For example, many Americans believe that members of Congress, the president, and other executive personnel partake in insider trading based on the unique knowledge their positions bestow on them. Among those accused of benefitting from nonpublic knowledge is Representative Spencer Bachus (R-AL). "60 Minutes" broke the story in November 2011 that Bachus, a member of the House Financial Services Committee, was included in closed-door hearings on the economy with Ben Bernanke and Hank Paulson in 2008, and is being investigated by the Office of Congressional Ethics for trades he conducted around the time of the bailout. Bachas retired from Congress when his term ended in 2015.

Since over half of the members of Congress own stock, many with stock investments exceeding $100,000 (excluding mutual funds and other holdings) and given that a majority of lawmakers are millionaires (as of 2014), their legislative actions can be affected by such financial ties to businesses. They may be aware of nonpublic information regarding pending legislative proposals that could be helpful to companies where they have investments. This could influence the decisions of stockholding lawmaker actions on legislation, regulations, subsidies, taxes or contract awards (Hill, Ridge, & Ingram, 2017).

Congress has taken to burnishing their public image regarding financial transactions. The Stop Trading on Congressional Knowledge (STOCK) Act passed in 2012 prohibits elected officials and senior government personnel from trading on confidential information they are privileged to by virtue of their positions. To promote honesty and improve public trust the bill also mandates that these officials (about 28,000) disclose their stock trades, real estate transactions, bonds, and other securities within 45 days of the transaction occurring. Transparency is one of the truest safeguards of democracy. In a nearly unanimous vote, Congress took steps to ensure its place in government affairs. Unfortunately, a year later, Congress unanimously amended the STOCK Act, quietly repealing the plan for Internet financial disclosure, effectively taking the teeth out of the regulations.

They did so without a hearing or a recorded vote in either the House or Senate, thereby undermining the intent of the law that was to ensure that government officials did not profit from nonpublic information. "The Daily Show"'s John Stewart issued a blistering critique of Congress for this one step forward, one step back approach. It is still legally permissible for stockholding lawmakers to sponsor legislation that could benefit the firms family members have investments in (Abad-Santos, 2012).

Potential solutions to these issues exist: requiring members of Congress to put their investment holdings in blind trusts and to recuse themselves from votes where conflicts of interest are involved as well as improving the accuracy and timeliness of reporting on stock holdings of members of Congress and expanding the disclosure system to encompass congressional staff (Hill et al., 2017; Public Citizen, 2017, June 22).

QUESTIONS TO CONSIDER

1. Why do you think Congress repealed the plan for Internet financial disclosure?

2. Can insider trading by public officers be stopped? If not, why not? If so, how?

Sources: Abad-Santos (2012); Pear (2012); Margasak (2012); Lawder and Cowan (2013); Feldman (2013); Hill, et al. (2017).

ETHICS AND LEGISLATIVE DECISION MAKING

Ethics cases involving members of Congress have received considerable attention in recent years—sometimes corroborated with substantial evidence, other times politically motivated and without merit—and the push for ethics reform continues despite questions about the likelihood of success (Public Citizen, 2017a). A brief review of past cases illustrates the increasing prominence of the problem of legislative corruption.

Some of the most visible incidents involving legislators and ethics since the 1950s have been detailed by Tolchin and Tolchin (2001). One case involves Senator Joe McCarthy, condemned for disgracing the institution of the Senate with his anticommunist vendetta. In another, Senator Herman Talmadge is denounced for financial carelessness. Still others detail Representative Adam Clayton Powell's censure for tax evasion, travel junkets, and additional offenses, and Senator Bob Packwood's threatened expulsion for sexual misconduct, which led to his resignation. Sex, money, and power remain strong temptations for ethical misconduct. Two cases that garnered considerable attention are Abscam and the Keating Five.

Abscam (an abbreviation of Abdul, a cliché for an Arab name, and Scam) was the most complete investigation and prosecution of legislative corruption in U.S. history, bringing down more members of Congress than any other scandal. The operation began with an FBI sting operation in the late 1970s and early 1980s targeting traffickers in stolen securities and art objects that quickly morphed into a public corruption investigation. Agents posing as Middle Eastern sheikhs offered bribes to numerous congressmen and senators in exchange for promised assistance with business and immigration problems. Politicians were video recorded receiving tens of thousands of dollars in bribes for agreeing to offer requested services. The investigation led to the conviction of a U.S. senator, five members of the House of Representatives, and other federal, state, and local officials (for details, see Grossman, 2008; Marion, 2010; Tolchin & Tolchin, 2001).

The Keating Five exposé refers to a 1989 imbroglio involving Charles Keating, owner of California-based Lincoln Savings and Loan, and U.S. Senators Alan Cranston (D-CA), Dennis DeConcini (D-AZ), John Glenn (D-OH), John McCain (R-AZ), and Donald Riegle (D-MI). When Keating ran into financial problems, the federal government prepared to take over Lincoln Savings and Loan. Keating gave hefty political donations to five senators, requesting that they assist him in avoiding regulation. The Senate Ethics Committee formally rebuked the senators for intervening on Keating's behalf with regulators after accepting large campaign contributions from him.

Although the Abscam scandal is a clear case of wrongdoing, the Keating Five case illustrates the vague boundaries between corruption and constituent service. The Keating revelation involved campaign contributions or charitable contributions, not money for their own pockets. While as candidates for reelection they would benefit from the monies, the funds were for political rather than personal use. Nonetheless, the senators' intervention with regulators was seen as unfair, disrupting the mythical "level playing field" implying fair treatment for all in the regulatory process. The case also illustrated how vague ethics rules make deliberations about wrongdoing difficult to judge. The ignominious Abscam law enforcement sting was not problematic in that regard—it involved legislators lining their own pockets for personal gain.

Among the factors that determine congressional action are partisanship and publicity. Partisanship explains the use of ethics charges—deserved or not—to attack political opponents and provide justifications for retaliation. Party politics comes into play when determining punishment for ethical transgressions—condemnation, denunciation, expulsion, censorship, reprimand, rebuke. There is a tendency for legislators to consider "there but for the Grace of God go I," suggesting that they, too, feel uneasy about the boundaries of appropriate behavior and are reluctant to be too harsh in judging colleagues. Legislators also defer to loyalty, evident in their hesitance to condemn their allies. Such forces can lead to the "ethical fading," discussed in Chapter 7, and act as a deterrent to the whistleblowing, considered in Chapter 10.

Publicity is one potentially effective way to nudge Congress to take action on ethical issues; while they may be reluctant to condemn, they do not want to be seen as condoning unethical behavior. Another strategy is to overcome loyalty—to the institution, the party, and fellow members of Congress. As Tolchin and Tolchin (2001, 47) opine, "[M]ost lawmakers have to be pushed hard before they will go after a colleague, however low those colleagues may have fallen," suggesting that loyalty has its limits and will give way when public pressure is intense.

Dennis Thompson (1981a) warns against the dangers of "excuses of roles," pointing out that officials need to retain a sense of moral responsibility above and beyond their political responsibility. This is reinforced by the three-pronged model of ethical obligation for government officials: process, general duty of beneficence (public interest), and colleagues/subordinates (Moore, 1981). With regard to process, Moore cites the obligation of officials to share authority with others and to subject governmental actions to the scrutiny of citizens. Beneficence implies the exercise of government authority to effectively, efficiently, and decently achieve public purposes. Treating colleagues and subordinates with respect implies engaging in honest and fair dealings with them on a daily basis. These potentially conflicting roles and obligations are evident in the case of Robert Torricelli.

CASE STUDY 11.3

Robert Torricelli and the CIA

In the early 1990s, two murders in the jungles of Guatemala caught the attention of the public. One victim was an American innkeeper, the other a Guatemalan rebel leader. The faraway murders burst onto the media scene when evidence of U.S. involvement began to surface. The widows of the victims tried desperately to obtain information from the White House, but their efforts were conducted in vain until Rep. Robert Torricelli (D-NJ) stepped into the fray. Torricelli, a member of the House Intelligence Committee, suddenly went public with some disturbing classified information—the Guatemalan military officials responsible for the deaths were linked to the Central Intelligence Agency (CIA), and the agency had withheld information about the murders from the president. While the public was outraged at these allegations of a CIA cover-up, Torricelli's colleagues were furious that he had disclosed information he had obtained as a member of the Intelligence Committee. Despite attacks from both Democrats and Republicans, Torricelli stood firmly by his decision, declaring, "No oath imposed by the leadership can ask a member of Congress to conceal criminal activity" (quoted in Tolchin & Tolchin, 2001, 105).

Torricelli felt the ends—peace for the widows—justified the means—exposing the CIA. He weighed his loyalty to Congress against his personal, micro-level commitment to a higher order—a moral obligation to shed light on appalling CIA meso-level ethics permissive of such practices. His position on the issue matched prevailing public opinion. Had he not taken on the problem—and relentlessly pursued answers—it is unlikely that the resultant reform of congressional oversight of the CIA would have occurred through normal committee hearings or inquiries. Torricelli was guided by his character and by his perception of his role as a policymaker at the micro level. The next section examines these two influences—character and roles—on elected officials.

QUESTIONS TO CONSIDER

1. Do you think Torricelli was justified in disclosing this confidential information? Why or why not?

2. Would Torricelli have been right to allow the CIA to conceal criminal activity? Why or why not?

THE INFLUENCE OF CHARACTER AND ROLES ON ELECTED OFFICIALS

What is the appropriate role of members of Congress: Are they primarily emissaries (delegates) or leaders (trustees) of the people? As emissaries, they represent their constituents, remaining aware of what their support base is likely to advocate or oppose, and voting accordingly. As Frank E. Smith, former congressman from Mississippi, volunteers, "All members of Congress have a primary interest in being reelected. Some members have no other interest" (quoted in Falvey, 1991, 323). The role of conviction or belief is less significant if the primary duty is seen as serving the will of the people and the primary objective is self-preservation: The people are the true masters.

The leader or trustee, meanwhile, has an agenda. She identifies the most important issues, proposes solutions, explains the advantages and disadvantages, and persuades the voters of her views. This is consistent with Edmund Burke's (1774) advice to voters in Bristol regarding a representative's role, "Your representative owes you, not his industry only, but his judgment; and he betrays instead of serving you if he sacrifices it to your opinion." The role requirements of the leader are more demanding, the consequences less certain, than those of the emissary. When addressing new issues, the trustee would rely on her conscience, even when confronting opposition, with the intent of responding both to the demands of constituents and personal convictions.

Modern-day presidents and legislators are more accurately characterized as emissaries than leaders. Typically, they keep a finger elevated to gauge prevailing winds when making decisions. Emissaries in Congress are usually reluctant to be closely identified with a president during campaigns, only publicly supporting him when he has high ratings in their district or state. Why are there so few leaders? In part, because politicians are risk averse. As former Senator William Saxbe said, "If you don't stick your neck out, you don't get it chopped off" (quoted in Mayhew, 2004, 11). Elected officials want to retain power, some sacrificing their ethical beliefs to do so. Also, partisanship requires a certain amount of conformity to party leader preferences, because politics is a team sport. There is a price to pay when legislators go against the party, evidenced by the late Speaker Sam Rayburn's advice to Congressional freshmen, "You have to go along to get along" (quoted in MacNeil, 1963).

Given the differences in roles of officeholders and the paucity of leadership, what criteria can be used to evaluate their behavior? What principles and values can be reasonably expected from politicians regardless of trustee/delegate style to exhibit so that she might be held accountable? Scholars have identified moral criteria (see Carter, 1996, 1998; Cooper & Wright, 1992; Dobel, 1999; Planas, 2012; Thompson, 1995), including several discussed in earlier chapters:

- *Integrity*—having incorruptible honesty, playing by the rules, not being unduly influenced by friendship and family in conducting affairs of government, leading by example.
- *Civility*—respecting one's co-workers, displaying sportsmanlike conduct.
- *Upholding principles*—drawing on one's religious or philosophical moral values, taking the high road, following one's convictions, avoiding judgment of one's opponents.
- *Sincerity*—being forthright, avoiding hypocrisy and cynicism, not having a hidden agenda.
- *Political sensitivity*—seeking the good of the nation as a whole, responding to the needs of all citizens, showing compassion to those in need, being concerned about issues and problems.
- *Honor*—acting to bring credit and worth to one's work, profession, and institution.

- *Conviction*—having strong and consistent beliefs and the courage to stand by one's values while being open to new information and change where warranted.

Michael Josephson (2006) has posited "The Six Pillars of Character," to include trustworthiness, respect, responsibility, fairness, caring, and citizenship. These core values, together with those summarized above, provide a yardstick for evaluating the ethical behavior of elected as well as appointed officials. One form of recognition singles out public servants with core values and character. An example is the Profile in Courage Award given to selected appointed and elected officials. Winners displayed courage of conscience by putting their careers at risk by pursuing the public interest in opposition to popular opinion or political pressures. Prominent recipients include Gerald Ford and John Lewis. But in today's climate of polarized politics, the character of elected officials is sorely tested.

POLARIZATION OF POLITICS AND ETHICAL IMPLICATIONS

By now, every American has seen signs of the hyperpolarization that characterizes the contemporary political environment, from the bumper stickers either lauding or lambasting political figures, to the "talking heads" on radio and TV deflecting charges of bias right back at their competitors, and to elected officials who, instead of reaching across party lines, choose to lob accusations across the aisle. Collective political discourse suggests partisan differences have surpassed mere bickering to enter a state of animosity. As Mike Lofgren, former long-term Republican staffer, observed, "[L]egislating has now become war minus the shooting" (quoted in Mann & Ornstein, 2012, 55). Indeed, it appears the turning point of polarization has been reached. Beyond it, a wall separates acceptable and stable forms of politics that fall short of consensus from the slippery slope of incivility that fuels feuding and strife and leads ultimately to violence (see Figure 11.1).

Despite incivility in political discourse, the historical nadir of partisanship was characterized by the doctrine of nullification (a doctrine devised by Jefferson and Madison to

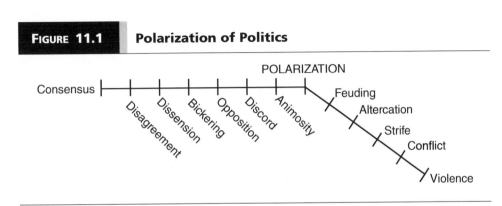

FIGURE 11.1   **Polarization of Politics**

Source: Adapted from Planas (2012).

circumvent the acts of their political rival, President John Adams). Nevertheless, the state-led constitutional challenge of the 2010 Affordable Care Act and the fiercely partisan nomination hearings for Supreme Court justices suggest American government is at least heading in that direction (Nivola, 2010). Studies show that uncivil speech on the floors of both congressional chambers is on the rise (Ahuja, 2008; Jamieson & Falk, 2000; Maisel, 2012; Uslaner, 2000) and that the accompanying party polarization has contributed to legislative gridlock (Binder, 2003; Dodd & Schraufnagel, 2012; Jones, 2001; Schraufnagel, 2011). Mann and Ornstein (2012) call attention to the asymmetric partisan polarization attributing this in large measure to the growing ideological gap between the two political parties. The environment is so polarized that some politicians will vote against issues that they are for if they believe the other party will benefit as a result. If they block whatever their opponents support, it is thought that it will weaken their rivals.

While the political consequences of polarization are clear, the ethical implications are subtler. As observed above, whether as an emissary or a leader, an elected official bears a solemn responsibility to serve the interests of her constituents. However, when these politicians are preoccupied with partisan attacks and thereby foreclose the possibility of compromise, they generate a status quo bias that blocks the passage of policies necessary to promote the greater good (Gutmann & Thompson, 2010, 1129).

In fact, unwillingness or inability to compromise strikes at the very core of the American democratic political system. As Gutmann and Thompson (2010, 1130) observe:

> When parties enter into negotiations in bad faith, deliberately misrepresent their opponents' positions, and refuse to cooperate even on matters on which they could find common ground, they undermine relationships of respect that are necessary to sustain any morally justified democracy.

Problematically, the "uncompromising mindset" only serves to compound the effects of polarization, yet is an integral part of the democratic process. The uncompromising stance is a staple of successful political campaigns and a source of the type of principled argumentation that can nourish a democracy.

Yet, as Gutmann and Thompson (2010, 2012) demonstrate, there exists an urgent need to distinguish between the exigencies of campaigning and those of governing. To gain power in a democracy, elected officials must assume a firmly principled mindset. But to wield this power in accordance with their overriding ethical duties to their constituents, they must take on a more compromising posture. It is therefore a matter of duty for elected officials, regardless of the political climate, to keep politics off the dangerous slope to the acrid discourse that thwarts progress and corrodes mutual respect. It may not be clear exactly what this obligation implies. Does this mean that candidates have to do away with negative campaigning? In the next section, the ethics of officials are put to the test in deciding whether to participate in that sort of activity.

NEGATIVE CAMPAIGNING

The strongest argument in favor of negative campaigning is that it works. Both the public and political candidates perceive it as an effective part of running for office (Geer, 2006). But is it ethical? Former Senate Majority Leader Tom Daschle has asserted that "negative advertising is the crack cocaine of politics" (Rich, 2012). It is widespread and addictive, especially in swing states and close elections. While most would agree that candidates should inform voters of any potential negative outcomes that would result from their opponents' policies or character, they would also likely contend that this should be done within the boundaries of civility and decorum. Deterioration of campaigns into the "ethics of the jungle"—name calling, distortion, disinformation, false insinuations—where anything goes should be avoided.

Planas (2012, Chapter 13) makes the important distinction between "how things are and how they should be." "All's fair in love and politics" is an oft-used expression; indeed, it inspired the title of Matalin and Carville's classic 1994 campaign primer, but crossing the "fairness line" does raise ethical concerns. While negative ads that are mean, rude, deceptive, insensitive, and vicious may be effective, applying the core values above would not lead to the conclusion that these "ought to be made the practice of politics" (382).

In recent years, nonpartisan organizations such as FactCheck.org and PolitiFact.com, along with organizations including Project Vote Smart and visual devices such as "Truth-O-Meters," have provided information to help voters sift through false claims generated by negative campaigning. These websites and organizations challenge duplicitous statements from both ends of the political spectrum. They can enable citizens to determine the truth behind campaign statements, news stories, and advertisements.

Yet the cost has been lowered for politicians as fact checkers have become an unremarkable part of the process, and politicians seemingly pay little price for fabrications. Ideology trumps facts; slogans trump reality. Flatly, grossly, and shamefully untrue statements are often repeated as if they were true. No one is condemned for mendacity, to say nothing of its consequences for democratic governance. As one commentator observed, there is now a "liberty to lie"; truth has lost its honor and falsehoods have lost their stigma (Blow, 2012).

The issue for candidates is whether they are willing to take charge of their campaigns and remove staffers who engage in questionable strategies. If elected, whether as a result of negative or positive campaign tactics, other ethical tests await them. Can it be expected that newly elected politicians will suddenly turn their backs on special interests that supported their campaigns financially? If so, how far can elected officials be obliged to go in their quest to be ethical? Should they do as Supreme Court justices are expected to do—recuse themselves from voting on matters related to special interest groups who may have contributed to their campaign? Should they refuse any financial support (e.g., meals, trips) paid for by special interest groups? Where is the line drawn on such matters if the law is unclear? Fuzzy limitations tempt unethical behavior, particularly when enforcement of campaign violations is slow and ineffective. Unfortunately, these questions are not being either asked or answered by policymakers in today's toxic political environment.

In sum, candidates and legislators must deal with a host of ethical dilemmas. The examples discussed above highlight a wide range of issues confronting members of Congress, including insider trading, conflict of interest, inappropriate constituent service, ideological vendettas, financial and sexual misconduct, bribe taking, uncivil speech, unfair treatment on behalf of campaign contributors, negative campaigning, and unauthorized disclosure of privileged information. While most of these concerns are illegal, government incumbents can also encounter the ethically troubling "dirty hands" problem, a subject discussed next.

THE PROBLEM OF DIRTY HANDS

The problem of "dirty hands" is traceable to Machiavelli, who advised that the Prince "must learn how not to be good." Political theorist Michael Walzer (1974) gave Machiavelli's principle the title of dirty hands, adapting the term from a play by Jean-Paul Sartre. The issue is thus: Sometimes the wrong thing is the right thing to do. But, Walzer qualifies, only in situations of dire or "supreme" emergency is the disutility of abiding by the prohibitions or rules great enough to override the utilitarian value of keeping to the rules (Coady, 2009). A classic example: A political leader must decide whether to torture a terrorist to find the whereabouts of a bomb. Without this coercion, innocent people could die (Cunningham, 1992, 239; see also Case Study 11.4).

Walzer argued that the dirty hands conundrum "is posed most dramatically in politics," where officials sometimes face violating their principles for the sake of achieving some morally weighty political end. This then is not just a problem, but a paradox. Dovi's (2005, 130) recommendation to citizens is to "accept the paradox and seek what solace is available by choosing political actors who are willing to get their hands dirty and will feel guilty doing so." The condition of guilt serves as an information mechanism of public accountability, given the assumption that guilty politicians will be disposed to confess their violations of moral principles or willingly subject their decisions to scrutiny.

Walzer (1974, 160) further claims the pervasiveness of dirty hands in politics as "a central feature of political life, one that arises not merely as an occasional crisis in the career of this or that unlucky official but systematically and frequently." He divides political actors into two broad categories: consequentialists who ignore the obligations of morality and make decisions based solely on the considerations of expediency, and absolutists who act solely according to their moral principles. Like the contrasting styles of congressional representatives, both absolutists and consequentialists are needed for a morally healthy polity. Without the presence of some individuals refusing to compromise on their integrity, polity would suffer, and Dovi cautions against the cumulative effects individual dirty-handed decisions can have. Continually compromising principles can result in officials—and the public witnessing the compromising—weakening their commitment to political ideals. A second cumulative effect is narrowing the scope of availability of policy options. Repeated exposure to dirty-handed decisions—even those made for morally important gains—can dull the intensity of certain commitments. If more and more decision makers accept torturing or bribing for preferable political ends, then the ordinariness and routine of these practices can numb moral repulsion. Politicians, soldiers, law enforcement agents, public defense attorneys, and resistance fighters are all people who often operate in dirty arenas and must constantly struggle against losing their moral sensitivity (Cunningham, 1992, 244).[1]

No precise decision procedure exists to inform people in advance when they can or must embrace evil to minimize it, or when they can forsake the battle against evil without becoming a partner in crime. The ethics triad, nonetheless, can aid in the decision procedure, illustrated in Case Study 11.4.

Presidents, too, cannot avoid ethical quagmires and must decide how to deal with them. Some of the same issues that confront Congress also confront presidents (see, e.g., "The Bad President" Tabletop Exercise at the end of the chapter). However, one special concern singled out for attention here is adherence to truthfulness, the topic of the next section.

CASE STUDY 11.4

Applying Philosophical and Behavioral Ethics Approaches: Interrogation Methods

You are Major Smith, the new counterintelligence operations officer for a battalion deployed last week to support Operation A. The infantry brigade is deployed throughout a major city, patrolling the streets. Things have not been going well in the last month. A number of soldiers have been killed by improvised explosive devices (IEDs) set by insurgents. As the senior officer, you get a call from your commander, who reports he just caught an insurgent leader. The commander says the leader is bragging that a car bomb has been set to go off in the next 30 minutes and said, "There's nothing you can do about it." The company commander is prepared to do some "serious persuasion" to find out where the bomb is, saying, "Your interrogators are too far away. I know the new directives say they have to do all interrogations by the book—but time is running out. I know how to make a man talk, so I can get the information. These attacks have to come to an end. Request guidance, sir." What should you do, Major?

A similar case occurred in the reality of war in Afghanistan (Operation Enduring Freedom), resulting in the deaths of two detainees in the Bagram Theater Internment Facility in December 2002. In February 2003, Lieutenant General Daniel K. McNeill, commander of American forces in Afghanistan in 2002 and 2003, said prisoners Mullah Habibullah and Dilawar had died of natural causes. He did not disclose that military pathologists had described both deaths as homicides caused by beatings.

Sergeant James P. Boland watched a subordinate beat prisoner Habibullah. Boland chained the hands of Dilawar above his shoulders and denied him medical care. Nearly two years later, the Army charged Sergeant Boland with criminal offenses in the Dilawar case ranging from dereliction of duty to maiming and involuntary manslaughter. The findings of the military investigation support accounts by former Afghan prisoners that they were subject to abuse. The interrogation methods described were authorized in Guantanamo Bay, Cuba—not Bagram—including removal of clothing, isolation for long periods, stress positions, and sleep and light deprivation. Three men arrested with Dilawar said they were hooded with their arms raised and chained to the ceiling for hours and days at a time in Bagram. One of the three men said he was forced to lie on his stomach and a solider jumped on his back. Was the price of immorality of abuse worth paying? Did obtaining intelligence from the prisoners constitute a supreme emergency?

Results-Based Analysis. The two cases (based on Gall & Rohde, 2004; Kern, 2006) can be analyzed using the ethics triumvirate. Concentrating first on results—the greatest good for the greatest number—both the company commander in the first case and Sergeant Boland in the second thought they could obtain actionable intelligence by using "enhanced" interrogation techniques. In the best-case scenario the insurgent suffers but lives are saved if accurate information is divulged. The end of preventing the car bombing or obtaining information from detainees at Bagram justifies means of unauthorized interrogation methods. The major and the sergeant may believe that their action requires moral courage and that their decisions would lead to the greater good—fewer American casualties.

There is no certainty, however, that the fictional insurgent leader or the real-life detainees had the information necessary to prevent the bombing or advance the military mission in Afghanistan. Use of extreme methods may or may not have extracted useful intelligence. Subjecting others to harsh treatment undoubtedly takes a toll not only on the victim of the extreme tactics, but also on those administering it, especially if the information gleaned fails to yield expected results. In the first case, authorizing unlawful methods could irreparably damage the major's reputation and media coverage could erode public support for the military.

Rule-Based Analysis. Assessing rules and principles, neither organizational rules nor the fundamental ethical rule "what is good for one is good for all" endorse the methods used to obtain information about enemy actions. The officers violated established procedures regarding the conduct of interrogations. Recall the Department of Justice memos used to authorize torture. In the first scenario, the major should not authorize the company commander to engage in actions that fall outside the rules and that violate moral principles. He might have done so because of giving higher priority to loyalty to his fellow soldiers and innocent civilians. The second case violated both the law and ethics with flagrant examples of detainee abuse. Following the moral minimum (avoid and correct social injury) and the Kew Gardens principles (they felt there was a compelling need, they were in proximity, possessed capability, and, at least in the first case, the major may have considered himself the last resort), they might argue that their choice was reasonable: The soldiers and the mission come first.

Under the extreme circumstances in the first case, wherein time was of the essence—delay could mean deaths—the major might have authorized unorthodox methods and subsequently defended his actions to his superiors claiming that he had to do a wrong thing to do the right (obtain information that would prevent harm and loss of life), the "dirty-hands" defense. While there is no assurance that the information would be accurate and achieve the desired result, the major is able to justify his decision and is willing to accept the consequences of his action if it comes to a court-martial. He may believe that anyone confronting this specific dilemma would be willing to endorse the universality of such action. Engaging in unauthorized interrogation caused harm and pain to the insurgents and involved techniques that, in the latter case, violated the law, resulting in criminal charges against Sergeant Boland.

Virtue-Based Analysis. From a virtue theory perspective, the action will be influenced by the ingrained dispositions of the decision maker. Moral courage will be required whichever choice is made. It takes courage to act when the stakes are so high, taking responsibility for the lives and well-being of others. In the first case, the major did not have time to think it over; there were two stark options with no middle course available. Prudence and thoughtful deliberation had to give way to decisiveness and valor. He had to act in the moment and make a snap decision. The major and the sergeant then must live with their decisions and the way their actions will be viewed by those they respect. Will their conduct survive the self-evaluation test posed when they look at themselves in the mirror and ask, "Is this someone who did what a moral exemplar would do?" Will it pass the after-event assessment by review boards who will render a judgment on the action? Ultimately, both of them will have to decide whether they are comfortable with the rightness—or wrongness—of their decision: That is what makes it a moral choice.

Behavioral Ethics-Based Analysis. The first and second case can be further considered using some concepts from behavioral ethics. Ethical fading is a form of self-deception whereby people fail to recognize the moral dimension of an issue. This is most likely to occur when a visceral response occurs around a high-stress decision point. The major in this scenario, while he no doubt realizes his decision has moral implications, is forced to make a high-stakes decision with inadequate information. There is little time for System 2 thinking (slow-paced, cool and deliberative) given the circumstances, so it is not surprising that System 1 thinking (rapid, intuitive, gut reaction) is used even though System 2 might be preferred. Depending on the outcome, the major may regret that his "want" self prevailed over his "should" self in approaching the interrogation, a concern that may become more apparent after the event itself. Under the circumstances, the major was forced to decide quickly and later may be required to think more carefully when he is asked to justify his actions.

The overarching difficulty with concocted and—far rarer—actual "ticking bomb" cases is that they tend to obscure the need to think clearly not only about the limits of routine interrogations, but also what happens after the decision to torture is made. Impossible questions arise: How many people must be endangered? How certain must decision makers be of the danger? How convinced must they be that the victim will be susceptible to brutality? If necessary, are they prepared to engage in cruelty against his family to obtain accurate information? Stated differently, the argument for torture has no beginning and has no end (Fried & Fried, 2011; also see Exhibit 8.4).

PRESIDENTS AND TRUTHFULNESS

For a moment the lie becomes the truth.

—Fyodor Dostoevsky

Consider Lyndon Johnson and the Vietnam War, Richard Nixon and Watergate, Jimmy Carter and Iranian hostages, Ronald Reagan and the Iran-Contra affair, George H. W. Bush and tax increases, Bill Clinton and the Monica Lewinsky affair, George W. Bush and the Iraq War, Barack Obama and Guantanamo, Donald Trump and campaign promise keeping. In each case, be it policy or politics, private or public behavior, the president had to decide whether to be truthful or deceptive. While a broken promise is not technically the same as a lie, "promise keeping" is an important principle and breaking a promise suggests one is untrustworthy. This requires qualification: If the promise is broken because of something you could not control, it is not a lie, but if it is betrayed for no good reason, it is a lie:

- Lyndon Johnson deliberately suppressed information about the Vietnam War, selectively revealing reports about the war's progress to put the best possible face on American success, thereby creating "an illusion of imminent victory" (Ekman, 2009, 307).
- Richard Nixon lied to cover up the fact that people working for the White House were caught at the Watergate complex while breaking in to the Democratic Party headquarters. Audiotapes of conversations in the Oval Office indicated that he was abusing the power of his office, concealing a crime to stay in power, and deceiving the people.
- Jimmy Carter misled the public when he said at a January 8, 1980, press conference that a military rescue of American hostages who had been seized by Iranian militants at the U.S. embassy in Tehran "would almost certainly end in failure and almost certainly end in the death of the hostages." He said this knowing that he had secretly authorized military training for just such a rescue operation.
- Ronald Reagan lied to the nation about the extent of American involvement in Iranian affairs. When an Iranian newspaper broke the story that the administration had secretly sold weapons to Iran through Israel in the hopes of triggering the release of hostages, Reagan at first categorically denied the allegations. He then backpedaled and asserted that the arms sale was simply a minor one, and then days later went back to denying the sale altogether. When it was later discovered that the funds from the Iranian arms sale were diverted to fund rebels in Nicaragua, in contravention of a congressional prohibition of such funding, the administration quickly became entangled in the infamous Iran-Contra scandal (Alterman, 2004).
- George H. W. Bush in August 1988 accepted the Republican Party's nomination for president, saying in his acceptance speech, "The Congress will push me to raise taxes, and I'll say no. And they'll push, and I'll say no, and they'll press again. And all I can say to them is read my lips. No new taxes." In retrospect, this is reminiscent of the joke about lies told by politicians: "How can you tell when a politician is lying? When he moves his lips." He reneged on his unequivocal "no new taxes" pledge two years later when he signed the 1990 Omnibus Budget Reconciliation Act.
- Bill Clinton's infamous statement, "I did not have sexual relations with that woman, Miss Lewinsky," was a lie to the nation about his extramarital sex life. David Gergen, editor at large of *U.S. News and World Report*, who had experience working for Reagan, Nixon, and Clinton, took particular umbrage at Clinton's lie. "The deep and searing violation took place when he not only lied to the country, but co-opted his friends and lied to them" (quoted in Alterman, 2004, 11; also see Kinzer, 2007).

- George W. Bush was interviewed by NBC's Matt Lauer on November 8, 2010, and said, in reference to dealings with Iraq, "I gave diplomacy every chance to work." Yet insider accounts from inside Bush's national security team (e.g., Clarke, 2009) and others (e.g., Fromkin, 2010; Isikoff & Corn, 2006) indicate that a year prior to the invasion and immediately after 9/11, the administration had its sights set on military action against Iraq.

- Barack Obama made many promises to the American people during the campaign of 2008. According to PolitiFact.com's "Obamameter," composed of 533 of the president's promises, by the end of his eight years in office he had kept 48 percent of his promises and broken 24 percent of them, while another 28 percent were part of a compromise. One of the more prominent broken promises listed was Obama's pledge to close Guantanamo detention center, but the decision was not completely under his control (Congress refused to support closure of the prison).

- Donald Trump also made promises to the public during the 2016 campaign. PolitiFact.com's "Trump-O-Meter" identified 97 promises, by late October 2017 PolitiFact concluded he had kept eight promises, with 42 "in the works," 32 stalled and 15 were not yet rated. Two of the most widely publicized promises—repealing Obamacare and building a wall that Mexico would pay for—were among those "in the works." PolitiFact also had a Truth-O-Meter making fact checks on Trump's statements and those of other elected officials classifying them as mostly true, half true, mostly false, false, or "pants on fire." Trump did not fare well on this "truth" criterion or standards used by other fact-checking sources reported in the press (see, e.g., Leonhardt & Thompson, 2017, July 21; Kessler, Kelly, & Lewis, 2018, January 2). His most controversial comments are often qualified by phrases such as "people think" or "some say" or "I was told that" (Blow, 2017, October 19).

Patrick Dobel (1999) has argued that prudence is a virtue of political leaders. "Diligence in obtaining information . . . and attentiveness to the fit and proportionality of means and ends" is required because of their "responsibility for the welfare of the polity" (57–75). Robert Dallek (2010) concludes that presidential deception is ethical in foreign policy if it is necessary for national security and produces substantially better outcomes. He maintains, however, that deception culminating in foreign policy debacles (e.g., George W. Bush and Iraq; Johnson and Vietnam) is unethical. One drawback of this view is that it explicitly links ethical judgments to outcomes. Dallek is right to focus on the pragmatic element of presidential deception, but there will always be factors outside of the president's control for which he should not necessarily be held responsible.

What is the purpose behind the lie? Jimmy Carter lied about a rescue mission for the Iranian hostages. Ekman's (2009, 304–306) analysis of this deception concludes that he had to lie to "gain an advantage over the enemy." The attempt failed, but Carter was held responsible for only the failure and not the falsehood. When assessing an untrue statement by an official, it is crucial to determine the motivation for lying and to whom the lie is addressed. When evaluating the ethics of presidential deception, it is important to remember a now famous question asked by Howard Baker, then U.S. Senator and ranking minority member of the Senate committee investigating the Watergate scandal—"What did the President know and when did he know it?"

In making judgments regarding truthfulness and character, Dennis Thompson (2010, 24) cautions that "ethical character is fragmented," and one needs to consider both private and public virtues. Presidents sometimes fail to display both private and public rectitude (e.g., Clinton's lies about the Lewinsky affair), but the question is whether they need to exhibit both. In his view, the qualities that constitute "Constitutional character" should take priority—"the disposition to act, and to motivate others to act, according to the principles that constitute the democratic process" (24). Actions in this regard may vary according to the respective responsibilities of different public offices, but they would include things like sensitivity to basic rights of citizenship, respect for due process, sense of responsibility, tolerance of opposition, willingness to justify decisions, and commitment to candor. Private virtues might make a president more capable or respectable, Thompson maintains, but constitutional virtues should be required as a condition for holding office.

Yet the behavior of politicians too often fails to reflect the core values and Constitutional character described here (e.g., see Exhibit 11.2). In what ways do citizens' and media's dealings with officials affect their ethical behavior? This is the topic of the final section.

THE INFLUENCE OF CITIZENS AND THE MEDIA ON POLITICIANS

The populace and the media have subjected the private lives of officials to increased scrutiny with the advent of 24/7 "gotcha media" and the citizens' voracious appetite for tabloid stories. Back in the 1880s, when President Chester A. Arthur said, "I may be president, but my private life is nobody's damned business" (Hagopian Institute, 2008), he may have been able to make it stick. Now it is common to see headlines discussing the drinking habits, driving record, sexual conduct, and family life of presidents and other officials. This led Dennis Thompson (1981b, 2006) to examine when the private life of public servants should become an issue of public concern. Privacy laws provide limited clarity, and ethical principles sometimes conflict on this issue, making it difficult to identify precise rules regarding officials' rights to privacy.

Thompson (1981b) provides the following distinction between instrumental and intrinsic justification for the value of privacy: Instrumental arguments maintain that privacy is linked to liberty by enabling a person to engage in certain activities unhampered by observation or intrusive interventions; intrinsic arguments focus on the nature of intimate relations (love, friendship) and trust, which typically require privacy to develop. Clearly, officials must surrender some of their privacy rights, but how much and what kind? Here, Thompson considers the "principle of diminished privacy," which can be justified on utilitarian grounds—the interests of the many (citizens) trump the rights of the few (elected officials), with limitations on the privacy rights of elected officials, but not to an unlimited extent. In general, the more influential the position, the less privacy protection is afforded. The nature and type of the issues dealt with by the official (intimate/personal vs. policy/job related) and the effect of those issues (public/media perception; adverse impact on the job) are also important.

EXHIBIT 11.2   **Mendacity and American Democracy: An Editorial**

"When you tell a lie, you steal someone's right to the truth."

—Khaled Hosseini

Today's political environment presents unprecedented challenges to holding government accountable: a flagrant disregard of truth, censorship of public information, and disrespect for ethical norms. The nature of the dishonesty—its sheer volume and spontaneity as well as its repetition of easily disproved statements—distracts, confuses, and overwhelms the public and punditry alike. It leads to familiarity and familiarity leads to acceptance, ultimately rendering those who would question government ineffectual. It is difficult to have meaningful dialogue with those who do not believe in facts.

Among the numerous widely spread false claims are disinformation about September 11 celebrations, Iraq war opposition, Iraq war spending, the birther conspiracy, inaugural crowd size, the Electoral College majority, voter fraud, the status of the Affordable Care Act, tax cut beneficiaries, the United States having the highest taxes in the world, the North American Free Trade Agreement, the Iran nuclear deal, contributions to NATO, Mexican and Muslim immigrants, the unemployment rate, the murder rate, and sexual harassment.

Indifference to facts, and no penalty for being wrong, represents a societal breakdown in the ability to face objective reality, as well as to morally and intellectually compromise government. Post-truth politics undermines the very idea of facts; the issue becomes not what is right, but what you can get away with. PolitiFact rates nearly 70 percent of presidential statements as mostly false, false, or "pants on fire" (this site keeps track of all assertions on a daily basis: https://www.washingtonpost.com/news/fact-checker/wp/2017/07/20/president-trumps-first-six-months-the-fact-check-tally/?utm_term=.d5d4af8b7a63. Easy falsehoods often sound more true than hard facts, as humans are often swayed more by fiction than reality. Mark Twain observed that it is easier to fool a person than to convince him that he has been fooled. Incriminating truth is seldom preferred over flattering fabrications that win applause. Incapable of acknowledging wrongdoing, it is not a deception if top officials believe it.

With no standard of propriety, the disdain for truth embodies contempt for democracy and a challenge to legitimacy of its institutions. In an apparent "us-against-them" attacks on the rule of law and constitution government, separation of powers (the courts, the Congress, executive agency secretaries, the intelligence community, the military), Gold Star families, political party allies, defense treaties, the free press, labor unions, as well as business advisory councils erode the sense of trust in society—and ourselves.

Democracies depend upon acceptance of shared facts such as the certification of elections as valid (including accurate counting of votes and the absence of illegally cast votes) as well as respect for the electoral process and one's opponents. The existence of facts, a conception of truth outside of what government says is true, as well as the force of law are foundational to, and a test of, democracy. Duplicity distracts attention from other ethical concerns such as undermining the capacity for evidence-based governing and upholding laws policymakers are sworn to protect. Falsification, deceit, denial, habitual lying, imperviousness to correction, and political chicanery must be called out for what they are. Ethical competence is not to be confused with confidence, attitude is not the same as aptitude. "When you tell a lie," writes Khaled Hosseini, "you steal someone's right to tell the truth."

Sources: Gold (2017), Hohmann (2017, August 2), Jurecic (2017, January 27), Kessler, Lee, and Kelly (2017, July 20), Paul and Matthews (2016), Sargent (2017, March 6).

What is the benefit and cost of exposure of the private lives of public servants? On the upside, Thompson argues that it enables citizens to form judgments about an official's physical and moral competence, the likelihood that they would put the public interest ahead of private interests and support politically popular policies. Public exposure offers clues about officials' or candidates' moral sensitivity, and provides a basis for holding them accountable. In the 2012 presidential campaign, Republican nominee Mitt Romney told a group of Florida donors that 47 percent of the citizenry would not vote for the GOP because they were, essentially, parasitic "takers" dependent on government largess. An enterprising bartender taped the "private" talk, and *Mother Jones* magazine broke the story. This reinforced a stereotype that Democrats had been pushing of Romney as an out-of-touch plutocrat, too aloof and arrogant to care about the needs of less privileged voters. Was this recording of the speech an invasion of privacy? While some may doubt it, others may see it as a public service, as Wasserman (2013) opined in an op-ed for the *Miami Herald*: "[W]hat it revealed and what might not have been heard otherwise" justified its reporting.

On the downside, exposure is a distraction from the more significant issues of the day. The amount of the media's time and space devoted to salacious stories and the viewer's/reader's attention to such matters means the decision-maker's time and attention likely will be occupied by these concerns as well—diverting them from the more substantive policy matters for which they were elected to deliberate. Also, "the private lives of public officials deserve protection because the privacy of all citizens has value" (Thompson, 1981b, 240), and these rights have been progressively eroded for politicians as well as candidates. For example, *Mother Jones* also published reports of Senate minority leader Mitch McConnell planning with campaign aides to release an unflattering secret video of film star Ashley Judd, a rumored challenger for McConnell's seat. It included comments about her history of mental instability and personal, private comments she had made that were likely to annoy Kentucky voters. (Judd opted not to run prior to publication of the article.) Clearly, the zone of candidate privacy, like that of elected incumbents, has diminished considerably. Some aspects of the private lives of public officials and those seeking office, such as sexual orientation and gender identity, have no bearing on their performance. Media exposure of such characteristics (especially when the person wishes them to remain confidential) is unethical when it causes undue professional or personal harm (Case Study 11.5).

Some balance must be struck between the public's right to be informed about the actions of their elected officials or candidates and the officials' and candidates' right to privacy (Chapter 14).

CASE STUDY 11.5

Applying Philosophical and Behavioral Ethics Approaches: A Transgender City Manager

Susan Stanton, then known as Steve, had been working as city manager for the city of Largo, Florida, for more than 14 years and was a recent recipient of a sizable merit pay increase. In 2007, someone leaked to the local newspaper the fact that Stanton was in the midst of a gender transition. The *Saint Petersburg Times* published the story and "outed" Stanton against her wishes. Stanton's wife was already aware of her circumstances, but her 13-year-old son was not. Stanton rushed home the afternoon before the story broke to share her struggle firsthand with her son, whom she feared would be harassed at school following the disclosure.

The news about Stanton's new identity came as a shock to the citizens of Largo, who had known Steve Stanton as an esteemed community member and as their city manager for years. Once the news was published, there was an immediate outcry from residents demanding that Stanton be fired. City Commission members were inundated with phone calls and emails denouncing Stanton as "disgusting." One religious official went so far as to publicly claim that Jesus would want Stanton fired. Prior to this, Stanton's job performance was never in question—indeed, Stanton had proved competent and effective at managing the city. Stanton wanted to continue in her position, a job that she enjoyed and at which she was successful (Escobedo, 2010). A minority cohort of community members rallied in support of Stanton, arguing that job retention should be based on merit, and not on aspects of identity. There were, however, no legal protections in Largo that prohibited discrimination on the basis of gender identity or expression. What should the City Commission do?

The ethics triad can help provide a defensible evaluation to an ethical conflict derived from a comprehensive consideration of three elements: results, rules, and virtue. This framework allows for the interplay of the competing interests involved in decision making. However, the tripartite analysis can be perverted as well. For it to work as intended the results must be based on the greatest good, not self-interest; the rules interests must pivot on a sense of justice and fairness, not organizational rules; and the value interests must be predicated on integrity, not conformity.

Results-Based Analysis. This case presents an example of instances when results interests may not lead to sound ethical decision making. The greatest good is served if the city manager is discharged because that is what the community desires and the community is an emblem of the greatest good. However, serving the greatest good by meeting public demands is unethical in this context because its motives are driven by prejudice and ignorance. Therefore, even though retaining the city manager will cause discontent, it is nevertheless the proper course of action.

Rule-Based Analysis. The council should look to its code of ethics, its oath to protect and serve the public interest, its employment contract with the city manager, as well as state and federal employment laws when evaluating how to address the issue. The rules contained in each of these documents will help inform the council of the best course of action. Likely, such rules will support retaining the manager—as long as her personal transition does not interfere with her ability to fulfill her professional responsibilities. And even if the rules do not direct the council how to proceed ethically, the underlying notions of justice and fairness inherent in the rules interests should indeed inform the council that prejudice and ignorance serve no purpose in ethical decision making. "What is good for one is good for all" is the key criterion in rule-based decision making.

Virtue-Based Analysis. The virtue interests involved in this conflict will be determined by the values that the city council chooses to demonstrate through its actions. Robert Greenleaf's (2002) theory of Servant Leadership suggests that the council should be attentive to the concerns of constituents and empathize with them. This theory would justify heeding the call of citizens who wish to see the city manager fired. However, such a decision would undoubtedly violate several of the "Six Pillars of Character" espoused by Michael Josephson (2002), namely, respect, fairness, and caring. Therefore, a decision to terminate the manager would reflect poor character on the part of the city council members.

Actual Outcome. Within days of the initial newspaper article, Largo's City Commission held a highly emotional emergency hearing. At the conclusion, it voted to terminate Stanton's employment. Several commissioners cited as justification their belief that the public had "lost confidence" in the manager and, under those circumstances, Stanton could not be retained. In making this decision, the Commission stood with the majority of vocal residents, and argued that their actions led to a "good" outcome for the maximum possible number of people ("Susan Stanton's Story," 2012). In October 2012, Stanton was hired as the city manager of Greenfield, California.

Lesson. This scenario should not present an ethical conflict. If the city manager were somehow unable to perform at the same caliber because of being transgendered, then the scenario could merit termination. But for the Commission to make such an evaluation based solely on citizen outcry—any credence to the employee's actual performance notwithstanding—is wholly improper and sends a signal to the community that it is acceptable to be biased and ill informed.

QUESTIONS TO CONSIDER

1. Did the *Saint Petersburg Times* dutifully fulfill a journalistic duty to publish the story that "outed" Stanton, despite being against her wishes?

2. Does one's gender identity affect his or her ability to fulfill professional responsibilities?

3. Was the Commission correct in hearing citizen comments regarding Stanton's transition in a public forum?

4. Should the public's opinion regarding a personal element of an official's life influence the official's employment standing?

5. Did Stanton have an obligation to make her transition known to the Commission prior to the article being published?

Behavioral Ethics-Based Analysis. The language of behavioral ethics can be used to further dissect this scenario. System 1 thinking based on rapid, intuitive, visceral reactions characterized the general reaction to Stanton's gender reassignment, precluding more reflective and deliberative System 2 consideration of the matter. By becoming the "political issue," Stanton misjudged the reaction of her colleagues and community, perceiving them to be more progressive in their attitudes than they were. Alternatively, she knew of the risks and decided to go public with her gender reassignment anyway. The bias and stereotypic thinking demonstrated by the press, the Commission, and the vocal portions of the community compromised Stanton's ability to continue in her managerial role. The absence of transgender support groups and an ethics code with teeth provided no counterweight to the overwhelming negative response to Stanton's transgender status.

CONCLUSION

The distinction between political ethics and administrative ethics is often overdrawn. Many of the same values and ethical principles—problems and dilemmas—are encountered by both appointed and elected public servants. Conflicts of interest, insider trading, competing roles and obligations, significance of personal character, temptations to compromise, the value of ethical principles—these challenges are present regardless of whether one is elected or appointed. However, some issues are more pronounced for elected officials. Citizen and media scrutiny is often more intense, legal requirements are more ambiguous, and political polarization and partisanship make decision making slower and more treacherous. Expectations for performance are higher for elected officials than for appointed officials, vulnerability to personal attack is greater, and privacy rights are less protected. Similarly, external pressures are more overt, job security is less certain, and accountability is regularly demanded.

Elected legislators and executives face particular challenges. They can be leaders or emissaries, truthful or deceptive. They can be guided by core values and public service obligations, or succumb to the pressures and temptations that lead to compromising ethical principles and violating their oath of office. The citizenry, unfortunately, is exposed to too many instances of the latter and too few of the former. Recall the epigram opening this chapter ("Art, like morality, consists of drawing the line somewhere"). Public officials—elected or appointed—have to make distinctions between what they "should" and "should not" do, realizing that some lines are drawn for them, and some are drawn by them. Then they need the moral courage to do the right thing.

***

The whole art of government consists in the art of being honest.

—Thomas Jefferson

NOTE

1. For a compelling argument that virtue ethics (Chapter 6) is a way to deal with the struggle, see Tholen (2013); also consult Anderson (2014).

FOR DISCUSSION

1. How would you assess the effectiveness of the House and Senate Ethics Committees? Read Appendix 11.1 before answering. What reforms would you propose for handling ethical wrongdoing by members of Congress? How likely is it that your suggestions would be feasible and effective?

2. Discuss the following statements and questions:

   - "We expect leaders to be truthful even though we suspect that they will not be."
   - Where is the line drawn between constituent service and conflict of interest? Current methods of campaign finance amount to informal bribery. How would you refute or support this assertion?
   - How can insider trading among public officials be stopped? Is new legislation needed? How likely is it that your suggestions would be feasible and effective?
   - "All members of Congress have a primary interest in being reelected. Some members have no other interest."
   - Why are there far more emissaries than leaders among today's politicians?
   - What criteria can and should be used to evaluate the performance of politicians? What role should ethics play in such assessments?
   - What can be done to curb polarization of politics? How likely is it that your suggestions would be efficacious?
   - Which of the examples of presidential deception listed is most egregious? Why?

3. In a polarized political climate, many legislators vote the "party line," seemingly irrespective of the merits of issues or what is for the greater good. Using the ethics triad and the tenets of behavioral ethics (Chapter 7), is such conduct ethical? Why or why not?

4. The chapter ends by discussing how public servants often confront difficult choices and need political courage to act. Consider the advice that Eleanor Roosevelt ("Do what you feel in your heart to be right, for you'll be criticized anyway") and Ernest Hemingway ("I know only that what is moral is what you feel good after and what is immoral is what you feel bad after") offer as officials respond to compelling challenges.

EXERCISES

1. Identify any one of the 535 members of the current Congress who you believe meets the qualifications of a moral exemplar (consider criteria discussed in this chapter). Write a two-page essay justifying your selection of this person and the criteria used.

2 Visit PolitiFact.com's Truth-O-Meter and examine the facts provided on an issue or candidate. How useful is such a source in determining whether to support candidates for public office? Why?

3. **Bad Actor Tabletop Exercise 4:** "The Bad President." Instructions (see Chapter 3, Exercise 5)

Senator John Ross III is currently running for office as the President of the United States of America. The public is wary of Senator Ross because of his position on a number of issues during his time on the Senate. Ross knows that his chances of being elected will be much higher if he changes his stance on critical issues during his campaign. He plans to release a campaign video making promises to push issues during his presidency that he did not support in the Senate. If elected, the Senator has no intention of keeping those promises.

Role 1: Independent Journalist

You are a journalist who hears from a credible source that Senator Ross plans on breaking his campaign promises. The source is willing to go on record. In light of this information, how do you react? Consider your obligations, ethical and otherwise. To whom are you accountable as an independent journalist? What factors impact your decision?

Role 2: Campaign Manager

You are Senator Ross' campaign manager. As you have firsthand knowledge of the Senator's platform, Ross comes to you to advise him regarding this new campaign video. Do you support his decision or try to persuade him to take a different approach? Consider your obligations, ethical and otherwise. To whom are you accountable as campaign manager? What factors impact your decision?

Role 3: Running Mate

Senator Ross has tapped you to run alongside him during his Presidential campaign. You become aware of his intent to make false campaign promises. How do you react? Do you accept the Senator's offer or decline? Consider your obligations, ethical and otherwise. To whom are you accountable as the potential Vice President of the United States? What factors impact your decision?

Role 4: Industry Executive/Donor

You are a top executive in a leading industry. You have been negotiating with Senator Ross, who is seeking funding from you for his campaign. In return, you expect to have some influence on forthcoming policy that impacts your industry. You are informed of the Senator's intent to renege on the campaign promises. How does this knowledge impact your decision to fund his campaign? Consider your obligations, ethical and otherwise. To whom are you accountable as a professional? What factors impact your decision?

Role 5: Public Official/Supporter

You are a public official in the same state as Senator Ross. As such, you have decided to publicly support his campaign. Just before you have made your statement, you become aware that he has been making false campaign promises. Does this impact your decision to support the Senator? Do you feel obligated to inform the public of his intentions? Consider your obligations, ethical and otherwise. To whom are you accountable as an official? What factors impact your decision?

REFERENCES

Abad-Santos, A. (2012, October 8). Lucky for Congress, blatant conflict of interest is still perfectly legal. *The Atlantic*. Retrieved from https://www.theatlantic.com/.../lucky-congress-blatant-conflict-interest-still-perfectly-legal/322790/

Ahuja, S. (2008). *Congress behaving badly: The rise of partisanship and incivility and the death of public trust*. Westport, CT: Praeger.

Alterman, E. (2004). *When presidents lie: A history of official deception and its consequences*. New York: Penguin.

Anderson, J. (2014). An open letter to "dirty hands" theorists from a public manager. *Public Integrity*, 16(3), 305–316.

Binder, S. (2003). *Stalemate: Causes and consequences of legislative gridlock*. Washington, DC: Brookings Institution.

Blow, C. (2012, November 1). Liberty to lie. *New York Times*. Retrieved from http://campaign stops.blogs.nytimes.com/2012/11/01/liberty-to-lie/

Blow, C. (2017, October 19). Trump isn't Hitler, but the lying . . . *New York Times*. Retrieved from https://nyti.ms/2zlXjPA

Burke, E. (1774). *Speech to the electors of Bristol*. Retrieved from http://press-pubs.uchicago.edu/founders/documents/v1ch13s7.html

Carter, S. (1996). *Integrity*. New York: Harper Perennial.

Carter, S. (1998). *Civility*. New York: Basic Books.

Clarke, R. (2009). *Against all enemies: Inside America's war on terror*. New York: Free Press.

Coady, C. (2009). The problem of dirty hands. In E. N. Zalta (Ed.), *The Stanford encyclopedia of philosophy* (summer 2011 ed.). Retrieved from http://plato.stanford.edu/archives/sum2011/entries/dirty-hands/

Cooper, T. & Wright, D. (1992). *Exemplary public administrators: Character and leadership in government*. San Francisco: Jossey-Bass.

Cunningham, A. (1992). The moral importance of dirty hands. *Journal of Value Inquiry*, 26(2), 239–250.

Dallek, R. (2010). Presidential fitness and presidential lies. *Presidential Studies Quarterly*, 40, 9–22.

Dobel, J. (1999). *Public integrity*. Baltimore, MD: Johns Hopkins University Press.

Dodd, L., & Schraufnagel, S. (2012). Congress and the polarity paradox: Party polarization, member incivility, and enactment of landmark legislation, 1891–1994. *Congress & the Presidency*, 39, 109–132.

Dovi, S. (2005). Guilt and the problem of dirty hands. *Constellations*, 12(1), 128–146.

Ekman, P. (2009). *Telling lies: Clues to deceit in the marketplace, politic and marriage*. New York: W. W. Norton.

Escobedo, T. (2010, March 12). *Journey from Steven to Susan captured in new documentary*. Retrieved from http:/ww//cnn.com/2010/LIVING/03/10/her.name.was.steven/index.html

Falvey, J. (1991). The congressional ethics dilemma: Constituent service or conflict of interest. *American Criminal Law Review, 28*, 323–382.

Feldman, J. (2013, April 23). John Stewart tears up Congress for quietly scaling back insider trading law: The "f*cker Act." Retrieved from http://www.mediaite.com/tv/jon-stewart-tears-up-congress-for-quietly-scaling-back-insider-trading-law-the-fcker-act/

Fried, C., & Fried, G. (2011, May 5). Torture apologists stain triumph over bin Laden. *Washington Post*. Retrieved from http://articles.washingtonpost.com/2011-05-05/opinions/35232191_1_osama-bin-laden-abbottabad-torture

Fromkin, D. (2010). The two most essential, abhorrent, intolerable lies of George W. Bush's memoir. *HuffingtonPost*. Retrieved from http://www.huffingtonpost.com/2010/11/22/the-two-most-essential-a_n_786219.html

Gall, C., & Rohde D. (2004, September 17). New charges raise questions on abuse at Afghan prisons. *New York Times*. Retrieved from http://www.nytimes.com/2004/09/17/international/asia/17afghan.html?_r=0

Geer, J. G. (2006). *In defense of negativity: Attack ads in presidential campaigns*. Chicago: University of Chicago Press.

Gold, D. (2017) The challenge: Making truth-telling the norm. *Whistleblower*, Spring, p. 3.

Greenleaf, R. K. (2002). *Servant leadership: A journey into the nature of legitimate power and greatness*. New York: Paulist.

Grossman, M. (2008). *Political corruption in America*. Amenia, NY: Grey House.

Gutmann, A., & Thompson, D. (2010). The mindsets of political compromise. *Perspectives on Politics, 8*, 1125–1143.

Gutmann, A., & Thompson, D. (2012). *The spirit of compromise: Why governing demands it and campaigning undermines it*. Princeton, NJ: Princeton University Press.

Hagopian Institute. (2008). *Quote junkie presidents edition: Hundreds of the greatest quotes from the greatest men ever to run our fine country*. CreateSpace Independent.

Hill, A., Ridge, J., & Ingram, A. (2017, February 24). The growing conflict-of-interest problem in the U.S. Congress. *Harvard Business Review*. Retrieved from https://hbr.org/2017/02/the-growing-conflict-of-interest-problem-in-the-u-s-congress

Hohmann, J. (2017, August 2). The Daily 202: Jeff Flake delivers the most courageous conservative rebuttal of Trump yet. *Washington Post*. Retrieved from https://www.washingtonpost.com/news/powerpost/paloma/daily-202/...

Isikoff, M., & Corn, D. (2006). *Hubris: The inside story of spin, scandal, and the selling of the Iraq War*. New York: Crown.

Jamieson, K., & Falk, E. (2000). Continuity and change in civility in the House. In J. R. Bond & R. Fleisher (Eds.), *Polarized politics: Congress and the president in an artisan era* (pp. 96–108). Washington, DC: CQ Press.

Jones, D. (2001). Party polarization and legislative gridlock. *Political Research Quarterly, 54*, 125–141.

Josephson, M. (2002). *Making ethical decisions*. Los Angeles: Josephson Institute of Ethics.

Josephson, M. (2006). The six pillars of character. In J. West & E. Berman (Eds.), *The ethics edge* (pp. 18–23). Washington, DC: International City/County Management Association.

Jurecic, Q. (2017, January 27). Can a president who disregards the truth uphold his oath of office? *Washington Post*. Retrieved from https://www.washingtonpost.com/posteverything/wp/2017/01/27/can-a...

Kern, J. (2006). The use of the "ethical triangle" in military decision making. *Public Administration and Management*, *11*(1), 22–43.

Kessler, G., Kelly, M., & Lewis, N. (2017, July 20). President Trump has made 1,950 false or misleading claims over 347 days. *Washington Post*. Retrieved from https://www.washington post.com/news/fact-checker/wp/2017/07/20/president-trumps-first-six-months-the-fact-check-tally/?utm_term=.d5d4af8b7a63

Kinzer, S. (2007). *Blood of brothers: Life and war in Nicaragua*. Cambridge, MA: Harvard University Press.

Lawder, D., & Cowan, R. (2013, April 12). U.S. Congress quietly repeals plan for internet financial disclosures. Retrieved from http://www.reuters.com/assets/print/aid-USL.2N0C120 130412

Leonhardt, D., & Thompson, S. (2018, January 2). Trump's Lies. *New York Times*. Retrieved from https://www.nytimes.com/interactive/2017/06/23/opinion/trumps-lies.html?_r=0

Levine, N. (2017, August 10). Bridging the gap between political appointees and civil servants. Retrieved from www.govexec.com/excellence/promising-practices/2-17/08/bridging-gap-between-political-appointees-and-civil-servants/140146/WY97?BocJrhM.email

Lipton, E. (2011, September 5). A congresswoman's cause is often her husband's gain. *New York Times*. Retrieved from http://www.nytimes.com/2011/09/06/us/06berkley.html?page wanted=all

MacNeil, N. (1963). *Forge of democracy: The House of Representatives*. New York: D. McKay.

Maisel, L. (2012). The negative consequences of uncivil political discourse. *PS: Political Science & Politics*, *45*, 405–411.

Mann, T., & Ornstein, N. (2012). *It's even worse than it looks: How the American constitutional system collided with the new politics of extremism*. New York: Basic Books.

Margasak, L. (2012, February 28). Insider trading in Congress: New regulations to open window into transactions. *Huffington Post*. Retrieved from http://www.huffingtonpost.com/2012/02/28/insider-trading-congress-stock-act_n_1306301.html

Marion, N. (2010). *The politics of disgrace*. Durham, NC: Carolina Academic Press.

Mayhew, D. (2004). *Congress: The electoral connection*. New Haven, CT: Yale University Press.

McBride, A. (1990). Ethics in Congress: Agenda and action. *George Washington Law Review*, *58*, 451–487.

Moore, M. (1981). Realms of obligation and virtue. In J. Fleishman, L. Liebman, & M. Moore (Eds.), *Public duties: The moral obligations of government officials* (pp. 3–21). Cambridge, MA: Harvard University Press.

Nivola, P. (2010). Partisanship in perspective. *National Affairs*, *5*, 91–104.

Paul, C., & Matthews, M. (2016). The Russian "firehose of falsehood" propaganda model: Why it might work and options to counter it. RAND Corporation Perspective Series Paper. Retrieved from https://www.rand.org/pubs/perspectives/PE198.html

Pear, R. (2012, March 22). Insider trading ban for lawmakers clears Congress. *New York Times*.

Retrieved from http://www.nytimes.com/2012/03/23/us/politics/insider-trading-ban-for-law makers-clears-congress.html

Planas, R. (2012). I'm right, you're wrong no, you're wrong, I'm right. *Reason & Politics*. Retrieved from http://www.reasonandpolitics.com/home.html

Public Citizen (2017). Congressional ethics. Retrieved from https://www.citizen.org/our-work/ government-reform/government-ethics-and-lobbying-reform/congressional-ethics

Public Citizen (2017, June 22). The impact of the STOCK act on stock trading activity by U.S. senators, 2009–2015. Retrieved from https://www.citizen.org/system/files/case_documents/ 2017_stock_act_report.pdf

Rich, F. (2012, June 17). Frank Rich: Nuke 'em. *New York Times*. Retrieved from http://nymag. com/news/frank-rich/negative-campaigning-2012-6/

Sargent, G. (2017, March 6). At the root of Trump's new fury: Total contempt for American democracy. *Washington Post*. Retrieved from https://www.washingtonpost.com/blogs/plum-line/wp/2017/03/06/at…

Schraufnagel, S. (2011). Testing the implications of incivility in the United States Congress, 1977–2000: The case of judicial confirmation delay. *Journal of Legislative Studies*, *11*, 216–234.

Straus, J. (2011a). *Enforcement of Congressional rules of conduct: An historical overview* (Congressional Research Service Report). Retrieved from http://www.fas.org/sgp/crs/misc/ RL30764.pdf

Straus, J. (2011b). *House Committee on Ethics: A brief history of its evolution and jurisdiction* (Congressional Research Service Report). Retrieved from http://ethics.house.gov/sites/ethics. house.gov/files/HouseCommitteEthics3%202011%20Straus.pdf

Straus, J. (2011c). *House Office of Congressional Ethics: History, authority, and procedures* (Congressional Research Service Report). Retrieved from http://waxman.house.gov/sites/ waxman.house.gov/files/House%20Office%20of%20Congressional%20Ethics%20 History%20Authority%20and%20Procedures.pdf

Straus, J. (2011d). *Senate Select Committee on Ethics: A brief history of its evolution and juris-diction* (Congressional Research Service Report). Retrieved from http://www.fas.org/sgp/crs/ misc/RL30650.pdf

Susan Stanton's Story. (2012, January 19). Unitarian Universalist Association of Congregations. Retrieved from http://www.uua.org/re/tapestry/adults/ethics/workshop3/workshopplan/stor ies/191788.shtml

Tholen, B. (2013). Dirty hands or political virtue? Walzer's and MacIntyre's answers to Machiavelli's challenge. *Public Integrity*, *15*, 187–202.

Thompson, D. (1981a). Moral responsibility and the New York City financial crisis. In J. Fleishman, L. Liebman, & M. Moore (Eds.), *Public duties: The moral obligations of government officials* (pp. 266–289). Cambridge, MA: Harvard University Press.

Thompson, D. (1981b). The private lives of public officials. In J. Fleishman, L. Liebman, & M. Moore (Eds.), *Public duties: The moral obligations of government officials* (pp. 221–248). Cambridge, MA: Harvard University Press.

Thompson, D. (1995). *Ethics in Congress*. Washington, DC: Brookings Institution.

Thompson, D. (2006). Private life and public office. In J. West & E. Berman (Eds.), *The ethics edge* (pp. 156–166). Washington, DC: International City/County Management Association.

Thompson, D. (2010). Constitutional character: Virtues and vices in presidential leadership. *Presidential Studies Quarterly, 40*, 23–37.

Tolchin, M., & Tolchin, S. (2001). *Glass houses*. Boulder, CO: Westview Press.

U.S. House of Representatives Committee on Ethics. (n.d.). *Policies underlying disclosure*. Retrieved from http://ethics.house.gov/financial-dislosure/policies-underlying-disclosure

Uslaner, E. (2000). Is the Senate more civil than the House? In B. Loomis (Ed.), *Esteemed colleagues: Civility and deliberation in the Senate* (pp. 32–56). Washington, DC: Brookings Institution.

Waldo, D. (2009). Public administration and ethics: A prologue to a preface. In R. Stillman (Ed.), *Public administration: Concepts and cases* (pp. 472–482). Boston, MA: Wadsworth.

Walzer, M. (1974). Political action: The problem of dirty hands. In M. Cohen, T. Nagel., & T. Scanlon (Eds). *War and moral responsibility*. Princeton, NJ: Princeton University Press, 62–82.

Wasserman, E. (2013, April 22). Privacy invasion requires good reason. *Miami Herald*, p. 13A.

Appendix 11.1

Ethics Committees

Article I, Section 5 of the Constitution delegates to the House and Senate the exclusive authority to draft rules of conduct for their members, as well as sole discretion to discipline and expel them. However, for much of the nation's history, Congress operated without a formalized code of ethics or standardized procedures for adjudicating allegations of improper conduct. It was not until the 1960s that Congress began to shift away from the regime of informal rules and *ad hoc* procedures that left punishment to be meted out mainly by public opinion and electoral outcomes. In 1964, in the wake of a bribery scandal involving the secretary to the Senate Majority Leader, the Senate created the Select Committee on Standards and Conduct (now the Select Committee on Ethics). The House followed suit in 1967, establishing the Committee on Standards of Official Conduct (now the Committee on Ethics). Both committees immediately went to work on drafting codes for their respective members, staff, and employees. When first drafted, they covered such topics as campaign finance and financial disclosure. They have since been amended to include rules governing gifts, outside earned income, conflicts of interest, foreign travel, franking, political advertising, and lobbying.

Both committees are unique in that their membership is constituted in a bipartisan fashion. They consist of equal numbers of members from each party (five from each party in the House and three from each party in the Senate). Such a balanced structure is intended to avoid the politicization of the ethics process. The work of each committee is divided between advising members and staff on rules of conduct and investigating and adjudicating cases of misconduct. Yet it is here that the similarities between the two committees end. While the structure and jurisdiction of the Senate committee has remained fairly static over the years, the House committee has a more colorful history, which has resulted in a more complex structure that has expanded to include an external review body. The three major periods of House ethics reform—1989, 1997, and 1998—serve to illustrate the structural and procedural differences between the two chambers' ethics committees.

While many minor procedural changes were adopted in the 1970s, substantive House ethics reform was not seriously considered until 1989, a high-profile year for ethical controversy in the House. That year the Savings and Loan crisis precipitated numerous investigations into the "constituent service" activities of members. These investigations did not stop at the Keating Five in the Senate. Speaker of the House Jim Wright was forced to resign after the Ethics Committee found evidence of upwards of 60 violations of House rules. He was followed out by the Majority Whip. The sights were set on the Minority Whip who had begun the investigation, and then the chairmen of the Banking Committee and Defense Appropriations Subcommittee (Falvey, 1991; McBride, 1990).

Out of the chaos emerged the Ethics Reform Act of 1989, which stipulated, among other things, a meso-ethics strategy that the investigative and adjudicative functions of the committee be segregated. Thus, when allegations of ethics violations are brought to the committee, an *ad hoc* investigative subcommittee is convened. If this subcommittee discovers any violations and submits formal charges to the chair, a separate *ad hoc* adjudicative subcommittee consisting of the chair, ranking member, and the committee members who did not participate in the investigative subcommittee is formed. In contrast, the Senate committee does not require that the investigation and adjudication of ethics violations proceed separately. The full Senate committee also assumes the burden of advisory and educational (i.e., ethics training) responsibilities, which the 1989 Act delegated to a separate Office of Advice and Education in the House Committee on Ethics.

The legislation addressed the meso-level of ethics by attempting to alter the organizational culture of the institution. The presence of impartial committees with genuine jurisdiction over ethical violations is a signal to members in the House and Senate that ethics is taken seriously. The 1997 House Ethics Reform Task Force analyzed some of the lingering concerns over the process. Most notably, the Task Force recommended a requirement that nonmembers be prohibited from filing an ethics complaint unless a member can certify that the complaint is submitted in good faith and warrants consideration. No such requirements exist in the Senate, where anybody inside or outside of Congress can bring forth charges of ethical impropriety against a senator. Ten years later, in 2007, another task force, the Special Task Force on Ethics Enforcement in the House of Representatives, was established to consider whether establishing an outside enforcement entity would address growing concerns over the closed nature of the Committee on Ethics' proceedings. The following year the House voted to create the Office of Congressional Ethics composed of six members jointly appointed by House leaders, which can initiate independent investigations of allegations lodged by the general public. The Senate has not created a corresponding external entity. Its Select Committee on Ethics continues to collect and investigate internally all allegations of senatorial misconduct.

Sources: Unless otherwise noted, the narrative is drawn from Straus (2011a, 2011b, 2011c, 2011d).

12 Organizational Gaming and Performance Measurement

Integrity is one of several paths. It distinguishes itself from the others because it is the right path, and the only one upon which you will never get lost.

—M. H. McKee

This chapter is limited in scope to efforts by organizations to take advantage of "loopholes in the rules and system" and, even more specifically, to "manipulate performance criteria" or "gaming" (Bohte & Meier, 2000, 175; Fisher & Downes, 2008, 248). While Chapter 9 presented an overview of both individual and organizational corruption, here the focus is exclusively on this narrower concept of organizational cheating. Chapter objectives include examining:

- what motivates organizational gaming,
- ways to ethically evaluate cheating,
- types of institutional manipulation,
- a program design to affect organizational "fudging,"
- the link between performance measurement and gaming behaviour,
- the consequences of fraud, and
- strategies to prevent or minimize fakery.

The epigram above alludes to integrity as the right path whereupon one will never be lost. Manipulation would be a wrong path that often—but not always—leads to bad outcomes. Stated differently, manipulation is an example of what Stephen Carter (1996, 13) refers to as *unintegrity*. Repeated acts of this kind can result in getting away with things known to be wrong. The discussion begins by considering some of the pressures that contribute to cheating, and the nexus between performance measurement and manipulation. Attention then turns to different types of gaming, followed by a brief section on the role of politicians and public opinion. The last two topics, prior to the conclusion, consider ethical evaluation of fudging and ways to prevent or minimize it.

DUPLICITY PRESSURES

What stresses contribute to cheating? In a competitive economy, the need to perform, meet expectations, achieve standards, and avoid failure is intense in all sectors of the economy. As contracting and outsourcing have become more common, governments and nonprofit organizations have had to step up their game to retain their monopoly power or to have their service contracts renewed. The more competitive the environment, the greater temptations there are to deceive, especially when safeguards against wrongdoing are absent. There are often substantial rewards associated with fraud, at least in the short term. Indeed, as Callahan (2004, Chapter 6) has observed, a "trickle-down" effect occurs when people make up their own moral code because they think the system is not fair; they start cheating a little more, and then it accelerates into cheating a lot. The same effect can occur in organizations (Haines, 2003–2004). Such spillover occurs between the micro, meso, and macro levels of ethics. Individuals within an organization can alter the institution as a whole (micro–meso), and organizations can influence markets and civil society (meso–macro).

Coupled with external pressures are those internal to the organization. Sometimes there are counterintuitive influences—setting goals can actually incentivize unethical decision making. For example, the overcharging of customers and hiding of financial losses conducted by Sears and Enron employees can be traced back to how goals were set for the corporations. Sears set difficult sales goals ($147/hour) and linked commissions to meeting these quotas. Enron established a "performance unit plan" whereby executives received large bonuses based on the company's financial success (Barsky, 2008, 63–64).

Similar goal setting and performance plans are created in government and nonprofit organizations, often mandated by law or required by contract (Berman, 2006; Cooper, 2000; DeHoog & Salamon, 2002; Liff, 2014). For instance, the 1993 Government Performance and Results Act requires that every federal department submit a strategic plan to Congress, plans that typically include productivity measures. Such measurement gone awry can lead to gaming the system. To use some examples from local government, consider solid waste haulers who water down the garbage before weighing the truck (to gain rewards based on performance targets measured by the full truck weight), school enrollment specialists (who inflate the number of enrollees in order to get more state funds), or police officers who increase the number of tickets issued (to meet a standard and earn a reward).

Autocratic goal setting led to Air Force officers cheating on exams measuring ICBM launching ability because commanders insisted on a 100 percent test score and used the exam as the only promotion criterion (Cooper, 2014). The Department of Veteran Affairs faced with too many service demands from returning veterans and too few staff, imposed an unrealistic work standard that each veteran be seen within 14 days of requesting an appointment, thereby incentivizing cheating as staff misreported the number of veterans asking for and waiting for care in order to meet the standard (Jaffe & Hicks, 2017). In other words, goals can have a downside when: employees are too fixated on them (neglecting non-goal areas), when goals prompt risky behavior, when external motivators override intrinsic motivation, and when objectives nudge employees toward more unethical behaviors than they would engage in absent the goal (Ordonez et al., 2009).

The conceptual link between falsification and performance measurement is that democratic governance requires both a large technical bureaucracy as well as accountability. Because it is difficult to gauge the often intangible ends of public service delivery, elected officials frequently fall back on shorthand indicators when judging agency action. The resultant problem? "Rather than measuring the final *outcomes* of bureaucratic activity, those who evaluate the performance of public bureaucracies often pay more attention to the *outputs* these agencies produce" (Bohte & Meier, 2000, 174). This can result in goal displacement, as "agencies focus on generating numbers that please political officials, rather than devoting their energies to achieving more meaningful policy outcomes" (174). This myopia is a dangerous dynamic because continued political and financial support is predicated on a measurement scale that does not necessarily match up with the overarching mission of the organization. Thus, the dilemma: "Engage in goal displacement and seek to meet the standard even if it affects performance in a detrimental manner, or continue to seek the larger goal and hope that success in the actual mission will also produce success on the performance standard" (179–180). This can encourage gaming—reliance on loopholes and manipulation of evaluation criteria to meet expectations. Considerable vulnerability occurs when monitoring of service providers is limited and bureaucracies are decentralized, as is often the case in social welfare, health, and education programs. This is especially true in institutions wherein resources are scarce and expectations are overwhelming—a typical circumstance in many jurisdictions. "Outside observers demand results, regardless of how intractable an agency's task may be" (180).

As such, the nature of goal setting in organizations generates natural/internal incentives to cheat/game. However, these internal incentives can be compounded by tangible, external incentives, such as incentive-based structures embedded in program designs. Some structures abet manipulation to receive program benefits, like cities that dismissed employees, later hiring them back with federal monies available under the Comprehensive Employment and Training Act of 1973 or school districts that offer bonuses to teachers, contingent on student test scores. In more than a few cases, teachers or principals have been involved in erasing or correcting student answers on exams to boost performance ratings (see Case Study 12.1 and Exercise 3, the "Bad Teacher"; see also Chapter 7). Thus, the incentive structure is decisive in influencing the decision to game the system.

Organizational Cheating in Education

During the last generation, cheating has permeated the education system. From elementary to university levels, and from student to administrative perpetrators, it has become a grave issue in American education. In light of reforms such as President George W. Bush's No Child Left Behind and President Barack Obama's Race to the Top initiatives—as well as growing pressures placed both on students and on teachers to increase performance—the country has become a petri dish for cheating experimentation. Students have been compelled to achieve certain numerical scores on standardized tests and school examinations to succeed through the increasingly competitive university application and selection process. Similarly, public schools have felt great pressure under the implementation of teacher performance measures tied directly to student achievement, federal grants linked to standardized test scores, and cash bonuses for improved test results.

The Atlanta Public School System, like many others across the country, revolves around a standardized test to measure student success, teacher ability, and, most significantly, state and federal funding. The state of Georgia has received recognitions for its improvement in elementary education. These acknowledgments are attached to monetary aid and depend directly on the results of the state's Criterion Reference Competency Test (CRCT). Bonuses were given to every employee of the schools with high passing rates. Georgia's superintendent at the time, Beverly Hall, focused solely on the exam scores to begin measuring teacher achievement rather than student aptitude (Aviv, 2014; Frysh, 2011). Over 178 teachers and principals were investigated in 44 schools and charged with cheating on the statewide examination; later, nearly three dozen would be indicted on racketeering, false statements, and theft (Brumback, 2013; Strauss, 2011). Using several different methods, these professionals directly and indirectly altered exam results to keep their jobs, receive bonuses, and ensure federal and state funding. The national attention the case received spurred investigations in Denver, Washington, DC, and elsewhere.

State auditors in Denver found that school administrators had been allegedly erasing student responses on state standardized exams and filling in the correct answer, much like their colleagues in Georgia. In Denver, two teachers "met with the School's [Beach Court Elementary] Administration to discuss the fact that their students' Colorado Student Assessment Program scores were not reflective of the students' classroom performance" (Auge, 2012). In Washington, DC, 103 schools "had test erasure rates that indicated possible cheating from 2008 to 2010" (Whitesell, 2012). In DC, however, it was the teachers, who feel great stress over job stability and the need for federal aid, who had been allegedly participating in the scandal.

While they were not changing answers on exams, other school districts resorted to misusing and misreporting data to receive funding. For example, in Ohio, several districts were found to have been tampering with attendance records to improve school and district report cards. Over 2 million absences were wiped from the system in a practice known as "scrubbing": dropping students from the roster and adding them later in the year, because scores for students who are not enrolled from beginning to end do not affect the school's report card (Zhao, 2012). In essence, administrators were cherry picking pupils who perform well as the only determinants of the school report card, omitting the scores of underperforming students resulting in misreported and false data.

Claremont McKenna College, along with many other universities, is not exempt from the gaming phenomenon. With the heightened weight given to college rankings, higher education has also fallen into cheating through the misreporting of data to climb the ranks. For the last 25 years, the small university had fallen outside of the rankings' top 10 liberal arts colleges. That all changed in the years following 2005. Since then, Claremont McKenna has boasted the ninth and 10th spots on the popular ranking in *U.S. News & World Report*. However, in 2012, the president of Claremont McKenna, Pamela Gann, revealed that a manager of the admissions office had been inflating student SAT scores by 10–20 points to remain competitive in nationwide rankings (Strauss, 2012). Colleges such as Baylor University, Villanova University, and Iona College have all been found guilty of similar fraudulent and deceptive actions resulting in higher application rates and improved rankings (Perez-Pena & Slotnik, 2012).

In light of rampant cheating throughout the country, the Obama administration took steps to reform the system and help diminish the need and ability to cheat. The U.S. Department of Education requested that educators and administrators provide ideas on the causes and issues surrounding cheating, including how to restore credibility to a school or district following a scandal. The department also planned to host a symposium and publish manuals concerning cheating (Whitesell, 2012). However, many critics and scholars believe that cheating is inherent in the system that has developed. For example, Leonie Haimson (2012), writing for the *New York Times*, states that "Campbell's Law predicts that any time huge stakes are attached to quantitative data, the data itself will become inherently unreliable and distorted through cheating and gaming the system."

As long as standardized tests and rankings dominate the system, cheating is unlikely to stop. To change the climate in school districts, there needs to be a shift in focus from quantitative data to a holistic approach in which student and teacher assessments go beyond the scores of a single exam. Until such time, there is a small, but growing national movement to "opt out" of standardized testing on the grounds that it encourages how to answer multiple-choice questions at the expense of reasoning and critical thinking. Some school administrators have called for a testing moratorium (Layton, 2013).

QUESTIONS TO CONSIDER

1. What are the pros and contras of quantitative performance measurement systems?

2. How can actions gaming the system be reduced?

TYPES OF GAMING

Gaming can take a variety of additional forms: ratchet effects, output distortion, output tunnel vision, cherry picking, favorable focus, and cutting corners (Hendrick & Yazici, 2011).

Ratchet Effects

This phenomenon involves a deliberate attempt by managers to freeze existing performance levels to avoid having expectations ratcheted up in the future. Navy recruiters, for example, are required to be part of a program that rewards high performance. Asch (1990) found that recruiters would calibrate and time their effort to win rewards. In some cases, recruiters stalled their efforts until the deadline for the award was near, or they ramped up their effort by amassing an inventory of potential recruits but deliberately failed to enlist them until their eligibility for an award was established. Once an award is earned, productivity drops, in part because intense effort to gain the reward requires recruiters to scale back and rest, but also because, "in order to win a reward they pursued enlistments that they otherwise would have garnered in future months" (104).

Output Distortion

This strategy is among the most common gaming practices. It involves intentional manipulation of results by modifying information and misrepresenting performance. In some instances, it includes outright falsification of data (Bohte & Meier, 2000, 175). This makes it difficult for policymakers to know what is going on. Congressional oversight committees and watchdogs are at an "information disadvantage" relative to the agencies they oversee because they cannot keep track of all their activities. Output distortion gives the advantage to managers capitalizing on these "information asymmetries" by divulging to policymakers distorted data that convey a rosy picture while downplaying less favorable information. Figure 12.1 reports the levels of deceit, from less honest to more honest, in communication manipulation, of both quantitative and qualitative data.

The Environmental Protection Agency's Superfund toxic waste cleanup program under the leadership of Rita Lavelle is one example (Meier, 1985, 64–65). She deliberately misrepresented her record of inspecting toxic waste sites, claiming that objective criteria were used, when it was really political criteria that guided enforcement. Bohte and Meier (2000, 175) caution that "lying essentially violates the trust between bureaucrats and politicians that is necessary for effective governance"; therefore it is "an extremely high-risk method of cheating." Other high-profile examples of such misleading claims include exaggerated body counts in Vietnam or undercounting "collateral damage," including civilian deaths in Afghanistan.

Exposure of blatant cheating can be a costly deterrent, but cheating is harder to prevent when it is interwoven into the organizational rules and processes. This interweaving, Meier (2008, 4) asserts, is especially evident in educational organizations, given their tendency to sort and classify students. Bohte and Meier (2000) found a "moderate amount of cheating" in Texas school districts, with some schools illegitimately exempting low-scoring students from the Texas Assessment of Academic Skills exam under the guise of being special education students or limited English proficiency pupils. This was especially the case in low-income school districts. Similarly, Figlio and Getzler (2002) discovered that Florida schools reclassified

FIGURE 12.1   **Levels of Deceit in Data and Information Manipulation**

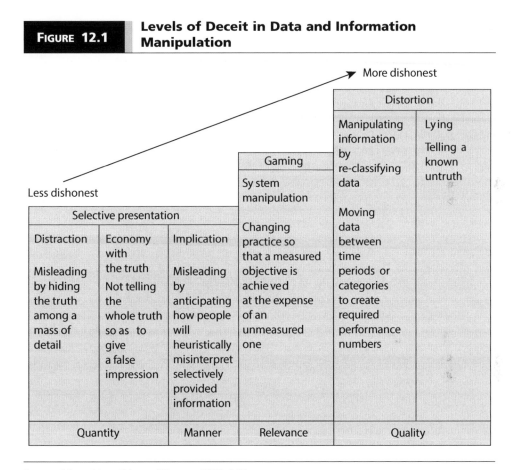

Source: Adapted from Fisher and Downes (2008, 247).

low-income and previously low-performing students as disabled—and therefore ineligible to contribute to the school's aggregate Florida Comprehensive Assessment Test score.

Figlio's (2005, 5) subsequent study found that schools "act on the incentive to re-shape the testing pool through selective discipline in response to accountability pressures," a "high-stakes testing regime" implemented in accordance with the No Child Left Behind Act of 2001. Some Florida schools went so far as to allocate longer suspensions to potentially low-performing students than to their high-performing counterparts to ensure that the high performers would be present at test time and low performers would not. Figlio and Winicki (2005) further revealed that schools experiencing accountability pressures upped the caloric content of school lunches in an apparent attempt to improve short-term student cognitive performance on test days.

Output distortion is also documented in the airline industry, federal job training programs, and health care (Table 12.1). Gormley and Weimer (1999, 149) reported that "an

TABLE 12.1	Types of Gaming	
Type of Gaming	**Behavior Involved**	**Examples**
Ratchet Effects	Deliberately restraining current performance to avoid having to achieve higher levels in the future	Navy incentive program to reward high performance—recruiters calibrated effort to reward
Output Distortion	Deliberately manipulating data and results by various forms of cheating, including altering performance data or misreporting performance	Faked improvements in U.K. A&E hospital wait times to improve rating
Output Tunnel Vision	Improving performance only for qualities that can be measured at the expense of qualities that cannot be or are not measured	Effort substitution to reduce A&E wait times at expense of quality care
Cherry Picking	Reporting on or servicing only cases where high performance can be achieved more easily while neglecting or not reporting hard cases that are costly to handle	Self-selection by police of easy-to-clear crimes vs. more difficult cases
Favorable Focus	Supplying, developing, or promoting performance measures that are easy to obtain and favorable of abandoning those that are hard to obtain or unfavorable	Elected officials selecting easy performance targets to reap electoral benefits
Cutting Corners	Doing sloppy work or quick-and-dirty delivery of services in order to boost performance measures	Quick-and-dirty regulatory inspections to look tough on regulation

Source: Adapted from Hendrick and Yazici (2011, 7).

airline may improve its 'on-time' punctuality performance by 'increasing the predicted length of a flight,'" thus improving "their official statistics without actually improving their performance." Courty and Marschke (2003) examined gaming in federal job training by observing student dismissal patterns in the training system. Training centers were directed to set up programs targeting the economically disadvantaged, and those encountering serious employment barriers, so they could gain needed job skills, achieve better income and reduce reliance on welfare.

The researchers found that discretion given to centers to terminate enrolees produced sub-optimal results. To cover up poor findings, "centers could postpone terminating enrollees who were unemployed, or if employed, had low wages" because the termination date corresponded to the measurement date of a particular center's employment and wage rates (Courty & Marschke, 2003, 908). In response, the U.S. Department of Labor implemented a 90-day rule that required training agencies not only to measure performance on the termination date, but also to discharge any participant who had not received any services for 90 days. The response triggered more cheating.[1]

Police have long recognized the value of gaming the system by relying on number manipulation. Don Winslow in his 2017 novel, *The Force*, illustrates this by showing how administrators, "suits," use numbers as "moneyball" tactics to demonstrate crime reduction: "The suits love their numbers. . . . This new 'management' breed of cops are like the sabermetrics baseball people—they believe the numbers say it all. And when the numbers don't say what they want them to, they massage them . . . until they get a happy ending" (p. 37) Winslow shows how this is done:

> The . . . way to manipulate the numbers is to let officers know they should downgrade charges from felonies to misdemeanors. So you call a straight up robbery a "petit larceny," a burglary becomes "lost property," a rape a "sexual assault." Boom—crime is down. Moneyball. (p. 38)

The final example of output distortion is based on research in U.K. hospital emergency rooms. In 2003, the Department of Health, which oversees the National Health Service (NHS), announced a new initiative regarding wait times in "accident and emergency" (A&E) (equivalent to the American ER) departments. Wait times would be included in the "star rating" system used to rank hospitals. The following year, it was announced that £100,000 would be given to hospitals that showed an increase in the percentage of patients treated within four hours. The Department announced that the A&E performance measurements would be conducted in the final week of March. *The Guardian* reported on the efficacy of the reform: "Two-thirds of NHS A&E departments faked improvements in their wait times during the week chosen by ministers to measure their performance" (Carvel, 2003, 12).

Output Tunnel Vision

This technique seeks to improve achievement, but only for measurable quantities at the expense of qualities incapable of measurement. As Kelman and Friedman (2009, 922–923) point out, "the focusing function of performance measures—'what gets measured gets *noticed*'—can have a dark side—'what gets *measured* gets noticed.'" Examples of "effort substitution" or output tunnel vision include reduced wait time at the expense of quality care, resource transfers (e.g., doctors and nurses) from nonemergency activities to A&E to achieve wait-time goals, and redistribution of wait times so patients who would normally experience short wait times are left waiting for nearly four hours to focus attention on patients who would normally exceed the four-hour threshold.

Cherry Picking

This next form of trickery involves focusing exclusively on cases where high performance is achievable, while costly and difficult cases are neglected or disappear from reports. Cherry picking (sampling bias) occurs in law enforcement agencies as they classify crimes. When officers are evaluated based on clearance rates rather than public safety, there is an incentive to focus on solving crimes. The more difficult cases to solve (break-ins and burglaries) may be classified as "unfounded" in reports, instead of classifying them as real crimes. When assessing probabilities, personnel may conclude that the probability of catching some law breakers (prostitutes, drug dealers) is higher than that of catching a burglar. To achieve high clearance rates, police tend to focus on the easier crimes with less attention to the more diffi-cult cases (Bohte & Meier, 2000, 174; Stone, 1988, 141). This tendency is not restricted to local police; self-selection of easy-to-clear crimes was also a tactic of the FBI under J. Edgar Hoover (Bohte & Meier, 2000, 181). Managers may also focus on highly visible cases, neglecting or excluding those less visible.

Another kind of cherry picking is "cream skimming." This happens when it is clear that a program fails to contribute to a jobseeker's employment prospects, and administrators claim credit for success that would have occurred without the program (Kelman & Friedman, 2009, 925). Further, this effort that added no value (assisting someone who was easy to place) might have been devoted to aiding the prospects of the hard-to-place person.

Favorable Focus

This fifth type of cheating occurs when selecting performance measures that are readily available, easy to get, and favorable, while abandoning measures that are harder to obtain and unfavorable. Arguably, this occurred at the executive level in the British hospital case when the Department of Health chose A&E wait times as the key measure. Hood, Dixon, and Beeston (2008) theorized that elected officials are confronted with political incentives to formulate "ambitious performance target systems" to reap electoral or symbolic benefits. They are likely to choose those targets that will be most likely to bring the desired benefits, and not accurate assessment parameters.

Cutting Corners

This final form of fraud occurs when performance measures are selected with an eye to conserving resources. This might be viewed as a "quick fix" by those choosing the metric that enables them to claim they are enhancing achievement. If the measure is based on a "more is better" mentality, it conveys the message to service recipients that the emphasis is on quantity of output rather than quality. This can be seen when regulatory agencies or financial auditors resort to "quick-and-dirty" inspections or audits to increase the overall number they conduct as a means of appearing tough on those regulated. During the 1960s, Federal Housing Administration housing inspectors were found "guilty of conducting inspections from their cars" (Bohte & Meier, 2000, 175). In the United Kingdom study, patients coming into the A&E with serious injuries that could not be treated within four hours were admitted to inpatient wards, taking up valuable space and resources. If an A&E were too crowded, ambulances would stay outside with the patient still inside to delay the four-hour countdown from starting until the hospital was ready (Kelman & Friedman, 2009).

In sum, there are many types of organizational falsification, cheating or gaming, but the results of all types of deception present adverse effects on citizens. Metric manipulation misleads the public and makes it difficult to accurately assess service efficacy. Service users are forced to be skeptical of claims by providers, reinforcing public cynicism. The next section moves from the six-item gaming typology to briefly explore issues involving cheating, politicians, and public opinion.

CHEATING, POLITICIANS, AND PUBLIC OPINION

Elected officials are notorious for claiming credit whenever positive outcomes occur and for "blaming the bureaucrats" when negative outcomes result. In bureaucracies, executives make the good-news announcements, but distance themselves and blame subordinates for bad news. Likewise, administrators face incentives to "[take] credit when times are good but [find] ways to pass blame back to politicians (by claiming inadequate resources, lack of authority, backdoor interference) when adverse events occur" (Hood, 2002, 326). The pessimistic takeaway from these "blame-game" cheating tendencies is that:

> [I]n the rare cases where politicians and other actors do not cheat by heavily encroaching on public managers' decision space, the latter will find it harder to escape blame and may therefore be led to play a highly defensive type of blame game . . . a managerial approach geared toward limitation of liability and tight control of potentially damaging information rather than bold and open initiatives—exactly the opposite of what managerial regimes were ostensibly designed to achieve. (329)

Hood also notes the inclinations of managers to fail to comply or engage in "creative compliance" when confronted with freedom of information requests or other transparency requirements (328; also see Chapter 11).

Cheating can affect public opinion: Elected officials might construe citizen opinion as a form of performance system, which then raises the question of cheating. For example, presidents routinely try to stoke public opinion in support of an agenda (Chapter 14). Meier (2007, 6) asks, "If enough administration spokespersons contend that weapons of mass destruction were found in Iraq, will the public believe it?" Analogously, this is equivalent to school districts changing answers on tests to generate better scores.

A subtler form of gaming occurs by omission. This occurs when managers fail to exercise due diligence by being too willing to believe information they are given. Hood (2006, 519) detects "an eagerness by the central managers of the system to accept 'good news' performance data at face value without putting substantial resources into probing those numbers." Having considered the forces prompting duplicity, the motivations behind gaming, and the forms of cheating, the discussion now shifts to ethical evaluation and strategies to reduce this form of wrongdoing.

ETHICALLY EVALUATING AND MINIMIZING CHEATING

Integrity is like the weather: everybody talks about it but nobody knows what to do about it.
—Stephen Carter

How can cheating be ethically evaluated? Selected decision frameworks, such as the ethics triad, were presented in Chapter 7. They could be applied to any one of the six types of cheating discussed here to aid in determining the appropriateness of implementation in the organization.

Doing so, all three components of the trilogy—results, rules, virtue—suggest that cheating is unethical. It does not represent the greatest good, causes harm, and reflects poorly on personal integrity. But sometimes the consequences of cheating may be good, coloring judgments about character. For example, doctors deceiving insurance companies to help patients (Callahan, 2004, 61) or law enforcement tricking suspected criminals in sting operations (see discussion of Abscam in Chapter 11). But virtue ethics is a double-edged sword—it can restrain people while at the same time giving them latitude to stray from the ethical within those restraints (see, e.g., Ariely, 2012; see also Exhibit 12.1).

Yet since cheating is considered unethical, how can it be minimized? Sometimes management's desire to detect and correct unproductive or unethical work behavior can lead

---

EXHIBIT 12.1   **The Fudge Factor: The Dishonesty of Honest People**

From an adult filling out tax returns to a student taking an exam, scholars argue that everyone may be unethical to a certain degree at one time or another. As fallible human beings, people tend to cheat a little here and a little there every day. But it is blatant and extensive dishonesty that most find disturbing. Rather than weigh every decision in light of traditional economic cost-benefit analysis, new studies show that there is more that comes into play when considering a decision. Individuals try to maintain a balance between cheating and still view themselves as dignified, honest people. Dan Ariely (2012), professor of behavioral economics and psychology at Duke University, calls this phenomenon the *fudge factor.*

After conducting experiments both in academic, controlled settings and out in the real world, Ariely discovered that the further away an individual is from the unethical act—the more steps between a person and the dishonest action he is engaging in—the more likely the individual is to carry it out. As the nation moves to a cashless society, Ariely wonders whether our moral compass is more likely to slip. Is stealing a credit card number easier from a moral standpoint than taking cash from someone's purse? Using the game of golf, where lies and cheating are not unknown, he observes that players are more likely to move the ball with their shoe or their club than with their own hand. Since people want to be able to think of themselves as morally just individuals, the degree and the manner in which they cheat is downplayed and fudges moral boundaries.

Source: Adapted from Ariely (2012, Ch. 2B).

to decisions with unanticipated adverse consequences. Case 12.2 on electronic surveillance shows that using monitoring software and videotaping to address "cyberlollygagging" and low productivity can yield both positive and negative results.

CASE STUDY 12.2

Applying Philosophical and Behavioral Ethics Approaches: Electronic Surveillance in the Workplace

Marisol Sanchez is the newly appointed director of the productivity improvement unit in the metropolitan county government of a Southwestern state. After surveying the performance of the major departments during her first year on the job and benchmarking productivity indicators against those from comparable jurisdictions elsewhere, she is convinced that changes are needed. She is considering installing new monitoring software on all office computers because of concerns about "cyberlollygagging" (wasting time on non-work-related websites). This will allow her to examine employee browsing patterns and determine whether they are visiting websites that the software categorizes as "productive," "unproductive," or "neutral." The software makes it possible to grade employees according to their browsing habits, singling out the most frequent users and the most commonly visited websites. She could also use the software to search emails and close access to objectionable websites. While she has been assured by general counsel that this strategy is legally acceptable, she has some ethical reservations about proceeding.

Consider Marisol's dilemma using the philosophical approach to decision making followed by behavioral ethics.

Results-Based Analysis. From a results perspective, Marisol believes this program will improve productivity, reduce wasted time, and keep employees honest. She thinks it will help employees as well as employers—workers are aided in reaching their career goals free of distractions, and employers can reward high-performing employees. It also helps to foster a positive, task-focused organizational culture and professional work environment. It will likely be cost effective and advance government's core purpose. It can also result in improved citizen service and reinforce the idea that time at work should be spent working.

The downside may be that employees resent the intrusion by the employer and feel the psychological contract—shared perceptions of expectations and obligations—has been broken. They may respond with anger and consider the monitoring to be an invasion of privacy. Surveillance may increase competition and stress while simultaneously lowering morale and eroding trust. Employees may object to the initiative, especially if the employer's motives are suspect or if they think the severity of the problem is insufficient to warrant management's overreaching with the monitoring approach.

Rule-Based Analysis. When rules or principles become the focus it is the agency's prerogative to make and implement workplace policies. Legal counsel has assured Marisol that the policy has been tailored in a way that complies with existing statutes. It is Marisol's duty to work responsibly to improve employee performance and public service. Monitoring helps managers to manage. By implementing monitoring in all departments, it is applied fairly. As stewards of government resources, officials can be confident that government property (computers) is being used for government work. "What is good for one, is good for all."

Among the disadvantages of overreliance on surveillance is that employees may believe their privacy rights are violated. They may resent not being included in the formulation of the policy and object to the secrecy of its implementation. They may feel their trust has been violated, reinforcing feelings of alienation from management. They may question whether due diligence will be observed regarding the access and use of the gathered information. It may be that highly productive employees are able to finish a task and be refreshed by a brief diversion browsing the Internet. The means (privacy invasion) do not justify the ends (productivity).

Virtue-Based Analysis. Virtue ethics provides a third lens in assessing this program. Aristotle argued for balance and the need to avoid both excesses and deficiencies. Marisol may feel that the surveillance is balanced, respecting both the county's interests and employee's rights. She believes this action is necessary and that data will not be misused. It is a way to hold employees accountable. Abusers deserve to be caught. Those who are not violating policy should not mind. Protecting government property from misuse is an obligation of management. Surveillance indicates the caring of government in promoting government's public service function. Marisol thinks that the program will make her a better manager and likewise will improve metropolitan government.

Employees may feel that their rights are being compromised by overly aggressive, intrusive management monitoring. They could believe that surveillance disrupts the power balance between employer and employee and fear the misuse of data collected. Workers may think that the program is unfair, likely to result in fewer rewards or undeserved punishment. The monitoring might be seen as a violation of civil liberties. Some will likely try to "work around" the policy (use their own iPad or cell phone) and point to the "chilling effect" surveillance has on the work environment. Performance could suffer if the worry, concern, and dislike of employees negatively alter the organizational climate. In the interest of integrity, employers should respect and protect employee privacy.

Outcome. After weighing the electronic surveillance issue, Marisol decides to buy and install the new monitoring software. Indeed, she goes so far as secretly installing videotaping equipment in all offices to further monitor employee work. It does not take long for Marisol to begin getting employee feedback about these initiatives. Two cases cause her to second-guess her decisions: (i) Bonnie Albright was surprised and distressed to find out that her employer, Metropolitan County Government, had secretly videotaped her office 24/7 for several months because of concern about subpar performance in her department. Bonnie often changed clothes in her office before leaving for the day, having no knowledge that this was caught on videotape. She was mortified that she had not been told of this practice, especially when she discovered that the employer had viewed the tapes. (ii) Burton Christianson complained when he saw his supervisor printing out emails sent among his fellow employees.

QUESTIONS TO CONSIDER

1. How do you assess Marisol's strategy for improving county performance?

2. Is there anything that could or should have been done prior to implementation?

3. Are there any design flaws in these two productivity improvement initiatives?

4. What ethical problems can you identify?

5. What advice would you give to Marisol regarding her efforts to monitor employees?

Behavioral Ethics-Based Analysis. Recall that the approach used above is considered incomplete because it ignores the importance of emotions and tacit understandings in behavior. Behavioral ethics, thus, introduces considerations like ethical fading, focalism, and motivated blindness that provide insights into the case. Marisol's mono-focus on curbing employee "cyberlollygagging" and improving productivity has led her to downplay privacy concerns. This form of ethical fading can lead to motivated blindness that unintentionally minimized legitimate moral concerns. It may be that the initial introduction of monitoring software was implemented with few objections and resulted in limited legal exposure, but the subsequent intrusive video-taping led to escalating legal and ethical concerns. Failure to involve employees in designing the policy and to inform them of the videotaping was—surprisingly—an unanticipated error. Supervisors circulating employee emails to co-workers shows bad judgment and suggests the absence of guidelines on appropriate use of information technology and protection of employee privacy rights. Identify other behavioral ethics phenomena that shed light on what happened.

Bohte and Meier (2000, 180) argue, "The most likely proposed solution, and perhaps the least likely to work, is to simply add rules to circumscribe the behavior." However, adding rules may lead to a vicious cycle in which stricter rules prompt more efforts to "circumvent control," which, in turn, produces even stricter policies, decreasing productivity and morale, because increasing rules implies distrust of employees. An extreme case of strict enforcement of rules that occurred in the JC Penney Company ended in mass firings.

In 2012, the 4,800 employees of Penney's headquarters watched a combined 5 million YouTube videos while working, using over 30 percent of the headquarters' bandwidth. CEO Ron Johnson brought in Michael Kramer, chief operating officer, to transform the company's culture. Kramer's "transformation" reduced the number of employees at headquarters by 1,600 people. Despite research such as the 2009 University of Melbourne study that found Internet browsing at work boosts productivity, companies like JC Penney take a hardline position on "cyber loafing"—lay off the YouTube videos or be laid off ("JC Penney Exec," 2013).

Professional or organizational norms to control cheating are a more likely effective corrective, according to Bohte and Meier (2000), because they involve a broader understanding of organizational goals and the possible inconsistencies between these goals and the narrower incentive system in place. Such norms are also likely to take into account the difficult tasks assigned to employees. They need to be buttressed by procedures and structures, including policies that look beyond short-term gains. It is also important to pay attention to the incentive structure (the basis for rewards and sanctions) and the kind of behavior it encourages.

Before attempting to prevent or minimize fakery, managers need to understand why it is occurring. A common form of cheating is metric manipulation. Prevention efforts can be aided by increased awareness of the motivation behind cheating via measurement manipulation and the organizational contexts that give rise to it. Fisher and Downes (2008, 249–250) identified seven reasons that help explain why people and organizations manipulate target and performance measures: (1) to avoid the hassle and scrutiny of managers, (2) because current metrics are inappropriate or unfair, (3) because there is the perception that the data are misleading or untrue, (4) the desire to achieve a target that yields a big bonus, (5) the desire to achieve a target that yields a small bonus, (6) to make performance appear worse that it really is as a way to argue for more resources, and (7) to make productivity appear better than it is in cases where income is tied to organization targets. Governance can be improved with performance measurement by removing inducements that trigger manipulative actions and providing inducements that encourage good practice.

Subtle reminders that others within the organization are observing behavior are sometimes sufficient to quell cheating. For years, an office kitchen operated in a manner that relied on employee honesty. Tea and coffee were available, along with a suggested price list and an "honors system" box into which people were expected to contribute. A poster was placed above the box that alternated between an image of a flower and an image of eyes. When it showed eyes staring at the employee, there was a spike in the money put in the box. The experiment illustrates that even simple symbolic reminders can deter cheating (Kahneman, 2011, 57–58). In organizations in which performance is scrutinized, there is less likely to be flagrant dishonesty.

Schweitzer, Ordonez, and Douma (2004, 422) found that "in addition to motivating constructive effort, goal setting motivates *unethical* behavior when people fall short of their goals." Thus, "when employees are close to a goal or a deadline, managers should be particularly vigilant," because under conditions of low transparency and asymmetric information, vulnerability to cheating is high (430). Recall the Sears case mentioned earlier—when difficult goals for automotive service advisors were set, repairs were unnecessary 90 percent of the time. Managers need to employ risk-assessment strategies and consider an ethics audit to determine their vulnerability to cheating behaviors.

Unlike incentive-based systems, performance measurement—the collection and analysis of information on program outputs and impacts—can be harnessed for ethical governance. Honest measurement promotes efficiency and effectiveness because it encourages dialogue between stakeholders and contributes to transparency. However, performance measurement is effective only when it is not "simply viewed as a system for accountability" (de Lancer Julnes, 2009, 1–2). Instead, the development and use of performance systems should include training that emphasizes ethical considerations. For example, systems can be designed and used to evaluate individual achievement in an ethically responsible way, according to Drongelen and Fisscher (2003, 55–57). Their suggestions are valuable for individual evaluation as well as for program assessment:

1. Be upfront and candid about the intended use of performance information. Avoid changing intended uses without proper consultation with relevant stakeholders.

2. Choose a variety of well-balanced measures.

3. Select measures that are closely aligned with program goals and realities.

4. Ensure that data collection methods are an appropriate fit for the task.

5. Offer feedback so that necessary changes can be made to achieve program goals.

6. Use accessible information to clearly explain the selected indicators.

7. Involve citizens in the overall process.

It is critical to recognize that accountability provided by productivity measures can both encourage and hinder the use of information (de Lancer Julnes, 2006, 2009). Thoughtful evaluation of a performance measurement after its implementation aids in weighing the costs and benefits of permanent adoption.

Thus, while performance measurement can support the value of accountability, it can also support other values (efficiency, effectiveness, responsiveness, equity) essential to advance public welfare. Managers need to consider some of the strategies discussed here to minimize fabrication. Formulating rules, establishing organizational norms, increasing awareness of the reasons for cheating, providing periodic reminders, routinely monitoring operations, and carefully designing program assessments are potentially useful strategies.

CONCLUSION

Cheating or gaming the system occurs in government as a result of both external (economic, political, and social) forces and internal pressures (high-performance goals). Goal setting and performance measurement are worthwhile activities that can enhance productivity and improve perceptions of public service. Citizens are likely to be concerned about the quality of services and their relative standing vis-à-vis other jurisdictions, departments, or vendors. Agencies are ranked and rated, the equivalent of organizational report cards, on a variety of measures at federal, state, and local levels, just as businesses and nonprofit organizations are evaluated.

Unfortunately, a by-product of relying heavily on targets and metrics is that it can be dysfunctional, as this chapter illustrates. Pressures to do well on rankings have resulted in fudging the numbers or manipulating the metrics, especially when substantial rewards or sanctions are linked to performance, deadlines are looming, and scrutiny is lacking. Cheating can be ethically evaluated by focusing on results, rules or virtues and gaming behavior often comes up short on one or more of them.

While not all gaming harms citizens, it nevertheless misleads them and erodes trust in business practices, government statistics, or nonprofit data. Falsified data mask the effort that went into performance when metrics are deceitfully raised or lowered, making legitimate comparisons among units impossible. When these actions come to light—and they often do—it can harm careers, tarnish reputations, and embarrass individuals and institutions that skirt the rules or manipulate evaluation criteria.

Organizational cheating will never be eradicated completely, but strategies exist that can be used to minimize it: risk assessments, new rules, organizational and professional norms, ethics training, managerial attentiveness, stakeholder participation, and honest reporting. As Stephen Carter (1996) said, "repeated acts of unintegrity often result in getting away with things that are known to be wrong." Integrity, in contrast, "is the right path . . . upon which you will never get lost," according to M. H. McKee. Public administrators need to use prudent leadership to keep public service on the right path.

***

What lies behind us and what lies before us are tiny matters compared to what lies within us.

—Ralph Waldo Emerson

NOTE

1. Enrollees who had jobs at the end of the training were usually terminated at that time. Those who were unemployed on the last day of training, but obtained jobs within 90 days, were discharged when employment started. Enrollees who did not gain jobs were usually released on the final day of the 90-day period.

   The terminations served to maximize performance scores of the training centers because the centers would have achieved an employment rate outcome substantially lower if they had been required to terminate enrollees (and record their performance results) on the day trainees completed training. However, the researchers concluded "the kind of monitoring of the caseload necessary to optimally time termination diverts resources from training activities" (Courty & Marschke, 2003, 908–909), resulting in lower quality training, thereby undermining the overarching goal of the program.

   Courty and Marschke's broader discovery delineates a "trial-and-error" dynamic, "characterized by a feedback loop" (904), whereby the federal agency implements measures, local managers game them, the feds discover the gaming and revise the metrics thereby promoting possible new gaming, and so on. This dynamic highlights a lesson for those implementing a performance management system—accurate assessment is a challenge that requires careful monitoring and continuous improvement.

For Discussion

1. It is claimed that cheating in the classroom pervades American schools. Have you witnessed this behavior? What was the cause(s)? If it was discovered, what, if anything, was done about it by students, instructors, or administrators? Are there exemplary models (e.g., institutions with effective honor codes) where dishonesty is rare or absent?

2. In a climate where cheating becomes so pervasive that people use the excuse "everybody does it" (see Tuckness, 2010, for a commentary on this rationalization in the

workplace) employees may be inclined to discount ethics because they do not want to put themselves at a competitive disadvantage when they conform to the official policies rather than the *real* policies. Discuss examples of when this might occur in public service settings and what managers can do to avoid or correct it.

3. Some organizations are too relaxed and others are too stressed. When the work environment is being revitalized, it can create excessive pressure to perform, causing uncertainty, anxiety, stress, and sometimes impaired ethical judgment. Discuss (a) examples of how wrongdoing can occur under such circumstances and (b) ways that institutions might achieve the golden mean between too much comfort and too much pressure.

EXERCISES

1. This chapter presented six different types of gaming, and ways in which to distinguish one from the other. Using this information and your own experience, provide two examples for each of the types (other than those provided in the chapter). How can selected types of gaming be avoided?

	Example 1	Example 2
Ratchet Effects		
Output Distortion		
Output Tunnel Vision		
Cherry Picking		
Favorable Focus		
Cutting Corners		

2. Ethically evaluating cheating is an important part of this chapter. Using the ethics triumvirate, evaluate the situations presented below from a rules, results, and virtue perspective:

Scenario 1
You are a fifth-grade teacher in a low-performing school working with underprivileged students. You have just been informed that the new principal has made it clear that if scores do not dramatically increase, the teachers with low-scoring classrooms will lose their jobs. The state standardized exam begins next week, and you know your students are not prepared. In a desperate effort to keep your job, you decide to walk around the room and "help" students on questions.

    Results:
    Rules:
    Virtue:

Scenario 2
You have just finished your master's in business administration and are now working for a prestigious lending company. After your first week successfully assisting people in

setting up their loans, and providing them with the information they need and telling them of their best options, you are confused when your boss calls you in to discuss your performance. After the meeting, you now know that your boss encourages subprime loans for all clients rather than the safer options that you know are the proper thing to offer. However, you begin offering clients risky subprime loans, assuring them that there is low risk and that their money is safe.

Results:
Rules:
Virtue:

Recalling the research results on behavioral ethics from Chapter 7, what are the possible explanations for and implications of the actions taken in this case?

Scenario 3

Samantha works for the administrative offices of Memorial Hospitals in a large metropolitan area. Her office is the managing body that oversees a chain of hospitals in the region. Samantha's recent task is to interpret performance measurement data that has been submitted in light of recent changes to hospital protocol. In an effort to improve efficiency and reputation, management had implemented a series of targets that the hospitals meet with regard to re-admission rates and emergency room wait time.

A few months after implementation, it is Samantha's duty to analyze the reports from the hospitals and provide her supervisor with feedback concerning performance in relation to the new targets. Samantha realized that one of the hospitals provided reports in which the hospital met every target, yet Samantha's own observations indicated it was falling short of each objective. When Samantha informed her supervisor of the inconsistencies between her report and the hospital's, her supervisor was not alarmed or surprised, and advised her to analyze the reports "as is." After that encounter, Samantha got the impression that her supervisor was more concerned with publishing reports that look good even if the information they represent is incorrect.

Results:
Rules:
Virtue:

Based on behavioral ethics findings, how might the conduct here be understood? What explains the dishonesty of honest people? T. S. Eliot thought, "Half of the harm that is done in this world is due to people who want to feel important . . . they do not mean to do harm . . . they are absorbed in their endless struggle to think well of themselves." What do you think?

3. **Bad Actor Tabletop Exercise:** The Bad Teacher. Instructions (see Chapter 3, Exercise 5 for instructions)

Miss English is a history teacher at Breakwood High School. She teaches 9th through 12th grade American and world history. In order to encourage teachers to perform according to standards, the school awards bonuses based on student performances on state exams. Knowing this, Miss English purposefully neglects any information that is not included in the scope of state exams. Although her students do well in the exams, the course does not cover the majority of the material outlined in her approved curriculum. Instead, students are pressured to study on their own right before test time and spend most of the year watching videos and completing marginally relevant assignments.

Role 1: Principal

You are the principal, and it has come to your attention that Miss English has been deviating from her approved curriculum and "teaching to the test." You know that this is frowned upon, but English's students are among the highest performing in state exams, which reflects well on the school. Do you feel compelled to address this issue with English? Why or why not? Consider your obligations, ethical and otherwise. To whom are you accountable as a school principal? What factors impact your decision?

Role 2: Co-worker

You are also a history teacher at the school. You go to Miss English for advice on improving your students' performances on state exams, and she informs you of her teaching methods. You know that teaching to the test is wrong, but it seems to be working for her. What do you do? Do you report English's behavior? Why or why not? Consider your obligations, ethical and otherwise. To whom are you accountable as an educator? What factors impact your decision?

Role 3: Student

You are a student in English's 12th grade world history course. You have always been interested in history and want to major in that field in college. After having swapped English for American history, you know that you will not be challenged academically, and will need a strong foundation to go into your major next year. What do you do? Do you complain to the principal and seek a transfer? Consider your obligations, ethical and otherwise. To whom are you accountable as a student? What factors impact your decision?

Role 4: PTA President

You are the president of the parent teacher association at Breakwood High. You have heard of Miss English's teaching practices and are aware that some parents and students are concerned about the quality of their education. You also know that English's students test well at the state level. How do you manage this situation? Consider your obligations, ethical and otherwise. To whom are you accountable as the PTA president? What factors impact your decision?

Role 5: Member of the Board of Education

You are on the Board of Education which is meeting to discuss taking punitive action against Miss English. Knowing the details of her teaching methods and her students' results on exams, do you vote in favor or against taking action? Why? Consider your obligations, ethical and otherwise. To whom are you accountable as a board member? What factors impact your decision?

REFERENCES

Ariely, D. (2012). *The (honest) truth about dishonesty*. New York: HarperCollins.

Asch, B. J. (1990). Do incentives matter? The case of Navy recruiters. *Industrial and Labor Relations Review*, *43*, 89S–106S.

Auge, K. (2012, June 7). "Principal-level" cheating on CSAP at Denver school, probe finds. *Denver Post*. Retrieved from http://www.denverpost.com/breakingnews/ci_20800253/principal-level-cheating-csap-at-denver-school

Aviv, R. (2014, July 21). Wrong Answer. *The New Yorker*. Retrieved from https://www.newyorker.com/magazine/2014/07/21/wrong-answer

Barsky A. (2008). Understanding the ethical cost of organizational goal-setting: A review and theory development. *Journal of Business Ethics*, *81*(1), 63–81.

Berman, E. (2006). *Performance and productivity in public and nonprofit organizations* (2nd ed.). Armonk, NY: M. E. Sharpe.

Bohte, J., & Meier, K. J. (2000). Goal displacement: Assessing the motivation for organizational cheating. *Public Administration Review*, *60*, 173–182.

Brumback, K. (2013, March 29). 3 dozen indicted in Atlanta cheating scandal. *Washington Post*. Retrieved from http://www.washingtonpost.com/politics/3-dozen-indicted-in-atlanta-cheating-scandal/2013/03/29/86711356-98c2-11e2-97cd-3d8c1afe4f0f_allComments.html

Callahan, D. (2004). *The cheating culture*. New York: Mariner Books.

Carter, S. (1996). *Integrity*. New York: Harper Perennial.

Carvel, J. (2003, May 13). Hospitals "faked" wait times test. *The Guardian*. Retrieved from http://www.guardian.co.uk/society/2003/may/13/hospitals.nhs

Cooper, H. (2014, February 14). For a new air force secretary, a baptism by fire. *New York Times*. Retrieved from https://www.nytimes.com/2014/02/14/us/for-new-air-force-secretary-a-baptism-by-fire.html

Cooper, P. (2000). *Public law and public administration*. Itasca, IL: F. E. Peacock.

Courty, P., & Marschke, G. (2003). Making government accountable: Lessons from a federal job training program. *Public Administration Review*, *67*, 904–916.

de Lancer Julnes, P. (2006). Performance measurement: An effective tool for government accountability? The debate goes on. *Evaluation*, *12*(2), 219–235.

de Lancer Julnes, P. (2009, October). *The role of performance measurement in ethical and effective government*. Paper presented at the Fourteenth International Congress of CLAD (Latin-American Center of Administration for Development) on Reform of the State and Public Administration, Salvador de Bahia, Brazil.

DeHoog, R., & Salamon, L. (2002). Purchase of service contracting. In L. Salamon (Ed.), *The tools of government: A guide to the new governance* (pp. 319–339). New York: Oxford University Press.

Drongelen, I., & Fisscher, O. (2003). Ethical dilemmas in performance measurement. *Journal of Business Ethics*, *45*, 51–63.

Figlio, D. (2005). *Testing, crime and punishment* (Working Paper 11194). Cambridge, MA: National Bureau of Economic Research. Retrieved from http://www.nber.org/papers/w11194

Figlio, D., & Getzler, L. (2002). *Accountability, ability and disability: Gaming the system* (Working Paper 9307). Cambridge, MA: National Bureau of Economic Research. Retrieved from http://www.nber.org/papers/w9307

Figlio, D., & Winicki, J. (2005). Food for thought: The effects of school accountability plans on school nutrition. *Journal of Public Economics*, *89*, 381–394.

Fisher, C., & Downes, B. (2008). Performance measurement and metric manipulation in the public sector. *Business Ethics: A European Review*, *17*, 245–258.

Frysh, P. (2011, August 8). Cheating report confirms teacher's suspicions. *CNN*. Retrieved from http://www.cnn.com/2011/US/08/05/atlanta.public.schools.scandal/index.html

Gormley, W. T., & Weimer, D. L. (1999). *Organizational report cards*. Cambridge, MA: Harvard University Press.

Haimson, L. (2012, July 29). Tests don't assess what really matters. *New York Times*. Retrieved from http://www.nytimes.com/roomfordebate/2012/07/29/can-school-performance-be-measured

Haines, D. (2003–2004). Fatal choices: The routinization of deceit, incompetence, and corruption. *Public Integrity*, *6*, 5–24.

Hendrick, R., & Yazici, N. (2011, June). *Strategic behavior and performance measurement in government*. Paper presented at the Seventh Transatlantic Dialogue on Strategic Management of Public Organizations, Rutgers School of Public Affairs and Administration, Newark, NJ.

Hood, C. (2002). Control, bargains, and cheating: The politics of public-service reform. *Journal of Public Administration Research and Theory*, *12*, 309–332.

Hood, C. (2006). Gaming in targetworld: The targets approach to managing British public services. *Public Administration Review*, *66*, 515–521.

Hood, C., Dixon, R., & Beeston, C. (2008). Rating the rankings: Assessing international rankings of public service performance. *International Public Management Journal*, *11*, 298–328.

Jaffe, G., & Hicks, J. (2014, June 9). VA audit: 57,000 veterans waiting more than 90 days for appointment at medical facilities. *Washington Post*. Retrieved at https://www.washingtonpost.com/politics/va-audit-57000-veterans-waiting-more-than-90-days-for-appointment-at-medical-facilities/2014/06/09/599d26ee-f014-11e3-9ebc-2ee6f81ed217_story.html?utm_term=.00fc6e4b7b5f

JC Penney exec admits its employees harbored enormous YouTube addiction. (2013, February 25). *Wall Street Journal*, p. A12.

Kahneman, D. (2011). *Thinking, fast and slow*. New York: Farrar, Straus, & Giroux.

Kelman, S., & Friedman, J. N. (2009). Performance improvement and performance dysfunction: An empirical examination of distortionary impacts of the emergency room wait-time target in the English National Health Service. *Journal of Public Administration Research and Theory*, *19*, 917–946.

Layton, N. (2013, April 14). Bush, Obama focus on standardized testing leads to "opt-out" parents' movement. *Washington Post*. Retrieved from http://articles.washingtonpost.com/2013-04-14/local/38537469_1_no-child-students-such-testing

Liff, S. (2014). *98 opportunities to improve management in government*. Tysons Corner, VA: Management Concepts Press.

Meier, K. J. (1985). *Regulation: Politics, economics and bureaucracy*. New York: St. Martin's Press.

Meier, K. J. (2007). The public administration of politics, or what political science could learn from public administration. *PS: Political Science and Politics*, *40*, 3–9.

Meier, K. J. (2008). The scientific study of public administration: A short essay on the state of the field. *International Review of Public Administration*, *13*, 1–10.

Ordonez, L., Schweitzer, M., Galinsky, A., Bazerman, M. (2009). On good scholarship, goal setting, and scholars gone wild. *Academy of Management Perspectives*, *23*(3), 82–87.

Perez-Pena, R., & Slotnik, D. E. (2012, January 31). Gaming the college rankings. *New York Times*. Retrieved from http://www.nytimes.com/2012/02/01/education/gaming-the-college-rankings.html?_r=1&pagewanted=print

Schweitzer, M. E., Ordonez, L., & Douma, B. (2004). Goal setting as a motivator of unethical behavior. *Academy of Management Journal*, *47*, 422–432.

Stone, D. (1988). *Policy paradox and political reason*. New York: HarperCollins.

Strauss, V. (2011, July 5). Probe: Widespread cheating on tests detailed in Atlanta. *Washington Post*. Retrieved from http://www.washingtonpost.com/blogs/answer-sheet/post/probe-widespread-cheating-on-tests-detailed-in-atlanta/2011/07/05/gHQAURaczH_blog.html

Strauss, V. (2012, January 31). College admits inflating SAT scores to boost ranking. *Washington Post*. Retrieved from http://www.washingtonpost.com/blogs/answer-sheet/post/college-admits-inflating-sat-scores-to-boost-ranking/2012/01/31/gIQA00H1fQ_blog.html

Tuckness, A. (2010). "Everybody does it": An analysis of a common excuse. *Public Integrity*, *12*, 261–272.

Whitesell, G. (2012, January 20). Government seeks help to stop teacher-led cheating. *USA Today*. Retrieved from http://www.usatoday.com/news/education/story/2012-01-19/teacher-testing-cheating/52683838/1

Winslow, D. (2017). *The force*. New York: William Morrow.

Zhao, E. (2012, July 27). Ohio state auditor will launch investigation into school cheating, attendance record tampering. *Huffington Post*. Retrieved from http://www.huffingtonpost.com/2012/07/27/ohio-state-auditor-will-1_n_1711448.html

13 At-Will Employment

Those who are fear'd, are hated.

—Benjamin Franklin

The nature of the employer–employee relationship has undergone change during the last generation from a long-term career system to a short-term employment system (Bowman & West, 2006b). The risks of management decisions and market fluctuations, previously borne by institutions, have increasingly been shifted to individuals. As a result, the traditional social contract at work—job security in exchange for organization loyalty—has been eroded (Stone, 2004; West, 2013). One of the most sweeping measures is the at-will employment doctrine. It has been used to eliminate existing employee protections not only in private companies, but also in government service (Hays & Sowa, 2006).

This chapter analyzes the at-will doctrine by emphasizing the complementarity and interdependence of results-based utilitarian ethics, rule-based duty ethics, and virtue-based character ethics. Chapter objectives include examining:

- the importance of the problem,
- its evolution and current status,
- evaluation of the employment at-will doctrine, and
- implications of the findings.

In so doing, Lord Acton's (1834–1902) adage—"Power tends to corrupt and absolute power corrupts absolutely"—provides a useful perspective on contemporary trends in employment relations.

THE EMPLOYMENT AT-WILL DOCTRINE

Historical Development

Early American labor-management law was based on British master–servant law, which assumed employment would last one year.[1] However, consistent with the laissez-faire capitalism of the Industrial Revolution, the approach was abandoned for the American Rule near the end of the 19th century. Under this rule, employees work for an unspecified period of time at the will of the employer (Hugh, 2001; also see Holger, 2004; Werhane, Radin, & Bowie, 2004). The relationship would be defined by the freedom to contract where neither party was compelled to create the affiliation and either party could terminate it at will. The discipline of the free market would ensure the societal efficiency of these voluntary agreements as both parties would have incentives to recover their investments made in each other (Epstein & Rosen, 1984). With the exception of unionized industries and most civil servants, the majority of the U.S. workforce today works at will.

In concept, the absolute right of the employer to discharge a worker coincides with the sovereignty doctrine in the public sector. Because employment is a privilege, not a right, it was subject to terms specified by government. Government is sovereign; it is inappropriate to dilute its management rights (e.g., no person has a right to a public job). Indeed for much of the 1800s—the last time that at-will employment was used in public service—the spoils system dominated personnel policy. Citizens sought a position not on the basis of character or competence but on political connections, and they could be terminated on the same basis. Public office was perverted into a private fiefdom as arrogance, greed, and opportunism prevailed over honor, openness, and prudence.

Favoritism, cronyism, intimidation, corruption, and rampant dismissals were widespread in that squalid era. Rather than emphasizing good government and policy, the system encouraged mediocre governance—its highest priority was to reward its friends, to grant favors for favors given. To protect the legitimacy of the state from private interests and to cleanse public service of partisan interference, English merit principles (including entrance examinations, job tenure, career service, political neutrality) were adopted in the 1883 Pendleton Act (and state "mini-Pendleton" laws) as well as the 1912 Lloyd-LaFollette Act. As the spoils system gradually eroded (only 10 percent of employees were initially covered by the Pendleton Act), the merit system, as well as the federal courts, progressively strengthened employee rights under the Constitution.

A merit-based civil service—as a moral guardian of democracy—would shield employees from politically inspired employment actions. Public servants would be loyal to the system of government, not to a particular political party. They would only give free and candid advice if their positions were safeguarded. Clean government would mean effective government as job security facilitated government responsiveness and ensured efficient service delivery. Competence would be the foundation of ethical public management; government would be run like a business when organized by administrative principles, led by an executive, and staffed by nonpartisan employees shielded from unscrupulous politicians.

Although the merit system was created to "clean up government" by eradicating spoils, it is not surprising that with the passage of time the past would be forgotten. Toward the end of the 20th century, a simpler, private sector-inspired employment model gained favor. Based on a liberal market ethos, it stresses a laissez-faire employment relationship that celebrates self-interested behaviors and economic incentives. The New Public Management/ Reinventing Government movement emphasized "letting managers manage" by increasing their discretion and using corporate management styles to ensure improved performance and results (Ferlie, Ashburner, & Pettigrew, 1996; Gore, 1993; Pollitt, 1990; Salamon & Elliott, 2002). Relaxing job protections for civil servants has been seen as a key method to accomplish these objectives. Policy advocates favor substituting tenured employees for contract workers who are obliged to provide specific outputs with few job guarantees (Pollitt & Bouckaert, 2004; Sulieman, 2003). At-will employment, in short, is now seen as solving, instead of causing, public management problems.

Contemporary Reform

Fueled by entrepreneurial strategies, budget cutbacks, and devolution, the reform movement (Condrey & Maranto, 2001) has gained exceptions from merit systems across the nation by expanding management prerogatives and restricting employee rights (Kellough & Nigro, 2006). In recent years, a variety of federal departments received full or partial waivers from Title 5 of the U.S. Code, which covers the merit system. Further, in the wake of the September 11, 2001, attacks, the Transportation Security Agency established at-will employment for its personnel. Subsequently, the Departments of Homeland Security and Defense were authorized in the name of the "war on terror" to create new human resource management systems that strengthen administrative discretion and diminish employee protections. Reformers sought to use these approaches as templates for government-wide change.

At the state level, major reform examples also exist: Texas nullified its merit system in 1985, making all state employees at will; a 1996 Georgia law mandated that all new civil servants be hired on an at-will basis; and in 2001, Florida eliminated job tenure for most incumbent middle managers (Walters, 2002). South Carolina and Arkansas recently abolished their merit systems; less dramatically, many states including Indiana, Delaware, and Kansas are reclassifying career service positions to unclassified ones as a consequence of reorganizations, reductions-in-force, or attrition. Such strategies are often mutually reinforcing in a manner that promotes the ongoing decline of career public service.

The effect is that the status and role of the public employee today is not too different than that found in business (Hays & Sowa, 2006). Changes reducing or abolishing job security (and otherwise altering basic merit system tenets), then, have occurred throughout the country, despite International Labor Organization standards that forbid unjust dismissal.

APPLYING THE ETHICS TRIAD TO AT-WILL EMPLOYMENT

The spread of at-will employment has led to concerns about whether the doctrine is ethical. As discussed in Chapter 7, various ethical models may be helpful, but one is particularly useful because its comprehensive nature reduces the chances of an incomplete, flawed judgment. The decision-making tool acknowledges the imperatives in three approaches based on (1) expected results of an action (consequentialism or teleology), (2) application of pertinent rules (duty ethics or deontology), and (3) personal rectitude or character (virtue ethics).[2] Although the synthesis developed from triangulation does not provide definitive solutions, it does offer guidance by identifying the underlying logic by which decisions are justified (for further discussion, see Bowman, West, & Beck, 2010, Chapter 3). The goal is to strive for balance; governance is not geometry, but the art of the possible. Ethical theories may lead to different evaluations of at-will employment, but Acton's epic-warning challenges decision makers to confront these differences, not suppress them. Management ethics need not be an oxymoron. The at-will doctrine will be analyzed below using the three perspectives.

Results-Based Analysis

In consequentialism, the best policy results in "the greatest good for the greatest number." What is right is that which creates the largest amount of human happiness with the least harm. This school of thought is associated with John Stuart Mill's ideas that "[d]ecisions are judged by their consequences depending on the results to be maximized" (Frederickson, 1997, 167–168). A similar emphasis is found in G. W. F. Hegel's (1821/1996, 113) writings where he articulates the principle, "[J]udge an act by its consequences, and make them the standard of what is right and good." This approach is useful for administrators seeking the common good for the public. Accordingly, consideration of an employment at-will policy examines affirmative and negative arguments on (a) productivity, (b) flexibility, (c) responsiveness, (d) merit, and (e) loyalty grounds.

In Support of At-Will Employment. Reformers maintain that use of a corporate-style "bottom-line" standard results in exemplary performance. Overprotective employment requirements entitle civil servants to their jobs regardless of results achieved (Howard, 2001). Moving from "protection to performance" means employees are not shielded by procedural requirements if they fail to produce (Florida Council of One Hundred, 2000). The threat of job loss is needed to keep employees motivated; they will have incentive to perform because they can be replaced at any time by others willing to work harder (Bardwick, 1995).

Among the benefits are gains in *productivity* (Epstein & Rosen, 1984). Charged with the responsibility to serve the public interest, political leaders have considerable leverage over at-will employees. When serving "at the pleasure of" the appointing official, efficiency is maximized and waste minimized. Time and resources expended dealing with burdensome due process rights and "just cause" dismissal rules are thereby saved for regular business that increases effectiveness. This assurance is grounded in employee confidence that government officials make decisions based on their merits. Prime beneficiaries of increased productivity are citizens who pay for and receive public services.

Running government like a business produces not only cost savings and enhanced efficiency, but also greater *flexibility* in implementing the will of the voters. Elected officials are responsible to the people and, in turn, civil servants must be held accountable. Absent the protection of job security, elected officials can pinpoint responsibility and ensure accountability from civil servants. At-will status, for example, can disempower "bureaucratic guerillas" who directly or indirectly subvert plans of their organizational superiors (O'Leary, 2006). Political appointees, in short, can expect that civil servants will be more *responsive* when their job is at risk. With emphasis on performance, it follows that *merit* can be readily rewarded, using programs such as pay for performance. The overall result is that employee *loyalty* is assured (Epstein & Rosen, 1984; Maitland, 1989).

In the 21st century, then, absolute power does not corrupt (as it might have done in Lord Acton's time) because it is limited by legal safeguards such as antidiscrimination statutes. Running government like a business by encouraging productivity, flexibility, and responsiveness enables the will of the people to be fulfilled. The payoff is greater workforce merit and loyalty, as well as enhanced public trust. Because the marketplace does not naturally produce job security contracts, this demonstrates that they are inefficient. For all these reasons, it is evident that removing job tenure and instituting at-will employment serves the greatest good for the greatest number.

In Opposition to At-Will Employment. Skeptics argue that reformers base their views on "common sense" or anecdotes that are suspect justifications for abandoning constraints on power that so concerned Lord Acton. There is a lack of empirical evidence of improved *productivity* when workers lose job security (e.g., McCall, 2003). Indeed, tenure, together with other workplace initiatives (e.g., employee participation, empowerment, incentive programs), is associated with higher productivity (see literature review in Levine & Tyson, 1990; also review Freeman & Medoff, 1984; Ichniowski, 1992; Pfeffer, 1998). Substantial cost saving can be incurred with a stable and loyal workforce (Reichheld, 1996).

Job tenure, in addition, does not require employers to retain unproductive workers or require them to keep employees if economic conditions mandate reductions in force. The real problem is not employment security provisions, but rather that administrators "do not want to go through the aggravation of giving marginal employees an unsatisfactory rating. If that is so, wouldn't managers under the new system also be reluctant to do so?" (Underhill & Oman, 2006). Finally, critics hold that fear of job loss is a poor motivator, because "KITA" (Kick in the Ass) is counterproductive (Herzberg, 1987). Indeed, they see "Theory X" managerial control policies, and its assumptions about human nature that guide reform (McGregor, 1960), as unfortunate throwbacks to an earlier era. Expectations of enhanced productivity are likely to be dashed, with heightened cynicism and low morale preventing even plausible outcomes as employees spend more time concerned "about antagonizing the current political party" than providing citizen services (Bowman & West, 2006a, 150). There is a paucity of evidence, in brief, that job security is related to productivity losses.

Defenders of "just cause" standards also point out that existing public personnel systems provide for ample *flexibility* when officials understand procedures, take advantage of opportunities to provide feedback, and use progressive discipline. This can lead to increased *responsiveness* since the public service ethos, by definition, encourages service to the citizenry. The absence of assurance of a job in the future may lead to high turnover, and less capacity for responsiveness, as employees use their positions as stepping stones to higher paying openings elsewhere. Upholding the principles of *merit* has been the important distinguishing feature of modern personnel systems for many generations. Indeed, historically government has been a "model employer," as recruiting, rewarding and retaining employees based on merit characterized best practices in public management (Berman et al., 2012).

In contrast, at-will employment exemplifies "hard" human resource management derived from Taylorism and scientific management (Greenwood, 2001; Guest, 1987, 1998; Truss & Gratton, 1997). Its instrumental emphasis focuses on organizational ends, with employees seen simply as means in achieving these ends. The doctrine allows "inconsistent, even irrational, management behavior by permitting arbitrary, non work-related, treatment of employees—behavior that is not considered a good management practice" (Werhane et al., 2004, 197). "Soft" human resource management, however, grew out of the human relations movement, and values people as assets to be developed more than costs to be reduced. Organizations, in fact, have a moral obligation to treat individuals with dignity by pursuing exemplary practices such as staff empowerment, participation, training, and skill building (Greenwood, 2002, 269).

One way to meet this obligation is to invest in employee skills and abilities and to use them effectively over the long term. This is more apt to occur where people are valued and protected from wrongful discharge (Burke & Little, 2002–2003). It is also likely that jurisdictions will experience a return on this investment in the form of greater employee *loyalty*, satisfaction, job commitment, and cooperation (Ashford, Lee, & Bobko, 1989; Green et al., 2006; Guest, 1998; Lim, 1996; Niehoff & Paul, 2001; West & Bowman, 2004).

Absent security, people may well ask, "If the employer is not loyal to me, why should I be loyal in return?" If government employment is just a job and not a calling, and if the traditionally below-market pay is not compensated for by tenure, then key staff are likely to leave. Indeed, at-will employment and privatization often has meant public employees lose their positions and do the same work done previously, but now as contract "shadow workers," with no security or benefits. Those who remain in the more politicized workplace may displace their loyalties from serving the public to obeying political masters. Manipulating public servants as disposable commodities or interchangeable parts is demeaning and misguided. In brief, the greatest good for the greatest number is achieved not by Theory X, but rather by Theory Y management policies.

To summarize this section, in result-based ethics, only consequences matter. At-will advocates seek the greatest good by emphasizing expected results from corporate, bottom-line approaches said to enhance productivity, flexibility, responsiveness, merit, and loyalty. To do otherwise, by authorizing job tenure, risks employee self-serving, expedient behavior. On these same grounds, however, skeptics argue that abandoning the keystone of the merit system hardly serves the citizenry. Instead, it encourages not only managerial opportunistic behaviors, but also expedient and, ultimately, counterproductive actions. Further, little theoretical or empirical evidence exists to suggest that the at-will doctrine has the results supporters claim. Because an overemphasis on any one point of the ethics triangle may put a proposed policy at risk, attention now turns to another approach.

Rule-Based Analysis

Rule-based decision making provides a different lens for evaluating at-will employment. Certain actions are inherently right (e.g., promise keeping) or wrong (e.g., inflicting harm), irrespective of predicted consequences. This approach is useful for administrators who are obligated to follow the morality found in the Constitution, court cases, and laws and regulations (Rohr, 1988). Principle- or rule-based ethics is closely identified with Immanuel Kant's categorical imperative and Thomas Hobbes's social contract theory. Kant's (1785/1959, 17) imperative is to "act as if the maxim of your action was to become a universal law of nature," which, in turn, is rooted in the belief that humans are capable of rational thought and self-governance. Hobbes refers to "natural law" wherein human nature is a combination of all one's experiences and competencies, the consequence of which is a common understanding of right and wrong (Kem, 2006).

In a rule-based analysis, what is right is what conforms to moral rules; one must see one's duty and do it. In deciding what rule to apply, the person asks, "Would I want everyone else to make the decision I did?" Here the emphasis is on ethical principles such as autonomy, fairness/justice, and mutual respect in examining the affirmative and negative positions on civil service reform.

In Support of At-Will Employment. Proponents stress the importance of managerial proprietary rights and prerogatives, and their need for *autonomy* to run their agency (Epstein & Rosen, 1984; Werhane, 1985). At-will employment is justified because no one has a right to a government job; as such, employment is a privilege. Mandating employment security diminishes managerial authority and the right to do what is best. Any abuses arising from discretion can be controlled by formal procedures (in the form of internal auditors), informal norms (employee pressures), and the operations of the free market (Epstein & Rosen, 1984).

Savvy managers, in fact, would refrain from unjust adverse actions because arbitrary and capricious actions impair the organization's reputation, damage morale, lead to high quit rates, and impede recruitment. Thoughtlessly exercising management proprietary rights and prerogatives is clearly unwise. Since wrongful personnel actions and discharges diminish returns on investments in training and development, they are costly and infrequent. The at-will doctrine, then, actually serves to deter employer abuse. In addition, legislation exists to protect the rights of employees from unfair dismissal (e.g., civil rights laws, whistleblower protection). The concerns of Lord Acton, in short, are considerably circumscribed in modern times.

At bottom, then, each party is at liberty to terminate a relationship should either one fail to live up to expectations: workers can quit at will, employers can fire at will. It follows that *fairness* and *mutual respect* are accorded to each. Both parties are negotiators who attempt to arrive at employment arrangements that advance their interests. As a matter of autonomy and simple justice, once such commitments are freely made, the working conditions and responsibilities apply to the partners. The market assures fair treatment; as long as employees are paid for past work, they have been fully compensated and thus have no claim on future employment (McCall, 2003). Abuses can occur, but sensible protections exist, and the deficiencies of job tenure outweigh the benefits.

In Opposition to At-Will Employment. Skeptics, following Lord Acton, are apprehensive about the exercise of power. Employers are in a dominant position over employees because they own the means of production without which the employee could not make a living. It is evident that the employee needs the employer more than vice versa, jeopardizing *autonomy*. Because of the asymmetric power relationship and the resulting inequality in resources favoring employers, job security is a prerequisite to level the playing field (Gertz, 2008).

While acknowledging wrongful discharge legislation, critics point out that there are numerous ways to terminate someone that are not protected by law. The at-will doctrine, in effect, furnishes near-absolute power to managers to discharge a worker for any or no reason not contrary to the limited exceptions provided by statute. Because most people need work to survive, "there is a sense in which (they) are forced to work" (Bowie, 2005, 70). Genuine autonomy is impossible under such circumstances. Indeed, assuming that the market will deter abusive behavior overlooks the hundreds of thousands of employees annually whose contested terminations are found by arbitrators to be without cause (McCall, 2003). The very lack of power can also produce effects detrimental to both the individual and organization. As Werhane et al. (2004, 196) observe, the at-will creed "has, on numerous occasions, seemingly translated in a license for employers and employees to treat one another" unfairly.

The unbalanced nature of the doctrine violates basic *fairness* and *mutual respect*. Job loss can have serious economic and psychological repercussions for employees and their families, as well as exacerbate problems in the larger community (unemployment, poverty). Formal and informal pressures (internal auditors, co-worker monitoring) and legal protections (civil rights, age discrimination, and whistleblowing laws) are often insufficient to deter abuse. Further, at-will employment is seen as part of a package of policies that includes outsourcing, privatization, and civil service reform—all of which enhances management rights at the expense of employees. Might does not make right. Instead, there is a duty to offer people meaningful work; to treat them as ends, not means; and to show each person respect.

In short, at-will advocates see a fair, symmetrical relationship, one that preserves the autonomy of each party. The balance of power is maintained not only by the employer's enlightened self-interest, but also by wrongful discharge legislation. Any effort to unduly emphasize rule-based ethics at the expense of the rest of the ethics triangle is thereby circumscribed. At-will protagonists, as free-market fundamentalists, believe that everyone should be at will so that mutually beneficial agreements can be struck with little or no outside interference. In contrast, defenders of the "just cause" standard see the one-sided power relationship leading to a lack of mutual respect and fairness and encouraging overreaching, detrimental practices. It follows, then, that the at-will creed must not be made universal, but rather job protections should be widely available. Attention now turns to the final point of the ethics triangle.

Virtue-Based Analysis

In virtue ethics, answers to the question of "What to do?" have little to do with results or rules, and everything to do with the kind of person one is. Personal character offers a third perspective by asking, "What would a person of integrity decide?" when assessing the ethical advisability of employment at will. Virtue theory stems from the classical writings of Aristotle (e.g., *The Nicomachean Ethics*) and the modern views of Alasdair MacIntyre (1984).

As Geuras and Garofalo (2006, 59) note, the "theory considers an act to be good on the basis of the character trait or virtue that the act evidences." Virtuous conduct derives from a lifelong practice of self-discipline requiring commitment to ethical values.

Virtue ethics is enticing for policymakers because it is a more personal approach than cognitive ethics—decisions are informed not only by consequences and duties, but also by the quality of one's character. What is right is that which nurtures individual excellence and contributes to collective well-being. While there is no one list of traits (the idea of virtue theory is to transcend procedures and rules by emphasizing one's moral being), characteristics such as trustworthiness, integrity, and prudence are integral to moral nobility.

In Support of At-Will Employment. Reformers believe that voluntary employer–employee relationships, unencumbered by regulations, promote *trustworthiness*. Employers trust that those hired will perform and employees trust that appropriate work opportunities will be provided. Legal requirements assume that trust cannot be assured, thereby damaging mutual expectations. Because an employer cannot exist without an employee (and vice versa), the at-will doctrine services both parties. A freedom of contract, laissez-faire approach is best to ensure trust.

Integrity, the synthesis of virtues, is the capacity to understand one's obligations and ensure moral soundness as a member of a larger community. By striving for integrity in work, employees will be secure in their positions. People are not moral because of rules, but because of what they demand of themselves in character; externally imposed rules impair the development of authentic character. One's moral self grows from internal values; a person of integrity chafes at outside regulations in his relationships with others. The spirit of the at-will doctrine, then, enriches the association between the employer and employee.

Personal character, steeped in virtues, provides the disposition to take action. If moral rectitude directs one to the right end, then *prudence* (the ability to distinguish between right and wrong, and to act accordingly) directs one to the right means. The goal of individual freedom at work, in short, can be best pursued by employers and employees through the at-will principle.

In Opposition to At-Will Employment. Reintroducing the 19th-century at-will doctrine into government service reneges the social contract inherent in the merit system: job safeguards in exchange for modest compensation. Complementing legal protection in most workplaces is the existence of a "psychological contract," an understanding between an employee and employer that enhances loyalty and commitment (Berman & West, 2003; Niehoff & Paul, 2001; Rousseau, 1995; West, 2013). Because such a contract implies continued employment, the taking of such an entitlement is a betrayal of good faith. Having due process rights with orderly procedures (notice, opportunity to be heard, enforcement of rights) is an effective check on capricious behavior. When personnel know that they will be treated fairly, in brief, then *trustworthiness* in the employment relationship is fostered.

Without such protections, employment at will promotes a system in which *integrity* is difficult for employees to maintain. Even now, not only are civil servants unlikely to report fraud, waste, and abuse, but they may feel pressured to "go along to get along" (Gertz, 2008). A consequence of at-will employment is that staff will be increasingly reluctant to participate fully in decision making or to "speak truth to power" by criticizing inefficient or unethical policies, or may even feel compelled to participate in dubious policies when confronted with job loss. Absolute power, manifest in at-will employment, can corrupt absolutely: It heightens the probability that such corruption will occur and that the public interest will be compromised. If employees are unlikely to report untoward behavior for fear of retribution, truth-telling, so critical to integrity, is devalued.

Prudent decision making suggests a cautious approach to reform, thereby ensuring that proposed change will lead to desired improvements. As noted by Dobel (1998, 76), "Prudent judgment identifies salient moral aspects of a political situation which a leader has a moral obligation to attend to in making a decision." "Good judgment," he adds, "requires good information and a willingness to learn." However, many jurisdictions have seen the at-will doctrine as a seductive quick-fix to perceived problems. They have undertaken reform initiatives hastily and with little evidence demonstrating the efficacy of the change. They are victims of the "sin of superficial advice" (Meltsner, 2005, 412). Hastily adopting reform, for example, "amputation before diagnosis," results in misjudgments and dubious policies. Bowman, West, and Gertz (2006), for instance, note that the absence of reliable evidence, a distorted view of the business model, and ideological rigidity promoted radical reforms in Florida.

In a nutshell, at-will supporters argue that the mutual freedom to contract nurtures trust, regulations interfere with individual and collective integrity, and individual freedom creates prudence. Critics think the creed negates trust by breaking contracts, damages integrity by increasing fear, and undermines prudence by its panacea-like quality. Yet the strength of virtue theory (reliance on subjective assessment derived from personal character) is also its weakness: If at-will proponents and opponents believe that they are good, then it is not hard to believe that what they do is good.

SUMMARY AND CONCLUSION

Responsible policymakers develop virtues, respect rules, and consider results. The analytical decision-making process presented here is a conscious attempt to reconcile clashing values by highlighting an essential function of ethical management—developing different viewpoints, evaluating them, and producing a considered judgment. The approach offered is like a good map, presenting choices, not formula. Just as a map outlines a journey, the triad provides help in making the inevitable compromises, aiding skilled management of ethical ambiguity and independent thinking.

It is important to keep in mind potential pitfalls when just one school of thought is emphasized at the expense of the others. For example, the results approach may be problematic because it is difficult to anticipate all possible consequences and because it may lead to expedient action (thus, when choosing among appealing outcomes, rule-based ethics and virtue theory should also be applied). Similarly, rule-based ethics, if used alone, may lack compassion (Svara, 1997) when truth telling produces cold and inconsiderate behaviors (to compensate, benevolence in the virtue ethics might be applied). Last, the exclusive use of virtue theory is perplexing because of its intuitive and possibly self-serving nature (to be counterbalanced by utilizing the other two schools of thought). In short, an integrated approach helps to provide a defensible decision that takes into account results, rules, and virtues.

As part of New Public Management, the doctrine of employment at will has, after a long decline (Muhl, 2001), enjoyed a renaissance in recent years. As Schwab (2001) predicted, the principle of just cause protection against unfair dismissal would be eroded in the new century. Reformers believe that employees have no need of job security because modern civil rights and whistleblowing laws provide adequate protection and employers are generally honorable and rarely engage in egregious behavior.

Until a short time ago, one of the distinguishing features of public employment was the merit system and the neutral competence of the civil service, safeguarded from political pressures, cronyism, sycophancy, and corruption. The rise of at-will employment (and its functional equivalents such as hiring temporary employees) is seen by proponents as a way to re-energize the bureaucracy and by opponents as a return to the spoils system (Bowman, 2002; Bowman & West, 2006a). There are compelling, competing grounds found in the debate over civil service reform and at-will employment. The overall assessment of these contentions below will provide a synthesis, or at least a conclusion.

Result-based decision making, as discussed earlier, evaluates at-will employment as it relates to productivity, flexibility, responsiveness, merit, and loyalty, and how these contribute to the greatest good. Stakeholders are benefited or harmed by employment at will. Elected officials benefit from the increased responsiveness of civil servants that eliminating job security is thought to produce. Managers, due to enhanced flexibility, are not required to deal with procedural requirements when undertaking adverse actions. However, career public employees, lacking tenure, fear losing their positions if they choose to serve the long-term public interest when it conflicts with short-term political advantage. More generally, the at-will doctrine encourages the treatment of personnel as means to organizational ends, as costs to be controlled rather than assets to be developed.

The largest stakeholder, however, is the citizenry. Reformers suggest that productivity will soar when government is run like a business. Yet there is little documentation adduced by reformers to substantiate this view, perhaps because available data suggest productivity, morale, and loyalty may be placed in jeopardy when employee protections are removed. Further, government can adopt proven business tools such as competitive pay and teamwork and still provide job safeguards. Such action is not inconsistent with the New Public Management emphasis and preserves the existing social contract with employees. A policymaker using result-based ethics may find some politically attractive at-will employment arguments, but the evidence suggests that the greatest good is served by neutral competence in the public service.

Rule-based imperatives, the second perspective, emphasize the need for principles such as autonomy, fairness/justice, and mutual respect. At-will supporters argue that the doctrine allows for freedom of contract. When the decision maker takes into account the asymmetrical nature of the employer–employee relationship, however, it is evident that personnel can easily be subject to intimidation and unjust actions that violate their autonomy and rob them of respect.

Virtue-based ethics relies on intuitive character traits such as trustworthiness, integrity, and prudence, said to be nurtured by the at-will doctrine according to reformers. Yet doubters believe that trust is compromised when rights are diminished, and adverse actions lacking just cause occur. Integrity suffers in a fear-filled environment. To the extent that reforms are rushed into place, with questionable grounds to support them, prudence is violated.

Each of the three approaches contains arguments for and against at-will employment. Taken separately, the creed may appear ethical at some points and unethical at others; as Aristotle admonished, one should not expect more precision from a subject matter than it can allow. On balance, however, it is difficult to see how an employment doctrine that permits harm without cause can be ethical from a results-, rule-, or virtue-based perspective. To have power is to be morally responsible for one's actions. An employment relationship with few reciprocal obligations in which the employer recognizes little obligation to the employee compromises the greatest good, duty, and personal integrity. In so doing, it needlessly places the hallmark of modern civil service—neutral competence—at risk. Because all power needs to be restrained, such concerns should inspire public employers to unambiguously reject the at-will doctrine:

> When others crucially depend on and expect continued participation in a cooperative enterprise, it appears patently unfair to abruptly end the relationship without notice and without good reason, an idea we reflect in our common moral assessments of contexts as varied as marriage, housing, and access to traditional routes of public passage through private property. Thus . . . the power to terminate the relationship without due process . . . violates commonly held norms of fairness.. . . . It is especially unfair when one party has the preponderance of power. (McCall, 2003, 166)

Since arbitrary behavior is not tolerated in other areas of management such as finance, it should not be accepted in employment relations. Lord Acton would agree.

***

Only they deserve power who justify its use daily.

—Dag Hammarskjold

NOTES

1. This chapter is adapted from Bowman & West (2007) with permission from Springer Science and Business Media. Parts of the background section are condensed from Bowman and West (2006b).
2. While other philosophies might be used to evaluate the ethics of at-will employment, these three schools of thought are dominant in the literature on administrative ethics (see Cooper, 1987; Frederickson & Ghere, 2005; Garofalo & Geuras, 1999; Geuras & Garofalo, 2006; Richter, Burke, & Doig, 1990).

FOR DISCUSSION

1. Lord Acton's observation is one of the most well known in political history. Why?

2. People often hold strong views on employment at will. Identify the most convincing argument for the doctrine and the most compelling against it.

3. Can an at-will employee be terminated for having a cup of coffee or tea, wearing a long- or short-sleeve shirt, or smiling politely? Explain.

4. Are there other significant arguments in the at-will employment debate not included in the results, rules, and virtue trifocal analysis? To what extent, if any, does behavioral ethics (Chapter 7) shed light on the debate?

5. Contest this statement: The employment-at-will doctrine sees employees as commodities to be exploited and mistreated.

6. Are recent civil service reforms that include removal of tenure a harbinger of a neo-spoils system in government?

7. The chapter concluded that Lord Acton would endorse the view that arbitrary management behavior should not be tolerated. Discuss.

EXERCISES

1. A large majority of people in the American workforce, except most career civil servants, "work at will." Visit an employer and ask a manager about how the system operates in her organization. What legal protections exist against arbitrary adverse personal actions? Are they adequate?

2. Ask an employee who "works at will." Does he understand that he is vulnerable to termination for any or no reason not contrary of law?

REFERENCES

Aristotle. (1980). *The Nicomachean ethics* (D. Ross, Trans.). Oxford: Oxford University Press.

Ashford, S., Lee, C., & Bobko, P. (1989). Content, causes and consequences of job insecurity: A theory-based measure and substantive test. *Academy of Management Journal, 32*, 803–829.

Bardwick, J. (1995). *Danger in the comfort zone.* New York: AMACOM.

Berman, E., Bowman, J., West, J., & Van Wart, M. (2012). *Human resource management in public service: Paradoxes, problems, and processes* (4th ed.). Thousand Oaks, CA: Sage.

Berman, E., & West, J. (2003). Psychological contracts in local government: A preliminary survey. *Review of Public Personnel Administration, 23*, 267–285.

Bowie, N. (2005). Kantian ethical thought. In J. Budd & J. Scoville (Eds.), *The ethics of human resources and industrial relations* (pp. 61–88). Champaign, IL: Labor and Employment Relations Association.

Bowman, J. (2002). At-will employment in Florida: A naked formula to corrupt public service. *Working USA, 6,* 90–102.

Bowman, J., & West, J. (2006a). Ending civil service protections in Florida government: Experiences in state agencies. *Review of Public Personnel Administration, 26,* 139–157.

Bowman, J., & West, J. (2006b, March). *Removing employee protections: A "see no evil" approach to civil service reform.* Paper presented at the 2006 Western Political Science Association meeting, Albuquerque, NM.

Bowman, J., & West, J. (2007, August). Lord Acton and employment doctrines: Absolute power and the spread of at-will employment. *Journal of Business Ethics, 74*(2).

Bowman, J., West, J., & Beck, M. (2010). *Achieving public service competencies: The professional edge.* Armonk, NY: M. E. Sharpe.

Bowman, J., West, J., & Gertz, S. (2006). Florida's service first: Radical reform in the sunshine state. In J. Kellough & L. Nigro (Eds.), *Civil service reform in the states* (pp. 145–170). New York: SUNY Press.

Burke, D., & Little, B. (2002–2003). At-will employment: Just let it go. *Journal of Individual Employment Rights, 10,* 119–131.

Condrey, S., & Maranto, R. (Eds.). (2001). *Radical reform of the civil service.* New York: Lexington Books.

Cooper, T. (1987). Hierarchy, virtue, and the practice of public administration: A perspective for normative ethics. *Public Administration Review, 47,* 320–328.

Dobel, P. (1998). Political prudence and the ethics of leadership. *Public Administration Review, 58,* 74–81.

Epstein, R., & Rosen, S. (1984). In defense of contract at will. *University of Chicago Law Review, 51,* 947–988.

Ferlie, E., Ashburner, L., & Pettigrew, A. (1996). *The new public management in action.* Oxford: Oxford University Press.

Florida Council of One Hundred. (2000). *Modernizing Florida's civil service system: Moving from protection to performance.* Tampa, FL: Author.

Frederickson, H. G. (1997). *The spirit of public administration.* San Francisco: Jossey-Bass.

Frederickson, H. G., & Ghere, R. K. (Eds.). (2005). *Ethics in public management.* Armonk, NY: M. E. Sharpe.

Freeman, R., & Medoff, J. (1984). *What do unions do?* New York: Basic Books.

Garofalo, D., & Geuras, D. (1999). *Ethics in the public service.* Washington, DC: Georgetown University Press.

Gertz, S. (2008). At-will employment: Origins, applications, exceptions, and expansions. *International Journal of Public Administration, 31,* 489–514.

Geuras, D., & Garofalo, C. (2006). *Practical ethics in public administration* (2nd ed.). Vienna, VA: Management Concepts.

Gore, A. (1993). *From red tape to results: Creating a government that works better and costs less: Report of the national performance review.* Darby, PA: DIANE.

Green, R., Golden, A., Forbis, R., Nelson, S., & Robinson, J. (2006). On the ethics of at-will employment relations in the public sector. *Public Integrity, 8,* 305–327.

Greenwood, M. (2001). The importance of stakeholders: According to business. *Business and Society Review, 106*, 29–50.

Greenwood, M. (2002). Ethics and HRM: A review and conceptual analysis. *Journal of Business Ethics, 36*, 261–278.

Guest, D. (1987). Human resource management and industrial relations. *Journal of Management Studies, 24*, 5–25.

Guest, D. (1998). Is the psychological contract worth taking seriously? *Journal of Organizational Behavior, 19*, 649–64.

Hays, S., & Sowa, J. (2006). A broader look at the "accountability" movement: Some grim realities in state civil service systems. *Review of Public Personnel Administration, 26*, 102–117.

Hegel, G. W. F. (1996). *Philosophy of right* (S. Dyde, Trans.). Amherst, NY: Prometheus Books. [Original work published 1821]

Herzberg, F. (1987). One more time: How do you motivate employees? *Harvard Business Review, 65*, 109–120.

Holger, R. (2004). *Employment relations in the United States*. Thousand Oaks, CA: Sage.

Howard, P. (2001, September 6). Demand accountability from public employees. *Miami Herald*, p. B7.

Hugh, S. (2001, May 25). Employment at will, an idea whose time has come—and gone. *Workforce*. Retrieved from http://www.workforce.com/apps/pbcs.dll/article?AID=/20010525/NEWS02/305259993&template=printarticle

Ichniowski, C. (1992). Human resource management and productive labor relations. In D. Lewin, O. S. Mitchell, & P. D. Sherer (Eds.), *Research frontiers in industrial relations and human resources* (pp. 239–272). Madison, WI: Industrial Relations Research Association.

Kant, I. (1959). *Foundations of the metaphysics of morals* (L. Beck, Trans.). Indianapolis, IN: Bobbs-Merrill. [Original work published 1785]

Kellough, J., & Nigro, L. (Eds.). (2006). *Civil service reform in the states*. Albany, NY: SUNY Press.

Kem, J. (2006). *A pragmatic ethical decision making model for the army: The ethical triangle*. Unpublished manuscript, U.S. Army Command and General Staff College, Fort Leavenworth, Kansas.

Levine, D., & Tyson, L. (1990). Participation, productivity and the firm's environment. In A. Blinder (Ed.), *Paying for productivity* (pp. 183–236). Washington, DC: Brookings Institution.

Lim, V. (1996). Job security and its outcomes: moderating effects of work-based and non work-based social support. *Human Relations, 49*, 171–194.

MacIntyre, A. C. (1984). *After virtue: A study in moral theory* (2nd ed.). South Bend, IN: University of Notre Dame Press.

Maitland, I. (1989). Rights in the workplace: A Nozickian argument. *Journal of Business Ethics, 8*, 951–954.

McCall, J. (2003). A defense of just cause dismissal rules. *Business Ethics Quarterly, 13*, 151–175.

McGregor, D. (1960). *The human side of enterprise*. New York: McGraw-Hill.

Meltsner, A. (2005). The seven deadly sins of policy analysts. In J. Shafritz, K. Layne, & C. Borick (Eds.), *Classics of public policy* (pp. 409–415). New York: Pearson/Longman.

Muhl, C. (2001). The employment at-will doctrine: Three major exceptions. *Monthly Labor Review, 124*, 3–12.

Niehoff, B., & Paul, R. (2001). The just workplace: Developing and maintaining effective psychological contracts. *Review of Business, 22*, 5–8.

O'Leary, R. (2006). *The ethics of dissent: Managing guerilla government.* Washington, DC: CQ Press.

Pfeffer, J. (1998). *The human equation.* Boston, MA: Harvard Business School Press.

Pollitt, C. (1990). *Managerialism in the public sector.* Cambridge: Basil-Blackwell.

Pollitt, C., & Bouckaert, G. (2004). *Public management reform: A comparative analysis* (2nd ed.). Oxford: Oxford University Press.

Reichheld, F. (1996). *The loyalty effect: The hidden force behind growth, profits, and lasting value.* Boston, MA: Harvard Business School Press.

Richter, W., Burke, F., & Doig, J. (1990). *Combating corruption/encouraging ethics: Sourcebook for PA ethics.* Washington, DC: American Society for Public Administration.

Rohr, J. A. (1988). *Ethics for bureaucrats* (2nd ed.). New York: Marcel Dekker.

Rousseau, D. (1995). *Psychological contracts in organizations: Understanding written and unwritten agreements.* Thousand Oaks, CA: Sage.

Salamon, L. M., & Elliott, O. V. (2002). *The tools of government: A guide to the new governance.* Oxford: Oxford University Press.

Schwab, S. (2001). Predicting the future of employment law: Reflecting or refracting market forces? *Indiana Law Journal, 29*, 31–48.

Stone, K. (2004). *From widgets to digits: Employment regulation for the changing workplace.* Cambridge: Cambridge University Press.

Sulieman, E. (2003). *Dismantling democratic states.* Princeton, NJ: Princeton University Press.

Svara, J. (1997). The ethical triangle: Synthesizing the bases of administrative ethics. In J. Bowman (Ed.), *Public integrity annual* (pp. 33–41). Lexington, KY: Council of State Governments.

Truss, C., & Gratton, L. (1997). Soft and hard models of human resource management: A reappraisal. *Journal of Management Studies, 34*, 53–73.

Underhill, J., & Oman, R. (2006). A critical review of the sweeping federal civil service changes. *Review of Public Personnel Administration, 27*, 401–420.

Walters, J. (2002). *Life after civil service reform: The Texas, Georgia, and Florida experiences.* Arlington, VA: IBM Endowment for the Business of Government.

Werhane, P. (1985). *Persons, rights, and corporations.* Englewood Cliffs, NJ: Prentice Hall.

Werhane, P., Radin, T., & Bowie, N. (2004). *Employment and employee rights.* Malden, MA: Blackwell.

West, J. (2013). Employee-friendly policies and development benefits for millennials. In R. Sims & W. Sauser (Eds.), *Managing human resources from the millennial generation* (pp. 201–228). Charlotte, NC: Information Age Press.

West, J., & Bowman, J. (2004). Stakeholder analysis of civil service reform in Florida: A descriptive, instrumental, normative human resource management perspective. *State and Local Government Review, 36*, 20–34.

14 Open Government Case Study

Pay Disclosure

People in power gravitate toward the comfort and efficiency of secrecy.

—Tom O'Hara

Since the founding of the country, the First Amendment freedom and right to know information about government has been fundamental to the American political system.[1] "A popular government without popular information or the means of acquiring it," James Madison wrote (1865, 276), "is but a Prologue to a Farce or a Tragedy, or perhaps both." Open government laws shed light on decision making by mandating that meetings and governmental documents be readily accessible. The state of California legislation says it best:

> The people in delegating authority do not give their public servants the right to decide what is good for the people to know and what is not good for them to know. The people insist on remaining informed so that they may retain control over the instruments they have created. (Emerson, Menkus, & Van Ness, 2011, 70)

The result of open government measures can ensure transparency, encourage citizens to be well informed, and safeguard against corruption.

This chapter examines state legislation that discloses public employee salary information. It asks, "Is compensation disclosure legislation ethical?" The ethics triad introduced in Chapter 7 and used in Chapter 13 is used to analyze this question. Objectives include an understanding of:

- the importance of the problem,
- its evolution and current status,
- the ethics of salary disclosure, and
- the implications of the findings.

TRENDS AND TENSIONS IN OPEN GOVERNMENT

Today, all states have legal measures specifying varying degrees of transparency in government meetings and records. One component of this legislation is disclosure of civil servant compensation. Although a traditional, if mercurial, source of news stories (most notably during gubernatorial transitions), public records and salary information issues have received renewed attention in recent years for a variety of reasons.

First, technological advances have afforded Internet access to nearly all government employee compensation records in many states. Among the implications of this development are forms of criminal behavior like identity theft and abusive uses such as "fishing expeditions," intimidation of political adversaries, and the chilling of free speech ("Using Open-Records," 2011). Second, the dramatic expansion of outsourcing since the turn of the century raises questions about contractor remuneration (a government function may suddenly go "dark", while contractual requirements may include inspections for legal compliance, inspections are rare, pre-announced, or perfunctory). Third, revelations of outsized employee salaries in the small city of Bell, California, have been a catalyst in the larger, ongoing argument over public sector pay and benefits (Vives & Gottlieb, 2010).

Fourth, national security threats such as terrorist attacks and arguably WikiLeaks have sparked discussion over availability of records (such as building plans and airport documents). Fifth, lavish executive salaries and bonuses in the private sector (along with Security and Exchange Commission pay disclosure guidelines for publically traded companies) have contributed to compensation as a prominent societal issue. Finally, citizens are voicing increasing concern over their right to privacy and the involuntary sharing of personal data in today's "information age."

Indeed, a longstanding social norm is to keep pay information private (Bierman & Gely, 2004). This "code of silence" derives from American individualism and privacy rights, rendering discussion of wages a sensitive topic. It may be, in fact, the "last taboo" in an otherwise "tell-all" culture, as earnings can represent a person's value to an organization, societal prestige, and, sadly, perhaps even self-worth. One indication of the problem *Business Week* discovered is that "almost no one agreed to be named [in its article], citing company policy, legal concerns, or simple propriety ("Mind if I Peek," 2007, 3).

The extent to which pecuniary information is confidential is a foundational issue because citizens have ultimate control over the provision of public services in a democracy. Nonetheless, there may be no simple answers to whether salary disclosure is beneficial to employees, organizations, and the populace. Employee morale, pay satisfaction, privacy rights, workforce stability, workplace harmony, compensation management, and citizen trust are among the concerns that suggest there is no single right or wrong approach. Some of the same evidence can be used by both advocates and opponents of government in the sunshine.

As a result, the issue of pay disclosure is subject to debate and revision to the point that advocates claim that the effectiveness of open government legislation has been eroded in some jurisdictions (McLendon & Hearn, 2006, 648). In fact, the *Tampa Bay Times* referred to Florida governor Rick Scott as the "prince of darkness" for his alleged lack of respect for the constitutional rights of state citizens (Nickens, 2011).[2] The issue is also controversial at the national level, President Barack Obama's pledge to run the most transparent administration in history and his instructions to federal departments on his first day in office to "adopt a presumption in favor of disclosure" notwithstanding. Transparency advocates think that there is a substantial gap between the performance and rhetoric on the part of the administration (Ellington, 2013). Not only has the Obama administration released fewer records under the Freedom of Information Act than during the George W. Bush administration, but it even censored 192 pages of email messages involving its Open Government Directive (Ornstein & Limor, 2011).

Disclosure, then, reflects an inherent tension between desirable but competing goals—governmental accountability, individual rights, and an agency's mandate to fulfill its public function (Cleveland, 1985). Thus, at any one time or place, transparency laws represent the state of concern about pay disclosure and privacy rights in government. The discussion continues with the background to the problem, including its evolution and present status. After describing the method of analysis, the central part of the text evaluates the ethics of disclosing employee pay. The conclusion explores the implications of the findings.

BACKGROUND: INCREASING DEMAND FOR TRANSPARENCY

Although the nation's founders emphasized the need for open government, more than a century would pass before it became the subject of legislation. This section briefly traces the development of open pay systems, contrasts them with closed systems, and places these differing approaches in the context of contemporary civil service reform.

As part of the Progressive Era, Florida was one of the first states to enact sunshine legislation, which remains the "gold standard" in this policy arena. In 1909, the state legislature passed Public Records Law (Chapter 119, Florida Statutes) that became a model in a national campaign for open records. The act determined that government department records created in the course of business would be available for inspection; it did not define public record or specify what agencies were subject to the law. By the 1960s, and in the wake of historic legislative reapportionment, the state legislature approved the 1967 Government-in-the-Sunshine Law (Chapter 286, Florida Statutes), another landmark open government law that expanded the provisions of open records statutes and another for open meetings. Half of the states followed suit, requiring government documents and meetings be made open to the public (McLendon & Hearn, 2006, 646).

Scandals and corruption during the 1970s' Watergate era resulted in reforms focusing on accountability through transparency. All remaining states adopted "sunshine measures" or strengthened existing legislation. Each open government law contains provisions on purpose, coverage, definitions, exemptions, executive sessions, and sanctions (Cleveland, 1985). These measures remain in every state's constitution, laws—or both—to help ensure that public good rather than private gain is a factor in decision making (McLendon & Hearn, 2006, 647).

Considerable differentiation exists among the states. These differences include such critical matters as exemptions to the law (there are over 1,100 in Florida), remedies for violations, variations in implementation, the extent of privatization of public functions, as well as the sometimes burdensome problems associated with formal freedom-of-information applications. The net result, according to McLendon and Hearn (2006, 649–650), is that audits of this legislation have found "widespread ignorance" of the law and "widespread non-compliance" with information requests. In Florida, attorneys general and state courts have broadly construed open meeting and public document laws, and citizens have twice amended the state Constitution to reinforce their support for open government. Yet Weitzel (2006, 138) pointedly acknowledges that the state has experienced "frequent and often quite innovative efforts to skirt the law."

Despite diversity among states, a general consensus prevails that citizens should have access to information on how government spends their money, that civil servants work for the public and therefore the people have a right to know how their taxes are spent. This idea is echoed in a website approved by Florida's Governor Rick Scott (www.floridahasarighttoknow.com) that provides links to searchable databases with information about contracts and state spending, payroll, and pensions.

If the public service represents one end of a pay disclosure–secrecy continuum, then the private sphere anchors the other end. With the exception of executive compensation for stock exchange-listed companies (and similar requirements by the Internal Review Service for nonprofit organizations), pay secrecy is the longstanding practice in business. This secrecy is preserved despite National Labor Relations Board and federal court decisions' consistent rulings that such confidentiality rules and norms are an unfair—and illegal—labor practice (Colella et al., 2007; Gely & Bierman, 2003–2004). DeNisi and Griffin (2008) suggest a gradual movement toward disclosure is taking place as online salary surveys make strict confidentiality difficult. With limited reporting, secrecy remains a "fact of life" in the corporate world (Bohlander & Snell, 2010, 417).

Many companies practice confidentiality, sometimes to the point of forbidding managers from discussing their pay with co-workers. Compensation is treated as proprietary information and a source of competitive advantage. Secrecy arguably contributes to the manageability of the compensation function and recognizes the inevitable subjectivity of salary decisions. Less-than-perfect performance and pay systems mean that, although transparency is a laudable goal, confidentiality can be socially beneficial for an organization and its employees (Bierman & Gely, 2004; Edwards, 2005).

Against this backdrop of private and public sector pay practices, the role of government and the character of public service have been the subject of controversy in civil service reforms (Kellough & Nigro, 2006). Protagonists hold competing views on the appropriate administrative doctrine—the guardian model (a politically neutral, merit-based, impartial career bureaucracy) vs. the politico model (a politically sensitive, patronage-based, partisan noncareer bureaucracy). The guardian approach reflects the Wilsonian dichotomy separating politics from administration, the hallmark of orthodox public administration. Part of this philosophy is open government laws, a method to safeguard the merit principles by insulating civil servants from manipulation and protecting the public from corruption.

The politico strategy, common to business practices, emphasizes managerial discretion and flexibility, on the one hand, and employee performance and responsiveness, on the other. Arguing that there is no merit in the merit system (Condrey & Maranto, 2001; Ingraham, 2006), the New Public Management and governmental reform movements introduced commercial values into public service, increased the number of political appointees, eroded civil service protections, and hollowed out agencies by privatizing their management functions (Bowman & West, 2007). This reform philosophy, while not publicly rejecting transparency, regards open government laws as constraints on organizational efficiency and management control that tend to thwart effective decision making.

To summarize, the compensation function can be viewed along a pay disclosure–secrecy continuum. With Florida leading the way, all states have open government laws and some level of pay disclosure to foster an accountable government. In contrast, secrecy is common in business, where it is often regarded as generally desirable and supported by employers as well as employees (Bohlander & Snell, 2010, 417). Contemporary civil service reform debates over the guardian and politico administrative doctrines inform these two approaches—disclosure vs. secrecy—to sunshine legislation. As indicated at the outset, such legislation not only embodies abstract rights in conflict but also increasingly sparks debate in practice.

APPLYING THE ETHICS TRIAD TO PAY DISCLOSURE

Substantial impediments to examining open government laws exist in all 50 states—the obstacles are as "daunting as they are logistically complex, financially burdensome, and labor intensive" (McLendon & Hearn, 2006, 679). In the absence of a centralized data clearinghouse, a baseline analysis of these laws in the aggregate is provided here. Because ethics is often overlooked or submerged into other decision-making criteria, an exploration of the ethical ramifications of these statutes is useful. Employing the analytical technique discussed below, the evaluation draws on existing, widely scattered research. This material, as well as the Florida experience, was discussed with five Florida subject-matter experts representing the state executive branch, the legislature, employee unions, public interest groups, and the press in semi-structured, 45- to 60-minute interviews. A small convenience judgment sample of four rank-and-file state employees—the actual subjects of transparency laws—was contacted for examples of how these statutes affected them (they requested anonymity).

While a variety of decision-making models could illuminate whether or not open government laws are ethical, one is particularly helpful because its comprehensive scope reduces the chances of an incomplete assessment. This tool, introduced in Chapter 7, recognizes the competing emphases of three schools of thought based on (1) expected results of an action (consequentialism or teleology), (2) application of pertinent rules (duty ethics or deontology), and (3) personal rectitude or character (virtue ethics). It follows that this ethics trinity can furnish a balanced, defensible evaluation derived from consideration of results, rules, and virtues. Variations and further claims of the three approaches are knowingly subordinated, as noted below, in the interests of parsimony and clarity.

Each of the three schools provides a lens to clarify and reframe different aspects of a dilemma conundrum. Employing Ockham's Razor (use the simplest possible explanation and only make it more complex if absolutely necessary) to cut to the essence of an argument, three queries can be posed. Considering results, the question is, "Which policy produces the greatest good for the greatest number?" Contemplating ethical rules, the issue is, "Would I want everyone else to make the same decision that I did?" Pondering the virtue ethics vantage point, one asks, "What would a person of integrity do?" An overemphasis on one school, at the expense of the other approaches, risks expediency (results-based ethics), rigid rule application (rule-based ethics), and self-justification (virtue-based ethics). In view of the limits of the individual approaches, it is apparent that this eclectic method can be worthwhile.

Although the analysis may not provide conclusive answers, it provides direction by evaluating the logic by which decisions are explained. Individual ethical theories may lead to different evaluations of pay disclosure legislation, but these differences must be assessed, not passed over. Neither pay openness nor secrecy is obviously good or bad, as both strategies can be, and are, problematic. Disclosure of employee salaries will be analyzed using the three perspectives presented.

Results-Based Analysis

In consequentialism, the best policy produces "the greatest good for the greatest number." What is right is that which creates the largest amount of human happiness with the least harm. This approach is helpful for policymakers seeking the common good; government by, for, and of the people is used against this benchmark. Accordingly, consideration of salary disclosure examines affirmative and negative arguments on the grounds of (a) efficiency, (b) responsibility, (c) merit, and (d) public trust.

In Support of Disclosure. Advocates believe that these statutes increase *efficiency* by promoting civil service professionalism, as well as by reducing employee manipulation, employer favoritism, and organizational corruption. They also believe that transparency laws support pay equity, motivation, and productivity (Futrell & Jenkins, 1978; Longnecker & Krueger, 2007). Consistent with equity theory and performance pay (Snell & Bohlander, 2010), when pay is viewed as a proxy for ability, productive individuals will earn superior compensation and thereby encourage others to strive for reward.

Openness reminds officials that they work for the people and effectiveness of government is therefore improved by increasing *responsibility* and accountability to the citizenry (Johnson & Libecap, 1995). Former long-term Florida legislative staffer Ray Wilson emphasized that public sector transactions are involuntary (whereas in business, they are usually voluntary) and, it follows, "are the people's business" (personal communication, November 17, 2010). Modern *merit* principles shield employees from abuse; transparency laws serve a vital public interest by enhancing *trust* in government. By promoting the democratic ideals described, disclosure laws help maintain citizen faith in democracy.

In the absence of these statutes, secrecy provides a basis for suspicion that the organization has something to conceal. As Florida Department of Children and Families Secretary

Bob Butterworth stated, "We have nothing to hide, but more importantly we should have nothing to hide" (Gleason, 2007, 46). Openness can create confidence in and acceptance of the governing process. Without it, citizen participation in governance will be compromised and self-government jeopardized.

A significant public need, then, exists for a transparent civil service as a key element of popular government. The lesson is clear: "When a person agrees to be a public servant . . . the public gains access to information related to that person's salary" (Swanson, 2006, 1595). According to Pat Gleason, special counsel to the governor of Florida, "the people hire you to work for the public; if you think the money belongs to you, then work in business" (personal communication, November 23, 2010). The general counsel for the First Amendment Foundation, echoes Gleason, stating, "If you work for government, you may have a state constitutional right to privacy, but not for information in public records" (J. P. Rhea, personal communication, November 23, 2010).

In Opposition to Disclosure. The assumption that open systems foster good government is that there are few, if any, benefits to confidentiality. A different approach is to weigh open systems against the advantages of closed systems using the efficiency, responsibility, merit, and trust criteria.

First, closed systems facilitate control requirements for orderly personnel management. While there currently may be little or no legal or policy debate about salary disclosure, Pat Gleason believes that salary disclosure presents a difficult management challenge (personal communication, November 23, 2010). Disclosure leads to morale problems, job dissatisfaction, and staff turnover, thereby affecting *efficiency* (Colella et al., 2007). Stressing access to information at the expense of other important values can erode the purpose of sunshine laws—good government and good decision making. Second, for leaders to be *responsible*, they need the freedom to act, unfettered by the negative results of disclosure. Arguments over salary generate conflict, making it difficult to reward performance in the public interest. As Case (2001, 43) observes, "The problem isn't that the (salary) disparities *aren't* justified; it's the ones that *are*."

There are ample *merit* system protections and legal requirements in place (e.g., financial disclosure statutes, "just cause" dismissal procedures, grievance arbitration, union protection, and federal legislation) to avoid abuses that might come from closed pay systems. It is unnecessary to infringe on privacy rights of civil servants, making them second-class citizens. Not only does government lose people who wish not to have their rights negated, but society is also denied the contributions that they could make. Indeed, in their pursuit of good government, sunshine advocates exploit the hostile public stereotypes of bureaucrats and politicians.

The public's attitude toward information disclosure may be explained by the belief that government is the agent of their interests and they have a right to know how it distributes funding. Yet in a democratic republic, if legislators can act as trustees, then the need for unfettered access to information may be limited. Likewise, government auditors, charged with safeguarding the common interest, diminish the need for access to all information. Thus, public *trust* is increased when corporate-style, bottom-line standards are met.

Conversely, it may well be diminished when citizens have access to the sometimes execrable nature of policymaking. Cynicism can easily result. Accomplishing policy goals is also problematic if leaders are hampered by laws that limit leverage over subordinates. Absent such leverage, it is more difficult to serve the citizenry and earn their confidence. If abuse is the danger, then appropriate penalties should be established rather than depriving citizen-employees their rights. In brief, secrecy norms, "make both practical and economic sense" (Bierman & Gely, 2004, 191) in serving the greatest good.

Yet an overemphasis on any single approach may put a policy at risk. Open government advocates may assume that they have found the common good for the majority of citizens—at the expense of a minority. And closed government supporters may think that the greatest good is found in secrecy, but perhaps because it is merely expedient. Accordingly, attention now shifts to another school of thought.

Rule-Based Analysis

Rule-based decision making provides a different lens for evaluating public employee salary disclosure. Certain actions are inherently right (e.g., promise keeping) or wrong (e.g., inflicting harm), irrespective of predicted consequences; the end does not justify the means. What is right is what conforms to moral rules; one must see one's duty and do it. In deciding what rule to apply, the person asks, "Would I want everyone else to do what I did?" (Stated differently, "What is good for one is good for all.") The approach is useful for administrators who are obligated to follow the principles found in the Constitution, court cases, and laws and regulations (Rohr, 1988). Here the emphasis is on principles such as (a) fairness and (b) the commonweal in examining competing positions on pay systems.

In Support of Disclosure. Advocates hope to foster fair treatment of personnel and avoid capricious actions that further special interests at the expense of the public. Disclosure results in greater *fairness* for both employees and citizens by establishing safeguards to avoid untoward practices that harm civil servants and undermine citizen confidence. It provides a check on administrative prerogatives, while enabling the equitable allocation of resources and delivery of services. Indeed American Federation of State, County, and Municipal Employees representative Douglas Martin pointed out that "disclosure of employee salaries helps us make our case that state employees are underpaid" (personal communication, November 19, 2010).

Salary plan secrecy, in contrast, is a form of managerial control hampering the ability of personnel from being informed and empowered. For example, "Secrecy norms," as Edwards (2005, 59) found, "lead workers to believe that they have fewer legal rights than the law actually affords." Not enforcing sunshine legislation, and permitting employers to evade it, is an affront to the rule of law. Confidentiality feeds dissatisfaction, low motivation, and distrust (Colella et al., 2007) because it treats employees like children—they do not know what determines their salaries: chance, mistakes, or bias. This paternalistic approach denies adults accurate information about an important dimension of their work life.

Instead, people should be shown respect; what should be good for one should be good for all. If individuals are treated as ends in themselves, and never as means, then they should know what policies are implemented in their name. Secrecy as a universal principle has no place in democracy; as such it represents a violation of the *commonweal*. Pay confidentiality policies, in fact, may play a part in sex discrimination, which is one impetus for the oft-proposed (and House of Representatives-passed) Paycheck Fairness Act aimed at strengthening the federal 1963 Equal Pay Act.

In Opposition to Disclosure. Disclosure of salaries often overreaches, and is neither *fair* nor *necessary* in the name of the commonweal. Confidentiality may be preferred not only by employers (who understand clearly the discretion it provides) but also by employees (who wish to avoid embarrassment and invidious comparisons). Both find that job satisfaction may decrease and conflict increase with disclosure (Colella et al., 2007) as jealousy, resentment, humiliation, opportunism, and discontent can accompany the release of detailed pay information. This is shown below by discussing concerns involving between peers, position levels, and public and private sectors.

Regarding peer relationships, one female state employee experienced unwelcome conflict when traveling with co-workers to a departmental function (anonymous, personal communication, July 7, 2010). A colleague joked that she should "spring" for lunch since she "made more than everyone else in the car." The interviewee was quite uncomfortable because jokes can be rooted in resentment and have real consequences. A male worker had strong feelings of resentment toward peers on learning that his salary was less than theirs (anonymous, personal communication, July 2010). Finally, Trina Vielhauer, an administrator, explains how managers today have severely limited ability to give promotions, which further frustrates those displeased with their pay in relation to others (personal communication, July 7–8, 2010).

Disclosure of salaries may also affect employees differently depending on the level of their position. The state employees and administrators interviewed typically agreed that for those in low pay grades disclosure negatively affected job satisfaction due to humiliation or embarrassment (anonymous, personal communication, July 7, 2010). Jessica Cherry, an agency employee relations official, stated that most discontent due to pay disclosure comes from rank-and-file positions, and rarely from administrative or professional positions (personal communication, July 9, 2010). Administrators Larry George and Trina Vielhauer agreed that management-level personnel feel less threatened and better understand inherent variability in salaries (personal communication, July 7–8, 2010).

A final issue to consider when questioning the fairness and *commonweal* considerations of transparent salaries is that private sector workers—many performing similar work to that of public employees—are allowed the full range of privacy rights, yet their governmental counterparts are not. For instance, while Article I, Section 23 of Florida's constitution reads, "Every natural person has the right to be let alone and free from governmental intrusion into his private life except as otherwise provided herein," the next sentence states, "This section shall not be construed to limit the public's right of access to public records and meetings as provided by law." Thus, while the privacy provision exists to protect individual rights, the constitution also includes a broad clause to limit that right to only those citizens that do not work for a public entity. This inconsistency and double standard in the language of the law suggests the commonweal is best served by treating all employees, public and private, in a like manner.

In short, real or perceived pay inequities between peers, position level, and economic sectors are a source of friction. People generally are made to feel worse off by disclosure because it points to their relative standing in the organization and society. Job satisfaction depends not only on one's absolute earnings, but also on how that pay compares to others (Moretti et al., 2010). "Inequality, rather than want, is the cause of trouble," according to an ancient Chinese saying.

To summarize briefly, disclosure advocates see an ethical duty to treat people as ends, not means to some supposed good. Applied to salary transparency, the duty is not to hide facts. Critics see broad and deep disclosure policies as creating unnecessary harm. Relying exclusively on rule-based analysis, however, may provide inadequate guidance and induce rigidity. Attention now turns to the final approach, virtue theory.

Virtue-Based Analysis

In virtue ethics (Chapter 6), answers to the question of "What to do?" have little to do with results or rules and everything to do with the kind of person one is. Personal character offers a third perspective when assessing the ethical advisability of open pay laws. It asks, "Does a proposed decision improve individual and community character?"

This philosophy is compelling for public administrators because it is a personal approach to ethics—decisions are informed not only by consequences and duties, but also by the quality of one's character. A decision maker may not be able to control circumstances, but can control character. What is right is that which nurtures individual excellence and contributes to collective well-being. Indeed, a person cannot be understood apart from the larger community in which he participates.

As noted earlier in the book, no definitive set of virtues exists. Virtue, as an excellence or trait, is found between the extremes of excess and deficiency. In every situation, the person will determine the mean—neither excessive nor deficient—based on reason and experience appropriate to the circumstance. Preeminent virtues—(a) integrity (a product or synthesis of virtues such as honesty, moderation, justice) and (b) prudence (the capacity to recognize moral challenges and respond)—are integral to moral nobility. Such individuals are guided by principles, not popularity or expedience.

In Support of Disclosure. The career civil service is clearly vulnerable to manipulation. In fact, scandals including coercion of personnel and misuse of authority were often the catalyst for sunshine legislation. Such laws are designed to show respect for employees (and citizens) by signaling that the first loyalty of public servants is to the constitution and its purposes—their *integrity* should not be put at risk by making them susceptible to political and administrative pressures. This enables personnel to exercise *prudent* judgment when advising officials and implementing public programs.

Open pay systems also evince concern for the welfare of civil servants, and the populace, by protecting them from abuse. In doing so, these laws help ensure integrity among those in public service and thereby promote accountability to voters and taxpayers. This can spur devotion to public purposes rather than special interests. In government, perceptions are crucial, and the "appearance of impropriety" standard is quite real. "Everything is presumptively open," said James Parker Rhea, general counsel for the First Amendment Foundation (personal communication, November 23, 2010). Thus, while sunshine statutes tend to focus on one aspect of public interest—the citizen right to know—it is "in the areas identified as exempt from openness requirements," Cleveland (1985, 9) notes, "that the other two elements of public interest (privacy and institutional mandates to serve the public interest) are acknowledged."

In Opposition to Disclosure. The separation between politics and administration is deeply ingrained in civil service. Merit principles are widely recognized as cardinal imperatives, ethics codes reinforce these principles, and organizational structures are developed to implement these principles. Statutory law and common law protections exist, often buttressed by union contracts. These various elements create overlapping requirements that satisfactorily protect civil servants, negating the need for disclosure. Rather than open government regulations that may be inequitably enforced, nurturing of *integrity* among employees through training and development may be more fruitful than pay disclosure initiatives.

Open government policies that have outlived their usefulness are no longer necessary or *prudent* without compelling evidence of abuse or wrongdoing. Indeed, many citizens have negative views of government workers as unresponsive, unproductive, and unaccountable. Nondisclosure helps to ensure that government personnel are responsive to the will of the people as determined by electoral results. To have political accountability, elected leaders need to be able to expect that public servants are loyal to the current administration's values and objectives. Because disclosure does not indicate if an employee is performing well, it does little that is constructive, and panders to voyeurism (hardly virtuous behavior) (Gomez & Wald, 2010, 118).

From a virtue ethics perspective, in short, open pay systems enhance the integrity and professionalism of employees by focusing attention on the general public interest. Alternatively, it can be argued that adequate protections already exist to avoid or correct abusive practices. Cultivating personal integrity through training and organization development is preferable to heavy-handed regulation and reliance on past policies that are no longer needed. Yet virtue theory's strength—subjective judgments inferred from personal character—is also its shortcoming—if supporters and opponents of pay disclosure perceive they are good, it is likely for them to think that what they do is good.

SUMMARY

States have had decades of experience with open government laws. While there is controversy over these laws, they are broadly accepted. Still, the popularity of salary disclosure legislation does not invariably imply that it is desirable or effective—neither openness nor secrecy is problem free. Indeed, recent shifts in administrative doctrine from the guardian model to the politico model call into question the fundamental underpinning of the public service and provide impetus for corporate-style management practices.

After examining each of the three philosophies in sequence, what, then, is the greatest good for the greatest number? As indicated, salary disclosure laws contribute to serving the greatest good by emphasizing efficiency, holding personnel responsible for meeting citizen needs, securing merit-based decision making, and fostering employee and citizen trust. A significant public need is seen for an open civil service as a key element of a majoritarian form of government. However, the analysis above also shows that secrecy norms can be quite sensible in seeking the greatest good. The claims of open government supporters, furthermore, are not sufficient to limit constitutional freedoms of one-sixth of the nation's workforce. Finally, the drawbacks of disclosure laws are borne by employees, while purported and speculative benefits accrue to the diffuse, indifferent public.

However complacent, the largest stakeholder is the citizenry. Closed government supporters suggest that productivity will soar when government is run like a business. Yet there is little documentation to substantiate this view, perhaps because productivity, morale, and loyalty may be placed in jeopardy if secrecy is the norm. In addition, government can adopt proven business tools such as competitive pay, teamwork and still operate "in the sunshine." A policymaker using result-based ethics may find confidentiality arguments attractive, but the greatest good is served by open government legislation.

The second approach, rule-based ethics, stipulates what is good for one is good for all. While some transparency laws overreach, they provide a check on administrative prerogatives while enabling the equitable allocation of resources and delivery of services. Secrecy is contrary to the principles of a democratic republic. It fails to uphold the public trust by denying information to employees and the public to make informed decisions. Salary plan secrecy is contrary to the rule of law and feeds dissatisfaction, low motivation, and distrust.

Finally, virtue ethics seeks individual excellence and collective well-being. There may be no easy answers based on results or rules; a person must act in a manner to enhance integrity and prudence. Open pay systems show concern for the welfare of civil servants by protecting them from abuse. In doing so, such laws help ensure integrity among those in public service and thereby promote accountability to voters and taxpayers. This can spur devotion to public purposes rather than special interests. Alternatively, cultivating personal integrity is preferable to heavy-handed regulation and reliance on outmoded policies that are no longer needed. Nondisclosure helps to ensure that government workers are responsive to the will of the people as determined by electoral results. To have political accountability, in fact, elected leaders need to be able to expect that public servants are loyal to the current administration's values and objectives.

CONCLUSION: IMPLEMENTING BALANCE IN TRANSPARENCY POLICY

Despite certain advantages, pay confidentiality is ethically problematic from results-, rule-, and virtue-based perspectives. To hold public authority is to be responsible for one's actions. Salary disclosure provides a check on moral responsibility of those in power to the benefit of both the employees and citizens. Open compensation systems encourage justifiable salary decisions and help personnel to better understand the agency's mission, why they earn what they do, and what they should do to earn more. In comparison, a closed pay system can compromise the greatest good, duty, and personal integrity. In so doing, closed government needlessly imperils a hallmark of modern democratic government—a professional civil service ethic.

Disclosure requirements applied across the board to all employees, with no distinction regarding the nature of the work or position involved, disregards important distinctions that deserve consideration. There are alternative ways to disclose salary data without revealing individual identities.

Releasing this information by position, not personal names, at least partially protects privacy and may also reduce conflict, especially for lower level staff (the same can be said for salary ranges or "pay bands"). Another alternative to full disclosure is to institute a threshold of $100,000, as in Ontario's Public Sector Salary Disclosure Act (Gomez & Wald, 2010). Publishing salaries above a certain amount would address concerns held by lower level staff, while still providing the citizen access to earnings of the high officials. This strategy would, however, keep the public from knowing the wages of most civil servants, thereby inviting opportunities for nepotism and cronyism.

This strategy also requires constant updating to adjust for inflation, unless (as Gomez and Wald suggest) the threshold is based on a ratio of salaries from the top of the pay distribution, not a static salary amount. These solutions would require changes in law and may be difficult to implement because adding exemptions requires rulemaking changes which can sometimes be contentious and arduous, and assumes political support.

A third approach, perhaps used in combination with the above strategies, removes the exclusive focus on salary. McGregor states, "Although money has only limited value in satisfying many higher level needs, it can become the focus of interest if it is the *only* means available" (in Handel, 2003, 111). He identifies the various needs people seek to be met, including physiological, safety, social, ego, and self-fulfillment needs.

Possible avenues to motivate employees beyond pay, accordingly, include giving meaningful rewards and recognition, providing opportunities for challenge and training, creating a cooperative and friendly workplace environment, giving interesting assignments, and offering feedback focused on development. Focusing on motivation can not only potentially reduce discontent, but also mitigate issues of retention and productivity as well for all employees. If an agency is an exciting, engaging place to work, pay concerns, while certainly not unimportant, become secondary to getting the job done.

Due to the inevitable tensions in attempting to serve the public interest, Cleveland (1985) posits signal principles to guide policymaking: (a) community interests should supersede those of any one of its parts, (b) there should be a presumption of openness, and (c) while openness is key, it is only one element, in addition to privacy and institutional mandates to achieve their mission, that must be taken into account. It is evident that public interest and openness currently supersede other important values such as personal privacy and workplace harmony. Stated differently, what may be desirable in principle can be problematic in practice. What may work in practice, however, may be guided by three conditions. Open salary policies work best when (1) individual and group performance can be measured objectively, (2) performance measures can be developed for all job duties, and (3) effort and performance are related closely over short time periods (Cascio, 2009).

NOTES

1. This chapter is adapted from Bowman and Stevens (2012). Used with permission.
2. Despite an executive order on the first day of office re-establishing the Office of Open Government launched by his predecessor, Governor Scott acknowledged that he does not use email for work correspondence (because he does not want to create public records), reveal who accompanies him in his private plane, or make known who visits him at the governor's mansion. He also cancelled public records workshops in state government. His relations with the press corps are strained for a variety of similar reasons.

FOR DISCUSSION

1. Open government issues have become particularly prominent in recent years. This chapter identifies six reasons to explain the phenomenon. Critically analyze that discussion by adding, modifying, or replacing selected reasons. Hint: The analysis of the causes of corruption in Chapter 9 may be helpful.

2. Is open government legislation effective?

3. Compare and contrast public and private sector approaches to salary management.

4. Is salary information "the last taboo"? If so, why?

5. Identify and examine competing values at stake in pay disclosure.

6. What is the most compelling result, rule, or virtue argument for disclosure? Against disclosure? Identify behavioral ethics concepts that help illuminate this case.

7. Is it necessary for the salary disclosure laws to reveal individual identities?

8. Thomas Cooper said, "Fraud and falsehood only dread examination. Truth invites it." Discuss this claim in the context of open government initiatives.

EXERCISE

1. Preview Exercise 2—creating a personal plan for future ethical development—found in the next chapter.

REFERENCES

Bierman, L., & Gely, R. (2004). Love, sex and politics? Sure. Salary? No way: Workplace social norms and the law. *Berkeley Journal of Employment & Labor Law, 25,* 167–192.

Bohlander, G., & Snell, S. (2010). *Managing human resources* (15th ed.). Mason, OH: South-Western Cengage Learning.

Bowman, J., & Stevens, K. (2012, May). Public pay disclosure in state government: An ethical analysis. *American Review of Public Administration, 43*, 476–492.

Bowman, J., & West, J. (2007). *American public service: Radical reform and the merit system.* New York: Taylor & Francis.

Cascio, W. (2009). *Managing human resources* (8th ed.). Boston, MA: McGraw-Hill/Irwin.

Case, J. (2001). When salaries aren't secret. *Harvard Business Review, 5*, 37–49.

Cleveland, H. (1985). *The costs and benefits of openness: Sunshine laws and higher education.* Washington, DC: Association of Governing Boards of Universities and Colleges.

Colella, A., Paetzold, R. I., Zardkoohi, A., & Wesson, M. J. (2007). Exposing pay secrecy. *Academy of Management Review, 32*, 55–71.

Condrey, S., & Maranto, R. (Eds.). (2001). *Radical reform in the civil service.* New York: Lexington Books.

DeNisi, A., & Griffin, R. (2008). *Human resource management.* Boston, MA: Houghton-Mifflin.

Edwards, M. A. (2005). The law and social norms of pay secrecy. *Berkeley Journal of Employment & Labor Law, 26*, 41–64.

Ellington, T. (2013). The most transparent administration in history? An assessment of official secrecy in the Obama administration's first term. *Public Integrity, 15*, 133–148.

Emerson, S., Menkus, R., & Van Ness, K. (2011). *Public administrator's companion.* Washington, DC: CQ Press.

Futrell, C. M., & Jenkins, O. C. (1978). Pay secrecy versus pay disclosure for salesmen: A longitudinal study. *Journal of Marketing Research, 15*(2), 214–219.

Gely, R., & Bierman, L. (2003–2004). Pay secrecy/confidentiality rules and the National Labor Relations Act. *University of Pennsylvania Journal of Labor and Employment Law, 6*, 121–156.

Gleason, P. (2007). Public disclosure: A founding principle that boosts accountability today. *Journal of the James Madison Institute, 40*, 44–47.

Gomez, R., & Wald, S. (2010). When public-sector salaries become public knowledge: Academic salaries and Ontario's Public Sector Salary Disclosure Act. *Canadian Public Administration, 53*, 107–126.

Handel, M. J. (2003). *The sociology of organizations: Classic, contemporary, and critical readings.* Thousand Oaks, CA: Sage.

Ingraham, P. (2006). Building bridges over troubled waters: Merit as a guide. *Public Administration Review, 66*, 486–495.

Johnson, R. N., & Libecap, G. D. (1995). Courts, a protected bureaucracy, and reinventing government. *Arizona Law Review, 37*, 791.

Kellough, J. & Nigro, L. (Eds.). (2006). *Civil service reform in the states.* Albany, NY: SUNY Press.

Longnecker, B., & Krueger, J. (2007). The next wave of compensation disclosure. *Compensation and Benefits Review, 39*(1), 50–54.

Madison, J. (1865). Letter to W. T. Barry, August 4, 1822. In P. R. Fendall (Ed.), *Letters and other writings of James Madison* (Vol. 3, p. 276). Philadelphia: Lippinott.

McLendon, M. K., & Hearn, J. C. (2006). Mandated openness in public higher education: A field study of state sunshine laws and institutional governance. *Journal of Higher Education, 77,* 645–685.

Mind if I peek at your paycheck? (2007, June 18). *Business Week.* Retrieved from http://www.businessweek.com/stories/2007-06-17/mind-if-i-peek-at-your-paycheck

Moretti, E., Card, D., Mas, A., & Saez, E. (2010). *Inequality, peer salary disclosure, and job satisfaction: Evidence from the field.* Unpublished manuscript, University of California, Berkeley.

Nickens, T. (2011, March 27). The prince of darkness. *Tampa Bay Times.* Retrieved from http://www.tampabay.com/opinion/columns/the-prince-of-darkness/1159632

Ornstein, C., & Limor, H. (2011, March 31). Where's the transparency that Obama promised? *Washington Post.* Retrieved from http://www.washingtonpost.com/opinions/wheres-the-transparency-that-obama-promised/2011/03/31/AFipwHCC_story.html

Rohr, J. (1988). *Ethics for bureaucrats* (2nd ed.). New York: Marcel Dekker.

Snell, S., & Bohlander, G. W. (2010). *Principles of human resource management.* Mason, OH: South-Western Cengage Learning.

Swanson, K. (2006). The right to know: An approach to gun licenses and public access to government records. *UCLA Law Review, 56,* 1579–1628.

Using open-records laws to harass scholars. (2011, April 1). *Washington Post.* Retrieved from http://www.washingtonpost.com/opinions/using-open-records-laws-to-harass-scholars/2011/04/01/AFLInHXC_story.html

Vives, R., & Gottlieb, J. (2010, July 23). 3 Bell leaders to quit in pay scandal. *Los Angeles Times.* Retrieved from http://articles.latimes.com/print/2010/jul/23/local/la-me-bell-council-20100723

Weitzel, P. (2006). *The white paper: A narrative history of open government in Florida.* Tallahassee, FL: First Amendment Foundation. www.flordafaf.org

PART V

Future History

15 Choices and Strategies for the Years Ahead

It's an unnerving thought that we may be living the universe's supreme achievement and its worst nightmare simultaneously.

—Bill Bryson

Parts I–IV of the book have asked questions more than they have provided answers. Since it is better to know some of the questions than all the answers, the intent was to offer frameworks to raise important concerns. There is not a rule for everything; the core of ethical behavior is to learn how to act when no rule exists. Even when there is a standard, there may not be an unambiguous way to decide how to act on it. All an ethics text can do is leave readers with an understanding that they are moral agents, that they understand as much about honor as about rules, and that their choices in the public, private, and nonprofit workplace are between moral grandeur and decay, between civilization and barbarism. The key to praiseworthy action is knowing how to handle free will to expand ethical and reduce unethical behavior. This final chapter illustrates how to proceed by:

- comprehending moral grandeur using four transcendental dimensions of life,
- recognizing moral decay and confronting it by understanding ignominious behavior,
- developing guidelines to expand exemplary conduct in the future, and
- reinforcing the nature of the ethical professional.

MORAL GRANDEUR

Each day provides its own gifts.

—Marcus Aurelius

If Aristotle Ran General Motors by Tom Morris (1997) is not really about the Greek philosopher or one of the nation's largest corporations. But the title does effectively convey the symbolism of each—what might happen if four foundations of the human experience were used to run a modern organization? The book urges conscious recognition of the philosophical elements that enrich life. The four components are intellectual (truth), aesthetic (beauty), moral (goodness), and spiritual (unity) in character. These constituent dimensions produce individual and organizational excellence, and permit human flourishing so as to make the world a better place.[1]

Truth—disturbing or comforting—is the basis of all relationships. One must be true to self and in interactions with others. Believing in something is not the same as knowing something. As philosopher Soren Kierkegaard observed, "There are two ways to be fooled. One is to believe what isn't true; the other is to refuse to believe what is." There is no greater source of waste than speculation, gossip, and rumor that arise in the absence of truth. Nothing inspires people more than the truth.

Despite its elemental significance, "The simplest truths," Frederick Douglass observed, "often meet with sternest resistance and are slowest in getting general acceptance." Indeed, according to Arthur Schopenhauer, all truth must pass through three stages: "[F]irst it is ridiculed, second it is violently opposed, and third it is accepted as being self-evident." The classic example of the process of accepting a new truth is the earth-as-the-center-of-the-universe theory. For centuries, people were reluctant to abandon their beliefs about the nature of reality. Yet humanity cannot flourish without challenging ideas; without truth, progress perishes. Openness to transcendence is what distinguishes the disciplined process of inquiry and dialogue, a dynamic conversation that tests old conclusions and develops new ones (Palmer, 2007, 106, 109).

The world is too dangerous for anything except the truth. "Post-truth politics"—when feeling and emotions trump objective facts—reveals a profound contempt for democratic life by eroding the ability to distinguish veracity from falsehood. To govern is to choose; citizens must be up to the task of discernment. Engaging in fact-based deliberations and embracing democratic norms is a minimum standard for governance. The problem with the truth is that people are afraid of it and it is easier to lie. Liars attempt to deceive not only themselves, but also others; in the process, reality becomes increasingly distorted, so that decisions are corrupted.

It is better to deal with an ugly truth—to live authentically and responsibly—than mollified by a beautiful lie. Truth can set, and keep, you free—but only if there is the moral courage to use it (Chapter 5). "If you tell the truth," writes Charles Gordon, "you have infinite power supporting you; but if not, you have infinite power against you." It takes seconds to be honest and costs nothing. One of the beauties of truth is that it does not require many words to speak it. A lie takes time and effort, and costs everything when exposed. It is better, it follows, to admit mistakes before someone else exaggerates them.[2]

While essential, truth is not sufficient for fulfillment, since humans are not mere intellects. They must also have something attractive to motivate them—beauty. There is nothing, it has been said, that makes its way more directly to the soul than beauty. Like the need for truth, the experience of beauty is universal. Beauty, in fact, is the result of truth. The "beauty of beauty" is all around us. The aesthetic dimension includes not only external observational beauty (as in a sunset), but also internal performance beauty (e.g., excellent work); both are a "thing of beauty," a masterpiece, a way to evoke the best in people.

Ralph Waldo Emerson says it best: "We ascribe beauty to that which is simple; which has no superfluous parts; which exactly answers its end; which stands related to all things; which is the mean of many extremes." Beauty liberates, refreshes, inspires, and thereby nurtures well-being. "Everybody needs beauty," John Muir wrote, "as well as bread, place to play in and pray in, where nature may heal and give strength to body and soul." Human flourishing releases great energy. In contrast, ugliness depresses the spirit. Badly done work is rarely rewarding. If people are to do a good job, they must feel they have a good job, career, or better, a higher calling (see below).

Doing true, beautiful work, however, is incomplete, Morris (1997) argues. That which is beautiful is not always good, but that which is good is always beautiful. Leaders must be convinced of the essential goodness of what they are doing. Unethical work can be done with exquisite deception, just as data can be manipulated well but fraudulently. Goodness might be considered a special kind of truth and beauty—it is how humanity values itself. Paradoxically, humans are the only species capable of ethical awareness—and, therefore, also capable of ignoring that awareness. People are at their finest when engaged in a worthy task, one in which they can make a genuine difference, doing a job that the world needs done and one that they want to do. True goodness is attained through fidelity to a worthwhile purpose. It is better to suffer for doing good than for doing wrong.

As John Wesley writes in *Rules for Doing Good*, "Do all the good you can, in all the ways that you can, to all the people you can, in every place you can, at all the times you can, as long as you can." For the administrator, service to the public is the place to start. Doing right things right includes both effectiveness (doing the right thing) and efficiency (doing things right). To paraphrase Socrates, the source of good is knowledge and the source of evil is ignorance.

Truth, beauty, and goodness are still not enough, as humans must feel they are a part of something greater than themselves. Not content with knowing what they are doing, they must also know why they are working. Matters of spirit are intertwined with truth, beauty, goodness—the worth of person and the community to which she belongs. What is needed is a sense of the majesty of creation and the ability to be respectful in its presence. The Athenian Oath from ancient Greece, taken by all 17-year-old citizens, captures the idea of truth, beauty, goodness, and community of the human spirit:

> We will ever strive for the ideals and sacred things of the city, both alone
> and with many;
> we will unceasingly seek to quicken the sense of public duty;
> we will revere and obey the city's laws;
> we will transmit this city not only not less, but greater, better and more beautiful than
> it was transmitted to us.[3]

This oath constitutes a public spirit, ethic, and mission that are neither liberal nor conservative, neither Republican nor Democratic. Respecting the common welfare is less a method to make a decision and more a question to pose during the decision process to guide policymaking.

If Aristotle ran General Motors, he would foster integrity throughout the company by nourishing a culture based on the four transcendental values—truth, beauty, goodness, and unity. Living the ethical life centered on these values benefits the individual and organization. Practiced well, ethics distinguishes between the necessary and the secondary and the useful and the wasteful. Everyone in an organization must understand their role as a moral agent, believing anything worth doing is worth doing well. Transforming the organization—internalizing and institutionalizing the four dimensions of quality—is anyone and everyone's responsibility, but one that must be assumed by leaders (Morris, 1997). The keys to excellence lie before us; if things go wrong, do not go with them. Ethics is far more about creating strength than it is about avoiding trouble. "The difference between what we do and what we are capable of doing," Gandhi believed, "would suffice to solve most of the world's problems."

In fact, public service can be seen not simply as a job (a way to earn a living) or a career (a means for advancement), but as a calling (finding one's true place in the world). Philosophers have long proposed that well-being is the doorway to human flourishing, to come alive to the true meaning found in pursuits that command conviction and commitment in civic service. More than an employee, you are a public servant, a high calling indeed. "The only way to achieve success," Aristotle observed, "is to express yourself completely in service to society."

> Politics practiced well is the noblest of professions. No other arena requires as much wisdom, tenacity, foresight, and empathy. No other field places such stress on conversation and persuasion. The English word "idiot" comes from the ancient Greek word for the person who is uninterested in politics but capable only of running his or her own private life. (Brooks, 2017, August 1)

Public service is a means of preserving democracy, considered by many to be one of humankind's greatest achievements. Calling—that wonder from antiquity—gives voice by discerning purpose in what one does in government (see Bowman, 2011–2012). Service is something to be honored, not demeaned. The sustained demonization of government—a profoundly antidemocratic movement aimed at delegitimizing the American system—may prove to be unsustainable. At least in the long run, the service orientation of the millennial generation suggests that the public service is being revalued (Perry & Buckwalter, 2012), and that moral duty of politics is to appeal of our best instincts rather than our worst. In these times, nonetheless, it might be a mistake to believe that history is linear, moving gradually forward from past to present to a progressive, honorable future. Yet patriotism and integrity are what draw people to public service. Every employee who takes an "oath of office swears to protect the Constitution from all enemies, foreign and domestic. Rarely have those words echoed with more resonance than right now" (McEldowney, 2018, January 26).

MORAL DECAY

The best way to rob a bank is to own one.

—William K. Black

Internalizing the transcendental values into one's professional life is a challenging goal. Leaders in the public, private, and not-for-profit spheres all too frequently fail to rise to the task. While violent crimes have declined in the last decade, government—and particularly corporate—fraud, waste, and abuse have increased markedly (Chapter 9). The dollar amounts are substantial, and the types of untoward behavior have multiplied with the opportunities provided by the Internet (e.g., identity theft). This is at a time when the Federal Bureau of Investigation's white-collar crime unit has been cut back to emphasize the real, if more remote, threat of terrorism. To understand the nature of this problem, two issues are discussed here: (1) the nature of corporate, government, and nonprofit sector crime and (2) strategies managers can use to combat it.

The Nature of White-Collar Crime

Corporate. White-collar criminals in organizations inflict far more damage on society than all street crime combined (Chapter 9). As the *Corporate Crime Reporter* ("Twenty Things," 2007) states, "[W]hether in bodies or injuries or dollars lost, corporate crime and violence wins by a landslide." While neither the FBI nor the US Department of Justice keeps statistics on white-collar crime, what is known includes the following:

- Institutional crime is often "silent violence" as a result of criminal negligence involving occupational diseases, pollution, contaminated foods, hazardous consumer products, and hospital malpractice—yet deaths attributed to negligence are seldom prosecuted as homicides.
- Corporate violators are the only criminal class that lobbies and influences business laws to ensure that no legislation imposes criminal sanctions on knowing and willful violations of law.
- White-collar crime is under-prosecuted by a factor of approximately 100 (stated differently, prosecutors are underfunded by the same factor).
- Notorious corporate criminals, in sweetheart deals, do not plead guilty; instead they (a) agree not to violate the law again (a deferred prosecution agreement), (b) consent to pay a fine and change their conduct in exchange for no criminal record (a non-prosecution agreement), or (c) identify a unit of the firm that has no assets—or even a defunct entity—to plead guilty, leaving the organization as a whole innocent (Office of US Senator Elizabeth Warren, 2016).
- There are very few career prosecutors of corporate crime, as many see their jobs as a stepping stone to defending corporations.

- Having *de facto* immunity, not one executive responsible for fraud during the 2007–2008 metastasizing financial crisis, and became exceptionally wealthy as a result, was required to pay back the fraud proceeds or was imprisoned (for different, if strained, view see Bourtin, 2017, November 3).
- The market does not take most corporate prosecutions seriously because when settled, the stock prices go up. There is no serious consequence to company reputation and business practices remain largely intact.

In short, corporate malfeasance is a compelling problem with significant effects on society, but is unlikely to be prosecuted due to lack of resources, business-friendly statutes, and case settlements that protect companies from serious consequences of wrongdoing.

Government. Institutional crime, as discussed in Chapter 9, is hardly unknown in the public arena. Corruption cases dominate headlines across the nation. One indicator of the social cost of corruption is found in a 2017 *Forbes* report of results from a national survey that examined the level of fear of Americans across 80 different types of fear. Corruption of government officials ranked as the most significant fear with three-quarters of adult respondents saying it makes them either "afraid" or "very afraid" (McCarthy, 2017). The WashingtonBlog lists 70 bullet points cataloguing recent instances of corruption in American government (see How Corrupt is the American Government, 2016). Given the extent of corruption (Chapter 9), it is not surprising that anticorruption efforts are increasing. For example, TRACE International found that U.S. enforcement actions against bribing government officials doubled in 2016 (Webb, 2017).

Government corruption is not only a concern at the national level, but the state and local level as well. Table 15.1 provides a ranking of states based on the number of public corruption convictions between 2000 and 2010. Florida led the nation in federal corruption convictions of state officials over the past decade, ranking first among states five times between 1999 and 2010. The state's reputation has been tarnished, with adverse impacts on its economy and ability to attract new jobs. Furthermore, a *Forbes* ranking of America's Most Miserable Cities in 2012, which used corruption as a key factor, shows three Florida cities ranked (1) Miami, (4) West Palm Beach, and (11) Fort Lauderdale.

Such disturbing statistics spurred reformers to create Integrity Florida, a nonpartisan, nonprofit research institute with a mission to promote governmental integrity and expose improbity. This good-government group proposed a roadmap for reform that includes four steps to help citizens track and hold public officials accountable: (1) Put all campaign finance data online in an electronic, searchable downloadable form; (2) place all lobbying expenditures online; (3) deposit all government expenditures online; and (4) digitize financial disclosure information (Perry, 2012). Most of these suggestions were adopted by the Florida Commission on Ethics in their legislative agenda—and were passed by the state legislature in 2013. Like any reforms, they will be only as good as their enforcement. The group is seeking to (a) create a corruption hotline, (b) institute tougher penalties for violations, (c) strengthen the independence of inspector generals, (d) fortify whistleblower protections, (e) convene ethics reform coalitions throughout the state, and (f) empower the state ethics commission

| TABLE 15.1 | State Public Corruption Convictions, 2000–2010 |

State	Total Convictions
Florida	781
California	753
Texas	741
New York	670
Pennsylvania	593
Ohio	551
Illinois	541
New Jersey	457
Virginia	442
Louisiana	407
Washington, DC*	383
Kentucky	306
Alabama	285
Puerto Rico*	269
Tennessee	269
Michigan	256
Georgia	228
Maryland	228
Massachusetts	214
Mississippi	201
Missouri	196
North Carolina	193
Arizona	183
Indiana	151
Oklahoma	142
Wisconsin	126
Connecticut	108
Washington	101
Colorado	98
Arkansas	95
Guam*	95
West Virginia	78
Montana	75
Minnesota	70
South Carolina	66
Alaska	64
South Dakota	61
North Dakota	57
Iowa	53
New Mexico	52
Delaware	47
Hawaii	46
Kansas	43
Virgin Islands*	42
Nevada	41
Oregon	41
Utah	40
Maine	39
Idaho	28

State	Total Convictions
Rhode Island	28
Nebraska	26
New Hampshire	18
Vermont	17
Wyoming	17

Source: Adapted from Wilcox and Krassner (2012).
*Nonstate jurisdictions.

to begin its own investigations and have the authority to collect the fines that it imposes (Kennedy, 2012; Krassner, 2013).

Palm Beach County, Florida, provides a closer look at the history of profligacy and reform. At one time, the county had the national reputation as the "capital of corruption." This was based on scandalous behavior by city and county commissioners that led to the ouster of four county commissioners over a four-year period, three of whom were sentenced to prison. In the aftermath, sweeping reforms were passed, including a local ethics code, a county ethics enforcement agency with a budget of $476,000 and staff of five, and appointment of a county inspector general to investigate fraud and mismanagement (Wallman, 2012a, 2012b). The changes were modeled in part after those in Miami-Dade County, which has had a Commission on Ethics and Public Trust (see Exhibit 2.2) and Office of Inspector General since 1998. As of August 2012, the Palm Beach County Ethics Commission had vetted almost 100 alleged ethics violations, administered some punishments, and offered advisory opinions in 225 cases. The commission holds televised monthly meetings. The county's Internet home-page contains a prominent message for citizens to "REPORT! WASTE FRAUD OR ABUSE."

Nonprofits. Governments at the national, state and local levels outsource many functions to community-based nonprofits; however, it is estimated that more than 10 percent are insol-vent (even higher in human services) and nearly half have limited cash on hand or access to credit (Kaplan, 2017; MacIntosh, 2017). With cuts in federal discretionary spending, not-for-profits will feel the hit and have difficulty using fundraising or volunteers as ways to balance declining government payments. It is not surprising that as nonprofits face growing financial insecurity, the number of stories reporting on scandals is increasing. The examples are plentiful: The Breast Cancer Relief Fund raised large sums of money ($64 million) yet a paltry 2 percent was given to hospitals and cancer victims. Similarly, Kids Wish Network purports to raise money to help sick children and their families; however, in reality only three cents to the dollar actually go to helping kids (Kandt, 2016).

It is not surprising that confidence in the ethics of charities dropped precipitously fol-lowing disclosures that the Red Cross had redirected gifts intended for the victims of the September 11, 2001, attacks to other purposes. The image of nonprofits had been besmirched earlier when the CEO of United Way was convicted of 25 counts of illegal conduct in 1992, including using United Way funds for his personal benefit and for interstate transportation of fraudulently obtained money. In 1997, the president of Adelphi University was fired. He not only was arbitrary and capricious in dealing with those who opposed his initiatives, but also engaged in lavish spending at a time when he was the second highest paid university president (just behind Harvard) in the country. While the wrongdoing was not as egregious as that found in businesses like Enron and Goldman Sachs, such behaviors contradicted the "serving society" purpose that has long been part of the identity of not-for-profits.

If nonprofits are to be seen as the ethical sector of society, Doug White (2010) suggests, they need to shift their thinking away from money making and growth, cease paying exorbitant salaries to their top executives, focus less on next quarter's financial balance sheet and more on mid- to long-range goals they seek to accomplish, and avoid public relations gimmicks while reemphasizing their mission and purpose. Surveys find that the public ranks the ethical behavior of nonprofits ahead of either business or government.

However, according to an Ethics Resource Center (2007) survey, "[I]ntegrity in the nonprofit sector is eroding" and "misconduct is on the rise—especially financial fraud." In part, this is attributable to boards who fail to set clear ethical standards. A poll by Paul Light (2008) also reported skepticism regarding charitable performance, concluding that "confidence has not risen significantly since it hit bottom in 2003." Furthermore, fraud is costly—approximately $40 billion per year is stolen from charities by their employees, as an estimated 6 percent of their revenue is lost to fraud annually (White, 2010, 31).

The *Washington Post* analysed IRS 990 forms of 1,000 large nonprofits in 2013 and found what was termed "outrageous, egregious, large-scale corruption within organizations," specifically an "astounding" number that had serious financial irregularities" (Fine, 2013). Another study of corruption in U.S. non-profit organizations between 2008 and 2011 (Archambeault, Webber & Greenlee, 2015) examined 115 incidents of detected fraud and reported three key findings: First, the primary perpetrators of wrongdoing were operational or financial executives (e.g., president, CEO, executive director, treasurer, CFO) followed by accounting, finance, and other employees. Second, most instances of wrongdoing involved insiders victimizing the organization through check or credit card schemes, theft of assets through other means or theft of cash or deposits. The wrongdoing also victimizes the public and defrauds contributors (e.g., using funds for other than intended purposes). Further, it involves improperly claiming loans, grants or government funds, and other fraudulent activity. Third, the majority of settings in which nonprofit wrongdoing was uncovered was in health and human services organizations (Archambeault et al., 2015).

The effects of institutional crime in all three economic sectors include poor employee morale, difficulty in recruitment and retention of personnel, lowered trust in organizations, heightened fear among stakeholders, waste, and intervention by stockholders, legislators, and boards of directors. The result is the death of accountability, justice, and deterrence. Meanwhile regulators are underfunded and marginalized, newspapers no longer fund in-depth investigations, and corporate compliance units seldom question profit centers. No one expects the historically low white-collar crime prosecutions to increase.

Confronting White-Collar Crime

Richard Nielsen (1987) examines a wide variety of strategies managers can employ when confronted with white-collar crime. In an analysis of 10 cases, he discusses the advantages and disadvantages of not thinking about the problem, going along to get along, voicing protest, conscientious objection, leaving, several forms of whistleblowing, sabotage, and building consensus for change (Table 15.2).

While refusal to think about a problem or going along to avoid trouble will not produce change, the remaining approaches can be used to arrest decay in organizational ethics. Nielsen

TABLE 15.2	Reacting to Ethical Issues in Organizational Management: Advantages and Disadvantages		
Strategy		**Advantages**	**Disadvantages**
1. *Not thinking about it.* Identifying so closely with the organization that United Fruit officials helped overthrow the government of Guatemala.		Protect careers	No policy change Thoughtlessness
2. *Going along to get along.* A contract negotiated the sale of equipment to the Navy involving kickbacks.		Protect one's career	Thinking about, and cooperating with, dubious practices No policy change
3. *Protesting.* A salesman objects to the sale of unsafe products.		Do the right thing	Putting career at risk
4. *Conscientious objection.* A pharmaceutical researcher objects to the false advertising claims, refusing to have his name used in press releases or press conferences regarding the product.		Set an honorable example	Not regarded as a team player
5. *Leaving.* A drug company executive resigns after refusing to test a suspect drug on infants and the elderly.		Courage of convictions Signal to firm that it will lose good people	Someone else will cooperate Prevents learning and change
6. *Secretly blowing the whistle.* An executive of an electric company writes an anonymous letter to the Justice Department alleging bid-rigging among electrical contractors.		Positive impact on problem Avoid retaliation	Sneaky behavior May be exposed by company investigation—unless whistleblower lies Distrust
7. *Publicly blowing the whistle.* A high-level public manager and former business CEO reveals underbidding and cost overruns by Lockheed to Congress and the press.		Positive effect on problem Regarded as hero	Dissenter vilified Others discouraged from similar behavior Damages reputation of all agency and contractor employees

Strategy	Advantages	Disadvantages
8. *Secretly threatening to blow the whistle.* An insurance salesperson anonymously writes a letter to the sales manager threatening to send the state insurance commission a copy of unethical sales instructions.	Change behavior Protect identity	No dialogue on problem Prevents injured parties from seeking remedies
9. *Sabotage.* Instead of following an unethical and illegal order, a local social welfare manager creates a paperwork trail to funding agencies that undermined and delayed the order.	Positive effect Protect identity	No dialogue to solve problem Retaliation if exposed Is sabotage ethical?
10. *Negotiating and building a consensus for change.* Concerned that cutting costs would undercut pollution control requirements and that closing the mill would impact the community, a division director negotiates a plan to extend the cost reduction targets to permit gradual improvements in pollution control and productivity that permitted the mill to remain open.	Individual efforts can gain support from others Satisfaction in constructive solution	Ineffective when many benefit from existing situation Difficult process Some situations are win-lose

Source: Adapted from Nielsen (1987).

(1987) advocates the last strategy—negotiating and creating consensus for change—because it provides the opportunity to discover more about the situation through diverse points of view. However, negotiation may not be effective when there is insufficient time, others are not interested, and the case circumstances are win–lose, not win–win. When negotiation is not possible, Nielsen recommends either secretly threatening to blow the whistle or administrative sabotage. For the first option, the organization is provided time to improve and avoids negative publicity. If reform is not forthcoming, then blowing the whistle may produce the desired effect. For the second option, sabotage—surreptitiously making a change that deters unethical behavior—may be effective. It is, however, ethically dubious especially if more open and honest alternatives have not been tried.

As this work has shown, it is seldom ethically sufficient to say, "I had no choice," which, in effect, relinquishes ethical autonomy. Instead, Nielsen (1987, 318) writes, "[T]here are realistic alternative responses to consider and compare, that there are situational factors that can influence the decision, and that we do need to think about these issues and choose." Thus, there is genuine value in a contingency approach to decision making in an effort to do the right thing at the right time and place. Not all battles are worth fighting; those that are should be big enough to matter and small enough to win.[4] To summarize this section, remember that while there is much that is bad in the world, there is more that is good. U.S. Supreme Court justice Louis Brandeis's sage observation is apropos: "[M]ost of the things worth doing in the world had been declared impossible before they were done."

NEW CHALLENGES: THERE IS A DAWN IN EVERY DARKNESS

Continued discovery will produce increasing sophistication in existing technologies, as well as the advent of revolutionary technologies beyond imagination. Current and new scientific advances will bring novel challenges to ethics. Already, surveillance technology in the form of drones is raising concerns in the United States (Case Study 15.1; also see Exhibit 10.1 on National Security Agency surveillance programs).

Yet the utility of ethics is that ancient methods can be adapted and applied to unprecedented situations. Dueling, foot binding, slavery, "honor killings," and female genital mutilation were once widely accepted, but are now rejected by most people. Ethics, then, has matured, and will continue developing to make sense of the modern world (Appiah, 2011; Shermer, 2015). Industrial meat production, the prison system, institutionalized and isolation of the elderly, and environmental abuse are increasingly subject to evolving views of morality. The ethics triad will guide future decision makers, linked to their colleagues present and past by a commitment to the public good.

In short, the human experiment is deep and dark and bright and beautiful; savagery and nobility coexist. Every saint has a past, every sinner a future (Cole-Whitaker, 2001). As Martin Keogh believes:

> If you look at the science about what is happening on earth and aren't pessimistic, you don't understand the data. But if you meet the people who are working to restore this earth and the lives of the poor and you aren't optimistic, you haven't got a pulse.

America begins not with a place, but an ideal; its people are imperfect creatures who aspire to be better than they are.

GUIDELINES FOR ETHICAL CONDUCT

There is no greater glory than to work for the public's good.

—Edmund Burke

In an effort to encourage exemplary action, three guidelines are offered. The first advises learning to differentiate two types of rationality—functional (a focus on means or "how to") and substantive (an emphasis on goals or "why"). An exclusive stress on doing things right—functional rationality—can become the dominant moral code for some professionals, instead of ensuring that right things—substantive rationality—are pursued. While both are important, they should not be confused. As Einstein observed, "The perfection of means and the confusion of ends characterizes our age." Conservative commentator David Brooks (2012) argues that today's elite lacks a self-conscious leadership ethos. The language of success has overwhelmed the language of meaning. "They have no sense that they are guardians of institutions the world depends upon" (also see Zakaria, 2017, August 18). Divorced from ethics, leadership has been reduced to management technique.

Kohlberg's theory of moral development is useful in clarifying the role of reason in human thinking. At the individual level, his taxonomy (Chapter 4) seeks to explain why people reason the way they do and defines increasingly sophisticated types of reasoning. At the organizational level, the developmental, "high-road" commitment approach to ethics can foster honorable behavior in a manner absent from the punitive, "low-road" compliance strategy (Chapter 8). The substantive form of rationality counsels that there is never a wrong time to do the right thing.

The second guideline, to borrow a leaf from environmentalists, is to "think globally, act locally." While one might be discouraged by events beyond one's control, this should not affect what can be done in one's own life. "We can't do everything for everyone everywhere," Richard L. Evans observed, "but we can do something for someone somewhere." As Gandhi said, "Be the change you want to see in the world." And he likely would chuckle in agreement at the observation, "If you think you're too small to make a change, try getting in bed with a mosquito."

CASE STUDY 15.1

Applying Rational and Philosophical Ethics Approaches: Drones in Domestic Law Enforcement

Sheriff Alonzo Griffith of Metropolitan County Government in a Northeastern state was intrigued by the idea of using drones, smaller and less expensive versions of the aircraft used in military operations in Afghanistan, Iraq, and Iran. His interest was piqued last year when he learned that they could see through walls, use software for facial recognition, and intercept calls and emails, all with little regulation. He envisioned drones helping to find missing children or marijuana fields, detect wildfires, report accidents such as highway pileups or hazardous material spills, or track dangerous suspects. Yet he was aware that surveillance drones raise controversial issues of privacy. He learned many citizen groups strongly oppose their domestic use. Sheriff Griffith told his staff to arrange the purchase of two unmanned remote control aircraft as a law enforcement tool. Now, he is torn about the order, wondering if this was the ethically correct action. He decided to use the ethics triad to think carefully about the decision before acting.

Results-Based Analysis. Griffith started by considering the results of the pending purchase. He is confident that drones would serve the "greater good" and that law enforcement capabilities would increase with the new aircraft. He believes using drones is a more efficient, effective, and safer way to respond to critical situations. The FAA estimates 10,000 civilian drones will be in use in the United States within five years. He thinks these numbers will continue to increase rapidly. He does not want his department to become obsolete. He considers drones preferable to manned helicopters. Plus, they cost less (approximately $36,009 to $250,000 for a drone vs. $3 million for a helicopter and crew).

Griffith also knows that drones will be perceived by some as a threat to civil rights and liberties. Lawyers and media commentary will likely bemoan this initiative as another step toward a surveillance society and warn about "Big Brother" spying on citizens in an Orwellian police state. Law enforcement offices in Miami, Houston, Metro Nashville, and Seattle have purchased drones, generating controversy and the attention of state policymakers (Seattle officials subsequently cancelled their order). Smaller cities including Montgomery, Texas, and Gadsden, Alabama, have had similar experiences with backlash. Griffith is aware that aroused citizenry could threaten his career and job security. Protest groups are already planning demonstrations throughout the United States; he would like not to be host to such an event.

Rule-Based Analysis. He is also mindful of rules and principles as he mulls over his decision. While laws and rules on domestic drones including FAA guidelines are in their infancy, Griffith has read about increased legislative and administrative rulemaking activity bound to result in stricter regulation. He believes that oversight, privacy safeguards, transparency, and public input regarding the purpose and intended use of drones are appropriate. He is also aware that drones carrying infrared cameras with facial recognition capability, heat sensors, GPS, and automated license plate readers pose First Amendment risks (chilling the right to anonymity and association); if misused, Fourth Amendment rights (to be secure against unreasonable search and seizure) are threatened as well. Citizens' "reasonable expectation of privacy" could be compromised without restrictions on data storage and dissemination. He recalls the controversy over whole body imaging technology as a screening tool at airports. Similar problems could surface over drones, especially if monitoring by drones is done clandestinely. Public safety issues could also surface when drones operate alongside of commercial or private planes.

Virtue-Based Analysis. Sheriff Griffith is also concerned about virtue theory—does the purchase of drones make me and my community better? Citizen confidence is crucial and public trust has declined recently. If he were to announce the use of drones without first adequately preparing and involving the populace, he likely would be subject to criticism that would further erode trust. In light of these considerations, he would rather "be right slower than wrong faster." He feels it is important to take his time and engage citizens in an open conversation about the pros and cons of using drones before making a final decision.

Griffith cares about his community and the welfare of others. He wants to make a decision that is in the best interest of those in his jurisdiction. If he opts to purchase the drone it will be after prudent deliberation and due diligence. He intends to listen to the concerns of those who may oppose aerial surveillance, weighing their concerns and arguments carefully. He plans to clearly communicate his rationale regarding the advisability of taking advantage of this technology. He recognizes the need to balance law enforcement's obligation to protect society from major disruptions against an individual's right to be secure in their person and household effects.

Behavioral Ethics-Based Analysis. Behavioral ethics research cautions about easily overlooked tendencies such as bounded rationality, issue framing, over-optimism, ethical fading, and confirmation bias. Griffith's enthusiasm for drones may rest in the efficiency, effectiveness, and cost-saving benefits for law enforcement, which may be the way he understands (frames) and assesses the issue. In the process, his infatuation with this new technology may desensitize him to the potential ethical downside of this development with its threat to citizen privacy (ethical fading). As with anything new, there are unknowns that impede rational decision making; problems cannot always be anticipated; nevertheless, in the exuberance of the moment, Griffith may be overly optimistic about the benefits of drones. As he learns about them, he needs to be alert to confirmation bias—gathering information to reinforce existing beliefs.

The last guideline is one that was suggested early in the book—aim for the middle ground between naïve idealism and cynical pessimism, because of the very real dangers at either extreme; the former should not let the perfect become the enemy of the good, the latter should not let discouragement surrender to wrongdoing. Compromise is a moral virtue in a democracy. Any time the lion and lamb can be brought to the table, it is a worthy thing to do.

Using such guidelines—or developing better ones—should assist in knowing what to do and whether one is making a positive difference in people's lives. Life consists not in holding good cards, someone once observed, but in playing those you hold well. "Nobody who ever gave his best," according to legendary Chicago Bears coach George Halas, "regretted it." In fact, the classical definition—and vow—of a professional is leadership in technical and ethical competence (Bowman, West, & Beck, 2010). Public servants, accordingly, must not only do technical things right, but also do ethically right things. The ability to contemplate, enhance, and act on ethical situations is the essence of service to the people. The guidelines will aid in this pursuit.

There are many ways of being ethical. In the end, it is up to each person to figure out who she is and who she is not. There is only one way in which one can endure inhumanity to man, and that is to try in one's own life to exemplify man's humanity to man. Man is a promise that he must not break. "Real generosity toward the future," Albert Camus observed, "consists in giving all to what is present." The cases discussed in the chapters here happened to people just like you—except most were not as prepared to deal with the dilemmas as you will be, having read this book and appreciated the ethical obligations of public life.

Since the world is seldom simple and clear-cut, the purpose of ethics is to encourage thinking about difficult matters. The human mind may not be readily equipped to ask, much less answer, important questions; crushing rocks with a feather duster is no easy task. But ethics expands the imagination and helps appreciate the extent of human ignorance, the first step to reduce it. As an exercise in self-realization, the book has sought not only to better understand who you are already, but also to reconsider some of your most fundamental beliefs. Struggle and uncertainty are part of ethics, as they are part of life, and this is what makes it hard, intriguing, magnificent, and so full of possibility and promise. There is no time like the present to set higher standards. Striving to live by ethical guidelines, as difficult as it may be, is the best way to lead a life worth living. As Madeline Bridge observes, "Give the world the best you have, and the best will come to you."

Our ending is your beginning in expanding and enhancing individual and institutional responsibilities in public service ethics. As this book attests, people care deeply about ethics. It has tried to give readers tools to address dilemmas for themselves based on their own values. Despite the excrescence of decay, there is also the ethical exuberance of grandeur. No one can do everything, but everyone can do something to create a more honorable world. "When do any of us," asked Texas congresswoman Barbara Jordan, "ever do enough?"

***

The test of our progress is not whether we add more to the abundance of those who have much; it is whether we provide enough for those who have too little.

—Franklin D. Roosevelt

NOTES

1. This section is based on, and expanded from, the authors' work in Berman, Bowman, West, and Van Wart (2016, 501–504).
2. In a prescient observation, Charles Blow (2012) believed that the 2012 presidential election was a moment that "truth and lies lost their honor and stigma, respectively," that facts are fungible and disinformation acceptable, and that dishonesty exposed by fact checking is unremarkable and ignored.
3. As inscribed in the foyer at the Maxwell School of Citizenship and Public Affairs, Syracuse University.
4. Mark Twain once observed, "We go to heaven for the climate and we go to hell for the company." Exploring the strategies above may be useful when confronting decay and might reduce the number of the hell bound (!).

FOR DISCUSSION

1. "Corporate corruption in recent years is not just a corporate failure, but also a failure of governmental oversight gutted by deregulation." Comment.

2. Will the past bury the future or will the future bury the past?

3. Identify trends that illustrate grandeur and decay in moral life.

4. Add to, or subtract from, the guidelines for exemplary behavior.

5. "To the question of your life, you are the only answer. To the problems of your life, you are the only solution"—*Jo Coudert*. Discuss in the context of moral grandeur and decay.

6. Of what does humanity consist? Risen apes, fallen angels, or something else?

7. Consider these insights:

   "It is what it is, but it will become what you make it."—Anonymous

   "Don't judge each day by the harvest you reap, but by the seeds you plant."—Robert Louis Stevenson

   "Knowledge is the source of good and ignorance is the source of evil."—Socrates

   "My concern is not whether God is on our side. My greatest concern is to be on God's side."—Abraham Lincoln

   "There can be no final truth in ethics any more than in physics until the last man has had his experience and said his last."—William James

"Every gun that is made, every warship launched, every rocket fired signifies, in the final sense, a theft from those who hunger and are fed, those who are cold and are not clothed."—Dwight E. Eisenhower

"I hate quotations."—Anonymous

EXERCISES

1. Ethical self-assessments are readily found on the Internet:
   http://www.ethics.va.gov/ELSA.pdf
   http://www.ache.org/newclub/career/ethself.cfm
   http://www.walkthetalk.com/media/solution_finder/pdf/how_ethical_am_i.pdf
   Such tools can be helpful to identify areas of moral strength and vulnerability, and to provide opportunities for reflection. They are intended for personal use and should not be used to evaluate others; they generally avoid scoring schemes because ethical conduct neither can nor should be quantified.

2. Consider these challenges for self-development created by Rich Gee (http://richgee.com):

   • Explain where you are now to your earlier self (talking to your past self produces insights into what might have been done differently; this not only may help you in the future, but also will demonstrate that you can handle anything that life throws at you).
   • Look back from your future (imagine where you want to be, and what advice he or she might give you; with a lucid view of your goals, you can take concrete steps to achieve them).

3. Create an actual plan for developing your ethical effectiveness, for "it is today that we create the world of the future" (Eleanor Roosevelt). It should contain three components:

   Assessment
   Gather feedback about yourself and your decisions by taking ethics self-evaluation questionnaires, establishing a mentor relationship with a person whom you respect, and asking friends, colleagues, and family about your behavior.

   Challenges
   Identify opportunities to further augment your skills by volunteering for organizational tasks, leading committees, taking advantage of training activities, forming clubs, writing op-ed essays for the local newspaper, and so forth.

   Support
   Discuss your concerns with peers, have an ongoing ethics reading program for yourself, or locate support groups that nurture leadership in your community.
   Provide examples, ethical theories, personal behaviors, and references (journal/

checklists, course readings, news events) to substantiate each of the above components. Include goals, tools, actions, and deadlines for each (Johnson, 2017). Identify strengths and weaknesses in the plan, and strategies to address weaknesses.

Appendix 15.1 offers a student example of this assignment.

REFERENCES

Appiah, K. (2011). *The honor code: How moral revolutions happen*. New York: Norton.

Archambeault, D., Webber, S., & Greenlee, J. (2015). Fraud and corruption in U.S. nonprofit entities. *Nonprofit and Voluntary Sector Quarterly*. Retrieved from http://journals.sagepub.com.access.library.miami.edu/doi/full/10.1177/0899764014555987

Berman, E., Bowman, J., West, J., & Van Wart, M. (2016). *Human resource management in public service: Paradoxes, processes, and problems* (5th ed.). Thousand Oaks, CA: Sage.

Blow, C. (2012, November 1). Liberty to lie. *New York Times*. Retrieved from http://campaignstops.blogs.nytimes.com/2012/11/01/liberty-to-lie/

Bourtin, N. (2017, November 3). Five myths about white collar crime. *Washington Post*. Retrieved from https://www.washingtonpost.com/outlook/five-myths/five-myths-about-white-collar-crime/2017/11/03/5793fb3a-be6e-11e7-97d9-bdab5a0ab381_story.html

Bowman, J. (2011–2012). Public service as a calling: Reflections, retreat, revival, resolve. *Journal of Workplace Rights*, *16*, 47–61.

Bowman, J., West, J., & Beck, M. (2010). *Competencies in public service: The professional edge* (2nd ed.). Armonk, NY: M. E. Sharpe.

Brooks, D. (2012, July 13). Why our elites stink. *New York Times*. Retrieved from http://www.nytimes.com/2012/07/13/opinion/brooks-why-our-elites-stink.html?_r=0

Brooks, D. (2017, August 1). Before manliness lost its virtue. *The New York Times*. Retrieved from: https://www.nytimes.com/2017/08/01/opinion/scaramucci-mccain-masculinity-white-house.html

Cole-Whitaker, T. (2001). *Every saint has a past, every sinner a future*. New York: Tarcher.

Ethics Resource Center. (2007). National nonprofit ethics survey: An inside view of nonprofit sector ethics. Retrieved from http://www.ethics.org/files/u5/ERC_s_National_Nonprofit_Ethics_Survey.pdf

Fine, A. (2013, November 1). Everyday nonprofit corruption. Retrieved from https://allisonfine.com/2013/11/01/regular-nonprofit-corruption/

How corrupt is the American government? (2016, January 5). Retrieved from http://www.washingtonsblog.com/2016/01/corrupt-american-government.html

Johnson, C. (2017). *Meeting the ethical challenges of leadership: Casting light or shadow* (6th ed.). Thousand Oaks, CA: Sage.

Kandt, H. (2016, November 18). Nonprofit corruption and why society needs to care. Retrieved from https://www.linkedin.com/pulse/nonprofit-corruption-why-society-needs-care-hannah-kandt

Kaplan, L. (2017, March 31). 5 ways to fix dysfunctional government contracting. Retrieved from https://nonprofitquarterly.org/2017/03/31/5-ways-fix-dysfunctional-government-contracting/

Kennedy, J. (2012, June 6). Florida tops in public corruption, changes needed, watchdog says. *Palm Beach Post*. Retrieved from http://www.postonpolitics.com/2012/6/florida-tops-in-public-corruption-changes-needed

Krassner, D. (2013, September 9). Urgent reform needed for Florida's future. *Tallahassee Democrat*, p. 5A.

Light, P. (2008). *How Americans view charities: A report on charitable confidence*. Washington, DC: Brookings Institution.

MacIntosh, J. (2017, March 30) How the mayor can save nonprofits hired by the city. Retrieved from http://www.crainsnewyork.com/article/20170330/OPINION/170329881/how-the-mayor-can-save-nonprofits-hired-by-the-city

McCarthy, N. (2017, October 19). Corruption of government officials ranked Americans' top fear of 2017. *Forbes*. Retrieved from https://www.forbes.com/sites/niallmccarthy/2017/10/19/corruption-of-government-officials-ranked-americans-top-fear-of-2017-infographic/#4db608101dff

McEldowney, N. (2018, January 26). How to work for a president who loathes the civil service. *Washington Post*. Retrieved from https://www.washingtonpost.com/outlook/how-to-work-for-a-president-who-hates-the-civil-service/2018/01/26/34dbe95c-0204-11e8-bb03-722769454f82_story.html?utm_term=.1beb11803b27

Morris, T. (1997). *If Aristotle ran General Motors*. New York: Holt.

Nielsen, R. (1987). What can managers do about unethical management? *Journal of Business Ethics*, 6, 309–320.

Office of US Senator Elizabeth Warren. (2016). *Rigged justice: How weak enforcement lets corporate offenders off easily*. Washington, DC: US Senate.

Palmer, P. (2007). *The courage to teach: Exploring the inner landscape of a teacher's life* (10th anniversary ed.). San Francisco: Jossey-Bass.

Perry, J., & Buckwalter, N. (2012). The public service of the future. *Public Administration Review*, 70(Supplement 1), S238–S245.

Perry, M. (2012, May 29). Florida's newest good government group wants to clean up state ethics. *CLTampaBay Loaf*. Retrieved from http://cltampa.com/dailyloaf/archieves/2012/05/29/floridas-newest-good-government-group

Shermer, M. (2015). *The moral arc: How science makes us better people*. New York: St. Martin's Griffin.

Twenty things you should know about corporate crime. (2007, June 12). *Corporate Crime Reporter*. Retrieved from http://corporatecrimereporter.com/twenty061207.htm

Wallman, B. (2012a, August 8). No ethics investigations from corruption watchdog. *Sun Sentinel*. Retrieved from http://www.sun-sentinel.com/news/palm-beach/fl-inspector-general-20120805

Wallman, B. (2012b, August 7). Palm's reputation of corruption on way out, reformers say. *Sun Sentinel*. Retrieved from http://www.sun-sentinel.com/news/palm-beach/fl-inspector-general-performance-palm

Webb, J. (2017, March 2). Anti-bribery enforcement actions increase across the globe: Prosecutors crack down on corruption. *Forbes*. Retrieved from https://www.forbes.com/sites/

jwebb/2017/03/02/anti-bribery-enforcement-actions-increase-across-the-globe-prosecutors-crack-down-on-corruption/#836fca218191

White, D. (2010). *The nonprofit challenge: Integrating ethics into the purpose and promise of our nation's charities*. New York: Palgrave Macmillan.

Wilcox, B., & Krassner, D. (2012). Corruption risk report: Florida ethics laws. *Integrity Florida*. Retrieved from http://www.integrityfl.org/corruption-risk-report-florida-ethics-laws-3/

Zakaria, F. (2017, August 18). The mealy-mouthed cowardice of America's elites after Charlottesville. *Washington Post*. Retrieved from https://www.washingtonpost.com/opinions/the-mealy-mouthed-cowardice-of-americas-elites-after-charlottesville/2017/08/17/48913872-8396-11e7-b359-15a3617c767b_story.html?utm_term=.a4604acbfc65

Appendix 15.1
Sample Graduate Student Action Plan

The readings have made me aware of the potential ethical possibilities and pitfalls faced in the course of a career. One way to capitalize on the possibilities and avoid pitfalls is to expand my ethical capacity by creating an "action plan." My plan has four goals: Two have deadlines, and two are ongoing goals. I have also identified the tools I intend to use to achieve these goals. The last section discusses the overall development components of the plan.

Goals

1. Create a mission statement and identify the principles that are critical for ethical decision making: this January

    The readings examine several decision-making methods. I realize this is important as both a professional and an individual to identify the tenets that are most significant for me. This would be the first step towards leading a principle-based life. These principles will also provide me with a way to assess my decisions on a continuing basis.

    Tools: I will read Stephen Covey, *First Things First* and *Principle-Centered Leadership*, as well as Tom Morris' book discussed in this chapter; continue journal writing; do research into servant leadership; engage in ongoing discussions with my mentor and my spouse to develop and update the mission statement I prepared at the beginning of this class to nurture, per Morris, the intellectual, aesthetic, moral and spiritual dimensions of my life.

2. Investigate the potential hurdles for continuing study: this March

    My studies and past experiences offer an opportunity to grasp the complications and ethical issues faced by professional administrators. Understanding and recognizing the challenges to be confronted in the future creates awareness of potential problems. I intend to pursue another degree next year and would like to understand and recognize the dilemmas that characterize that field.

    Tools: I will investigate the typical duties and responsibilities in obtaining another degree and examine ethical cases found in that area. I will talk to students and professors about the ethical issues that one would encounter in these situations.

3. Because an ethical administrator always does his/her best work for all projects, I will continue to improve my professional capabilities: ongoing

    It is my responsibility to always perform my best; it simply is not acceptable to perform below my personal standards. Although this goal might be seen as problematic, it is extremely important, if one wants to retain the trust of his/her supervisors and my own self-confidence. In addition to maintaining the established standards, I should continue to enhance my skill set and capabilities.

    Tools: Maintain professional certification, through continuing educational activities. Complete the Ethics Self-Assessment (2017). Ache.org. (retrieved from https://www.ache.org/newclub/career/ethself.cfm) and Ethics Quiz (2017) ima.org (retrieved from https://icma.org/documents/ethics-quiz). Look for opportunities to learn new skills or improve existing skills.

4. Assess my ethical capacity on a regular basis and change the action plan based on the new challenges and needs: ongoing

    Like any other plan, this one is only as good as long as it is used. Therefore it is key to constantly refer to it and make changes as needed. I will place the plan near my office calendar so it cannot be overlooked. Once a week, on Sunday evening, I will review the decisions I made and match them with my ethical action plan to check my progress. As part of this, I will benefit from the answers to the self-assessment above as well as feedback from mentors, my spouse, and friends.

    Tools: Weekly review and revision.

Developmental Components

In addition to the above goals, the plan includes elements below.

Assessment. This allows an individual to recognize the gaps between the current performance and the aspirations in the action plan. I will use a multipronged approach to assess my performance on a regular basis: self-assessment, peer assessment, and supervisory assessment.

My new employer requires the supervisors to evaluate all the employees on a quarterly basis. During the next evaluation cycle, I will request my supervisor to add ethical decision making to the evaluation criteria and request his feedback on my performance. I will suggest that ethics be a regular agenda item at staff meetings. Agenda items could include guest speakers, a review of the agency's code of conduct, and examination of ethical dimensions of major decisions under consideration by the department.

Challenges. I am a member of my local American Society for Public Administration chapter and, in the next few months, I will initiate new activities for our chapter and will expand my leadership capabilities and organization skills. I will continue to improve my academic standing by participating in conferences and will work on publishing an article in a professional publication.

Prior to the start date of my new job with state government, I will write a plan to improve my ethicality with particular attention to the blind sports, vulnerabilities and irrational tendencies revealed by the behavioral sciences. I will also examine the state ethics code and determine if my department has more specific, complementary documents.

Support. I will request the support of my mentor in writing the mission statement and request her feedback on the other activities as they relate to this plan. I will start ethical discussions with my peers and provide support when needed.

Tentative Concluding Thoughts (to be regularly updated)

Responding thoughtfully to ethical dilemmas is crucial in order to reflect public values and have a meaningful career. Self-assessments have and will help me to understand my strengths and weaknesses. I am shaping my goals to move forward and marshaling resources to assist me in developing ethical capacity. I should be able to effectively discipline myself to become more ethical in my thoughts and actions.

Index